CRACKNELL'S STATUTES

Conflict of Laws

Edited by

Robert M MacLean
LLB, Dip LP, LLM, Solicitor

and

Gwyn Tovey
LLB, PGCE
Senior Lecturer in Law, University of Glamorgan

Series Editor

D G Cracknell LLB
of the Middle Temple, Barrister

Old Bailey Press

OLD BAILEY PRESS LIMITED
The Gatehouse, Ruck Lane, Horsmonden, Kent TN12 8EA

First Published 1996

© Old Bailey Press Ltd 1996

ISBN 1 85836 022 6

British Library Cataloguing-in-Publication.

A CIP Catalogue record for this book is available from the
British Library.

Printed and bound in Great Britain.

CONTENTS

Contents

PREFACE

The purpose of this book is to bring together all the statutory materials pertaining to the Conflict of Laws with which students need to be familiar. In order to provide a comprehensive compendium of materials, and to cover as many courses as possible, we have included a substantial number (57, in fact) of statutes. They have been edited down to their most relevant provisions and all amendments and substitutions have been incorporated.

The two main commercial statutes, the Civil Jurisdiction and Judgments Act 1982 and the Contracts (Applicable Law) Act 1990, are covered, as are those relating to the enforcement of non-Community judgments. The Protection of Trading Interests Act 1980 has also been included.

Family law aspects of this subject are dealt with by inclusion of, amongst others, the Maintenance Orders (Facilities for Enforcement) Act 1920, the Maintenance Orders (Reciprocal Enforcement) Acts 1972 and 1992, the Family Law Act 1986 and the Child Abduction and Custody Act 1985.

Many statutory provisions bearing on the relationship between English law and foreign sovereign entities have been reproduced, including those to be found in the Diplomatic Privileges Act 1964, the Consular Relations Act 1968 and the International Organisations Act 1968. Also, we have included the main provisions of the State Immunity Act 1978 which plays an increasingly important role in the resolution of commercial disputes involving foreign governments and state-owned entities.

Finally, the Private International Law (Miscellaneous Provisions) Act 1995, which makes substantial changes not only to statutory rules but also to general principles of common law, has been included after having recently received Royal Assent.

This book contains statutory provisions, in their present form, which were in force as at 23 November 1995. While we believe that the coverage may fairly be described as comprehensive, we would always be pleased to receive suggestions as to provisions which should be included in future editions

ALPHABETICAL TABLE OF STATUTES, ETC

WILLS ACT 1837
(7 Will 4 & 1 Vict c 26)

1   Meaning of certain words in this Act

The words and expressions hereinafter mentioned, which in their ordinary signification have a more confined or a different meaning, shall in this Act, except where the nature of the provision or the context of the Act shall exclude such construction, be interpreted as follows: (that is to say,) the word 'will' shall extend to a testament, and to a codicil, and to an appointment by will or by writing in the nature of a will in exercise of a power, and also to an appointment by will of a guardian of a child, and to any other testamentary disposition; and the words 'real estate' shall extend to manors, advowsons, messuages, lands, tithes, rents, and hereditaments, whether freehold, customary freehold, tenant right, customary or copyhold, or of any other tenure, and whether corporeal, incorporeal, or personal, and to any undivided share thereof, and to any estate, right, or interest (other than a chattel interest) therein; and the words 'personal estate' shall extend to leasehold estates, and other chattels real, and also to moneys, shares of government and other funds, securities for money (being not real estates), debts, choses in action, rights, credits, goods, and all other property whatsoever, which by law devolves upon the executor or administrator, and to any share or interest therein; and every word importing the singular number only shall extend and be applied to several persons or things as well as one person or thing; and every word importing the masculine gender only shall extend and be applied to a female as well as a male.

7   No will of a person under age valid

No will made by any person under the age of eighteen years shall be valid.

9   Signing and attestation of wills

No will shall be valid unless –

(a) it is in writing, and signed by the testator, or by some other person in his presence and by his direction; and

(b) it appears that the testator intended by his signature to give effect to the will; and

(c) the signature is made or acknowledged by the testator in the presence of two or more witnesses present at the same time; and

(d) each witness either –

(i) attests and signs the will; or

(ii) acknowledges his signature,

in the presence of the testator (but not necessarily in the presence of any other witness),

but no form of attestation shall be necessary.

10   Appointments by will to be executed like other wills, and to be valid, although other required solemnities are not observed

No appointment made by will, in exercise of any power, shall be valid, unless the same be executed in manner hereinbefore required; and every will executed in manner hereinbefore required shall, so far as respects the execution and attestation thereof, be a valid execution of a power of appointment by will, notwithstanding it shall have been expressly required that a will made in exercise of such power should be executed with some additional or other form of execution or solemnity.

18   Will to be revoked by marriage

(1) Subject to subsections (2) to (4) below, a will shall be revoked by the testator's marriage.

(2) A disposition in a will in exercise of a power of appointment shall take effect notwithstanding the testator's subsequent marriage unless the property so appointed would in default of appointment pass to his personal representatives.

(3) Where it appears from a will that at the time it was made the testator was expecting to be married to a particular person and that

he intended that the will should not be revoked by the marriage, the will shall not be revoked by his marriage to that person.

(4) Where it appears from a will that at the time it was made the testator was expecting to be married to a particular person and that he intended that a disposition in the will should not be revoked by his marriage to that person –

(a) that disposition shall take effect notwithstanding the marriage; and

(b) any other disposition in the will shall take effect also, unless it appears from the will that the testator intended the disposition to be revoked by the marriage.

18A Effect of dissolution or annulment of marriage on wills

(1) Where, after a testator has made a will, a decree of a court of civil jurisdiction in England and Wales dissolves or annuls his marriage or his marriage is dissolved or annulled and the divorce or annulment is entitled to recognition in England and Wales by virtue of Part II of the Family Law Act 1986, –

(a) provisions of the will appointing executors or trustees or conferring a power of appointment, if they appoint or confer the power on the former spouse, shall take effect as if the former spouse had died on the date on which the marriage is dissolved or annulled, and

(b) any property which, or an in interest in which, is devised or bequeathed to the former spouse shall pass as if the former spouse had died on that date,

except in so far as a contrary intention appears by the will.

(2) Subsection (1)(b) above is without prejudice to any right of the former spouse to apply for financial provision under the Inheritance (Provision for Family and Dependants) Act 1975.

(3) Where –

(a) by the terms of a will an interest in remainder is subject to a life interest; and

(b) the life interest lapses by virtue of subsection (1)(b) above,

the interest in remainder shall be treated as if it had not been subject to the life interest and, if it was contingent upon the termination of the life interest, as if it had not been so contingent.

NB Section 18A(1), as amended, has effect as respects a will made by a person dying on or after 1 January 1996, regardless of the date of the will and the date of the dissolution or annulment: s3(2) of the Law Reform (Succession) Act 1995.

As amended by the Statute Law Revision (No 2) Act 1888; Statute Law Revision Act 1893; Statute Law (Repeals) Act 1969; Family Law Reform Act 1969, s3(1)(a); Administration of Justice Act 1982, ss17, 18(1), (2); Family Law Act 1986, s53; Children Act 1989, s108(5), Schedule 13, para 1; Law Reform (Succession) Act 1995, s3(1).

BILLS OF EXCHANGE ACT 1882
(45 & 46 Vict c 61)

PART I

PRELIMINARY

2   Interpretation of terms

In this Act, unless the context otherwise requires, –

'Acceptance' means an acceptance completed by delivery or notification.

'Action' includes counter claim and set off.

'Banker' includes a body of persons whether incorporated or not who carry on the business of banking.

'Bankrupt' includes any person whose estate is vested in a trustee or assignee under the law for the time being in force relating to bankruptcy.

'Bearer' means the person in possession of a bill or note which is payable to bearer.

'Bill' means bill of exchange, and 'note' means promissory note.

'Delivery' means transfer of possession, actual or constructive, from one person to another.

'Holder' means the payee or indorsee or a bill or note who is in possession of it, or the bearer thereof.

'Indorsement' means an indorsement completed by delivery.

'Issue' means the first delivery of a bill or note, complete in form to a person who takes it as a holder.

'Person' includes a body of persons whether incorporated or note.

'Value' means a valuable consideration.

'Written' includes printed, and 'writing' includes print.

PART II

BILLS OF EXCHANGE

3   Bill of exchange defined

(1) A bill of exchange is an unconditional order in writing, addressed by one person to another, signed by the person giving it, requiring the person to whom it is addressed to pay on demand or at a fixed or determinable future time a sum certain in money to or to the order of a specified person, or to bearer.

(2) An instrument which does not comply with these conditions, or which orders any act to be done in addition to the payment of money, is not a bill of exchange.

(3) An order to pay out of a particular fund is not unconditional within the meaning of this section; but an unqualified order to pay, coupled with (a) an indication of a particular fund out of which the drawee is to re-imburse himself or a particular account to be debited with the amount, or (b) a statement of the transaction which gives rise to the bill is unconditional.

(4) A bill is not invalid by reason –

   (a) That it is not dated;
   (b) That it does not specify the value given, or that any value has been given therefor;
   (c) That it does not specify the place where it is drawn or the place where it is payable.

72   Rules where laws conflict

Where a bill drawn in one country is negotiated, accepted, or payable in another, the rights, duties, and liabilities of the parties thereto are determined as follows –

(1) The validity of a bill as regards requisites in form is determined by the law of the place of issue, and the validity as regards requisites in form of the supervening contracts, such as acceptance, or indorsement, or acceptance supra protest, is determined by the law of the place where such contract was made.

Provided that –

   (a) Where a bill is issued out of the United Kingdom it is not invalid by reason only that it is not stamped in accordance with the law of the place of issue;

(b) Where a bill, issued out of the United Kingdom, conforms, as regards requisites in form, to the law of the United Kingdom, it may, for the purpose of enforcing payment thereof, be treated as valid as between all persons who negotiate, hold, or become parties to it in the United Kingdom.

(2) Subject to the provisions of this Act, the interpretation of the drawing, indorsement, acceptance, or acceptance supra protest of a bill, is determined by the law of the place where such contract is made. Provided that where an inland bill is indorsed in a foreign country the indorsement shall as regards the payer be interpreted according to the law of the United Kingdom.

(3) The duties of the holder with respect to presentment for acceptance or payment and the necessity for or sufficiency of a protest or notice of dishonour or otherwise, are determined by the law of the place where the act is done or the bill is dishonoured.

(5) Where a bill is drawn in one country and is payable in another, the due date thereof is determined according to the law of the place where it is payable.

PART III

CHEQUES ON A BANKER

73 Cheque defined

A cheque is a bill of exchange drawn on a banker payable on demand.

Except as otherwise provided in this Part, the provisions of this Act applicable to a bill of exchange payable on demand apply to a cheque.

FOREIGN MARRIAGE ACT 1892
(55 & 56 Vict c 23)

1 Validity of marriages solemnised abroad in manner provided by Act

(1) All marriages between parties of whom at least one is a United Kingdom national solemnised in the matter in this Act provided in any foreign country or place by or before a marriage officer within the meaning of this Act shall be as valid as if the same had been solemnised in the United Kingdom with a due observance of all forms required by law.

(2) In this Act 'United Kingdom national' means a person who is –

(a) a British citizen, a British Dependant Territories citizen, a British Overseas citizen or a British National (Overseas); or

(b) a British subject under the British Nationality Act 1981; or

(c) a British protected person, within the meaning of that Act.

8 Solemnisation of marriage at office in presence of marriage officer and two witnesses

(1) After the expiration of fourteen days after the notice of an intended marriage has been entered under this Act, then, if no lawful impediment to the marriage is shown to the satisfaction of the marriage officer, and the marriage has not been forbidden in manner provided by this Act, the marriage may be solemnised under this Act.

(2) Every such marriage shall be solemnised –

(a) at the official house of the marriage officer, with open doors, between 8 am and 6 pm, in the presence of two or more witnesses;

(b) by the marriage officer or, if the parties so desire, by another person in his presence; and

(c) according to such form and ceremony as the parties see fit to adopt.

(3) Where (apart from this subsection) it would not be stated or otherwise indicated in the course of the ceremony adopted by the parties that neither of them knows of any lawful impediment to their marriage, then, in some part of the ceremony and in the presence of the marriage officer and witnesses, they shall each declare –

'I solemnly declare that I know not of any lawful impediment why I *AB [or CD]* may not be joined in matrimony to *CD [or AB]*.'

(4) Where (apart from this subsection) it would not be stated by each of the parties in the course of the ceremony adopted by them that he or she takes the other as wife or husband, then, in some part of the ceremony and in the presence of the marriage officer and witnesses, each of the parties shall say to the other –

'I call upon these persons here present to witness that I *AB [or CD]* take thee *CD [or AB]* to be my lawful wedded wife *[or husband]*'.

11   Marriage officers and their districts

(1) For the purposes of this Act the following officers shall be marriage officers that is to say:

(a) Any officer authorised in that behalf by a Secretary of State by authority in writing under his hand (in this Act referred to as a marriage warrant); and

(b) Any officer who, under the marriage regulations hereinafter mentioned, is authorised to act as marriage officers without any marriage warrant,

and the district of the marriage officer shall be the area within which the duties of his office are exercisable, or any such less area as is assigned by the marriage warrant or any other warrant of a Secretary of State, or is fixed by the marriage regulations.

(2) Any marriage warrant of a Secretary of State may authorise to be a marriage officer –

(a) a British ambassador residing in a foreign country to the government of which he is accredited, and also any officer prescribed as an officer for solemnising marriages in the official house of such ambassador;

(b) the holder of the office of British consul in any foreign country or place specified in the warrant; and

(c) a governor, high commissioner, resident, consular or other officer, or any person appointed in pursuance of the marriage regulations to act in the place of a high commissioner or resident, and this Act shall apply with the prescribed modifications to a marriage by or before a governor, high commissioner, resident, or officer so authorised by the warrant, and such an application shall not be limited to places outside Her Majesty's dominions.

(3) If a marriage warrant refers to the office without designating the name of any particular person holding the office, then, while the warrant is in force, the person for the time being holding or acting in such office shall be a marriage officer.

(4) A Secretary of State may, by warrant under his hand, vary or revoke any marriage warrant previously issued under this Act.

(5) Where a marriage officer has no seal of his office, any reference in this Act to the official seal shall be construed to refer to any seal ordinarily used by him, if authenticated by his signature with his official name and description.

19 Power to refuse solemnisation of marriage where marriage inconsistent with international law

A marriage officer shall not be required to solemnise a marriage, or to allow a marriage to be solemnised in his presence, if in his opinion the solemnisation thereof would be inconsistent with international law or the comity of nations:

Provided that any person requiring his marriage to be solemnised shall, if the officer refuses to solemnise it or allow it to be solemnised in his presence, have the right of appeal to the Secretary of State given by this Act.

22 Validity of marriages solemnised by chaplains of HM forces serving abroad and other persons

(1) A marriage solemnised in any foreign territory by a chaplain serving with any part of the naval, military or air forces of His Majesty serving in that territory or by a person authorised, either generally or in respect of the particular marriage, by the commanding officer of any part of those forces serving in that territory shall, subject as hereinafter provided, be as valid in law as

if the marriage had been solemnised in the United Kingdom with a due observance of all forms required by law.

(1A) Subsection (1) above shall not apply to a marriage unless –

(a) at least one of the parties to the marriage is a person who –

(i) is a member of the said forces serving in the foreign territory concerned or is employed in that territory in such other capacity as may be prescribed by Order in Council; or

(ii) is a child of a person falling within sub-paragraph (i) above and has his home with that person in that territory; and

(b) such other conditions as may be so prescribed are complied with.

(1B) In determining for the purposes of subsection (1A) above whether one person is the child of another –

(a) it shall be immaterial whether the person's father and mother were at any time married to each other; and

(b) a person who is or was treated by another as a child of the family in relation to any marriage to which that other is or was a party shall be regarded as his child.

(2) In this section the expression 'foreign territory' means territory other than:

(a) any part of His Majesty's dominions;

(b) any British protectorate; or

(c) any other country or territory under His Majesty's protection or suzerainty or in which His Majesty has for the time being jurisdiction:

Provided that His Majesty may by Order in Council direct that –

(i) any British protectorate or any such other country or territory as is referred to in paragraph (c) hereof; or

(ii) any part of His Majesty's dominions which has been occupied by a State at war with His Majesty and in which the facilities for marriage in accordance with the local law have not in the opinion of His Majesty been adequately restored;

shall, while the Order remains in force, be treated as foreign territory for the purposes of this section.

(3) Any reference in this section to foreign territory, to forces serving in foreign territory and to persons employed in foreign territory

shall include references to ships which are for the time being in the waters of any foreign territory, to forces serving in any such ship and to persons employed in any such ship, respectively.

(4) His Majesty may by Order in Council provide for the registration of marriages solemnised under this section.

(5) Where a marriage purports to have been solemnised under this section, it shall not be necessary in any legal proceedings touching the validity of the marriage to prove the authority of the person by or before whom it was solemnised, nor shall any evidence to prove his want of authority be given in any such proceedings.

(6) Any Order in Council made under the foregoing provisions of this section may be varied or revoked by a subsequent Order in Council, and any Order in Council made under this section shall be laid forthwith before each House of Parliament.

23 Saving

Nothing in this Act shall confirm or impair or in anywise affect the validity in law of any marriage solemnised beyond the seas, otherwise than as herein provided, and this Act shall not extend to the marriage of any of the Royal family.

As amended by the Foreign Marriage Act 1947, s2; Foreign Marriage (Amendment) Act 1988, ss1(1), (2), 4, 6, 7(2), Schedule.

EVIDENCE (COLONIAL STATUTES)
ACT 1907
(7 Edw 7 c 16)

1   Proof of statutes of British possessions

(1) Copies of Acts, ordinances, and statutes passed (whether before or after the passing of this Act) by the Legislature of any British possession, and of orders, regulations, and other instruments issued or made, whether before or after the passing of this Act, under the authority of any such Act, ordinance, or statute, if purporting to be printed by the Government printer, shall be received in evidence by all courts of justice in the United Kingdom without any proof being given that the copies were so printed.

(3) In this Act –

> The expression 'Government printer' means, as respects any British possession, the printer purporting to be the printer authorised to print the Acts, ordinances, or statutes of the Legislature of that possession, or otherwise to be the Government printer of that possession:

> The expression 'British possession' means any part of His Majesty's dominions exclusive of the United Kingdom, and, where parts of those dominions are under both a central and a local Legislature, shall include both all parts under the central Legislature and each part under a local Legislature. ...

PERJURY ACT 1911
(1 & 2 Geo 5 c 6)

1A False unsworn statement under Evidence (Proceedings in Other Jurisdictions) Act 1975

If any person, in giving any testimony (either orally or in writing) otherwise than on oath, where required to do so by an order under section 2 of the Evidence (Proceedings in Other Jurisdictions) Act 1975, makes a statement –

> (a) which he knows to be false in a material particular, or
>
> (b) which is false in a material particular and which he does not believe to be true,

he shall be guilty of an offence and shall be liable on conviction on indictment to imprisonment for a term not exceeding two years or a fine or both.

As inserted by the Evidence (Proceedings in Other Jurisdictions) Act 1975, s8(1), Schedule 1.

MAINTENANCE ORDERS (FACILITIES FOR ENFORCEMENT) ACT 1920
(10 & 11 Geo 5 c 33)

1   Enforcement in England and Ireland of maintenance orders made in His Majesty's dominions outside the United Kingdom

(1) Where a maintenance order has, whether before or after the passing of this Act, been made against any person by any court in any part of His Majesty's dominions outside the United Kingdom to which this Act extends, and a certified copy of the order has been transmitted by the governor of that part of His Majesty's dominions to the Lord Chancellor, the Lord Chancellor shall send a copy of the order to the prescribed officer of a court in England or Ireland for registration; and on receipt thereof the order shall be registered in the prescribed manner, and shall, from the date of such registration, be of the same force and effect, and, subject to the provisions of this Act, all proceedings may be taken on such order as if it had been an order originally obtained in the court in which it is so registered, and that court shall have power to enforce the order accordingly.

(2) The Court in which an order is to be so registered as aforesaid shall, if the court by which the order was made was a court of superior jurisdiction, be the Family Division of the High Court, or in Ireland the King's Bench Division (Matrimonial) of the High Court of Justice in Ireland, and, if the court was not a court of superior jurisdiction, be a court of summary jurisdiction.

2   Transmission of maintenance orders made in England or Ireland

Where a court in England or Ireland has, whether before or after the commencement of this Act, made a maintenance order against any person, and it is proved to that court that the person against whom the order was made is resident in some part of His Majesty's dominions outside the United Kingdom to which this Act extends, the court shall send to the Lord Chancellor for transmission to the governor of that part of His Majesty's dominions a certified copy of the order.

3   Power to make provisional orders of maintenance against persons resident in His Majesty's dominions outside the United Kingdom

(1) Where an application is made to a court of summary jurisdiction in England or Ireland for a maintenance order against any person, and it is proved that that person is resident in a part of His Majesty's dominions outside the United Kingdom to which this Act extends, the court may, in the absence of that person, if after hearing the evidence it is satisfied of the justice of the application, make any such order as it might have made if that person had been resident in England and Wales, had received reasonable notice of the date of the hearing of the application and had failed to appear at the hearing, but in such case the order shall be provisional only, and shall have no effect unless and until confirmed by a competent court in such part of His Majesty's dominions as aforesaid.

(2) The evidence of any witness who is examined on any such application shall be put into writing, and such deposition shall be read over to and signed by him.

(3) Where such an order is made, the court shall send to the Lord Chancellor for transmission to the governor of the part of His Majesty's dominions in which the person against whom the order is made is alleged to reside the depositions so taken and a certified copy of the order, together with a statement of the grounds on which the making of the order might have been opposed if the person against whom the order is made had been resident in England and Wales, had received reasonable notice of the date of the hearing and had appeared at the hearing, and such information as the court possesses for facilitating the identification of that person, and ascertaining his whereabouts.

(4) Where any such provisional order has come before a court in a part of His Majesty's dominions outside the United Kingdom to which this Act extends for confirmation, and the order has by that court been remitted to the court of summary jurisdiction which made the order for the purpose of taking further evidence, that court or any other court of summary jurisdiction appointed for the same

commission area (within the meaning of) the Justices of the Peace Act 1979 shall, after the prescribed notice, proceed to take the evidence in like manner and subject to the like conditions as the evidence in support of the original application.

If upon the hearing of such evidence it appears to the court that the order ought not to have been made, the court may revoke the order, but in any other case the depositions shall be sent to the Secretary of State and dealt with in like manner as the original depositions.

(5) The confirmation of an order made under this section shall not affect any power of a court of summary jurisdiction to vary or revoke that order:

Provided that on the making of a varying or revoking order the court shall send a certified copy thereof to the Lord Chancellor for transmission to the governor of the part of His Majesty's dominions in which the original order was confirmed, and that in the case of an order varying the original order the order shall not have any effect unless and until confirmed in like manner as the original order.

(6) The application shall have the same right of appeal, if any, against a refusal to make a provisional order as he would have had against a refusal to make the order had the person against whom the order is sought to be made been resident in England and Wales and received reasonable notice of the date of the hearing of the application.

(7) Where subsection (1) of section 60 of the Magistrates' Courts Act 1980 (revocation, variation etc of orders for periodical payment) applies in relation to an order made under this section which has been confirmed, that subsection shall have effect as if for the words 'by order on complaint', there were substituted 'on an application being made, by order'.

(8) In this section 'revoke' includes discharge.

4   Power of court of summary jurisdiction to confirm maintenance order made out of the United Kingdom

(1) Where a maintenance order has been made by a court in a part of His Majesty's dominions outside the United Kingdom to which this Act extends, and the order is provisional only and has no effect unless and until confirmed by a court of summary jurisdiction in England or Ireland, and a certified copy of the order, together with

the depositions of witnesses and a statement of the grounds on which the order might have been opposed has been transmitted to the Lord Chancellor, and it appears to the Lord Chancellor that the person against whom the order was made is resident in England or Ireland, the Lord Chancellor may send the said documents to the prescribed officer of a court of summary jurisdiction, with a requisition that a notice be served on the person informing him that he may attend a hearing at the time and place specified in the notice to show cause why that order should not be confirmed, and upon receipt of such documents and requisition the court shall cause such a notice to be served upon such a person.

(2) A notice required to be served under this section may be served by post.

(3) At the hearing it shall be open to the person on whom the notice was served to oppose the confirmation of the order on any grounds on which he might have opposed the making of the order in the original proceedings had he been a party to them, but on no other grounds, and the certificate from the court which made the provisional order stating the grounds on which the making of the order might have been opposed if the person against whom the order was made had been a party to the proceedings shall be conclusive evidence that those grounds are grounds on which objection may be taken.

(4) If at the hearing the person served with the notice does not appear or, on appearing, fails to satisfy the court that the order ought not to be confirmed, the court may confirm the order either without modification or with such modifications as to the court after hearing the evidence may seem just.

(5) If the person served with the notice appears at the hearing and satisfies the court that for the purpose of establishing any grounds on which he opposes the confirmation of the order it is necessary to remit the case to the court which made the provisional order for the taking of any further evidence, the court may so remit the case and adjourn the proceedings for the purpose.

(5A) Where a magistrates' court confirms a provisional order under this section, it shall at the same time exercise one of its powers under subsection (5B).

(5B) The powers of the court are –

    (a) the power to order that payments under the order be made

directly to the clerk of the court or the clerk of any other magistrates' court;

(b) the power to order that payments under the order be made to the clerk of the court, or to the clerk of any other magistrates' court, by such method of payment falling within section 59(6) of the Magistrates' Courts Act 1980 (standing order, etc) as may be specified;

(c) the power to make an attachment of earnings order under the Attachment of Earnings Act 1971 to secure payments under the order.

(5C) In deciding which of the powers under subsection (5B) it is to exercise, the court shall have regard to any representations made by the person liable to make payments under the order.

(5D) Subsection (4) of section 59 of the Magistrates' Courts Act 1980 (power of court to require debtor to open account) shall apply for the purposes of subsection (5B) as it applies for the purposes of that section but as if for paragraph (a) there were substituted –

'(a) the court proposes to exercise its power under paragraph (b) of section 4(5B) of the Maintenance Orders (Facilities for Enforcement) Act 1920, and'.

(6) Subject to subsection (6A), where a provisional order has been confirmed under this section, it may be varied or revoked in like manner as if it had originally been made by the confirming court.

(6A) Where the confirming court is a magistrates' court, section 60 of the Magistrates' Courts Act 1980 (revocation, variation etc of orders for periodical payment) shall have effect in relation to a provisional order confirmed under this section –

(za) as if in subsection (1) for the words 'by order on complaint' there were substituted 'on application being made, by order';

(a) as if in subsection (3) for the words 'paragraphs (a) to (d) of section 59(3) above' there were substituted 'section 4(5B) of the Maintenance Orders (Facilities for Enforcement) Act 1920';

(b) as if in subsection (4) for paragraph (b) there were substituted –

'(b) payments under the order are required to be made to the clerk of the court, or to the clerk of any other magistrates' court, by any method of payment falling within section 59(6) above (standing order, etc)';

and as if after the words 'the court' there were inserted 'which made the order';

(c) as if in subsection (5) for the words 'to the clerk' there were substituted 'in accordance with paragraph (a) of section 4(5B) of the Maintenance Orders (Facilities for Enforcement) Act 1920';

(d) as if in subsection (7), paragraph (c) and the word 'and' immediately preceding it were omitted;

(e) as if in subsection (8) for the words 'paragraphs (a) to (d) of section 59(3) above' there were substituted 'section 4(5B) of the Maintenance Orders (Facilities for Enforcement) Act 1920';

(f) as if for subsections (9) and (10) there were substituted the following subsections –

'(9) In deciding, for the purposes of subsections (3) and (8) above, which of the powers under section 4(5B) of the Maintenance Orders (Facilities for Enforcement) Act 1920 it is to exercise, the court shall have regard to any representations made by the debtor.

(10) Subsection (4) of section 59 above (power of court to require debtor to open account) shall apply for the purposes of subsections (3) and (8) above as it applies for the purposes of that section but as if for paragraph (a) there were substituted –

"(a) The court proposes to exercise its power under paragraph (b) of section 4(5B) of the Maintenance Orders (Facilities for Enforcement) Act 1920, and".'

(6B) Where on an application for variation or revocation the confirming court is satisfied that it is necessary to remit the case to the court which made the order for the purpose of taking any further evidence, the court may so remit the case and adjourn the proceedings for the purpose.

(7) Where an order has been so confirmed, the person bound thereby shall have the same right of appeal, if any, against the confirmation of the order as he would have had against the making of the order had the order been an order made by the court confirming the order.

4A Variation and revocation of maintenance orders

(1) This section applies to –

(a) any maintenance order made by virtue of section 3 of this Act which has been confirmed as mentioned in that section; and

(b) any maintenance order which has been confirmed under section 4 of this Act.

(2) Where the respondent to an application for the variation or revocation of a maintenance order to which this section applies is residing in a part of Her Majesty's dominions outside the United Kingdom to which this Act extends, a magistrates' court in England and Wales shall have jurisdiction to hear the application (where it would not have such jurisdiction apart from this subsection) if that court would have had jurisdiction to hear it had the respondent been residing in England and Wales. ...

(4) Where –

(a) the respondent to an application for the variation or revocation of a maintenance order to which this section applies does not appear at the time and place appointed for the hearing of the application by a magistrates' court in England and Wales, and

(b) the court is satisfied that the respondent is residing in a part of Her Majesty's dominions outside the United Kingdom to which this Act extends,

the court may proceed to hear and determine the application at the time and place appointed for the hearing or for any adjourned hearing in like manner as if the respondent had appeared at that time and place. ...

(6) In this section 'revocation' includes discharge.

NB This Act is repealed by s22(2) of the Maintenance Orders (Reciprocal Enforcement) Act 1972 as from a day which has yet to be appointed.

As amended by the Administration of Justice Act 1970, s1(6), Schedule 2, para 2; Domestic Proceedings and Magistrates' Courts Act 1978, s89(2)(a), Schedule 2, para 2; Justice of the Peace Act 1979, s71, Schedule 2, para 1; Maintenance Enforcement Act 1991, s10, Schedule 1, para 1; Transfer of Functions (Magistrates' Courts and Family Law) Order 1992, art 4; Maintenance Orders (Reciprocal Enforcement) Act 1992, s1(1), Schedule 1, Pt I, paras 1, 2, 3.

ADMINISTRATION OF JUSTICE ACT
1920
(10 & 11 Geo 5 c 81)

PART II

RECIPROCAL ENFORCEMENT OF JUDGMENTS IN THE UNITED KINGDOM AND IN OTHER PARTS OF HIS MAJESTY'S DOMINIONS

9   Enforcement in the United Kingdom of judgments obtained in superior courts in other British dominions

(1) Where a judgment has been obtained in a superior court in any part of His Majesty's dominions outside the United Kingdom to which this Part of this Act extends, the judgment creditor may apply to the High Court in England or [Northern] Ireland, or to the Court of Session in Scotland, at any time within twelve months after the date of the judgment, or such longer period as may be allowed by the court, to have the judgment registered in the court, and on any such application the court may, if in all the circumstances of the case they think it is just and convenient that the judgment should be enforced in the United Kingdom, and subject to the provisions of this section, order the judgment to be registered accordingly.

(2) No judgment shall be ordered to be registered under this section if –

(a) the original court acted without jurisdiction; or

(b) the judgment debtor, being a person who was neither carrying on business nor ordinarily resident within the jurisdiction of the original court, did not voluntarily appear or otherwise submit or agree to submit to the jurisdiction of that court; or

(c) the judgment debtor, being the defendant in the proceedings, was not duly served with the process of the original court and did not appear, notwithstanding that he was ordinarily resident or was carrying on business within the jurisdiction of that court or agreed to submit to the jurisdiction of that court; or

(d) the judgment was obtained by fraud; or

(e) the judgment debtor satisfies the registering court either that an appeal is pending, or that he is entitled and intends to appeal, against the judgment; or

(f) the judgment was in respect of a cause of action which for reasons of public policy or for some other similar reason could not have been entertained by the registering court.

(3) Where a judgment is registered under this section –

(a) the judgement shall, as from the date of registration, be of the same force and effect, and proceedings may be taken thereon, as if it had been a judgment originally obtained or entered up on the date of registration in the registering court;

(b) the registering court shall have the same control and jurisdiction over the judgment as it has over similar judgments given by itself, but in so far only as relates to execution under this section;

(c) the reasonable costs of and incidental to the registration of the judgment (including the costs of obtaining a certified copy thereof from the original court and of the application for registration) shall be recoverable in like manner as if they were sums payable under the judgment. ...

(5) In any action brought in any court in the United Kingdom on any judgment which might be ordered to be registered under this section, the plaintiff shall not be entitled to recover any costs of the action unless an application to register the judgment under this section has previously been refused or unless the court otherwise orders.

10 Issue of certificates of judgment obtained in the United Kingdom

(1) Where –

(a) a judgment has been obtained in the High Court in England or Northern Ireland, or in the Court of Session in Scotland, against any person; and

(b) the judgment creditor wishes to secure the enforcement of the judgment in a part of Her Majesty's dominions outside the United Kingdom to which this Part of this Act extends, the court shall, on an application made by the judgment creditor, issue to him a certified copy of the judgment.

(2) The reference in the preceding subsection to Her Majesty's dominions shall be construed as if that subsection had come into force in its present form at the commencement of this Act.

12 Interpretation

(1) In this Part of this Act, unless the context otherwise requires –

The expression 'judgment' means any judgment or order given or made by a court in any civil proceedings, whether before or after the passing of this Act, whereby any sum of money is made payable, and includes an award in proceedings on an arbitration if the award has, in pursuance of the law in force in the place where it was made, become enforceable in the same manner as a judgment given by a court in that place;

The expression 'original court' in relation to any judgment means the court by which the judgment was given;

The expression 'registering court' in relation to any judgment means the court by which the judgment was registered;

The expression 'judgment creditor' means the person by whom the judgment was obtained, and includes the successors and assigns of that person;

The expression 'judgment debtor' means the person against whom the judgment was given, and includes any person against whom the judgment is enforceable in the place where it was given.

(2) Subject to rules of court, any of the powers conferred by this Part of this Act on any court may be exercised by a judge of the court.

14 Extent of Part II of Act

(1) Where His Majesty is satisfied that reciprocal provisions have been made by the legislature of any part of His Majesty's dominions outside the United Kingdom for the enforcement within that part of His dominions of judgment obtained in the High Court in England, the Court of Session in Scotland, and the High Court in Ireland, His Majesty may by Order in Council declare that this Part of this Act shall extend to that part of His dominions, and on any such Order being made this Part of this Act shall extend accordingly.

(2) An Order in Council under this section may be varied or revoked by a subsequent Order.

(3) Her Majesty may by Order in Council under this section consolidate any Orders in Council under this section which are in force when the consolidating Order is made.

21   Short title, repeal and application

(3) This Act, except Part II thereof, applies only to England and Wales.

As amended by the Civil Jurisdiction and Judgments Act 1982, s35(2), (3).

ADMINISTRATION OF ESTATES ACT 1925

(15 & 16 Geo 5 c 23)

33 Trust for sale

(1) On the death of a person intestate as to any real or personal estate, such estate shall be held by his personal representatives –

(a) as to the real estate upon trust to sell the same; and

(b) as to the personal estate upon trust to call in sell and convert into money such part thereof as may not consist of money,

with power to postpone such sale and conversion for such a period as the personal representatives, without being liable to account, may think proper, and so that any reversionary interest be not sold until it falls into possession, unless the personal representatives see special reason for sale, and so also that, unless required for purposes of administration owing to want of other assets, personal chattels be not sold except for special reason. ...

45 Abolition of descent to heir, curtesy, dower and escheat

(1) With regard to the real estate and personal inheritance of every person dying after the commencement of this Act, there shall be abolished –

(a) all existing modes rules and canons of descent, and of devolution by special occupancy or otherwise, of real estate, or of a personal inheritance, whether operating by the general law or by the custom of gavelkind or borough english or by any other custom of any county, locality, or manor, or otherwise howsoever; and

(b) tenancy by the curtesy and every other estate and interest of a husband in real estate as to which his wife dies intestate, whether arising under the general law or by custom or otherwise; and

(c) dower and freebench and every other estate and interest of a wife in real estate as to which her husband dies intestate, whether arising under the general law or by custom or otherwise: Provided that where a right (if any) to freebench or other like right has attached before the commencement of this Act which cannot be barred by a testamentary or other disposition made by the husband, such right shall, unless released, remain in force as an equitable interest; and

(d) escheat to the Crown or the Duchy of Lancaster or the Duke of Cornwall or to a mesne lord for want of heirs.

(2) Nothing in this section affects the descent or devolution of an entailed interest.

46 Succession to real and personal estate on intestacy

(1) The residuary estate of an intestate shall be distributed in the manner or be held on the trusts mentioned in this section, namely –

(i) If the intestate leaves a husband or wife, then in accordance with the following Table:

TABLE

If the intestate –

(1) leaves –	the residuary estate shall be held in trust for the surviving husband or wife absolutely.
(a) no issue, and	
(b) no parent, or brother or sister of the whole blood, or issue of a brother or sister of the whole blood	
(2) leaves issue (whether or not persons mentioned in sub-paragraph (b) above also survive)	the surviving husband or wife shall take the personal chattels absolutely and, in addition, the residuary estate of the intestate (other than the personal chattels) shall stand charged with the payment of a fixed net sum [£125,000], free of death duties and costs, to the surviving husband or wife with interest thereon from the date of the death at such rate as the Lord

Chancellor may specify by order until paid or appropriated, and, subject to providing for that sum and the interest thereon, the residuary estate (other than the personal chattels) shall be held –

(a) as to one half upon trust for the surviving husband or wife during his or her life, and, subject to such life interest, on the statutory trusts for the issue of the intestate, and

(b) as to the other half, on the statutory trusts for the issue of the intestate.

(3) leaves one or more of the following, that is to say, a parent, a brother or sister of the whole blood, or issue of a brother or sister of the whole blood, but leaves no issue

the surviving husband or wife shall take the personal chattels absolutely and, in addition, the residuary estate of the intestate (other than the personal chattels) shall stand charged with the payment of a fixed net sum [£200,000], free of death duties and costs, to the surviving husband or wife with interest thereon from the date of the death at such rate as the Lord Chancellor may specify by order until paid or appropriated, and, subject to providing for that sum and the interest thereon, the residuary estate (other than the personal chattels) shall be held –

(a) as to one half in trust for the surviving husband or wife absolutely, and

(b) as to the other half –

(i) where the intestate leaves one parent or both parents (whether or not brothers or sisters of the intestate or their issue also survive) in trust for the parent absolutely or, as the case may be, for the two parents in equal shares absolutely,

(ii) where the intestate leaves no parent, on the statutory trusts for the brothers and sisters of the whole blood of the intestate.

The fixed net sums referred to in paragraphs (2) and (3) of this Table shall be of the amounts provided by or under section 1 of the Family Provision Act 1966.

(ii) If the intestate leaves issue but no husband or wife the residuary estate of the intestate shall be held on the statutory trusts for the issue of the intestate;

(iii) If the intestate leaves no husband or wife and no issue but both parents, then the residuary estate of the intestate shall be held in trust for the father and mother in equal shares absolutely;

(iv) If the intestate leaves no husband or wife and no issue but one parent, then the residuary estate of the intestate shall be held in trust for the surviving father or mother absolutely;

(v) If the intestate leaves no husband or wife and no issue and no parent, then the residuary estate of the intestate shall be held in trust for the following persons living at the death of the intestate, and in the following order and manner, namely –

First, on the statutory trusts for the brothers and sisters of the whole blood of the intestate; but if no person takes an absolutely vested interest under such trusts; then

Secondly, on the statutory trusts for the brothers and sisters of the half blood of the intestate; but if no person takes an absolutely vested interested under such trusts; then

Thirdly, for the grandparents of the intestate and, if more than one survive the intestate, in equal shares; but if there is no member of this class; then

Fourthly, on the statutory trusts for the uncles and aunts of the intestate (being brothers or sisters of the whole blood of a parent of the intestate); but if no person takes an absolutely vested interest under such trusts; then

Fifthly, on the statutory trusts for the uncles and aunts of the intestate (being brothers or sisters of the half blood of a parent of the intestate).

(vi) In default of any person taking an absolute interest under the foregoing provisions, the residuary estate of the intestate shall belong to the Crown or to the Duchy of Lancaster or to the Duke of Cornwall for the time being, as the case may be, as bona vacantia, and in lieu of any right to escheat.

The Crown or the said Duchy or the said Duke may (without prejudice to the powers reserved by section 9 of the Civil List Act 1910, or any other powers), out of the whole or any part of the property devolving on them respectively, provide, in accordance with the existing practice, for dependants, whether kindred or not, of the intestate, and other persons for whom the intestate might reasonably have been expected to make provision.

(1A) The power to make orders under subsection (1) above shall be exercisable by statutory instrument subject to annulment in pursuance of a resolution of either House of Parliament; and any such order may be varied or revoked by a subsequent order made under the power.

(2) A husband and wife shall for all purposes of distribution or division under the foregoing provisions of this section be treated as two persons.

(2A) Where the intestate's husband or wife survived the intestate but died before the end of the period of 28 days beginning with the day on which the intestate died, this section shall have effect as respects the intestate as if the husband or wife had nor survived the intestate.

(3) Where the intestate and the intestate's husband or wife have died in circumstances rendering it uncertain which of them survived the other and the intestate's husband or wife is by virtue of section 184 of the Law of Property Act 1925 deemed to have survived the intestate, this section shall, nevertheless, have effect as respects the intestate as if the husband or wife had not survived the intestate.

(4) The interest payable on the fixed net sum payable to a surviving husband or wife shall be primarily payable out of income.

NB Section 46(2A) has effect as respects an intestate dying on or after 1 January 1996: s1(3) of the Law Reform (Succession) Act 1995.

As amended by the Intestates Estates Act 1952, s1; Family Provision Act 1966, s1; Administration of Justice Act 1977, s28(1)(a)(i), (ii); Law Reform (Succession) Act 1995, s1(1).

EVIDENCE (FOREIGN, DOMINION AND COLONIAL DOCUMENTS) ACT 1933

(23 & 24 Geo 5 c 4)

1 Proof and effect of foreign, dominion and colonial registers and certain official certificates

(2) An Order in Council made under section 5 of the Oaths and Evidence (Overseas Authorities and Countries) Act 1963 may provide that in all parts of the United Kingdom –

(a) a register of the country to which the Order relates, being such a register as is specified in the Order, shall be deemed to be a public register kept under the authority of the law of that country and recognised by the courts thereof as an authentic record, and to be a document of such a public nature as to be admissible as evidence of the matters regularly recorded therein;

(b) such matters as may be specified in the Order shall, if recorded in such a register, be deemed, until the contrary is proved, to be regularly recorded therein;

(c) subject to any conditions specified in the Order and to any requirements of rules of court a document purporting to be issued in the country to which the Order relates as an official copy of an entry in such a register as is so specified, and purporting to be authenticated as such in the manner specified in the Order as appropriate in the case of such a register, shall, without evidence as to the custody of the register or of inability to produce it and without any further or other proof, be received as evidence that the register contains such an entry;

(d) subject as aforesaid a certificate purporting to be given in the country to which the Order relates as an official certificate of any such class as is specified in the Order, and purporting to be signed by the officer, and to be authenticated in the manner specified in the Order as appropriate in the case of a certificate of that class, shall be received as evidence of the facts stated in the certificate;

(e) no official document issued in the country to which the Order relates as proof of any matters for the proof of which provision is made by the Order shall, if otherwise admissible in evidence, be inadmissible by reason only that it is not authenticated by the process known as legislation.

(3) Official books of record preserved in a central registry and containing entries copied from original registers may, if those entries were copied by officials in the course of their duty, themselves be treated for the purposes of this section as registers. ...

As amended by the Oaths and Evidence (Overseas Authorities and Countries) Act 1963, s5.

FOREIGN JUDGMENTS (RECIPROCAL ENFORCEMENT) ACT 1933

(23 & 24 Geo 5 c 13)

PART I

REGISTRATION OF FOREIGN JUDGMENTS

1 Power to extend Part I of Act to foreign countries giving reciprocal treatment

(1) If, in the case of a foreign country, His Majesty is satisfied that, in the event of the benefits conferred by this Part of the Act being extended to, or to any particular class of, judgments given in the courts of that country or in any particular class of those courts, substantial reciprocity of treatment will be assured as regards the enforcement in that country of similar judgments given in similar courts of the United Kingdom, He may by Order in Council direct –

(a) that this part of this Act shall extend to that country;

(b) that such courts of that country as are specified in the Order shall be recognised courts in that country for the purposes of this Part of this Act; and

(c) that judgments of any such recognised court, or such judgments of any class so specified shall, if within subsection (2) of this section, be judgments to which this Part of this Act applies.

(2) Subject to subsection (2A) of this section, a judgment of a recognised court is within this subsection if it satisfies the following conditions, namely –

(a) it is either final and conclusive as between the judgment debtor and the judgment creditor or requires the former to make an interim payment to the latter; and

(b) there is payable under it a sum of money, not being a sum payable in respect of taxes or other charges of a like nature or in respect of a fine or other penalty; and

(c) it is given after the coming into force of the Order in Council which made that court a recognised court.

(2A) The following judgments of a recognised court are not within subsection (2) of this section –

(a) a judgment given by that court on appeal from a court which is not a recognised court;

(b) a judgment or other instrument which is regarded for the purposes of its enforcement as a judgment of that court but which was given or made in another country;

(c) a judgment given by that court in proceedings founded on a judgment of court in another country and having as their object the enforcement of that judgment.

(3) For the purposes of this section, a judgment shall be deemed to be final and conclusive notwithstanding that an appeal may be pending against it, or that it may still be subject to appeal, in the courts of the country of the original court.

(4) His Majesty may by subsequent Order in Council vary or revoke any Order previously made under this section.

(5) Any Order in Council made under this section before its amendment by the Civil Jurisdiction and Judgments Act 1982 which deems any court of a foreign country to be a superior court of that country for the purposes of this part of this Act shall (without prejudice to subsection (4) of this section) have effect from the time of that amendment as if it provided for that court to be a recognised court of that country for those purposes, and for any final and conclusive judgment of that court, if within subsection (2) of this section, to be a judgment to which this Part of the Act applies.

2 Application for, and effect of, registration of foreign judgment

(1) A person, being a judgment creditor under a judgment to which this Part of this Act applies, may apply to the High Court at any time within six years after the date of the judgment, or, where there have been proceedings by way of appeal against the judgment, after the date of the last judgment given in those proceedings, to have the judgment registered in the High Court, and on any such

application the court shall, subject to proof of the prescribed matters and to the other provisions of this Act, order the judgment to be registered: Provided that a judgment shall not be registered if at the date of the application –

(a) it has been wholly satisfied; or

(b) it could not be enforced by execution in the country of the original court.

(2) Subject to the provisions of this Act with respect to the setting aside of registration –

(a) a registered judgment shall, for the purposes of execution, be of the same force and effect; and

(b) proceedings may be taken on a registered judgment; and

(c) the sum for which a judgment is registered shall carry interest; and

(d) the registering court shall have the same control over the execution of a registered judgment;

as if the judgment had been a judgment originally given in the registering court and entered on the date of registration: Provided that execution shall not issue on the judgment so long as, under this Part of the Act and the Rules of Court made thereunder, it is competent for any party to make an application to have the registration of the judgment set aside, or, where such an application is made, until after the application has been finally determined.

(4) If, at the date of the application for registration the judgment of the original court has been partly satisfied, the judgment shall not be registered in respect of the whole sum payable under the judgment of the original court, but only in respect of the balance remaining payable at that date.

(5) If, on an application for the registration of a judgment, it appears to the registering court that the judgment is in respect of different matters and that some, but not all, of the provisions of the judgment are such that if those provisions had been contained in separate judgments those judgments could properly have been registered, the judgment may be registered in respect of the provisions aforesaid but not in respect of any other provisions contained therein.

(6) In addition to the sum of money payable under the judgment of the original court, including any interest which by the law of the country of the original court becomes due under the judgment up to the time of registration, the judgment shall be registered for the

reasonable costs of and incidental to registration, including the costs of obtaining a certified copy of the judgment from the original court.

3   Rules of court

(1) The power to make rules of court under section 84 of the Supreme Court Act 1981 shall, subject to the provisions of this section, include power to make rules for the following purposes –

(a) For making provision with respect to the giving of security for costs by persons applying for the registration of judgments;

(b) For prescribing the matters to be proved on an application for the registration of a judgment and for regulating the mode of proving those matters;

(c) For providing for the service on the judgment debtor of notice of the registration of a judgment;

(d) For making provision with respect to the fixing of the period within which an application may be made to have the registration of the judgment set aside and with respect to the extension of the period so fixed;

(e) For prescribing the method by which any question arising under this Act whether a foreign judgment can be enforced by execution in the country of the original court, or what interest is payable under a foreign judgment under the law of the original court, is to be determined;

(f) For prescribing any matter which under this Part of this Act is to be prescribed.

(2) Rules made for the purposes of this Part of this Act shall be expressed to have, and shall have, effect subject to any such provisions contained in Orders in Council made under section one of this Act as are declared by the said Orders to be necessary for giving effect to agreements made between His Majesty and foreign countries in relation to matters with respect to which there is power to make rules of court for the purposes of this Part of this Act.

4   Cases in which registered judgments must, or may, be set aside

(1) On an application in that behalf duly made by any party against whom a registered judgment may be enforced, the registration of the judgment –

(a) shall be set aside if the registering court is satisfied –

(i) that the judgment is not a judgment to which this Part of this Act applies or was registered in contravention of the foregoing provisions of this Act; or

(ii) that the courts of the country of the original court had no jurisdiction in the circumstances of the case; or

(iii) that the judgment debtor, being the defendant in the proceedings in the original court, did not (notwithstanding that process may have been duly served on him in accordance with the law of the country of the original court) receive notice of those proceedings in sufficient time to enable him to defend the proceedings and did not appear; or

(iv) that the judgment was obtained by fraud; or

(v) that the enforcement of the judgment would be contrary to public policy in the country of the registering court; or

(vi) that the rights under the judgment are not vested in the person by whom the application for registration was made;

(b) may be set aside if the registering court is satisfied that the matter in dispute in the proceedings in the original court had previously to the date of the judgment in the original court been the subject of a final and conclusive judgment by a court having jurisdiction in the matter.

(2) For the purposes of this section the courts of the country of the original court shall, subject to the provisions of subsection (3) of this section, be deemed to have had jurisdiction –

(a) in the case of a judgment given in an action in personam –

(i) if the judgment debtor, being a defendant in the original court, submitted to the jurisdiction of that court by voluntarily appearing in the proceedings; or

(ii) if the judgment debtor was plaintiff in, or counter-claimed in, the proceedings in the original court; or

(iii) if the judgment debtor, being a defendant in the original court, had before the commencement of the proceedings agreed, in respect of the subject matter of the proceedings, to submit to the jurisdiction of that court or of the courts of the country of that court; or

(iv) if the judgment debtor, being a defendant in the original court, was at the time when the proceedings were instituted resident in, or being a body corporate had its principal place of business in, the country of that court; or

(v) if the judgment debtor, being a defendant in the original court, had an office or place of business in the country of that court and the proceedings in that court were in respect of a transaction effected through or at that office or place;

(b) in the case of a judgment given in an action of which the subject matter was immovable property or in an action in rem of which the subject matter was movable property, if the property in question was at the time of the proceedings in the original court situate in the country of that court;

(c) in the case of a judgment given in an action other than any such action as is mentioned in paragraph (a) or paragraph (b) of this subsection, if the jurisdiction of the original court is recognised by the law of the registering court.

(3) Notwithstanding anything in subsection (2) of this section, the courts of the country of the original court shall not be deemed to have had jurisdiction –

(a) if the subject matter of the proceedings was immovable property outside the country of the original court; or

(c) if the judgment debtor, being a defendant in the original proceedings, was a person who under the rules of public international law was entitled to immunity from the jurisdiction of the courts of the country of the original court and did not submit to the jurisdiction of that court.

5 Powers of registering court on application to set aside registration

(1) If, on an application to set aside the registration of a judgment, the applicant satisfies the registering court either that an appeal is pending, or that he is entitled and intends to appeal, against the judgment, the court, if it thinks fit, may, on such terms as it may think just, either set aside the registration or adjourn the application to set aside the registration until after the expiration of such period as appears to the court to be reasonably sufficient to enable the applicant to take the necessary steps to have the appeal disposed of by the competent tribunal.

(2) Where the registration of a judgment is set aside under the last foregoing subsection, or solely for the reason that the judgment was not at the date of the application for registration enforceable by execution in the country of the original court, the setting aside of the registration shall not prejudice a further application to register the

judgment when the appeal has been disposed of or if and when the judgment becomes enforceable by execution in that country, as the case may be.

(3) Where the registration of a judgment is set aside solely for the reason that the judgment, notwithstanding that it had at the date of the application for registration been partly satisfied, was registered for the whole sum payable thereunder, the registering court shall, on the application of the judgment creditor, order judgment to be registered for the balance remaining payable at that date.

6   Foreign judgments which can be registered not to be enforceable otherwise

No proceedings for the recovery of a sum payable under a foreign judgment, being a judgment to which this Part of this Act applies, other than proceedings by way of registration of the judgment, shall be entertained by any court in the United Kingdom.

PART II

MISCELLANEOUS AND GENERAL

8   General effect of certain foreign judgments

(1) Subject to the provisions of this section, a judgment to which Part I of this Act applies or would have applied if a sum of money had been payable thereunder, whether it can be registered or not, and whether, if it can be registered, it is registered or not, shall be recognised in any court in the United Kingdom as conclusive between the parties thereto in all proceedings founded on the same cause of action and may be relied on by way of defence or counterclaim in any such proceedings.

(2) This section shall not apply in the case of any judgment –

(a) where the judgment has been registered and the registration thereof has been set aside on some ground other than –

(i) that a sum of money was not payable under the judgment; or

(ii) that the judgment had been wholly or partly satisfied; or

(iii) that at the date of the application the judgment could not be enforced by execution in the country of the original court; or

(b) where the judgment has not been registered, it is shown (whether it could have been registered or not) that if it had been registered the registration thereof would have been set aside on an application for that purpose on some ground other than one of the grounds specified in paragraph (a) of this subsection.

(3) Nothing in this section shall be taken to prevent any court in the United Kingdom recognising any judgment as conclusive of any matter of law or fact decided therein if that judgment would have been so recognised before the passing of this Act.

9 Power to make foreign judgments unenforceable in United Kingdom if no reciprocity

(1) If it appears to His Majesty that the treatment in respect of recognition and enforcement accorded by the courts of any foreign country to judgments given in the courts of the United Kingdom is substantially less favourable than that accorded by the courts of the United Kingdom to judgments of the courts of that country, His Majesty may by Order in Council apply this section to that country.

(2) Except in so far as His Majesty may by Order in Council under this section otherwise direct, no proceedings shall be entertained in any court in the United Kingdom for the recovery of any sum alleged to be payable under a judgment given in a court of a country to which this section applies.

(3) His Majesty may by a subsequent Order in Council vary or revoke any Order previously made under this section.

10 Provision for issue of copies of, and certificates in connection with, United Kingdom judgments

(1) Rules may make provision for enabling any judgment creditor wishing to secure the enforcement in a foreign country to which Part I of this Act extends of a judgment to which this subsection applies, to obtain, subject to any conditions specified in the rules –

(a) a copy of the judgment; and

(b) a certificate giving particulars relating to the judgment and the proceedings in which it was given.

(2) Subsection (1) applies to any judgment given by a court or tribunal in the United Kingdom under which a sum of money is payable, not being a sum payable in respect of taxes or other charges of a like nature or in respect of a fine or other penalty.

(3) In this section 'rules' –

(a) in relation to judgments given by a court, means rules of court;

(b) in relation to judgments given by any other tribunal, means rules or regulations made by the authority having power to make rules or regulations regulating the procedure of that tribunal.

10A Arbitration awards

The provisions of this Act, except sections 1(5) and 6, shall apply as they apply to a judgment, in relation to an award in proceedings on an arbitration which has, in pursuance of the law in force in the place where it was made, become enforceable in the same manner as a judgment given by a court in that place.

11 Interpretation

(1) In this Act, unless the context otherwise requires, the following expressions have the meanings hereby assigned to them respectively, that is to say –

'Appeal' includes any proceeding by way of discharging or setting aside a judgment or an application for a new trial or a stay of execution;

'Country of the original court' means the country in which the original court is situated;

'Court', except in section 10 of this Act includes a tribunal;

'Judgment' means a judgment or order given or made by a court in any civil proceedings, or a judgment or order given or made by a court in any criminal proceedings for the payment of a sum of money in respect of compensation or damages to an injured party;

'Judgment creditor' means the person in whose favour the judgment was given and includes any person in whom the rights under the judgment have become vested by succession or assignment or otherwise;

'Judgment debtor' means the person against whom the judgment was given, and includes any person against whom the judgment is enforceable under the law of the original court;

'Original court' in relation to any judgment means the court by which the judgment was given;

'Prescribed' means prescribed by rules of court;

'Registration' means registration under Part I of this Act, and the expressions 'register' and 'registered' shall be construed accordingly;

'Registering court' in relation to any judgment means the court to which an application to register the judgment is made.

(2) For the purposes of this Act, the expression 'action in personam' shall not be deemed to include any matrimonial cause or any proceedings in connection with any of the following matters, that is to say, matrimonial matters, administration of the estates of deceased persons, bankruptcy, winding up of companies, lunacy, or guardianship of infants.

As amended by the Administration of Justice Act 1977, ss4, 32(4), Schedule 5; Supreme Court Act 1981, ss152(1), 153(4), Schedule 4; Civil Jurisdiction and Judgments Act 1982, ss35(1), 54, Schedule 10, paras 1-5, Schedule 14.

NATIONAL ASSISTANCE ACT 1948
(11 & 12 Geo 6 c 29)

42 Liability to maintain wife or husband, and children

(1) For the purposes of this Act –

(a) a man shall be liable to maintain his wife and his children, and

(b) a woman shall be liable to maintain her husband and her children.

(2) Any reference in subsection (1) of this section to a person's children shall be construed in accordance with section 1 of the Family Law Reform Act 1987. ...

43 Recovery of cost of assistance from persons liable for maintenance

(1) Where assistance is given or applied for by reference to the requirements of any person (in this section referred to as a person assisted), the local authority concerned may make a complaint to the court against any other person who for the purposes of this Act is liable to maintain the person assisted.

(2) On a complaint under this section the court shall have regard to all the circumstances and in particular to the resources of the defendant, and may order the defendant to pay such sum, weekly or otherwise, as the court may consider appropriate.

(3) For the purposes of the application of the last foregoing subsection to payments in respect of assistance given before the complaint was made, a person shall not be treated as having at the time when the complaint is heard any greater resources than he had at the time when the assistance was given.

(4) In this section the expression 'assistance' means the provision of accommodation under Part III of this Act (hereinafter referred to as 'assistance under Part III of this Act'); and the expression 'the court'

means a court of summary jurisdiction appointed for the commission area (within the meaning of the Justices of the Peace Act 1979) where the assistance was given or applied for.

(5) Payments under subsection (2) of this section shall be made –

(a) to the local authority concerned, in respect of the cost of assistance, whether given before or after the making of the order, or

(b) to the applicant for assistance or any other person being a person assisted, or

(c) to such other person as appears to the court expedient in the interests of the person assisted,

or as to part in one such manner and as to part in another, as may be provided by the order.

(6) An order under this section shall be enforceable as a magistrates' court maintenance order within the meaning of section 150(1) of the Magistrates' Courts Act 1980. ...

As amended by the Domestic Proceedings and Magistrates' Courts Act 1978, s89(2)(a), Schedule 2, para 6; Justices of the Peace Act 1979, s71, Schedule 2, para 3; Family Law Reform Act 1987, s33(1), Schedule 2, para 6.

MARRIAGE ACT 1949
(12, 13 & 14 Geo 6 c 76)

1   Marriages within prohibited degrees

(1) A marriage solemnised between a man and any of the persons mentioned in the first column of Part 1 of the First Schedule to the Act, or between a woman and any of the persons mentioned in the second column of the said Part 1, shall be void.

(2) Subject to subsection (3) of this section, a marriage solemnised between a man and any of the persons mentioned in the first column of Part II of the First Schedule to this Act, or between a woman and any of the persons mentioned in the second column of the said Part II, shall be void.

(3) Any such marriage as is mentioned in subsection (2) of this section shall not be void by reason only of affinity if both the parties to the marriage have attained the age of twenty-one at the time of the marriage and the younger party has not at any time before attaining the age of eighteen been a child of the family in relation to the other party.

(4) Subject to subsection (5) of this section, a marriage solemnised between a man and any of the persons mentioned in the first column of Part III of the First Schedule to this Act or between a woman and any of the persons mentioned in the second column of the said Part III shall be void.

(5) Any such marriage as is mentioned in subsection (4) of this section shall not be void by reason only of affinity if both the parties to the marriage have attained the age of twenty-one at the time of the marriage and the marriage is solemnised –

    (a) in the case of a marriage between a man and the mother of a former wife of his, after the death of both the former wife and the father of the former wife;

    (b) in the case of a marriage between a man and the former wife of his son, after the death of both his son and the mother of his son;

(c) in the case of a marriage between a woman and the father of a former husband of hers, after the death of both the former husband and the mother of the former husband;

(d) in the case of a marriage between a woman and a former husband of her daughter, after the death of both her daughter and the father of her daughter.

2   Marriages of persons under sixteen

A marriage solemnised between persons either of whom is under the age of sixteen shall be void.

41   Registration of buildings

(1) Any proprietor or trustee of a building which has been certified as required by law as a place of religious worship may apply to the superintendent registrar of the registration district in which the building is situated for the building to be registered for the solemnisation of marriages therein.

(2) Any person making such an application as aforesaid shall deliver to the superintendent registrar a certificate, signed in duplicate by at least twenty householders and dated not earlier than one month before the making of the application, stating that the building is being used by them as their usual place of public religious worship and that they desire that the building should be registered as aforesaid, and both certificates shall be countersigned by the proprietor or trustee by whom they are delivered.

(3) The superintendent registrar shall send both certificates delivered to him under the last foregoing subsection to the Registrar General who shall register the building in a book to be kept for that purpose in the General Register Office.

(4) The Registrar General shall endorse on both certificates sent to him as aforesaid the date of the registration, and shall keep one certificate with the records of the General Register Office and shall return the other certificate to the superintendent registrar who shall keep it with the records of his office.

(5) On the return of the certificate under the last foregoing subsection, the superintendent registrar shall –

(a) enter the date of the registration of the building in a book to be provided for that purpose by the Registrar General;

(b) give a certificate of the registration signed by him, on durable materials, to the proprietor or trustee by whom the certificates delivered to him under subsection (2) of this section were countersigned; and

(c) give public notice of the registration of the building by advertisement in some newspaper circulating in the country in which the building is situated and in the London Gazette.

(6) For every entry, certificate and notice made or given under the last foregoing subsection the superintendent registrar shall be entitled to receive, at the time of the delivery of the certificates under subsection (2) of this section, the sum of £93.00.

(7) A building may be registered for the solemnisation of marriages under this section whether it is a separate building or forms part of another building.

46 Register office marriage followed by religious ceremony

(1) If the parties to a marriage solemnised in the presence of a superintendent registrar desire to add the religious ceremony ordained or used by the church or persuasion of which they are members, they may present themselves, after giving notice of their intention so to do, to the clergyman or minister of the church or persuasion of which they are members, and the clergyman or minister, upon the production of a certificate of their marriage before the superintendent registrar and upon the payment of the customary fees (if any), may, if he sees fit, read or celebrate in the church or chapel of which he is the regular minister the marriage service of the church or persuasion to which he belongs or nominate some other minister to do so.

(2) Nothing in the reading or celebration of a marriage service under this section shall supersede or invalidate any marriage previously solemnised in the presence of a superintendent registrar, and the reading or celebration shall not be entered as a marriage in any marriage register book kept under Part IV of this Act. ...

75 Offences relating to solemnisation of marriages ...

(2) Any person who knowingly and wilfully –

(a) solemnises a marriage (not being a marriage by special licence, a marriage according to the usages of the Society of

Friends or a marriage between two persons professing the Jewish religion according to the usages of the Jews) in any place other than –

(i) a church or other building in which marriages may be solemnised according to the rites of the Church of England, or

(ii) the registered building, office, approved premises or person's residence specified as the place where the marriage was to be solemnised in the notice of marriage and certificate required under Part III of this Act;

(aa) solemnises a marriage purporting to be in pursuance of section 26(1)(bb) of this Act on premises which are not approved premises;

(b) solemnises a marriage in any such registered building as aforesaid (not being a marriage in the presence of an authorised person) in the absence of a registrar of the district in which the registered building is situated;

(bb) solemnises a marriage in pursuance of section 26(1)(dd) of this Act, otherwise than according to the rites of the Church of England, in the absence of a registrar of the registration district in which the place where the marriage is solemnised is situated;

(c) solemnises a marriage in the office of a superintendent registrar in the absence of a registrar of the district in which the office is situated;

(cc) solemnises a marriage on approved premises in pursuance of section 26(1)(bb) of this Act in the absence of a registrar of the district in which the premises are situated;

(d) solemnises a marriage on the authority of a certificate of a superintendent registrar (not being a marriage by licence) within twenty-one days after the day on which the notice of marriage was entered in the marriage notice book; or

(e) solemnises a marriage on the authority of a certificate of a superintendent registrar after the expiration of three months from the said day on which the notice of marriage was entered as aforesaid;

shall be guilty of felony and shall be liable to imprisonment for a term not exceeding five years. ...

FIRST SCHEDULE

KINDRED AND AFFINITY

PART I

Prohibited degrees of relationship

Mother	Father
Adoptive mother or former adoptive mother	Adoptive father or former adoptive father
Daughter	Son
Adoptive daughter or former adoptive daughter	Adoptive son or former adoptive son
Father's mother	Father's father
Mother's mother	Mother's father
Son's daughter	Son's son
Daughter's daughter	Daughter's son
Sister	Brother
Father's sister	Father's brother
Mother's sister	Mother's brother
Brother's daughter	Brother's son
Sister's daughter	Sister's son

PART II

Degrees of affinity referred to in section 1(2) and (3) of this Act

Daughter of former wife	Son of former husband
Former wife of father	Former husband of mother
Former wife of father's father	Former husband of father's mother

Former wife of mother's father	Former husband of mother's mother
Daughter of son of former wife	Son of son of former husband
Daughter of daughter of former wife	Son of daughter of former husband

PART III

Degrees of affinity referred to in section 1(4) and (5) of this Act

Mother of former wife	Father of former husband
Former wife of son	Former husband of daughter

As amended by the Marriage Acts Amendment Act 1958, s1(1); Children Act 1975, s108(1)(a); Marriage Act 1983, s1(7), Schedule 1, paras 12, 20; Marriage (Prohibited Degrees of Relationship) Act 1986, s1(6), Schedule 1, paras 2, 8; Marriage (Registration of Buildings) Act 1990, s1(1); Marriage Act 1994, s1, Schedule, para 7; Registration of Births, Deaths and Marriages (Fees) Order 1994.

ARBITRATION ACT 1950
(14 Geo 6 c 27)

PART I

GENERAL PROVISIONS AS TO ARBITRATION

1   Authority of arbitrators and umpires to be irrevocable

The authority of an arbitrator or umpire appointed by or by virtue of an arbitration agreement shall, unless a contrary intention is expressed in the agreement, be irrevocable except by leave of the High Court or a judge thereof.

2   Death of party

(1) An arbitration agreement shall not be discharged by the death of any party thereto, either as respects the deceased or any other party, but shall in such an event be enforceable by or against the personal representative of the deceased.

(2) The authority of an arbitrator shall not be revoked by the death of any party by whom he was appointed.

(3) Nothing in this section shall be taken to affect the operation of any enactment or rule of law by virtue of which any right of action is extinguished by the death of a person.

3   Bankruptcy

(1) Where it is provided by a term in a contract to which a bankrupt· is a party that any differences arising thereout or in connection therewith shall be referred to arbitration, the said term shall, if the trustee in bankruptcy adopts the contract, be enforceable by or against him so far as relates to any such differences.

(2) Where a person who has been adjudged bankrupt had, before the commencement of the bankruptcy, become a party to an

arbitration agreement, and any matter to which the agreement applies requires to be determined in connection with or for the purposes of the bankruptcy proceedings, then, if the case is one to which subsection (1) of this section does not apply, any other party to the agreement or, with the consent of the creditors' committee established under section 301 of the Insolvency Act 1986, the trustee in bankruptcy, may apply to the court having jurisdiction in the bankruptcy proceedings for an order directing that the matter in question shall be referred to arbitration in accordance with the agreement, and that court may, if it is of opinion that, having regard to all the circumstances of the case, the matter ought to be determined by arbitration, make an order accordingly.

4 Staying court proceedings where there is submission to arbitration

(1) If any party to an arbitration agreement, or any person claiming through or under him, commences any legal proceedings in any court against any other party to the agreement, or any person claiming through or under him, in respect of any matter agreed to be referred, any party to those legal proceedings may at any time after appearance, and before delivering any pleadings or taking any other steps in the proceedings, apply to that court to stay the proceedings, and that court or a judge thereof, if satisfied that there is no sufficient reason why the matter should not be referred in accordance with the agreement, and that the applicant was, at the time when the proceedings were commenced, and still remains, ready and willing to do all things necessary to the proper conduct of the arbitration, may make an order staying the proceedings.

5 Reference of interpleader issues to arbitration

Where relief by way of interpleader is granted and it appears to the High Court that the claims in question are matters to which an arbitration agreement, to which the claimants are parties, applies, the High Court may direct the issue between the claimants to be determined in accordance with the agreement.

6 When reference is to a single arbitrator

Unless a contrary intention is expressed therein, every arbitration agreement shall, if no other mode of reference is provided, be deemed to include a provision that the reference shall be to a single arbitrator.

7   Power of parties in certain cases to supply vacancy

Where an arbitration agreement provides that the reference shall be to two arbitrators, one to be appointed by each party, then, unless a contrary intention is expressed therein –

(a) if either of the appointed arbitrators refuses to act, or is incapable of acting, or dies, the party who appointed him may appoint a new arbitrator in his place;

(b) if, on such a reference, one party fails to appoint an arbitrator, either originally, or by way of substitution as aforesaid, for seven clear days after the other party, having appointed his arbitrator, has served the party making default with notice to make the appointment, the party who has appointed an arbitrator may appoint that arbitrator to act as sole arbitrator in the reference and his award shall be binding on both parties as if he had been appointed by consent:

Provided that the High Court or a judge thereof may set aside any appointment made in pursuance of this section.

8   Umpires

(1) Unless a contrary intention is expressed therein, every arbitration agreement shall, where the reference is to two arbitrators, be deemed to include a provision that the two arbitrators may appoint an umpire at any time after they are themselves appointed and shall do so forthwith if they cannot agree.

(2) Unless a contrary intention is expressed therein, every arbitration agreement shall, where such a provision is applicable to the reference, be deemed to include a provision that if the arbitrators have delivered to any party to the arbitration agreement, or to the umpire, a notice in writing stating that they cannot agree, the umpire may forthwith enter on the reference in lieu of the arbitrators.

(3) At any time after the appointment of an umpire, however appointed, the High Court may, on the application of any party to the reference and notwithstanding anything to the contrary in the arbitration agreement, order that the umpire shall enter upon the reference in lieu of the arbitrators and as if he were a sole arbitrator.

9 Majority award of three arbitrators

Unless the contrary intention is expressed in the arbitration agreement, in any case where there is a reference to three arbitrators, the award of any two of the arbitrators shall be binding.

10 Power of court in certain cases to appoint an arbitrator or umpire

(1) In any of the following cases –

(a) where an arbitration agreement provides that the reference shall be to a single arbitrator, and all the parties do not, after differences have arisen, concur in the appointment of an arbitrator;

(b) if an appointed arbitrator refuses to act, or is incapable of acting, or dies, and the arbitration agreement does not show that it was intended that the vacancy should not be supplied and the parties do not supply the vacancy;

(c) where the parties or two arbitrators are required or are at liberty to appoint an umpire or third arbitrator and do not appoint him;

(d) where an appointed umpire or third arbitrator refuses to act, or is incapable of acting, or dies, and the arbitration agreement does not show that it was intended that the vacancy should not be supplied, and the parties or arbitrators do not supply the vacancy;

any party may serve the other parties or the arbitrators, as the case may be, with a written notice to appoint or, as the case may be, concur in appointing, an arbitrator, umpire or third arbitrator, and if the appointment is not made within seven clear days after the service of the notice, the High Court or a judge thereof may, on application by the party who gave the notice, appoint an arbitrator, umpire or third arbitrator who shall have the like powers to act in the reference and make an award as if he had been appointed by consent of all parties.

(2) In any case where –

(a) an arbitration agreement provides for the appointment of an arbitrator or umpire by a person who is neither one of the parties nor an existing arbitrator (whether the provision applies directly or in default of agreement by the parties or otherwise), and

(b) that person refuses to make the appointment or does not

make it within the time specified in the agreement or, if no time is so specified, within a reasonable time,

any party to the agreement may serve the person in question with a written notice to appoint an arbitrator or umpire and, if the appointment is not made within seven clear days after the service of the notice, the High Court or a judge thereof may, on the application of the party who gave the notice, appoint an arbitrator or umpire who shall have the like powers to act in the reference and make an award as if he had been appointed in accordance with the terms of the agreement.

(3) In any case where –

(a) an arbitration agreement provides that the reference shall be to three arbitrators, one to be appointed by each party and the third to be appointed by the two appointed by the parties or in some other manner specified in the agreement; and

(b) one of the parties ('the party in default') refuses to appoint an arbitrator or does not do so within the time specified in the agreement or, if no time is specified, within a reasonable time,

the other party to the agreement, having appointed his arbitrator, may serve the party in default with a written notice to appoint an arbitrator. ...

11 Power of official referee to take arbitrations

(1) An official referee may, if in all the circumstances he thinks fit, accept appointment as sole arbitrator, or as umpire, by or by virtue of an arbitration agreement.

(2) An official referee shall not accept appointment as arbitrator or umpire unless the Lord Chief Justice has informed him that, having regard to the state of official referees' business, he can be made available to do so.

(3) The fees payable for the services of an official referee as arbitrator or umpire shall be taken in the High Court.

(4) Schedule 3 to the Administration of Justice Act 1970 (which modifies this Act in relation to arbitration by judges, in particular by substituting the Court of Appeal for the High Court in provisions whereby arbitrators and umpires, their proceedings and awards are subject to control and review by the court) shall have effect in relation to official referees appointed as arbitrators or umpires as it

has effect in relation to judge-arbitrators and judge-umpires (within the meaning of that Schedule).

(5) Any jurisdiction which is exercisable by the High Court in relation to arbitrators and umpires otherwise than under this Act shall, in relation to an official referee appointed as arbitrator or umpire, be exercisable instead by the Court of Appeal.

(6) In this section 'official referee' means any person nominated under section 68(1)(a) of the Supreme Court Act 1981 to deal with official referees' business ...

12 Conduct of proceedings, witnesses, etc

(1) Unless a contrary intention is expressed therein, every arbitration agreement shall, where such a provision is applicable to the reference, be deemed to contain a provision that the parties to the reference, and all persons claiming through them respectively, shall, subject to any legal objection, submit to be examined by the arbitrator or umpire, on oath or affirmation, in relation to the matters in dispute, and shall, subject as aforesaid, produce before the arbitrator or umpire all documents within their possession or power respectively which may be required or called for, and do all other things which during the proceedings on the reference the arbitrator or umpire may require.

(2) Unless a contrary intention is expressed therein, every arbitration agreement shall, where such a provision is applicable to the reference, be deemed to contain a provision that the witnesses on the reference shall, if the arbitrator or umpire thinks fit, be examined on oath or affirmation.

(3) An arbitrator or umpire shall, unless a contrary intention is expressed in the arbitration agreement, have power to administer oaths to, or take the affirmations of, the parties to and witnesses on a reference under the agreement.

(4) Any party to a reference under an arbitration agreement may sue out a writ of subpoena ad testificandum or a writ of subpoena duces tecum, but no person shall be compelled under any such writ to produce any document which he could not be compelled to produce on the trial of an action, and the High Court or a judge thereof may order that a writ of subpoena ad testificandum or of subpoena duces tecum shall issue to compel the attendance before an arbitrator or umpire of a witness wherever he may be within the United Kingdom.

(5) The High Court or a judge thereof may also order that a writ of habeas corpus ad testificandum shall issue to bring up a prisoner for examination before an arbitrator or umpire.

(6) The High Court shall have, for the purpose of and in relation to a reference, the same power of making orders in respect of –

(a) security for costs;

(c) the giving of evidence by affidavit;

(d) examination on oath of any witness before an officer of the High Court or any other person, and the issue of a commission or request for the examination of a witness out of the jurisdiction;

(e) the preservation, interim custody or sale of any goods which are the subject matter of the reference;

(f) securing the amount in dispute in the reference;

(g) the detention, preservation or inspection of any property or thing which is the subject of the reference or as to which any question may arise therein, and authorising for any of the purposes aforesaid any persons to enter upon or into any land or building in the possession of any party to the reference, or authorising any samples to be taken or any observation to be made or experiment to be tried which may be necessary or expedient for the purpose of obtaining full information or evidence; and

(h) interim injunctions or the appointment of a receiver;

as it has for the purpose of and in relation to an action or matter in the High Court: Provided that nothing in this subsection shall be taken to prejudice any power which may be vested in an arbitrator or umpire of making orders with respect to any of the matters aforesaid.

13   Time for making award

(1) Subject to the provisions of subsection (2) of section 22 of this Act, and anything to the contrary in the arbitration agreement, an arbitrator or umpire shall have power to make an award at any time.

(2) The time, if any, limited for making an award, whether under this Act or otherwise, may from time to time be enlarged by order of the High Court or a judge thereof, whether that time has expired or not.

(3) The High Court may, on the application of any party to a

reference, remove an arbitrator or umpire who fails to use all reasonable dispatch in entering on and proceeding with the reference and making an award, and an arbitrator or umpire who is removed by the High Court under this subsection shall not be entitled to receive any remuneration in respect of his services.

For the purposes of this subsection, the expression 'proceeding with a reference' includes, in a case where two arbitrators are unable to agree, giving notice of that fact to the parties and to the umpire.

13A Want of prosecution

(1) Unless a contrary intention is expressed in the arbitration agreement, the arbitrator or umpire shall have power to make an award dismissing any claim in a dispute referred to him if it appears to him that the conditions mentioned in subsection (2) are satisfied.

(2) The conditions are –

(a) that there has been inordinate and inexcusable delay on the part of the claimant in pursuing the claim; and

(b) that the delay –

(i) will give rise to a substantial risk that it is not possible to have a fair resolution of the issues in that claim; or

(ii) has caused, or is likely to cause or to have caused, serious prejudice to the respondent.

(3) For the purpose of keeping the provision made by this section and the corresponding provision which applies in relation to proceedings in the High Court in step, the Secretary of State may by order made by statutory instrument amend subsection (2) above...

14 Interim awards

Unless a contrary intention is expressed therein, every arbitration agreement shall, where such a provision is applicable to the reference, be deemed to contain a provision that the arbitrator or umpire may, if he thinks fit, make an interim award, and any reference in this Part of this Act to an award includes a reference to an interim award.

15 Specific performance

Unless a contrary intention is expressed therein, every arbitration agreement shall, where such a provision is applicable to the reference, be deemed to contain a provision that the arbitrator or umpire shall have the same power as the High Court to order specific performance of any contract other than a contract relating to land or any interest in land.

16 Awards to be final

Unless a contrary intention is expressed therein, every arbitration agreement shall, where such a provision is applicable to the reference, be deemed to contain a provision that the award to be made by the arbitrator or umpire shall be final and binding on the parties and the persons claiming under them respectively.

17 Power to correct slips

Unless a contrary intention is expressed in the arbitration agreement, the arbitrator or umpire shall have power to correct in an award any clerical mistake or error arising from any accidental slip or omission.

18 Costs

(1) Unless a contrary intention is expressed therein, every arbitration agreement shall be deemed to include a provision that the costs of the reference and awards shall be in the discretion of the arbitrator or umpire, who may direct to and by whom and in what manner those costs or any part thereof shall be paid, and may tax or settle the amount of costs to be so paid or any part thereof, and may award costs to be paid as between solicitor and client.

(2) Any costs directed by an award to be paid shall, unless the award otherwise directs, be taxable in the High Court.

(3) Any provision in an arbitration agreement to the effect that the parties or any party thereto shall in any event pay their or his own costs of the reference or award or any part thereof shall be void, and this Part of this Act shall, in the case of an arbitration agreement containing any such provision, have effect as if that provision were not contained therein: Provided that nothing in this subsection shall invalidate such a provision when it is a part of an agreement to submit to arbitration a dispute which has arisen before the making of that agreement.

(4) If no provision is made by an award with respect to the costs of the reference, any party to the reference may, within fourteen days of the publication of the award or such further time as the High Court or a judge thereof may direct, apply to the arbitrator for an order directing by and to whom those costs shall be paid, and thereupon the arbitrator shall, after hearing any party who may desire to be heard, amend his award by adding thereto such directions as he may think proper with respect to the payment of the costs of the reference.

(5) Section 69 of the Solicitors Act 1932 (which empowers a court before which any proceeding is being heard or is pending to charge property recovered or preserved in the proceeding with the payment of solicitors' costs) shall apply as if an arbitration were proceeding in the High Court, and the High Court may make declarations and orders accordingly.

19 Taxation of arbitrator's or umpire's fees

(1) If in any case an arbitrator or umpire refuses to deliver his award except on payment of the fees demanded by him, the High Court may, on an application for the purpose, order that the arbitrator or umpire shall deliver the award to the applicant on payment into court by the applicant of the fees demanded, and further that the fees demanded shall be taxed by the taxing officer and that out of the money paid into court there shall be paid out to the arbitrator or umpire by way of fees such sum as may be found reasonable on taxation and that the balance of the money, if any, shall be paid out to the applicant.

(2) An application for the purposes of this section may be made by any party to the reference unless the fees demanded have been fixed by a written agreement between him and the arbitrator or umpire.

(3) A taxation of fees under this section may be reviewed in the same manner as a taxation of costs.

(4) The arbitrator or umpire shall be entitled to appear and be heard on any taxation or review of taxation under this section.

19A Power of arbitrator to award interest

(1) Unless a contrary intention is expressed therein, every arbitration agreement shall, where such a provision is applicable to the reference, be deemed to contain a provision that the arbitrator or

umpire may, if he thinks fit, award simple interest at such rate as he thinks fit –

(a) on any sum which is the subject of the reference but which is paid before the award, for such period ending not later than the date of the payment as he thinks fit; and

(b) on any sum which he awards, for such period ending not later than the date of the payment as he thinks fit.

(2) The power to award interest conferred on an arbitrator or umpire by subsection (1) above is without prejudice to any other power of an arbitrator or umpire to award interest.

20 Interest on awards

(1) A sum directed to be paid by an award shall, unless the award otherwise directs, carry interest as from the date of the award.

(2) The rate of interest shall be –

(a) the rate for judgment debts specified in section 17 of the Judgments Act 1838 at the date of the award; or

(b) if the power under subsection (3) below is exercised, the rate specified in the award.

(3) Where the sum is expressed in a currency other than sterling, the award may specify such rate as the arbitrator or umpire thinks fit instead of the rate mentioned in subsection (2)(a) above.

22 Power to remit award

(1) In all cases of reference to arbitration the High Court or a judge thereof may from time to time remit the matters referred, or any of them, to the reconsideration of the arbitrator or umpire.

(2) Where an award is remitted, the arbitrator or umpire shall, unless the order otherwise directs, make his award within three months after the date of the order.

23 Removal of arbitrator and setting aside of award

(1) Where an arbitrator or umpire has misconducted himself or the proceedings, the High Court may remove him.

(2) Where an arbitrator or umpire has misconducted himself or the

proceedings, or an arbitration or award has been improperly procured, the High Court may set the award aside.

(3) Where an application is made to set aside an award, the High Court may order that any money made payable by the award shall be brought into court or otherwise secured pending the determination of the application.

24 Power of court to give relief where arbitrator is not impartial or the dispute involves question of fraud

(1) Where an agreement between any parties provides that disputes which may arise in the future between them shall be referred to an arbitrator named or designated in the agreement, and after a dispute has arisen any party applies, on the ground that the arbitrator so named or designated is not or may not be impartial, for leave to revoke the authority of the arbitrator or for an injunction to restrain any other party or the arbitrator from proceeding with the arbitration, it shall not be a ground for refusing the application that the said party at the time when he made the agreement knew, or ought to have known, that the arbitrator, by reason of his relation towards any other party to the agreement or of his connection with the subject referred, might not be capable of impartiality.

(2) Where an agreement between any parties provides that disputes which may arise in the future between them shall be referred to arbitration, and a dispute which so arises involves the question whether any such party has been guilty of fraud, the High Court shall, so far as may be necessary to enable that question to be determined by the High Court, have power to order that the agreement shall cease to have effect and power to give leave to revoke the authority of any arbitrator or umpire appointed by or by virtue of the agreement.

(3) In any case where by virtue of this section the High Court has power to order that an arbitration agreement shall cease to have effect or to give leave to revoke the authority of an arbitrator or umpire, the High Court may refuse to stay an action brought in breach of the agreement.

25 Power of court where arbitrator is removed or authority of arbitrator is revoked

(1) Where an arbitrator (not being a sole arbitrator), or two or more arbitrators (not being all the arbitrators) or an umpire who has not

entered on the reference is or are removed by the High Court or the Court of Appeal, the High Court or the Court of Appeal, as the case may be, may, on the application of any party to the arbitration agreement, appoint a person or persons to act as arbitrator or arbitrators or umpire in place of the person or persons so removed.

(2) Where the authority of an arbitrator or arbitrators or umpire is revoked by leave of the High Court or the Court of Appeal, or a sole arbitrator or all the arbitrators or an umpire who has entered on the reference is or are removed by the High Court or the Court of Appeal, the High Court or the Court of Appeal, as the case may be, may, on the application of any party to the arbitration agreement, either –

(a) appoint a person to act as sole arbitrator in place of the person or persons removed; or

(b) order that the arbitration agreement shall cease to have effect with respect to the dispute referred.

(3) A person appointed under this section by the High Court or the Court of Appeal as an arbitrator or umpire shall have the like power to act in the reference and to make an award as if he had been appointed in accordance with the terms of the arbitration agreement.

(4) Where it is provided (whether by means of a provision in the arbitration agreement or otherwise) that an award under an arbitration agreement shall be a condition precedent to the bringing of an action with respect to any matter to which the agreement applies, the High Court or the Court of Appeal if it orders (whether under this section or under any other enactment) that the agreement shall cease to have effect as regards any particular dispute, may further order that the provision making an award a condition precedent to the bringing of an action shall also cease to have effect as regards that dispute.

26 Enforcement of award

(1) An award on an arbitration agreement may, by leave of the High Court or a judge thereof, be enforced in the same manner as a judgment or order to the same effect, and where leave is so given, judgment may be entered in terms of the award.

(2) If a county court so orders, the amount sought to be recovered shall be recoverable (by execution issued from the county court or

otherwise) as if payable under an order of that court and shall not be enforceable under subsection (1) above.

(3) An application to the High Court under this section shall preclude an application to a county court and an application to a county court under this section shall preclude an application to the High Court.

27 Power of court to extend time for commencing arbitration proceedings

Where the terms of an agreement to refer future disputes to arbitration provide that any claims to which the agreement applies shall be barred unless notice to appoint an arbitrator is given or an arbitrator is appointed or some other step to commence arbitration proceedings is taken within a time fixed by the agreement, and a dispute arises to which the agreement applies, the High Court, if it is of opinion that in the circumstances of the case undue hardship would otherwise be caused, and notwithstanding that the time so fixed has expired, may, on such terms, if any, as the justice of the case may require, but without prejudice to the provisions of any enactment limiting the time for the commencement of arbitration proceedings, extend the time for such period as it thinks proper.

28 Terms as to costs, etc

Any order made under this Part of this Act may be made on such terms as to costs or otherwise as the authority making the order thinks just.

29 Commencement of arbitration

(2) An arbitration shall be deemed to be commenced when one party to the arbitration agreement serves on the other party or parties a notice requiring him or them to appoint or concur in appointing an arbitrator, or, where the arbitration agreement provides that the reference shall be to a person named or designated in the agreement, requiring him or them to submit the dispute to the person so named or designated.

(3) Any such notice as is mentioned in subsection (2) of this section may be served either –

  (a) by delivering it to the person on whom it is to be served; or

(b) by leaving it at the usual or last known place of abode in England of that person; or

(c) by sending it by post in a registered letter addressed to that person at his usual or last known place of abode in England;

as well as in any other manner provided in the arbitration agreement; and where a notice is sent by post in manner prescribed by paragraph (c) of this subsection, service thereof shall, unless the contrary is proved, be deemed to have been effected at the time at which the letter would have been delivered in the ordinary course of post.

30 Crown to be bound

This Part of this Act shall apply to any arbitration to which His Majesty, either in right of the Crown or of the Duchy of Lancaster or otherwise, or the Duke of Cornwall, is a party.

31 Application of Part I to statutory arbitrations

(1) Subject to the provisions of section 33 of this Act, this Part of this Act, except the provisions thereof specified in subsection (2) of this section, shall apply to every arbitration under any other Act (whether passed before or after the commencement of this Act) as if the arbitration were pursuant to an arbitration agreement and as if that other Act were an arbitration agreement, except in so far as this Act is inconsistent with that other Act or with any rules or procedure authorised or recognised thereby.

(2) The provisions referred to in subsection (1) of this section are subsection (1) of section2, section 3, section 5, subsection (3) of section 18 and sections 24, 25, 27 and 29.

32 Meaning of 'arbitration agreement'

In this Part of this Act, unless the context otherwise requires, the expression 'arbitration agreement' means a written agreement to submit present or future differences to arbitration, whether an arbitrator is named therein or not.

33 Operation of Part I

This Part of this Act shall not affect any arbitration commenced (within the meaning of subsection (2) of section 29 of this Act) before the commencement of this Act, but shall apply to an arbitration so commenced after the commencement of this Act under an agreement made before the commencement of this Act.

34   Extent of Part I

None of the provisions of this Part of this Act shall extend to Scotland or Northern Ireland.

PART II

ENFORCEMENT OF CERTAIN FOREIGN AWARDS

35   Awards to which Part II applies

(1) This Part of this Act applies to any award made after the twenty-eighth day of July, nineteen hundred and twenty-four –

(a) in pursuance of an agreement for arbitration to which the protocol set out in the First Schedule to this Act applies; and

(b) between persons of whom one is subject to the jurisdiction of some one of such Powers as His Majesty, being satisfied that reciprocal provisions have been made, may by Order in Council declare each to be parties to the convention set out in the Second Schedule to this Act, and of whom the other is subject to the jurisdiction of some other of the Powers aforesaid; and

(c) in one of such territories as His Majesty, being satisfied that reciprocal provisions have been made, may by Order in Council declare to be territories to which the said convention applies;

and an award to which this Part of this Act applies is in this Part of this Act referred to as 'a foreign award'.

(2) His Majesty may by a subsequent Order in Council vary or revoke any Order previously made under this section.

(3) Any Order in Council under section 1 of the Arbitration (Foreign Awards) Act 1930, which is in force at the commencement of this Act shall have effect as if it had been made under this section.

36   Effect of foreign awards

(1) A foreign award shall, subject to the provisions of this Part of this Act, be enforceable in England either by action or in the same

manner as the award of an arbitrator is enforceable by virtue of section 26 of this Act.

(2) Any foreign award which would be enforceable under this Part of this Act shall be treated as binding for all purposes on the persons as between whom it was made, and may accordingly be relied on by any of those persons by way of defence, set off or otherwise in any legal proceedings in England, and any references in this Part of this Act to enforcing a foreign award shall be construed as including references to relying on an award.

37 Conditions for enforcement of foreign awards

(1) In order that a foreign award may be enforceable under this Part of this Act it must have –

(a) been made in pursuance of an agreement for arbitration which was valid under the law by which it was governed;

(b) been made by the tribunal provided for in the agreement or constituted in manner agreed upon by the parties;

(c) been made in conformity with the law governing the arbitration procedure;

(d) become final in the country in which it was made;

(e) been in respect of a matter which may lawfully be referred to arbitration under the law of England;

and the enforcement thereof must not be contrary to the public policy or the law of England.

(2) Subject to the provisions of this subsection, a foreign award shall not be enforceable under this Part of this Act if the court dealing with the case is satisfied that –

(a) the award has been annulled in the country in which it was made; or

(b) the party against whom it is sought to enforce the award was not given notice of the arbitration proceedings in sufficient time to enable him to present his case, or was under some legal incapacity and was not properly represented; or

(c) the award does not deal with all the questions referred or contains decisions on matters beyond the scope of the agreement for arbitration: Provided that, if the award does not deal with all the questions referred, the court may, if it thinks fit, either postpone the enforcement of the award or order its enforcement subject to the giving of such security by the person seeking to enforce it as the court may think fit.

(3) If a party seeking to resist the enforcement of a foreign award proves that there is any ground other than the non-existence of the conditions specified in paragraphs (a), (b) and (c) of subsection (1) of this section, or the existence of the conditions specified in paragraphs (b) and (c) of subsection (2) of this section, entitling him to contest the validity of the award, the court may, if it thinks fit, either refuse to enforce the award or adjourn the hearing until after the expiration of such period as appears to the court to be reasonably sufficient to enable that party to take the necessary steps to have the award annulled by the competent tribunal.

38 Evidence

(1) The party seeking to enforce a foreign award must produce –

(a) the original award or a copy thereof duly authenticated in manner required by the law of the country in which it was made; and

(b) evidence proving that the award has become final; and

(c) such evidence as may be necessary to prove that the award is a foreign award and that the conditions mentioned in paragraphs (a), (b) and (c) of subsection (1) of the last foregoing section are satisfied.

(2) In any case where any document required to be produced under subsection (1) of this section is in a foreign language, it shall be the duty of the party seeking to enforce the award to produce a translation certified as correct by a diplomatic or consular agent of the country to which that party belongs, or certified as correct in such other manner as may be sufficient according to the law of England.

(3) Subject to the provisions of this section, rules of court may be made under section 84 of the Supreme Court Act 1981 with respect to the evidence which must be furnished by a party seeking to enforce an award under this Part of this Act.

39 Meaning of 'final award'

For the purposes of this Part of this Act, an award shall not be deemed final if any proceedings for the purpose of contesting the validity of the award are pending in the country in which it was made.

40 Saving for other rights, etc

Nothing in this Part of this Act shall –

(a) prejudice any rights which any person would have had of enforcing in England any award or of availing himself in England of any award if neither this Part of this Act nor Part I of the Arbitration (Foreign Awards) Act 1930, had been enacted; or

(b) apply to any award made on an arbitration agreement governed by the law of England.

FIRST SCHEDULE

PROTOCOL ON ARBITRATION CLAUSES SIGNED ON BEHALF OF HIS MAJESTY AT A MEETING OF THE ASSEMBLY OF THE LEAGUE OF NATIONS HELD ON THE TWENTY-FOURTH DAY OF SEPTEMBER NINETEEN HUNDRED AND TWENTY-THREE

The undersigned, being duly authorised, declare that they accept, on behalf of the countries which they represent, the following provision:–

1. Each of the Contracting States recognises the validity of an agreement whether relating to existing or future differences between parties, subject respectively to the jurisdiction of different Contracting States by which the parties to a contract agree to submit to arbitration all or any differences that may arise in connection with such contract relating to commercial matters or to any other matter capable of settlement by arbitration, whether or not the arbitration is to take place in a country to whose jurisdiction none of the parties is subject.

Each Contracting State reserves the right to limit the obligation mentioned above to contracts which are considered as commercial under its national law. Any Contracting State which avails itself of this right will notify the Secretary-General of the League of Nations, in order that the other Contracting States may be so informed.

2. The arbitral procedure, including the constitution of the arbitral tribunal, shall be governed by the will of the parties and by the law of the country in whose territory the arbitration takes place.

The Contracting States agree to facilitate all steps in the procedure which require to be taken in their own territories, in accordance with the provisions of their law governing arbitral procedure applicable to existing differences.

3. Each Contracting State undertakes to ensure the execution by its authorities and in accordance with the provisions of its national laws of arbitral awards made in its own territory under the preceding articles.

4. The tribunals of the Contracting Parties, on being seized of a dispute regarding a contract made between persons to whom Article 1 applies and including an arbitration agreement whether referring to present or future differences which is valid in virtue of the said article and capable of being carried into effect, shall refer the parties on the application of either of them to the decision of the arbitrators.

Such reference shall not prejudice the competence of the judicial tribunals in case the agreement or the arbitration cannot proceed or becomes inoperative.

5. The present Protocol, which shall remain open for signature by all States, shall be ratified. The ratifications shall be deposited as soon as possible with the Secretary-General of the League of Nations, who shall notify such deposit to all the signatory States.

6. The present Protocol shall come into force as soon as two ratifications have been deposited. Thereafter it will take effect, in the case of each Contracting State, one month after the notification by the Secretary-General of the deposit of its ratification.

7. The present Protocol may be denounced by any Contracting State on giving one year's notice. Denunciation shall be effected by a notification addressed to the Secretary-General of the League, who will immediately transmit copies of such notification to all the other signatory States and inform them of the date on which it was received. The denunciation shall take effect one year after the date on which it was notified to the Secretary General, and shall operate only in respect of the notifying State.

8. The Contracting States may declare that their acceptance of the present Protocol does not include any or all of the under-mentioned territories: that is to say, their colonies, overseas possessions or

territories, protectorates or the territories over which they exercise a mandate.

The said States may subsequently adhere separately on behalf of any territory thus excluded. The Secretary General of the League of Nations shall be informed as soon as possible of such adhesions. He shall notify such adhesions to all signatory States. They will take effect one month after the notification by the Secretary General to all signatory States.

The Contracting States may also denounce the Protocol separately on behalf of any of the territories referred to above. Article 7 applies to such denunciation.

SECOND SCHEDULE

CONVENTION ON THE EXECUTION OF FOREIGN ARBITRAL AWARDS SIGNED AT GENEVA ON BEHALF OF HIS MAJESTY ON THE TWENTY-SIXTH DAY OF SEPTEMBER, NINETEEN HUNDRED AND TWENTY-SEVEN

ARTICLE 1

In the territories of any High Contracting Party to which the present Convention applies, an arbitral award made in pursuance of an agreement, whether relating to existing or future differences (hereinafter called 'a submission to arbitration') covered by the Protocol on Arbitration Clauses, opened at Geneva on September 24, 1923, shall be recognised as being and shall be enforced in accordance with the rules of the procedure of the territory where the award is relied upon, provided that the said award has been made in a territory of one of the High Contracting Parties to which the present Convention applies and between persons who are subject to the jurisdiction of one of the High Contracting Parties.

To obtain such recognition or enforcement, it shall, further, be necessary –

(a) That the award has been made in pursuance of a submission to arbitration which is valid under the law applicable thereto;

(b) That the subject-matter of the award is capable of settlement by arbitration under the law of the country in which the award is sought to be relied upon;

(c) That the award has been made by the arbitral tribunal

provided for in the submission to arbitration or constituted in the manner agreed upon by the parties and in conformity with the law governing the arbitration procedure;

(d) That the award has become final in the country in which it has been made, in the sense that it will not be considered as such if it is open to opposition, appel or pourvoi en cassation (in the countries where such forms of procedure exist) or if it is proved that any proceedings for the purpose of contesting the validity of the award are pending;

(e) That the recognition or enforcement of the award is not contrary to the public policy or to the principles of the law of the country in which it is sought to be relied upon.

ARTICLE 2

Even if the conditions laid down in Article 1 hereof are fulfilled, recognition and enforcement of the award shall be refused if the Court is satisfied:–

(a) That the award has been annulled in the country in which it was made;

(b) That the party against whom it is sought to use the award was not given notice of the arbitration proceedings in sufficient time to enable him to present his case; or that, being under a legal incapacity, he was not properly represented;

(c) That the award does not deal with the differences contemplated by or falling within the terms of the submission to arbitration or that it contains decisions on matters beyond the scope of the submission to arbitration.

If the award has not covered all the questions submitted to the arbitral tribunal, the competent authority of the country where recognition or enforcement of the award is sought can, if it think fit, postpone such recognition or enforcement or grant it subject to such guarantee as that authority may decide.

ARTICLE 3

If the party against whom the award has been made proves that, under the law governing the arbitration procedure, there is a ground, other than the grounds referred to in Article 1 (a) and (c), and Article 2 (b) and (c), entitling him to contest the validity of the award in a Court of Law, the Court may, if it thinks fit, either refuse recognition or enforcement of the award or adjourn the consideration thereof, giving such party a reasonable time within which to have the award annulled by the competent tribunal.

ARTICLE 4

The party relying upon an award or claiming its enforcement must supply, in particular:–

(1) The original award or a copy thereof duly authenticated, according to the requirements of the law of the country in which it was made;

(2) Documentary or other evidence to prove that the award has become final, in the sense defined in Article 1 (d), in the country in which it was made;

(3) When necessary, documentary or other evidence to prove that the conditions laid down in Article 1, paragraph 1 and paragraph 2 (a) and (c), have been fulfilled.

A translation of the award and of the other documents mentioned in this Article into the official language of the country where the award is sought to be relied upon may be demanded. Such translation must be certified correct by a diplomatic or consular agent of the country to which the party who seeks to rely upon the award belongs or by a sworn translator of the country where the award is sought to be relied upon.

ARTICLE 5

The provisions of the above Articles shall not deprive any interested party of the right of availing himself of an arbitral award in the manner and to the extent allowed by the law or the treaties of the country where such award is sought to be relied upon.

ARTICLE 6

The present Convention applies only to arbitral awards made after the coming into force of the Protocol on Arbitration Clauses, opened at Geneva on September 24th, 1923.

ARTICLE 7

The present Convention, which will remain open to the signature of all the signatories of the Protocol of 1923 on Arbitration Clauses, shall be ratified.

It may be ratified only on behalf of those Members of the League of Nations and non-Member States on whose behalf the Protocol of 1923 shall have been ratified.

Ratifications shall be deposited as soon as possible with the Secretary General of the League of Nations, who will notify such deposit to all the signatories.

ARTICLE 8

The present Convention shall come into force three months after it shall have been ratified on behalf of two High Contracting Parties. Thereafter, it shall take effect, in the case of each High Contracting Party, three months after the deposit of the ratification on its behalf with the Secretary General of the League of Nations.

ARTICLE 9

The present Convention may be denounced on behalf of any Member of the League or non-Member State. Denunciation shall be notified in writing to the Secretary General of the League of Nations, who will immediately send a copy thereof, certified to be in conformity with the notification, to all the other Contracting Parties, at the same time informing them of the date on which he received it.

The denunciation shall come into force only in respect of the High Contracting Party which shall have notified it and one year after such notification shall have reached the Secretary General of the League of Nations.

The denunciation of the Protocol on Arbitration Clauses shall entail, ipso facto, the denunciation of the present Convention.

ARTICLE 10

The present Convention does not apply to the Colonies, Protectorates or territories under suzerainty or mandate of any High Contracting Party unless they are specially mentioned.

The application of this Convention to one or more of such Colonies, Protectorates or territories to which the Protocol on Arbitration Clauses, opened at Geneva on September 24th, 1923, applies, can be effected at any time by means of a declaration addressed to the Secretary General of the League of Nations by one of the High Contracting Parties.

Such declaration shall take effect three months after the deposit thereof.

The High Contracting Parties can at any time denounce the Convention for all or any of the Colonies, Protectorates or territories referred to above. Article 9 hereof applies to such denunciation.

ARTICLE 11

A certified copy of the present Convention shall be transmitted by the Secretary-General of the League of Nations to every Member of the League of Nations and to every non-Member State which signs the same.

As amended by the Administration of Justice Act 1970, s4(4), Schedule 3, para 11; Arbitration Act 1975, s8(2); Administration of Justice Act 1977, s17(2); Arbitration Act 1979, s6(2), (3), (4), 8(3); Administration of Justice Act 1982, s15(6), Schedule 1, Pt IV; Insolvency Act 1986, s439(2), Schedule 14; Courts and Legal Services Act 1990, ss99, 101(1), 102, 103, 125(7), Schedule 20; High Court and County Courts Jurisdiction Order 1991, art 2(8), Schedule, Pt I; Statute Law (Repeals) Act 1993, Schedule 1, Pt XV; Private International Law (Miscellaneous Provisions) Act 1995, s3(1).

MARRIAGE (ENABLING) ACT 1960
(8 & 9 Eliz c 29)

1 Certain marriages not to be void

(1) No marriage hereafter contracted (whether in or out of Great Britain) between a man or a woman who is the sister, aunt or niece of a former wife of his (whether living or not), or was formerly the wife of his brother, uncle or nephew (whether living or not), shall by reason of that relationship be void or voidable under any enactment or rule of law applying in Great Britain as a marriage between persons within the prohibited degrees of affinity.

(2) In the foregoing subsection words of kinship apply equally to kin of the whole and of the half blood.

(3) This section does not validate a marriage, if either party to it is at the time of the marriage domiciled in a country outside Great Britain, and under the law of that country there cannot be a valid marriage between the parties.

OATHS AND EVIDENCE (OVERSEAS AUTHORITIES AND COUNTRIES) ACT 1963
(1963 c 27)

1   Taking of evidence for foreign civil proceedings

Any person appointed by a court or other judicial authority of any foreign country shall have power in the United Kingdom to administer oaths for the purpose of taking evidence for use in proceedings, not being criminal proceedings, carried on under the law of that country.

5   Amendment of 23 & 24 Geo 5 c 4

(1) If Her Majesty in Council is satisfied as respects any country that —

(a) there exist in that country public registers kept under the authority of the law of that country and recognised by the courts of that country as authentic records, and

(b) that the registers are regularly and properly kept,

Her Majesty may by Order in Council make in respect of that country and all or any of those registers such provision as is specified in subsection (2) of section 1 of the Evidence (Foreign, Dominion and Colonial Documents) Act 1933. ...

WILLS ACT 1963
(1963 c 44)

1 General rule as to formal validity

A will shall be treated as properly executed if its execution conformed to the internal law in force in the territory where it was executed, or in the territory where, at the time of its execution or of the testator's death, he was domiciled or had his habitual residence, or in a state of which, at either of those times, he was a national.

2 Additional rules

(1) Without prejudice to the preceding section, the following shall be treated as properly executed –

(a) a will executed on board a vessel or aircraft of any description, if the execution of the will conformed to the internal law in force in the territory with which, having regard to its registration (if any) and other relevant circumstances, the vessel or aircraft may be taken to have been most closely connected;

(b) a will so far as it disposes of immovable property, if its execution conformed to the internal law in force in the territory where the property was situated;

(c) a will so far as it revokes a will which under this Act would be treated as properly executed or revokes a provision which under this Act would be treated as comprised in a properly executed will, if the execution of the later will conformed to any law by reference to which the revoked will or provision would be so treated;

(d) a will so far as it exercises a power of appointment, if the execution of the will conformed to the law governing the essential validity of the power.

(2) A will so far as it exercises a power of appointment shall not be treated as improperly executed by reason only that its execution was not in accordance with any formal requirements contained in the instrument creating the power.

3   Certain requirements to be treated as formal

Where (whether in pursuance of this Act or not) a law in force outside the United Kingdom falls to be applied in relation to a will, any requirement of that law whereby special formalities are to be observed by testators answering a particular description, or witnesses to the execution of a will are to possess certain qualifications, shall be treated, notwithstanding any rule of that law to the contrary, as a formal requirement only.

4   Construction of wills

The construction of a will shall not be altered by reason of any change in the testator's domicile after the execution of the will.

6   Interpretation

(1) In this Act –

'internal law' in relation to any territory or state means the law which would apply in a case where no question of the law in force in any other territory or state arose;

'state' means a territory or group of territories having its own law of nationality;

'will' includes any testamentary instrument or act, and 'testator' shall be construed accordingly.

(2) Where under this Act the internal law in force in any territory or state is to be applied in the case of a will, but there are in force in that territory or state two or more systems of internal law relating to the formal validity of wills, the system to be applied shall be ascertained as follows –

   (a) if there is in force throughout the territory or state a rule indicating which of those systems can properly be applied in the case in question, that rule shall be followed; or

   (b) if there is no such rule, the system shall be that with which the testator was most closely connected at the relevant time, and for this purpose the relevant time is the time of the testator's death where the matter is to be determined by reference to circumstances prevailing at his death, and the time of execution of the will in any other case.

(3) In determining for the purposes of this Act whether or not the

execution of a will conformed to a particular law, regard shall be had to the formal requirements of that law at the time of execution, but this shall not prevent account being taken of an alteration of law affecting wills executed at that time if the alteration enables the will to be treated as properly executed.

7   Short title, commencement, repeal and extent

(2) This Act shall come into operation on 1 January 1964.

(4) This Act shall not apply to a will of a testator who died before the time of the commencement of this Act and shall apply to a will of a testator who dies after that time whether the will was executed before or after that time ...

DIPLOMATIC PRIVILEGES ACT 1964
(1964 c 81)

1 Replacement of existing law

The following provisions of this Act shall, with respect to the matters dealt with therein, have effect in substitution for any previous enactment or rule of law.

2 Application of Vienna Convention

(1) Subject to section 3 of this Act, the Articles set out in Schedule 1 to this Act (being Articles of the Vienna Convention on Diplomatic Relations signed in 1961) shall have the force of law in the United Kingdom and shall for that purpose be construed in accordance with the following provisions of this section.

(2) In those Articles –

'agents of the receiving State' shall be construed as including any constable and any person exercising a power of entry to any premises under any enactment (including any enactment of the Parliament of Northern Ireland);

'national of the receiving State' shall be construed as meaning citizen of the United Kingdom and Colonies;

'Ministry for Foreign Affairs or such other ministry as may be agreed' shall be construed as meaning the department of the Secretary of State concerned;

and, in the application of those Articles to Scotland, any reference to attachment or execution shall be construed as a reference to the execution of diligence, and any reference to the execution of diligence, and any reference to the execution of a judgment as a reference to the enforcement of a decree by diligence.

(3) For the purposes of Article 32 a waiver by the head of the mission of any State or any person for the time being performing his functions shall be deemed to be a waiver by that State.

(4) The exemption granted by Article 33 with respect to any services shall be deemed to except those services from any class of employment in respect of which contributions are payable under the enactments relating to social security..., but not so as to render any person liable to any contribution which he would not be required to pay if those services were not so excepted.

(5) Articles 35, 36 and 40 shall be construed as granting any privilege or immunity which they require to be granted.

(5A) The reference in Article 36 to customs duties shall be construed as including a reference to excise duties chargeable on goods imported into the United Kingdom and to value added tax charged in accordance with section 10 or 15 of the Value Added Tax Act 1994 (acquisitions from other member States and importations from outside the European Community).

(6) The references in Articles 37 and 38 to the extent to which any privileges and immunities are admitted by the receiving State and to additional privileges and immunities that may be granted by the receiving State shall be construed as referring respectively to the extent to which any privileges and immunities may be specified by Her Majesty by Order in Council and to any additional privileges and immunities that may be so specified.

3   Restriction of privileges and immunities

(1) If it appears to Her Majesty that the privileges and immunities accorded to a mission of Her Majesty in the territory of any State, or to persons connected with that mission, are less than those conferred by this Act on the mission of that State or on persons connected with that mission, Her Majesty may by an Order in Council withdraw such of the privileges and immunities so conferred from the mission of that State or from such persons connected with it as appears to Her Majesty to be proper.

(2) An Order in Council under this section shall be disregarded for the purposes of section 50(4) of the British Nationality Act 1981 (circumstances in which certain persons entitled to exemption under section 8(3) of the Immigration Act 1971 are to be regarded for the purposes of section 1(1) of the said Act of 1981 as settled in the United Kingdom).

4   Evidence

If in any proceedings any question arises whether or not any person is entitled to any privilege or immunity under this Act a certificate issued by or under the authority of the Secretary of State stating any fact relating to that question shall be conclusive evidence of that fact.

6   Orders in Council

(1) No recommendation shall be made to Her Majesty in Council to make an Order under section 2 of this Act unless a draft thereof has been laid before Parliament and approved by resolution of each House of Parliament; and any statutory instrument containing an Order under section 3 of this Act shall be subject to annulment in pursuance of a resolution of either House of Parliament.

(2) Any power to make an Order conferred by the foregoing provisions of this Act includes power to vary or revoke an Order by a subsequent Order.

7   Saving for certain bilateral arrangements

(1) Where any special agreement or arrangement between the Government of any State and the Government of the United Kingdom in force at the commencement of this Act provides for extending –

(a) such immunity from jurisdiction and from arrest or detention, and such inviolability of residence, as are conferred by this Act on a diplomatic agent; or

(b) such exemption from duties (whether of customs or excise) chargeable on imported goods, taxes and related charges as is conferred by this Act in respect of articles for the personal use of a diplomatic agent;

to any class of person, or to articles for the personal use of any class of person, connected with the mission of that State, that immunity and inviolability or exemption shall so extend, so long as that agreement or arrangement continues in force.

(2) The Secretary of State shall publish in the London, Edinburgh and Belfast Gazettes a notice specifying the States with which and the classes of person with respect to which such an agreement or arrangement as is mentioned in subsection (1) of this section is in

force and whether its effect is as mentioned in paragraph (a) or paragraph (b) of that subsection, and shall whenever necessary amend the notice by a further such notice; and the notice shall be conclusive evidence of the agreement or arrangement and the classes of person with respect to which it is in force.

8 Short title, interpretation, commencement, repeal and saving

(1) This Act may be cited as the Diplomatic Privileges Act 1964.

(3) This Act shall come into force on such day as Her Majesty may by Order in Council appoint.

(5) Any Order in Council under the Diplomatic Immunities Restriction Act 1955 which is in force immediately before the commencement of this Act shall, so far as it could have been made under section 3 of this Act, have effect as if so made.

SCHEDULE 1

ARTICLES OF VIENNA CONVENTION HAVING THE FORCE OF LAW IN THE UNITED KINGDOM

ARTICLE 1

For the purpose of the present Convention, the following expressions shall have the meanings hereunder assigned to them:

(a) the 'head of the mission' is the person charged by the sending State with the duty of acting in that capacity;

(b) the 'members of the mission' are the head of the mission and the members of the staff of the mission;

(c) the 'members of the staff of the mission; are the members of the diplomatic staff, of the administrative and technical staff and of the service staff of the mission;

(d) the 'members of the diplomatic staff' are the members of the staff of the mission having diplomatic rank;

(e) a 'diplomatic agent' is the head of the mission or a member of the diplomatic staff of the mission;

(f) the 'members of the administrative and technical staff' are the members of the staff of the mission employed in the administrative and technical service of the mission;

(g) the 'members of the service staff' are the members of the staff of the mission in the domestic service of the mission;

(h) a 'private servant' is a person who is in the domestic service of a member of the mission and who is not an employee of the sending State;

(i) the 'premises of the mission' are the buildings or parts of buildings and the land ancillary thereto, irrespective of ownership used for the purposes of the mission including the residence of the head of the mission.

ARTICLE 22

1. The premises of the mission shall be inviolable. The agents of the receiving State may not enter them, except with the consent of the head of the mission.

2. The receiving State is under a special duty to take all appropriate steps to protect the premises of the mission against any intrusion or damage and to prevent any disturbance of the peace of the mission or impairment of its dignity.

3. The premises of the mission, their furnishings and other property thereon and the means of transport of the mission shall be immune from search, requisition, attachment or execution.

ARTICLE 23

1. The sending State and the head of the mission shall be exempt from all national, regional or municipal dues and taxes in respect of the premises of the mission, whether owned or leased, other than such as represent payment for specific services rendered.

2. The exemption from taxation referred to in this Article shall not apply to such dues and taxes payable under the law of the receiving State by persons contracting with the sending State or the head of the mission.

ARTICLE 24

The archives and documents of the mission shall be inviolable at any time and wherever they may be.

ARTICLE 27

1. The receiving State shall permit and protect free communication on the part of the mission for all official purposes. In communicating with the Government and other missions and consulates of the sending State, wherever situated, the mission may employ all appropriate means, including diplomatic couriers and messages in code or cipher. However, the mission may install and use a wireless transmitter only with the consent of the receiving State.

2. The official correspondence of the mission shall be inviolable. Official correspondence means all correspondence relating to the mission and its functions.

3. The diplomatic bag shall not be opened or detained.

4. The packages constituting the diplomatic bag must bear visible external marks of their character and may contain only diplomatic documents or articles intended for official use.

5. The diplomatic courier, who shall be provided with an official document indicating his status and the number of packages constituting the diplomatic bag, shall be protected by the receiving State in the performance of his functions. He shall enjoy personal inviolability and shall not be liable to any form of arrest or detention.

6. The sending State or the mission may designate diplomatic couriers ad hoc. In such cases the provisions of paragraph 5 of this Article shall also apply, except that the immunities therein mentioned shall cease to apply when such a courier has delivered to the consignee the diplomatic bag in his charge.

7. A diplomatic bag may be entrusted to the captain of a commercial aircraft scheduled to land at an authorised port of entry. He shall be provided with an official document indicating the number of packages constituting the bag but he shall not be considered to be a diplomatic courier. The mission may send one of its members to take possession of the diplomatic bag directly and freely from the captain of the aircraft.

ARTICLE 28

The fees and charges levied by the mission in the course of its official duties shall be exempt from all dues and taxes.

ARTICLE 29

The person of a diplomatic agent shall be inviolable. He shall not be liable to any form of arrest or detention. The receiving State shall treat him with due respect and shall take all appropriate steps to prevent any attack on his person, freedom or dignity.

ARTICLE 30

1. The private residence of a diplomatic agent shall enjoy the same inviolability and protection as the premises of the mission.

2. His papers, correspondence and, except as provided in paragraph 3 of Article 31, his property, shall likewise enjoy inviolability.

ARTICLE 31

1. A diplomatic agent shall enjoy immunity from the criminal jurisdiction of the receiving State. He shall also enjoy immunity from its civil and administrative jurisdiction, except in the case of:

   (a) a real action relating to private immovable property situated in the territory of the receiving State, unless he holds it on behalf of the sending State for the purposes of the mission;

   (b) an action relating to succession in which the diplomatic agent is involved as executor, administrator, heir or legatee as a private person and not on behalf of the sending State;

   (c) an action relating to any professional or commercial activity exercised by the diplomatic agent in the receiving State outside his official functions.

2. A diplomatic agent is not obliged to give evidence as a witness.

3. No measures of execution may be taken in respect of a diplomatic agent except in the cases coming under sub-paragraphs (a), (b) and (c) of paragraph 1 of this Article, and provided that the measures concerned can be taken without infringing the inviolability of his person or of his residence.

4. The immunity of a diplomatic agent from the jurisdiction of the receiving State does not exempt him from the jurisdiction of the sending State.

ARTICLE 32

1. The immunity from jurisdiction of diplomatic agents and of persons enjoying immunity under Article 37 may be waived by the sending State.

2. The waiver must always be express.

3. The initiation of proceedings by a diplomatic agent or by a person enjoying immunity from jurisdiction under Article 37 shall preclude him from invoking immunity from jurisdiction in respect of any counter-claim directly connected with the principal claim.

4. Waiver of immunity from jurisdiction in respect of civil or administrative proceedings shall not be held to imply waiver of immunity in respect of the execution of the judgment, for which a separate waiver shall be necessary.

ARTICLE 33

1. Subject to the provisions of paragraph 3 of this Article, a diplomatic agent shall with respect to services rendered for the sending State be exempt from social security provisions which may be in force in the receiving State.

2. The exemption provided for in paragraph 1 of this Article shall also apply to private servants who are in the sole employ of a diplomatic agent, on condition:

   (a) that they are not nationals of or permanently resident in the receiving State; and

   (b) that they are covered by the social security provisions which may be in force in the sending State or a third State.

3. A diplomatic agent who employs persons to whom the exemption provided for in paragraph 2 of this Article does not apply shall observe the obligations which the social security provisions of the receiving State impose upon employers.

4. The exemption provided for in paragraphs 1 and 2 of this Article shall not preclude voluntary participation in the social security system of the receiving State provided that such participation is permitted by that State.

5. The provisions of this Article shall not affect bilateral or multilateral agreements concerning social security concluded

previously and shall not prevent the conclusion of such agreements in the future.

ARTICLE 34

A diplomatic agent shall be exempt from all dues and taxes, personal or real, national, regional or municipal except:

(a) indirect taxes of a kind which are normally incorporated in the price of goods or services;

(b) dues and taxes on private immovable property situated in the territory of the receiving State, unless he holds it on behalf of the sending State for the purposes of the mission;

(c) estate, succession or inheritance duties levied by the receiving State, subject to the provisions of paragraph 4 of Article 39;

(d) dues and taxes on private income having its source in the receiving State and capital taxes on investments made in commercial undertakings in the receiving State;

(e) charges levied for specific services rendered;

(f) registration, court or record fees, mortgage dues and stamp duty, with respect to immovable property, subject to the provisions of Article 23.

ARTICLE 35

The receiving State shall exempt diplomatic agents from all personal services, from all public service of any kind whatsoever, and from military obligations such as those connected with requisitioning, military contributions and billeting.

ARTICLE 36

1. The receiving State shall, in accordance with such laws and regulations as it may adopt, permit entry of and grant exemption from all customs duties, taxes, and related charges other than charges for storage, cartage and similar services, on:

(a) articles for the official use of the mission;

(b) articles for the personal use of a diplomatic agent or members of his family forming part of his household, including articles intended for his establishment.

2. The personal baggage of a diplomatic agent shall be exempt from inspection, unless there are serious grounds for presuming that it contains articles not covered by the exemptions mentioned in paragraph 1 of this Article, or articles the import or export of which is prohibited by the law or controlled by the quarantine regulations of the receiving State. Such inspection shall be conducted only in the presence of the diplomatic agent or of his authorised representative.

ARTICLE 37

1. The members of the family of a diplomatic agent forming part of his household shall, if they are not nationals of the receiving State, enjoy the privileges and immunities specified in Articles 29 to 36.

2. Members of the administrative and technical staff of the mission, together with members of their families forming part of their respective households, shall, if they are not nationals of or permanently resident in the receiving State, enjoy the privileges and immunities specified in Articles 29 to 35, except that the immunity from civil and administrative jurisdiction of the receiving State specified in paragraph 1 of Article 31 shall not extend to acts performed outside the course of their duties. They shall also enjoy the privileges specified in Article 36, paragraph 1, in respect of articles imported at the time of first installation.

3. Members of the service staff of the mission who are not nationals of or permanently resident in the receiving State shall enjoy immunity in respect of acts performed in the course of their duties, exemption from dues and taxes on the emoluments they receive by reason of their employment and the exemption contained in Article 33.

4. Private servants of members of the mission shall, if they are not nationals of or permanently resident in the receiving State, be exempt from dues and taxes on the emoluments they receive by reason of their employment. In other respects, they may enjoy privileges and immunities only to the extent admitted by the receiving State. However, the receiving State must exercise its jurisdiction over those persons in such a manner as not to interfere unduly with the performance of the functions of the mission.

ARTICLE 38

1. Except in so far as additional privileges and immunities may be granted by the receiving State, a diplomatic agent who is a national of or permanently resident in that State shall enjoy only immunity from jurisdiction and inviolability, in respect of official acts performed in the exercise of his functions.

2. Other members of the staff of the mission and private servants who are nationals of or permanently resident in the receiving State shall enjoy privileges and immunities only to the extent admitted by the receiving State. However, the receiving State must exercise its jurisdiction over those persons in such a manner as not to interfere unduly with the performance of the functions of the mission.

ARTICLE 39

1. Every person entitled to privileges and immunities shall enjoy them from the moment he enters the territory of the receiving State on proceeding to take up his post or, if already in its territory, from the moment when his appointment is notified to the Ministry for Foreign Affairs or such other ministry as may be agreed.

2. When the functions of a person enjoying privileges and immunities have come to an end, such privileges and immunities shall normally cease at the moment when he leaves the country, or on expiry of a reasonable period in which to do so, but shall subsist until that time, even in case of armed conflict. However, with respect to acts performed by such a person in the exercise of his functions as a member of the mission, immunity shall continue to subsist.

3. In case of the death of a member of the mission, the members of his family shall continue to enjoy the privileges and immunities to which they are entitled until the expiry of a reasonable period in which to leave the country.

4. In the event of the death of a member of the mission not a national of or permanently resident in the receiving State or a member of his family forming part of his household, the receiving State shall permit the withdrawal of the movable property of the deceased, with the exception of any property acquired in the country the export of which was prohibited at the time of his death. Estate, succession and inheritance duties shall not be levied on movable property the presence of which in the receiving State was due solely to the

presence there of the deceased as a member of the mission or as a member of the family of a member of the mission.

ARTICLE 40

1. If a diplomatic agent passes through or is in the territory of a third State, which has granted him a passport visa if such visa was necessary, while proceeding to take up or to return to his post, or when returning to his own country, the third State shall accord him inviolability and such other immunities as may be required to ensure his transit or return. The same shall apply in the case of any members of his family enjoying privileges or immunities who are accompanying the diplomatic agent, or travelling separately to join him or to return to their country.

2. In circumstances similar to those specified in paragraph 1 of this Article, third States shall not hinder the passage of members of the administrative and technical or service staff of a mission, and of members of their families, through their territories.

3. Third States shall accord to official correspondence and other official communications in transit, including messages in code or cipher, the same freedom and protection as is accorded by the receiving State. They shall accord to diplomatic couriers, who have been granted a passport visa if such visa was necessary, and diplomatic bags in transit the same violability and protection as the receiving State is bound to accord.

4. The obligations of third States under paragraphs 1, 2 and 3 of this Article shall also apply to the persons mentioned respectively in those paragraphs, and to official communications and diplomatic bags, whose presence in the territory of the third State is due to force majeure.

ARTICLE 45

If diplomatic relations are broken off between two States, or if a mission is permanently or temporarily recalled:

(a) the receiving State must, even in case of armed conflict, respect and protect the premises of the mission, together with its property and archives;

(b) the sending State may entrust the custody of the premises of the mission, together with its property and archives, to a third State acceptable to the receiving State;

(c) the sending State may entrust the protection of its interests and those of its nationals to a third State acceptable to the receiving State.

As amended by: the Social Security Act 1973, ss100, 101, Schedule 27, para 24; Social Security (Consequential Provisions) Act 1975, ss1(2), 5, Schedule 1, Pt I; Customs and Excise Management Act 1979, s177(1), Schedule 4, paras 3, 12; British Nationality Act 1981, s52(6), Schedule 7; Diplomatic and Consular Premises Act 1987, s6, Schedule 2, para 1; Finance (No 2) Act 1992, s14, Schedule 3, Pt III, para 87; Value Added Tax Act 1994, s100(1), Schedule 14, para 1.

CARRIAGE OF GOODS BY ROAD ACT 1965

(1965 c 37)

1 Convention to have force of law

Subjects to the following provisions of this Act, the provisions of the Convention on the Contract for the International Carriage of Goods by Road (in this Act referred to as 'the Convention'), as set out in the Schedule to this Act, shall have the force of law in the United Kingdom so far as they relate to the rights and liabilities of persons concerned in the carriage of goods by road under a contract to which the Convention applies.

4 Registration of foreign judgments

(1) Subject to the next following subsection, Part I of the Foreign Judgments (Reciprocal Enforcement) Act 1933 (in this section referred to as 'the Act of 1933') shall apply, whether or not it would otherwise have so applied, to any judgment which –

(a) has been given in any such action as is referred to in paragraph 1 of article 31 in the Schedule to this Act, and

(b) has been so given by any court or tribunal of a territory in respect of which one of the High Contracting Parties, other than the United Kingdom, is a party to the Convention, and

(c) has become enforceable in that territory.

(2) In the application of Part I of the Act of 1933 in relation to any such judgment as is referred to in the preceding subsection, section 4 of that Act shall have effect with the omission of subsections (2) and (3).

(3) The registration, in accordance with Part I of the Act of 1933, of any such judgment as is referred to in subsection (1) of this section shall constitute, in relation to that judgment, compliance with the

formalities for the purposes of paragraph 3 of article 31 in the Schedule to this Act.

7 Arbitrations

(1) Any reference in the preceding provisions of this Act to a court includes a reference to an arbitration tribunal acting by virtue of article 33 in the Schedule to this Act. ...

8 Resolution of conflicts between Conventions on carriage of goods

(1) If it appears to Her Majesty in Council that there is any conflict between the provisions of this Act (including the provisions of the Convention as set out in the Schedule to this Act) and any provisions relating to the carriage of goods for reward by land, sea or air contained in –

(a) any other Convention which has been signed or ratified by or on behalf of Her Majesty's Government in the United Kingdom before the passing of this Act, or

(b) any enactment of the Parliament of the United Kingdom giving effect to such a Convention,

Her Majesty may by Order in Council make such provision as may seem to Her to be appropriate for resolving that conflict by amending or modifying this Act or any such enactment.

(2) Any statutory instrument made by virtue of this section shall be subject to annulment in pursuance of a resolution of either House of Parliament.

8A Amendments consequential on revision of Convention

(1) If at any time it appears to Her Majesty in Council that Her Majesty's Government in the United Kingdom have agreed to any revision of the Convention, Her Majesty may by Order in Council make such amendment of –

(a) this Act; and

(c) section 5(1) of the Carriage by Air and Road Act 1979,

as appear to Her to be appropriate in consequence of the revision.

(2) In the preceding subsection 'revision' means an omission from,

addition to or alteration of the Convention and includes replacement of the Convention or part of it by another convention.

(3) An Order in Council under this section shall not be made unless a draft of the Order has been laid before Parliament and approved by a resolution of each House of Parliament.

As amended by the Carriage by Air and Road Act 1979, s3(3); International Transport Convention Act 1983, s9, Schedule 2, para 2.

CONSULAR RELATIONS ACT 1968
(1968 c 18)

1   Application of Vienna Convention

(1) Subject to sections 2 and 3(2) of this Act, the provisions set out in Schedule 1 to this Act (being Articles or parts of Articles of the Vienna Convention on Consular Relations signed in 1963) shall have the force of law in the United Kingdom and shall for that purpose be construed in accordance with subsections (2) to (11) of this section.

(2) In those provisions –

'authorities of the receiving State' shall be construed as including any constable and any person exercising a power of entry to any premises under any enactment (including any enactment of the Parliament of Northern Ireland);

'grave crime' shall be construed as meaning any offence punishable (on a first conviction) with imprisonment for a term that may extend to five years or with a more severe sentence;

'Ministry for Foreign Affairs' shall be construed as meaning the Department of the Secretary of State concerned;

'national of the receiving State' shall be construed as meaning –

(a) a British citizen, a British Dependent Territories citizen, a British National (Overseas) or a British Overseas citizen; or

(b) a person who under the British Nationality Act 1981 is a British subject; or

(c) a British protected person (within the meaning of that Act).

(3) The reference in paragraph 2 of Article 17 to any privileges and immunities accorded by customary international law or by international agreements shall be construed as a reference to any privileges and immunities conferred under the International Organisations (Immunities and Privileges) Act 1950 or the International Organisations Act 1968.

(4) The references in Article 44 to matters connected with the

exercise of the functions of members of a consular post shall be construed as references to matters connected with the exercise of consular functions by consular officers or consular employees.

(5) For the purposes of Article 45 and that Article as applied by Article 58 a waiver shall be deemed to have been expressed by a State if it had been expressed by the head, or any person for the time being performing the functions of head, of the diplomatic mission of that State or, if there is no such mission, of the consular post concerned.

(6) The exemption granted by Article 48 with respect to any services shall be deemed to except those services from any class of employment in respect of which contributions are payable under the enactments relating to social security ... but not so as to render any person liable to any contribution which he would not be required to pay if those services were not so excepted.

(7) Article 48 shall not affect any agreement made between the United Kingdom and any other State before the commencement of this Act and shall not be taken to prevent the making of any such agreement after the commencement of this Act.

(8) Articles 50, 51, 52, 54, 62 and 67 shall be construed as granting any privilege or immunity which they require to be granted.

(8A) The references in Articles 50 and 62 to customs duties shall be construed as including references to excise duties chargeable on goods imported into the United Kingdom and to value added tax charged in accordance with section 10 or 15 of the Value Added Tax Act 1994.

(9) The reference in Article 57 to the privileges and immunities provided in Chapter 11 shall be construed as referring to those provided in Section II of that Chapter.

(10) The reference in Article 70 to the rules of international law concerning diplomatic relations shall be construed as a reference to the provisions of the Diplomatic Privileges Act 1964.

(11) The references in Article 71 to additional privileges and immunities that may be granted by the receiving State or to privileges and immunities so far as these are granted by the receiving State shall be construed as referring to such privileges and immunities as may be specified by Her Majesty by Order in Council.

2   Restriction of privileges and immunities

If it appears to Her Majesty that the privileges and immunities accorded to a consular post of the United Kingdom in a territory of any State, or to persons connected with such a consular post, are less than those conferred by this Act on a consular post of that State or on persons connected with such a consular post, Her Majesty may by Order in Council withdraw such of the privileges and immunities so conferred from all or any of the consular posts of that State or from such persons connected therewith as appears to Her Majesty to be proper.

3   Agreements providing for additional or reduced privileges and immunities

(1) Where any agreement made, whether before or after the passing of this Act, between the United Kingdom and any other State provides for according to consular posts and persons connected with them privileges and immunities not accorded to them by the other provisions of this Act, Her Majesty may by Order in Council exercise, with respect to the consular posts of that State and persons connected with them, the powers specified in Schedule 2 to this Act so far as may be necessary to give effect to that agreement.

(2) Where any agreement made, whether before or after the passing of this Act, between the United Kingdom and any other State provides for according to consular posts and persons connected with them some but not all of the privileges and immunities accorded to them by the other provisions of this Act, Her Majesty may by Order in Council provide for excluding, with respect to consular posts of that State and persons connected with them, any of those privileges and immunities which are not provided for by the agreement.

4   Civil jurisdiction concerning service on board ship or aircraft

Her Majesty may by Order in Council make provision for excluding or limiting the jurisdiction of any court in the United Kingdom to entertain proceedings relating to the remuneration or any contract of service of the master or commander or a member of the crew of any ship or aircraft belonging to a State specified in the Order, except where a consular officer of that State has been notified of the intention to invoke the jurisdiction of that court and has not objected within such time as may be specified by or under the Order.

5 Jurisdiction over offences committed on board ship

(1) Her Majesty may by Order in Council make provision for securing that, where an offence is alleged to have been committed on board any ship by the master or a member of the crew and the ship belongs to a State specified in the Order, proceedings for the offence instituted otherwise than at the request or with the consent of a consular officer of that State are not entertained by any court in the United Kingdom, unless –

(a) the offence is alleged to have been committed by or against a person who is a citizen of the United Kingdom and Colonies or is otherwise comprised in the definition of 'national of the receiving State' in section 1(2) of this Act, or against a person other than the master or a member of the crew; or

(b) the offence is one involving the tranquillity or safety of a port, or the law relating to safety of life at sea, public health, oil pollution, wireless telegraphy, immigration or customs or is of any other description specified in the Order; or

(c) the offence is one comprised in the definition of 'grave crime' in section 1(2) of this Act.

(1A) In subsection (1)(b) of this section the expression 'the law relating to customs', to the extent that it refers to the law relating to duties on goods, refers to the law relating to duties (whether of customs or excise) for the time being chargeable on goods imported into the United Kingdom.

(2) For the purposes of this section, an offence which affects the property of any person shall be deemed to have been committed against him.

(3) For the purposes of this section, any document purporting to be signed by or on behalf of a consular officer and stating that he has requested or consented to the institution of any proceedings shall be sufficient proof of that fact unless the contrary is shown.

6 Detention on board ship for disciplinary offences

Her Majesty may by Order in Council designate any State for the purposes of this section; and where a State is so designated, a member of the crew of a ship belonging to that State who is detained in custody on board for a disciplinary offence shall not be deemed to be unlawfully detained unless –

(a) his detention is unlawful under the laws of that State or the conditions of detention are inhumane or unjustifiably severe; or

(b) there is reasonable cause for believing that his life or liberty will be endangered for reasons of race, nationality, political opinion or religion, in any country to which the ship is likely to go.

10   Right of diplomatic agents and consular officers to administer oaths and do notarial acts in certain cases

(1) A diplomatic agent or consular officer of any State may, if authorised to do so under the laws of that State, administer oaths, take affidavits and do notarial acts –

(a) required by a person for use in that State or under the laws thereof; or

(b) otherwise required by a national of that State but not for use in the United Kingdom except under the laws of some other country.

(2) Her Majesty may by Order in Council exclude or restrict the provisions of the preceding subsection in relation to the diplomatic agents or consular officers of any State if it appears to Her that in any territory of that State diplomatic agents or consular officers of the United Kingdom are not permitted to perform functions corresponding in nature and extent to those authorised by that subsection.

(3) Her Majesty may by Order in Council make provision for applying section 6 of the Commissioners for Oaths Act 1889 (powers as to oaths and notarial acts abroad) to countries within the Commonwealth or the Republic of Ireland by requiring the section to be construed as if –

(a) the references therein to a foreign country or place included such country or place as may be specified in the Order; and

(b) the diplomatic ranks specified in that section, included such ranks of any United Kingdom mission in a country specified in the Order as may be so specified in relation to that country.

(4) In this section 'diplomatic agent' has the same meaning as in the Diplomatic Privileges Act 1964.

11 Evidence

If in any proceedings any question arises whether or not any person is entitled to any privilege or immunity under this Act, a certificate issued by or under the authority of the Secretary of State stating any fact relating to that question shall be conclusive evidence of that fact.

12 Privileges and immunities in connection with Commonwealth and Irish establishments

(1) Her Majesty may, in relation to any such Commonwealth representatives as are described in subsection (2) below, provide by Order in Council for conferring all or any of the privileges and immunities which are conferred by or may be conferred under this Act on consular posts or persons connected with consular posts...

(2) The Commonwealth representatives in relation to whom this section applies are:

(a) persons in the service of the Government of any country within the Commonwealth (other than the United Kingdom) who hold offices appearing to Her Majesty to involve the performance of duties substantially corresponding to duties which, in the case of a foreign sovereign power, would be performed by a consular officer; and

(b) any person for the time being recognised by Her Majesty's Government in the United Kingdom as the chief representative in the United Kingdom of a state or province of a country within the Commonwealth.

(3) The privileges and immunities which may be conferred under this section shall include those which in other cases may, if an agreement so requires, be conferred by virtue of Schedule 2 of this Act.

(4) The provisions of this section shall have effect in relation to persons in the service of the Government of the Republic of Ireland as they have effect in relation to persons in the service of the Government of a country within the Commonwealth.

14 Orders in Council

(1) No recommendation shall be made to Her Majesty in Council to make an Order containing such provision as is mentioned in section

1(11) o section 3(1) of this Act unless a draft thereof has been laid before and approved by resolution of each House of Parliament.

(2) Any other statutory instrument made under the foregoing provisions of this Act shall be subject to annulment in pursuance of a resolution of either House of Parliament.

(3) Any power to make an Order conferred by this Act includes power to vary or revoke such an Order by a subsequent Order.

16 Short title, interpretation, commencement and repeal

(1) This Act may be cited as the Consular Relations Act 1968.

(2) For the purposes of section 4, 5 or 6 of this Act a ship, and for the purposes of section 4 an aircraft, shall be treated as belonging to a State in such circumstances as may be so specified by an Order in Council under that section; and different circumstances may be so specified with respect to different States and different classes of ship or aircraft ...

SCHEDULE 1

PROVISONS OF VIENNA CONVENTION HAVING THE FORCE OF LAW IN THE UNITED KINGDOM

ARTICLE 1

1. For the purposes of the present Convention, the following expressions shall have the meanings hereunder assigned to them:

(a) 'consular post' means any consulate-general, consulate, vice-consulate or consular agency;

(b) 'consular district' means the area assigned to a consular post for the exercise of consular functions;

(c) 'head of consular post' means the person charged with the duty of acting in that capacity;

(d) 'consular officer' means any person, including the head of a consular post, entrusted in that capacity with the exercise of consular functions;

(e) 'consular employee' means any person employed in the administrative or technical service of a consular post;

(f) 'member of the service staff' means any person employed in the domestic service of a consular post;

(g) 'member of the consular post' means consular officers, consular employees and members of the service staff;

(h) 'members of the consular staff' means consular officers, other than the head of a consular post, consular employees and members of the service staff;

(i) 'member of the private staff' means a person who is employed exclusively in the private service of a member of the consular post;

(f) 'consular premises' means the buildings or parts of buildings and the land ancillary thereto, irrespective of ownership, used exclusively for the purposes of the consular post;

(k) 'consular archives' includes all the papers, documents, correspondence, books, films, tapes and registers of the consular post, together with the ciphers and codes, the card-indexers and any article of furniture intended for their protection or safekeeping.

2. Consular officers are of two categories, namely career consular officers and honorary consular officers. The provisions of Chapter II of the present Convention apply to consular posts headed by career consular officers; the provisions of Chapter III governs consular posts headed by honorary consular officers.

3. The particular status of members of the consular posts who are nationals or permanent residents of the receiving State is governed by Article 71 of the present Convention.

CHAPTER I – CONSULAR RELATIONS IN GENERAL

Section I – Establishment and conduct of consular relations

ARTICLE 5

Consular functions consist in:

(a) protecting in the receiving State the interests of the sending State and of its nationals, both individuals and bodies corporate, within the limits permitted by international law;

(b) furthering the development of commercial, economic, cultural and scientific relations between the sending State and the receiving State and otherwise promoting friendly relations between them in accordance with the provisions of the present Convention;

(c) ascertaining by all lawful means conditions and developments in the commercial, economic, cultural and scientific life of the receiving State, reporting thereon to the Government of the sending State and giving information to persons interested;

(d) issuing passports and travel documents to nationals of the sending State and visas or appropriate documents to persons wishing to travel to the sending State;

(e) helping and assisting nationals, both individuals and bodies corporate, of the sending State;

(f) acting as notary and civil registrar and in capacities of a similar kind, and performing certain functions of an administrative nature, provided that there is nothing contrary thereto in the laws and regulations of the receiving State;

(g) safeguarding the interests of nationals, both individuals and bodies corporate, of the sending State in cases of succession mortis causa in the territory of the receiving State, in accordance with the laws and regulations of the receiving State;

(h) safeguarding, within the limits imposed by the laws and regulations of the receiving State, the interests of minors and other persons lacking full capacity who are nationals of the sending State, particularly where any guardianship or trusteeship is required with respect to such persons;

(i) subject to the practices and procedures obtaining in the receiving State, representing or arranging appropriate representation for nationals of the sending State before the tribunals and other authorities of the receiving State, for the purpose of obtaining, in accordance with the laws and regulations of the receiving State, provisional measures for the preservation of the rights and interests of these nationals, where, because of absence or any other reason, such nationals are unable at the proper time to assume the defence of their rights and interests;

(j) transmitting judicial and extra-judicial documents or executing letters rogatory or commissions to take evidence for the courts of the sending State in accordance with international agreements in force or, in the absence of such international agreements, in any other manner compatible with the laws and regulations of the receiving State;

(k) exercising rights of supervision and inspection provided for in the laws and regulations of the sending State in respect of vessels having the nationality of the sending State, and of aircraft registered in that State, and in respect of their crews;

(l) extending assistance to vessels and aircraft mentioned in sub-paragraph (k) of this Article and to their crews, taking statements regarding the voyage of a vessel, examining and stamping the ship's papers, and, without prejudice to the powers of the authorities of the receiving State, conducting investigations into any incidents which occurred during the voyage, and settling disputes of any kind between the master, the officers and the seamen in so far as this may be authorised by the laws and regulations of the sending State;

(m) performing any other functions entrusted to a consular post by the sending State which are not prohibited by the laws and regulations of the receiving State or to which no objection is taken by the receiving State or which are referred to in the international agreements in force between the sending State and the receiving State.

ARTICLE 15

1. If the head of a consular post is unable to carry out his functions or the position of head of consular post is vacant, an acting head of post may act provisionally as head of the consular post.

2. The full name of the acting head of post shall be notified either by the diplomatic mission of the sending State or, if that State has no such mission in the receiving State, by the head of the consular post, or, if he is unable to do so, by any competent authority of the sending State, to the Ministry for Foreign Affairs of the receiving State or to the authority designated by that Ministry. As a general rule, this notification shall be given in advance. The receiving State may make the admission as acting head of post of a person who is neither a diplomatic agent nor a consular officer of the sending State in the receiving State conditional on its consent.

3. The competent authorities of the receiving State shall afford assistance and protection to the acting head of post. While he is in charge of the post, the provisions of the present Convention shall apply to him on the same basis as to the head of the consular post concerned. The receiving State shall not, however, be obliged to grant to an acting head of post any facility, privilege or immunity which the head of the consular post enjoys only subject to conditions not fulfilled by the acting head of post.

4. When, in the circumstances referred to in paragraph 1 of this Article, a member of the diplomatic staff of the diplomatic mission of the sending State in the receiving State is designated by the sending State as an acting head of post, he shall, if the receiving State does not object thereto, continue to enjoy diplomatic privileges and immunities.

ARTICLE 17

1. In a State where the sending State has no diplomatic mission and is not represented by a diplomatic mission of a third State, a consular officer may, with the consent of the receiving State, and without affecting his consular status, be authorised to perform diplomatic acts. The performance of such acts by a consular officer shall not confer upon him any right to claim diplomatic privileges and immunities.

2. A consular officer may, after notification addressed to the receiving State, act as representative of the sending State to any inter-governmental organisation. When so acting, he shall be entitled to enjoy any privileges and immunities accorded to such a representative by customary international law or by international agreements; however, in respect of the performance by him of any consular function, he shall not be entitled to any greater immunity from jurisdiction than that to which a consular officer is entitled under the present Convention.

Section II – End of consular functions

ARTICLE 27

1. In the event of the severance of consular relations between two States:

(a) the receiving State shall, even in case of armed conflict, respect and protect the consular premises, together with the property of the consular post and the consular archives;

(b) the sending State may entrust the custody of the consular premises, together with the property contained therein and the consular archives, to a third State acceptable to the receiving State;

(c) the sending State may entrust the protection of its interests and those of its nationals to a third State acceptable to the receiving State.

2. In the event of the temporary or permanent closure of a consular post, the provisions of sub-paragraph (a) of paragraph 1 of this Article shall apply. In addition,

(a) if the sending State, although not represented in the receiving State by a diplomatic mission, has another consular post in the territory of that State, that consular post may be entrusted with the custody of the premises of the consular post which has been closed, together with the property contained therein and the consular archives, and, with the consent of the receiving State, with the exercise of consular functions in the district of that consular post; or

(b) if the sending State has no diplomatic mission and no other consular post in the receiving State, the provisions of sub-paragraphs (b) and (c) of paragraph 1 of this Article shall apply.

CHAPTER II – FACILITIES; PRIVILEGES AND IMMUNITIES RELATING TO CONSULAR POSTS, CAREER CONSULAR OFFICERS AND OTHER MEMBERS OF A CONSULAR POST

Section I – Facilities, privileges and immunities relating to a consular post

ARTICLE 31

1. Consular premises shall be inviolable to the extent provided in this Article.

2. The authorities of the receiving State shall not enter that part of the consular premises which is used exclusively for the purpose of the work of the consular post except with the consent of the head of the consular post or of his designee or of the head of the diplomatic mission of the sending State. The consent of the head of the consular post may, however, be assumed in case of fire or other disaster requiring prompt protective action.

3. Subject to the provisions of paragraph 2 of this Article, the receiving State is under a special duty to take all appropriate steps to protect the consular premises against any intrusion or damage and to prevent any disturbance of the peace of the consular post or impairment of its dignity.

4. The consular premises, their furnishings, the property of the consular post and its means of transport shall be immune from any form of requisition for purposes of national defence or public utility. If expropriation is necessary for such purposes, all possible steps shall be taken to avoid impeding the performance of consular functions, and prompt, adequate and effective compensation shall be paid to the sending State.

ARTICLE 32

1. Consular premises and the residence of the career head of consular post of which the sending State or any person acting on its behalf is the owner or lessee shall be exempt from all national, regional or municipal dues and taxes whatsoever, other than such as represent payment for specific services rendered.

2. The exemption from taxation referred to in paragraph 1 of this Article shall not apply to such dues and taxes if, under the law of the receiving State, they are payable by the person who contracted with the sending State or with the person acting on its behalf.

ARTICLE 33

The consular archives and documents shall be inviolable at all times and wherever they may be.

ARTICLE 35

1. The receiving State shall permit and protect freedom of communication on the part of the consular post for all official purposes. In communicating with the Government, the diplomatic missions and other consular posts, wherever situated, of the sending State, the consular post may employ all appropriate means, including diplomatic or consular couriers, diplomatic or consular bags and messages in code or cipher. However, the consular post may install and use a wireless transmitter only with the consent of the receiving State.

2. The official correspondence of the consular post shall be inviolable. Official correspondence means all correspondence relating to the consular post and its functions.

3. The consular bag shall be neither opened nor detained. Nevertheless, if the competent authorities of the receiving State have serious reason to believe that the bag contains something other than the correspondence, documents or articles referred to in paragraph 4 of this Article, they may request that the bag be opened in their presence by an authorised representative of the sending State. If this request is refused by the authorities of the sending State, the bag shall be returned to its place of origin.

4. The packages constituting the consular bag shall bear visible external marks of their character and may contain only official correspondence and documents or articles intended exclusively for official use.

5. The consular courier shall be provided with an official document indicating his status and the number of packages constituting the consular bag. Except with the consent of the receiving State, he shall be neither a national of the receiving State, nor, unless he is a national of the sending State, a permanent resident of the receiving State. In the performance of his functions he shall be protected by the receiving State. He shall enjoy personal inviolability and shall not be liable to any form of arrest or detention.

6. The sending State, its diplomatic missions and its consular posts may designate consular couriers ad hoc. In such cases the provisions of paragraph 5 of this Article shall also apply except that the immunities therein mentioned shall cease to apply when such a courier has delivered to the consignee the consular bag in his charge.

7. A consular bag may be entrusted to the captain of a ship or of a commercial aircraft scheduled to land at an authorised port of entry. He shall be provided with an official document indicating the number of packages constituting the bag, but he shall not be considered to be a consular courier. By arrangement with the appropriate local authorities, the consular post may send one of its members to take possession of the bag directly and freely from the captain of the ship or of the aircraft.

ARTICLE 39

1. The consular post may levy in the territory of the receiving State the fees and charges provided by the laws and regulations of the sending State for consular acts.

2. The sums collected in the form of the fees and charges referred to in paragraph 1 of this Article, and the receipts for such fees and charges, shall be exempt from all dues and taxes in the receiving State.

Section II – Facilities, privileges and immunities relating to career consular officers and other members of a consular post

ARTICLE 41

1. Consular officers shall not be liable to arrest or detention pending trial, except in the case of a grave crime and pursuant to a decision by the competent judicial authority.

2. Except in the case specified in paragraph 1 of this Article, consular officers shall not be committed to prison or liable to any other form of restriction on their personal freedom save in execution of a judicial decision of final effect.

ARTICLE 43

1. Consular officers and consular employees shall not be amenable to the jurisdiction of the judicial or administrative authorities of the receiving State in respect of acts performed in the exercise of consular functions.

2. The provisions of paragraph 1 of this Article shall not, however, apply in respect of a civil action either:

(a) arising out of a contract concluded by a consular officer or a consular employee in which he did not contract expressly or impliedly as an agent of the sending State; or

(b) by a third party for damage arising from an accident in the receiving State caused by a vehicle, vessel or aircraft.

ARTICLE 44

1. Members of a consular post may be called upon to attend as witnesses in the course of judicial or administrative proceedings. A consular employee or a member of the service staff shall not, except in the cases mentioned in paragraph 3 of this Article, decline to give

evidence. If a consular officer should decline to do so, no coercive measure or penalty may be applied to him.

2. The authority requiring the evidence of a consular officer shall avoid interference with the performance of his functions. It may, when possible, take such evidence at his residence or at the consular post or accept a statement from him in writing.

3. Members of a consular post are under no obligation to give evidence concerning matters connected with the exercise of their functions or to produce official correspondence and documents relating thereto. They are also entitled to decline to give evidence as expert witnesses with regard to the law of the sending State.

ARTICLE 45

1. The sending State may waive, with regard to a member of the consular post, any of the privileges and immunities provided for in Articles 41, 43 and 44.

2. The waiver shall in all cases be express, except as provided in paragraph 3 of this Article, and shall be communicated to the receiving State in writing.

3. The initiation of proceedings by a consular officer or a consular employee in a matter where he might enjoy immunity from jurisdiction under Article 43 shall preclude him from invoking immunity from jurisdiction in respect of any counter-claim directly connected with the principal claim.

4. The waiver of immunity from jurisdiction for the purposes of civil or administrative proceedings shall not be deemed to imply the waiver of immunity from the measures of execution resulting from the judicial decision; in respect of such measures, a separate waiver shall be necessary.

ARTICLE 48

1. Subject to the provisions of paragraph 3 of this Article, members of the consular post with respect to services rendered by them for the sending State, and members of their families forming part of their households, shall be exempt from social security provisions which may be in force in the receiving State.

2. The exemption provided for in paragraph 1 of this Article shall apply also to members of the private staff who are in the sole employ of members of the consular post, on condition:

(a) that they are not nationals of or permanently resident in the receiving State; and

(b) that they are covered by the social security provisions which are in force in the sending State or a third State.

3. Members of the consular post who employ persons to whom the exemption provided for in paragraph 2 of this Article does not apply shall observe the obligations which the social security provisions of the receiving State impose upon employers.

4. The exemption provided for in paragraphs 1 and 2 of this Article shall not preclude voluntary participation in the social security system of the receiving State, provided that such participation is permitted by that State.

ARTICLE 49

1. Consular officers and consular employees and members of their families forming part of their households shall be exempt from all dues and taxes, personal or real, national, regional or municipal, except:

(a) indirect taxes of a kind which are normally incorporated in the price of goods or services;

(b) dues or taxes on private immovable property situated in the territory of the receiving State, subject to the provisions of Article 32;

(c) estate, succession or inheritance duties, and duties on transfers, levied by the receiving State, subject to the provisions of paragraph (b) of Article 51;

(d) dues and taxes on private income, including capital gains, having its source in the receiving State and capital taxes relating to investments made in commercial or financial undertakings in the receiving State;

(e) charges levied for specific services rendered;

(f) registration, court or record fees, mortgage dues and stamp duties, subject to the provisions of Article 32.

2. Members of the service staff shall be exempt from dues and taxes on the wages which they receive for their services.

3. Members of the consular post who employ persons whose wages or salaries are not exempt from income tax in the receiving State shall observe the obligations which the laws and regulations of that State impose upon employers concerning the levying of income tax.

ARTICLE 50

1. The receiving State shall, in accordance with such laws and regulations as it may adopt, permit entry of and grant exemption from all customs duties, taxes, and related charges other than charges for storage, cartage and similar services, on:

(a) articles for the official use of the consular post;

(b) articles for the personal use of a consular officer or members of his family forming part of his household, including articles intended for his establishment. The articles intended for consumption shall not exceed the quantities necessary for direct utilisation by the persons concerned.

2. Consular employees shall enjoy the privileges and exemptions specified in paragraph 1 of this Article in respect of articles imported at the time of first installation.

3. Personal baggage accompanying consular officers and members of their families forming part of their households shall be exempt from inspection. It may be inspected only if there is serious reason to believe that it contains articles other than those referred to in sub-paragraph (b) of paragraph 1 of this Article, or articles the import or export of which is prohibited by the laws and regulations of the receiving State or which are subject to its quarantine laws and regulations. Such inspection shall be carried out in the presence of the consular officer or member of his family concerned.

ARTICLE 51

In the event of the death of a member of the consular post or of a member of his family forming part of his household, the receiving State:

(a) shall permit the export of the movable property of the deceased, with the exception of any such property acquired in the receiving State the export of which was prohibited at the time of his death;

(b) shall not levy national, regional or municipal estate,

succession or inheritance duties, and duties on transfers, on movable property the presence of which in the receiving State was due solely to the presence in that State of the deceased as a member of the consular post or as a member of the family of a member of the consular post.

ARTICLE 52

The receiving State shall exempt members of the consular post and members of their families forming part of their households from all personal services, from all public service of any kind whatsoever, and from military obligations such as those connected with requisitioning, military contributions and billeting.

ARTICLE 53

1. Every member of the consular post shall enjoy the privileges and immunities provided in the present Convention from the moment he enters the territory of the receiving State on proceeding to take up his post or, if already in its territory, from the moment when he enters on his duties with the consular post.

2. Members of the family of a member of the consular post forming part of his household and members of his private staff shall receive the privileges and immunities provided in the present Convention from the date from which he enjoys privileges and immunities in accordance with paragraph 1 of this Article or from the date of their entry into the territory of the receiving State or from the date of their becoming a member of such family or private staff, whichever is the latest.

3. When the functions of a member of the consular post have come to an end, his privileges and immunities and those of a member of his family forming part of his household or a member of his private staff shall normally cease at the moment when the person concerned leaves the receiving State or on the expiry of a reasonable period in which to do so, whichever is the sooner, but shall subsist until that time, even in case of armed conflict. In the case of the persons referred to in paragraph 2 of this Article, their privileges and immunities shall come to an end when they cease to belong to the household or to be in the service of a member of the consular post provided, however, that if such persons intend leaving the receiving State within a reasonable period thereafter, their privileges and immunities shall subsist until the time of their departure.

4. However, with respect to acts performed by a consular officer or a consular employee in the exercise of his functions, immunity from jurisdiction shall continue to subsist without limitation of time.

5. In the event of the death of a member of the consular post, the members of his family forming part of his household shall continue to enjoy the privileges and immunities accorded to them until they leave the receiving State or until the expiry of a reasonable period enabling them to do so, whichever is the sooner.

ARTICLE 54

1. If a consular officer passes through or is in the territory of a third State, which has granted him a visa if a visa was necessary, while proceeding to take up or return to his post or when returning to the sending State, the third State shall accord to him all immunities provided for by the other Articles of the present Convention as may be required to ensure his transit or return. The same shall apply in the case of any member of his family forming part of his household enjoying such privileges and immunities who are accompanying the consular officer or travelling separately to join him or to return to the sending State.

2. In circumstances similar to those specified in paragraph 1 of this Article, third States shall not hinder the transit through their territory of other members of the consular post or of members of their families forming part of their households.

3. Third States shall accord to official correspondence and to other official communications in transit, including messages in code or cipher, the same freedom and protection as the receiving State is bound to accord under the present Convention. They shall accord to consular couriers who have been granted a visa, if a visa was necessary, and to consular bags in transit, the same inviolability and protection as the receiving State is bound to accord under the present Convention.

4. The obligations of third States under paragraphs 1, 2 and 3 of this Article shall also apply to the persons mentioned respectively in those paragraphs, and to official communications and to consular bags, whose presence in the territory of the third State is due to force majeure.

ARTICLE 55

2. The consular premises shall not be used in any manner incompatible with the exercise of consular functions.

3. The provisions of paragraph 2 of this Article shall not exclude the possibility of offices of other institutions or agencies being installed in part of the building in which the consular premises are situated, provided that the premises assigned to them are separate from those used by the consular post. In that event, the said offices shall not, for the purposes of the present convention, be considered to form part of the consular premises.

ARTICLE 57

2. Privileges and immunities provided in this Chapter shall not be accorded:

(a) to consular employees or to members of the service staff who carry on any private gainful occupation in the receiving State;

(b) to members of the family of a person referred to in sub-paragraph (a) of this paragraph or to members of his private staff;

(c) to members of the family of a member of a consular post who themselves carry on any private gainful occupation in the receiving State.

CHAPTER III – REGIME RELATING TO HONORARY CONSULAR OFFICERS AND CONSULAR POSTS HEADED BY SUCH OFFICERS

ARTICLE 58

1. Articles 35 and 39, paragraph 3 of Article 54 and paragraphs 2 and 3 of Article 55 shall apply to consular posts headed by an honorary consular officer. In addition, the facilities, privileges and immunities of such consular posts shall be governed by Articles 60, 61 and 62.

2. Articles 43, paragraph 3 of Article 44, Articles 45 and 53 shall apply to honorary consular officers. In addition, the facilities, privileges and immunities of such consular officers shall be governed by Articles 66 and 67.

3. Privileges and immunities provided in the present Convention shall not be accorded to members of the family of an honorary consular officer or of a consular employee employed at a consular post headed by an honorary consular officer.

ARTICLE 59

The receiving State shall take such steps as may be necessary to protect the consular premises of a consular post headed by an honorary consular officer against any intrusion or damage and to prevent any disturbance of the peace of the consular post or impairment of its dignity.

ARTICLE 60

1. Consular premises of a consular post headed by an honorary consular officer of which the sending State is the owner or lessee shall be exempt from all national, regional or municipal dues and taxes whatsoever, other than such as represent payment for specific services rendered.

2. The exemption from taxation referred to in paragraph 1 of this Article shall not apply to such dues and taxes if, under the laws and regulations of the receiving State, they are payable by the person who contracted with the sending State.

ARTICLE 61

The consular archives and documents of a consular post headed by an honorary consular officer shall be inviolable at all times and wherever they may be, provided that they are kept separate from other papers and documents and, in particular, from the private correspondence of the head of a consular post and of any person working with him, and from the materials, books or documents relating to their profession or trade.

ARTICLE 62

The receiving State shall, in accordance with such laws and regulations as it may adopt, permit entry of, and grant exemption from all customs duties, taxes, and related charges other than charges for storage, cartage and similar services on the following articles, provided that they are for the official use of a consular post headed by an honorary consular officer: coats-of-arms, flags, signboards, seals and stamps, books, official printed matter, office furniture, office equipment and similar articles supplied by or at the instance of the sending State to the consular post.

ARTICLE 66

An honorary consular officer shall be exempt from all dues and taxes on the remuneration and emoluments which he receives from the sending State in respect of the exercise of consular functions.

ARTICLE 67

The receiving State shall exempt honorary consular officers from all personal services and from all public services of any kind whatsoever and from military obligations such as those connected with requisitioning, military contributions and billeting.

CHAPTER IV – GENERAL PROVISIONS

ARTICLE 70

1. The provisions of the present Convention apply also, so far as the context permits, to the exercise of consular functions by a diplomatic mission.

2. The names of members of a diplomatic mission assigned to the consular section or otherwise charged with the exercise of the consular functions of the mission shall be notified to the Ministry for Foreign Affairs of the receiving State or to the authority designated by that Ministry....

4. The privileges and immunities of the members of a diplomatic mission referred to in paragraph 2 of this Article shall continue to be governed by the rules of international law concerning diplomatic relations.

ARTICLE 71

1. Except in so far as additional facilities, privileges and immunities may be granted by the receiving State, consular officers who are

nationals of or permanently resident in the receiving State shall enjoy only immunity from jurisdiction and personal inviolability in respect of official acts performed in the exercise of their functions, and the privilege provided in paragraph 3 of Article 44.

2. Other members of the consular post who are nationals of or permanently resident in the receiving State and members of their families, as well as members of the families of consular officers referred to in paragraph 1 of this Article, shall enjoy facilities, privileges and immunities only in so far as these are granted to them by the receiving State. Those members of the families of members of the consular post and those members of the private staff who are themselves nationals of or permanently resident in the receiving State shall likewise enjoy facilities, privileges and immunities only in so far as these are granted to them by the receiving State.

SCHEDULE 2

PROVISIONS FOR GIVING EFFECT TO OTHER AGREEMENTS

1. The like exemption from dues and taxes may be extended to the residence of any member of a consular post as is accorded under Article 32 in Schedule 1 to this Act to the residence of the career head of a consular post.

2. Paragraph 1 of Article 49 in that Schedule may be extended to members of the service staff.

3. Paragraph 2 of Article 50 in that Schedule may be applied as if it were among the Articles mentioned in paragraph 2 of Article 58 in that Schedule, as if the reference to consular employees included members of the service staff and also such members of the families of consular employees or of members of the service staff as form part of their households, and as if the words 'in respect of articles imported at the time of first installation' were omitted.

4. Articles 29 and 31 in Schedule 1 to the Diplomatic Privileges Act 1964 (inviolability and immunity from jurisdiction and arrest of diplomatic agents and exemption from duty to give evidence) may be extended to members of a consular post and members of their families forming part of their households.

5. Article 22 in Schedule 1 to the Diplomatic Privileges Act 1964 (inviolability and protection of mission) may be extended to consular premises and paragraph 1 of Article 30 in that Schedule

(inviolability of private residence) may be extended to the residences of consular officers.

6. Article 27 in Schedule 1 to the Diplomatic Privileges Act 1964 (freedom of communications) may be extended to the communications of a consular post.

As amended by the International Organisations Act 1968, s12(2); Diplomatic and other Privileges Act 1971, s4, Schedule; Social Security Act 1973, ss100, 101, Schedule 27, para 78; Social Security (Consequential Provisions) Act 1975, ss1(2), 5, Schedule 1, Pt I; Customs and Excise Management Act 1979, s177(1), Schedule 4, paras 6, 7; British Nationality Act 1981, s52(6), Schedule 7; Hong Kong (British Nationality) Order 1986, art 8, Schedule 1; Diplomatic and Consular Premises Act 1987, s6, Schedule 2, paras 3–6; Finance (No 2) Act 1992, s14, Schedule 3, Pt III, para 89(1); Value Added Tax Act 1994, s100(1), Schedule 14, para 3.

INTERNATIONAL ORGANISATIONS ACT 1968
(1968 c 48)

1 Organisations of which United Kingdom is a member

(1) This section shall apply to any organisation declared by Order in Council to be an organisation of which –

(a) the United Kingdom, or Her Majesty's Government in the United Kingdom, and

(b) any other sovereign Power or the Government of any other sovereign Power,

are members.

(2) Subject to subsection (6) of this section, Her Majesty may by Order in Council made under this subsection specify an organisation to which this section applies and make any one or more of the following provisions in respect of the organisation so specified (in the following provisions of this section referred to as 'the organisation'), that is to say –

(a) confer on the organisation the legal capacities of a body corporate;

(b) provide that the organisation shall, to such extent as may be specified in the Order, have the privileges and immunities set out in Part I of Schedule 1 to this Act;

(c) confer the privileges and immunities set out in Part II of Schedule 1 to this Act, to such extent as may be specified in the Order, on persons of any such class as is mentioned in the next following subsection;

(d) confer the privileges and immunities set out in Part III of Schedule 1 to this Act, to such extent as may be specified in the Order, on such classes of officers and servants of the organisation (not being classes mentioned in the next following subsection) as may be so specified.

(3) The classes of persons referred to in subsection (2)(c) of this section are –

(a) persons who (whether they represent Governments or not) are representatives to the organisation or representatives on, or members of, any organ, committee or other subordinate body of the organisation (including any sub-committee or other subordinate body of a subordinate body of the organisation);

(b) such number of officers of the organisation as may be specified in the Order, being the holders (whether permanent, temporary or acting) of such high offices in the organisation as may be so specified; and

(c) persons employed by or serving under the organisation as experts or as persons engaged on missions for the organisation.

(4) Where an Order in Council is made under subsection (2) of this section, the provisions of Part IV of Schedule 1 to this Act shall have effect by virtue of that Order (in those provisions, as they so have effect, referred to as 'the relevant Order'), except in so far as that Order otherwise provides.

(5) Where an Order in Council is made under subsection (2) of this section, then for the purpose of giving effect to any agreement made in that behalf between the United Kingdom or Her Majesty's Government in the United Kingdom and the organisation Her Majesty may by the same or any subsequent Order in Council make either or both of the following provisions, that is to say –

(a) confer the exemptions set out in paragraph 13 of Schedule 1 to this Act, to such extent as may be specified in the Order, in respect of officers and servants of the organisation of any class specified in the Order in accordance with subsection (2)(d) of this section and in respect of members of the family of any such officer or servant who form part of his household;

(b) confer the exemptions set out in Part V of that Schedule in respect of –

(i) members of the staff of the organisation recognised by Her Majesty's Government in the United Kingdom as holding a rank equivalent to that of a diplomatic agent, and

(ii) members of the family of any such member of the staff of the organisation who form part of his household.

(6) Any Order in Council made under subsection (2) or subsection (5) of this section shall be so framed as to secure –

(a) that the privileges and immunities conferred by the Order are not greater in extent than those which, at the time when the Order takes effect, are required to be conferred in accordance with any agreement to which the United Kingdom or Her Majesty's Government in the United Kingdom is then a party (whether made with any other sovereign Power or Government or made with one or more organisations such as are mentioned in subsection (1) of this section), and

(b) that no privilege or immunity is conferred on any person as the representative of the United Kingdom, or of Her Majesty's Government in the United Kingdom, or as a member of the staff of such a representative.

2 Specialised agencies of United Nations

(1) Where an Order in Council under section 1(2) of this Act is made in respect of an organisation which is a specialised agency of the United Nations having its headquarters or principal office in the United Kingdom, then for the purpose of giving effect to any agreement between the United Kingdom or Her Majesty's Government in the United Kingdom and that organisation Her Majesty may by the same or any other Order in Council confer the exemptions, privileges and reliefs specified in the next following subsection, to such extent as may be specified in the Order, on officers of the organisation who are recognised by Her Majesty's Government in the United Kingdom as holding a rank equivalent to that of a diplomatic agent.

(2) The exemptions, privileges and reliefs referred to in the preceding subsection are –

(a) the like exemption or relief from income tax, capital gains tax and rates as, in accordance with Article 34 of the 1961 Convention Articles, is accorded to a diplomatic agent, and

(aa) the like exemption or relief from being liable to pay anything in respect of council tax as in accordance with that Article is accorded to a diplomatic agent, and

(b) the exemptions, privileges and reliefs specified in paragraphs 10 to 12 of Schedule 1 to this Act and the exemption comprised in paragraph 9 of that Schedule from vehicle excise duty (that is to say, duty under section 1 of the Vehicles (Excise) Act 1971, whether chargeable by virtue of that section or otherwise, or any corresponding duty under an enactment of the Parliament of Northern Ireland).

(3) Where by virtue of subsection (1) of this section any of the exemptions, privileges and reliefs referred to in subsection (2)(b) of this section are conferred on persons as being officers of the organisation, Her Majesty may by the same or any other Order in Council confer the like exemptions, privileges and reliefs on persons who are members of the families of those persons and form part of their households.

(4) The powers conferred by the preceding provisions of this section shall be exercisable in addition to any power exercisable by virtue of subsection (2) or subsection (5) of section 1 of this Act; and any exercise of the powers conferred by those provisions shall have effect without prejudice to the operation of subsection (4) of that section.

(5) Subsection (6) of section 1 of this Act shall have effect in relation to the preceding provisions of this section as it has effect in relation to subsections (2) and (5) of that section.

(6) In this section 'specialised agency' has the meaning assigned to it by Article 57 of the Charter of the United Nations.

4 Other organisations of which United Kingdom is not a member

Where an organisation of which two or more sovereign Powers, or the Governments of two or more such Powers, are members but of which neither the United Kingdom nor Her Majesty's Government in the United Kingdom is a member, maintains or proposes to maintain an establishment in the United Kingdom, then for the purpose of giving effect to any agreement made in that behalf between the United Kingdom or Her Majesty's Government in the United Kingdom and that organisation, Her Majesty may by Order in Council specifying the organisation make either or both of the following provisions in respect of the organisation, that is to say –

(a) confer on the organisation the legal capacities of a body corporate, and

(b) provide that the organisation shall, to such extent as may be specified in the Order, be entitled to the like exemption or relief from taxes on income and capital gains as is accorded to a foreign sovereign Power.

4A International commodity organisations

(1) In this section, 'international commodity organisation' means any such organisation as is mentioned in section 4 of this Act

(international organisations of which the United Kingdom is not a member) which appears to Her Majesty to satisfy each of the following conditions –

(a) that the members of the organisation are States or the Governments of States in which a particular commodity is produced or consumed;

(b) that the exports or imports of that commodity from or to those States account (when taken together) for a significant volume of the total exports or imports of that commodity throughout the world; and

(c) that the purpose or principal purpose of the organisation is –

(i) to regulate trade in that commodity (whether as an import or an export or both) or to promote or study that trade; or

(ii) to promote research into that commodity or its uses or further development.

(2) Subject to the following provisions of this section, an Order made under section 4 of this Act with respect to an international commodity organisation may, for the purpose there mentioned and to such extent as may be specified in the Order –

(a) provide that the organisation shall have the privileges and immunities set out in paragraphs 2, 3, 4, 6 and 7 of Schedule 1 to this Act;

(b) confer on persons of any such class as is mentioned in sub-section (3) of this section the privileges and immunities set out in paragraphs 11 and 14 of that Schedule;

(c) provide that the official papers of such persons shall be inviolable; and

(d) confer on officers and servants of the organisation of any such class as may be specified in the Order the privileges and immunities set out in paragraphs 13, 15 and 16 of that Schedule.

(3) The classes of persons referred to in subsection (2)(b) of this section are –

(a) persons who (whether they represent Governments or not) are representatives to the organisation or representatives on, or members of, any organ, committee or other subordinate body of the organisation (including any sub-committee or other subordinate body of a subordinate body of the organisation);

(b) persons who are members of the staff of any such representative and who are recognised by Her Majesty's

Government in the United Kingdom as holding a rank equivalent to that of a diplomatic agent.

(4) An Order in Council made under section 4 of this Act shall not confer on any person of such class as is mentioned in sub-section (3) of this section any immunity in respect of a civil action arising out of an accident caused by a motor vehicle or other means of transport belonging to or driven by such a person, or in respect of a traffic offence involving such a vehicle and committed by such a person.

(5) In this section 'commodity' means any produce of agriculture, forestry or fisheries, or any mineral, either in its natural state or having undergone only such processes as are necessary or customary to prepare the produce or mineral for the international market.

5   International judicial and other proceedings

(1) Her Majesty may by Order in Council confer on any class of persons to whom this section applies such privileges, immunities and facilities as in the opinion of Her Majesty in Council are or will be required for giving effect –

(a) to any agreement to which, at the time when the Order takes effect, the United Kingdom or Her Majesty's Government in the United Kingdom is or will be a party, or

(b) to any resolution of the General Assembly of the United Nations.

(2) This section applies to any persons who are for the time being –

(a) judges or members of any international tribunal, or persons exercising or performing, or appointed (whether permanently or temporarily) to exercise or perform, any jurisdiction or functions of such a tribunal;

(b) registrars or other officers of any international tribunal;

(c) parties to any proceedings before any international tribunal;

(d) agents, advisers or advocates (by whatever name called) for any such parties;

(e) witnesses in, or assessors for the purposes of, any proceedings before any international tribunal.

(3) For the purposes of this section any petition, complaint or other communication which, with a view to action to be taken by or before an international tribunal, –

(a) is made to the tribunal, or

(b) is made to a person through whom, in accordance with the constitution, rules or practice of the tribunal, such a communication can be received by the tribunal,

shall be deemed to be proceedings before the tribunal, and the person making any such communication shall be deemed to be a party to such proceedings.

(4) Without prejudice to subsection (3) of this section, any reference in this section to a party to proceedings before an international tribunal shall be construed as including a reference to –

(a) any person who, for the purposes of any such proceedings, acts as next friend, guardian or other representative (by whatever name called) of a party to the proceedings, and

(b) any person who (not being a person to whom this section applies apart from this paragraph) is entitled or permitted, in accordance with the constitution, rules or practice of an international tribunal, to participate in proceedings before the tribunal by way of advising or assisting the tribunal in the proceedings.

(5) In this section 'international tribunal' means any court (including the International Court of Justice), tribunal, commission or other body which, in pursuance of any such agreement or resolution as is mentioned in subsection (1) of this section, –

(a) exercises, or is appointed (whether permanently or temporarily) for the purpose of exercising, any jurisdiction, or

(b) performs, or is appointed (whether permanently or temporarily) for the purpose of performing, any functions of a judicial nature or by way of arbitration, conciliation or inquiry,

and includes any individual who, in pursuance of any such agreement or resolution, exercises or performs, or is appointed (whether permanently or temporarily) for the purpose of exercising or performing, any jurisdiction or any such functions.

5A   Orders under ss1 and 4 extending to United Kingdom conferences

(1) An Order in Council made under section 1 of this Act in respect of any organisation, or under section 4 of this Act in respect of an international commodity organisation, may to such extent as may be

specified in the Order, and subject to the following provisions of this section –

(a) confer on persons of any such class as may be specified in the Order, being persons who are or are to be representatives (whether of Government or not) at any conference which the organisation may convene in the United Kingdom –

(i) in the case of an Order under section 1, the privileges and immunities set out in Part II of Schedule 1 to this Act;

(ii) in the case of an Order under section 4, the privileges and immunities set out in paragraphs 11 and 14 of that Schedule; and

(b) in the case of an Order under section 4, provide that the official papers of such persons shall be inviolable.

(2) Where in the exercise of the power conferred by subsection (1)(a) of this section an Order confers privileges and immunities on persons of any such class as is mentioned in that paragraph, the provisions of paragraphs 19 to 22 of Schedule 1 to this Act shall have effect in relation to the members of the official staffs of such persons as if in paragraph 29 of that Schedule 'representative' were defined as a person of such a class.

(3) The powers exercisable by virtue of this section may be exercised notwithstanding the provisions of any such agreement as is mentioned in section 1(6)(a) or 4 of this Act, but no privilege or immunity may thereby be conferred on any such representative, or member of his staff, as is mentioned in section 1(6)(b) of this Act.

(4) In this section 'international commodity organisation' has the meaning given by section 4A(1) of this Act.

(5) This section is without prejudice to section 6 of this Act.

6   Representatives at international conferences in United Kingdom

(1) This section applies to any conference which is, or is to be, held in the United Kingdom and is, or is to be, attended by representatives –

(a) of the United Kingdom, or of Her Majesty's Government in the United Kingdom, and

(b) of any other sovereign Power or the Government of any other sovereign Power.

(2) Her Majesty may by Order in Council specify one or more classes of persons who are, or are to be, representatives of a sovereign Power (other than the United Kingdom) or of the Government of such a Power, at a conference to which this section applies, and confer on persons of the class or classes in question, to such extent as may be specified in the Order, the privileges and immunities set out in Part II of Schedule 1 to this Act.

(3) Where an Order in Council is made under subsection (2) of this section in relation to a particular conference, then, except in so far as that Order otherwise provides, the provisions of paragraphs 19 to 22 of Schedule 1 to this Act shall have effect in relation to members of the official staffs of persons of a class specified in the Order in accordance with that subsection as if in paragraph 19 of that Schedule 'representative' were defined as a person of a class so specified in the Order.

7   Priority of telecommunications

So far as may be necessary for the purpose of giving effect to the International Telecommunication Convention done at Montreux on 12 November 1965 or any subsequent treaty or agreement whereby that Convention is amended or superseded, priority shall, wherever practicable, be given to messages from, and to replies to messages from, any of the following, that is to say –

(a) the Secretary General of the United Nations;

(b) the heads of principal organs of the United Nations; and

(c) the International Court of Justice.

8   Evidence

If in any proceedings a question arises whether a person is or is not entitled to any privilege or immunity by virtue of this Act or any Order in Council made thereunder, a certificate issued by or under the authority of the Secretary of State stating any fact relating to that question shall be conclusive evidence of that fact.

9   Financial provisions

Any amount refunded under any arrangement made in accordance with any provisions of Schedule 1 to this Act relating to refund of customs duty, value added tax or car tax –

(a) if the arrangements were made by the Secretary of State, shall be paid out of moneys provided by Parliament, or

(b) if the arrangements were made by the Commissioners of Customs and Excise, shall be paid out of the moneys standing to the credit of the General Account of those Commissioners.

10 Orders in Council

(1) No recommendation shall be made to Her Majesty in Council to make an Order under any provision (other than section 6) of this Act unless a draft of the Order has been laid before Parliament and approved by a resolution of each House of Parliament.

(2) Any Order in Council made under section 6 of this Act shall be subject to annulment in pursuance of a resolution of either House of Parliament.

(3) Any power conferred by any provision of this Act to make an Order in Council shall include power to revoke or vary the Order by a subsequent Order in Council made under that provision.

11 Interpretation

(1) In this Act 'the 1961 Convention Articles' means the Articles (being certain Articles of the Vienna Convention on Diplomatic Relations signed in 1961) which are set out in Schedule 1 to the Diplomatic Privileges Act 1964, and 'the International Court of Justice' means the court set up by that name under the Charter of the United Nations.

(2) Expressions used in this Act to which a meaning is assigned by Article 1 of the 1961 Convention Articles, and other expressions which are used both in this Act and in those Articles, shall, except in so far as the context otherwise requires, be construed as having the same meanings in this Act as in those Articles.

(3) For the purpose of giving effect to any arrangements made in that behalf between Her Majesty's Government in the United Kingdom and any organisation, premises which are not premises of the organisation but are recognised by that Government as being temporarily occupied by the organisation for its official purposes shall, in respect of such period as may be determined in accordance with the arrangements, be treated for the purposes of this Act as if they were premises of the organisation.

(4) Except in so far as the context otherwise requires, any reference in this Act to an enactment is a reference to that enactment as amended or extended by or under any other enactment.

12 Consequential amendments, repeals and transitional provisions

(3) References in any enactment to the powers conferred by the International Organisations (Immunities and Privileges) Act 1950 shall be construed as including references to the powers conferred by this Act.

(5) Any Order in Council which has been made, or has effect as if made, under an enactment repealed by subsection (4) of this section and is in force immediately before the passing of this Act shall continue to have effect notwithstanding the repeal of that enactment and, while any such Order in Council continues to have effect in relation to an organisation –

(a) the enactment in question shall continue to have effect in relation to that organisation as if that enactment had not been repealed, and

(b) section 8 of this Act shall have effect as if in that section any reference to this Act or an Order in Council made thereunder included a reference to that enactment or that Order in Council.

(6) Any such Order in Council as is mentioned in subsection (5) of this section –

(a) if made, or having effect as if made, under section 1 of the International Organisations (Immunities and Privileges) Act 1950, may be revoked or varied as if it had been made under section 1 of this Act;

(b) if made, or having effect as if made, under section 3 of that Act, may be revoked or varied as if it had been made under section 5 of this Act.

SCHEDULE 1

PRIVILEGES AND IMMUNITIES

PART I

1. Immunity from suit and legal process.

2. The like inviolability of official archives and premises of the organisation as, in accordance with the 1961 Convention Articles, is accorded in respect of the official archives and premises of a diplomatic mission.

3. (1) Exemption or relief from taxes, other than duties (whether of customs or excise) and taxes on the importation of goods.

(2) The like relief from rates as in accordance with Article 23 of the 1961 Convention Articles is accorded in respect of the premises of a diplomatic mission.

4. Exemption from duties (whether of customs or excise) and taxes on the importation of goods imported by or on behalf of the organisation for its official use in the United Kingdom, or on the importation of any publications of the organisation imported by it or on its behalf, such exemption to be subject to compliance with such conditions as the Commissioners of Customs and Excise may prescribe for the protection of the Revenue.

5. Exemption from prohibitions and restrictions on importation or exportation in the case of goods imported or exported by the organisation for its official use and in the case of any publication of the organisation imported or exported by it.

6. Relief, under arrangements made either by the Secretary of State or by the Commissioners of Customs and Excise, by way of refund of duty (whether of customs or excise) paid on imported hydrocarbon oil (within the meaning of the Hydrocarbon Oil Duties Act 1979) or value added tax paid on the importation of such oil which is brought in the United Kingdom and used for the official purposes of the organisation, such relief to be subject to compliance with such conditions as may be imposed in accordance with the arrangements.

7. Relief, under arrangements made by the Secretary of State, by way of refund of car tax paid on any vehicles and value added tax paid on the supply of any goods or services which are used for the official purposes of the organisation, such relief to be subject to

compliance with such conditions as may be imposed in accordance with the arrangements.

PART II

8. For the purpose of conferring on any person any such exemption, privilege or Schedule, any reference in that paragraph to the representative or officer shall be construed as a reference to that person.

9. The like immunity from suit and legal process, the like inviolability of residence, and the like exemption or relief from taxes and rates, other than customs duties and taxes on the importation of goods, as are accorded to or in respect of the head of a diplomatic mission.

9A. The like inviolability of official premises as is accorded in respect of the premises of a diplomatic mission.

9B. The like exemption or relief from being liable to pay anything in respect of council tax, as is accorded to or in respect of the head of a diplomatic mission.

10. The like exemption from duties (whether of customs or excise) and taxes on the importation of articles imported for the personal use of the representative or officer or of members of his family forming part of his household, including articles intended for his establishment and the like privilege as to the importation of such articles, as in accordance with paragraph 1 of Article 36 of the 1961 Convention Articles is accorded to a diplomatic agent.

11. The like exemption and privileges in respect of the personal baggage of the representative or officer as in accordance with paragraph 2 of Article 36 of those Articles are accorded to a diplomatic agent, as if in that paragraph the reference to paragraph 1 of that Article were a reference to paragraph 10 of this Schedule.

12. Relief, under arrangements made either by the Secretary of State or by the Commissioners of Customs and Excise, by way of refund of duty (whether of customs or excise) paid on imported hydrocarbon oil (within the meaning of the Hydrocarbon Oil Duties Act 1979) or value added tax paid on the importation of such oil which is bought in the United Kingdom by or on behalf of the representative or officer, such relief to be subject to compliance with such conditions as may be imposed in accordance with the arrangements.

13. Exemptions whereby, for the purposes of the enactments relating to social security ... –

(a) services rendered for the organisation by the representative or officer shall be deemed to be excepted from any class of employment in respect of which contributions under those enactments are payable, but

(b) no person shall be rendered liable to pay any contribution which he would not be required to pay if those services were not deemed to be so excepted.

PART III

14. Immunity from suit and legal process in respect of things done or omitted to be done in the course of the performance of official duties.

15. Exemption from income tax in respect of emoluments received as an officer or servant of the organisation.

16. The like exemption from duties (whether of customs or excise) and taxes on the importation of articles which –

(a) at or about the time when an officer or servant of the organisation first enters the United Kingdom as such an officer or servant are imported for his personal use or that of members of his family forming part of his household, including articles intended for his establishment, and

(b) are articles which were in his ownership or possession or that of such a member of his family, or which he or such a member of his family was under contract to purchase, immediately before he so entered the United Kingdom,

and the like privilege as to the importation of such articles as in accordance with paragraph 1 of Article 36 of the 1961 Convention Articles is accorded to a diplomatic agent.

17. Exemption from duties (whether of customs or excise) and taxes on the importation of any motor vehicle imported by way of replacement of a motor vehicle in respect of which the conditions specified in sub-paragraphs (a) and (b) of paragraph 16 of this Schedule were fulfilled, such exemption to be subject to compliance with such conditions as the Commissioners of Customs and Excise may prescribe for the protection of the Revenue.

18. The like exemption and privileges in respect of the personal baggage of an officer or servant of the organisation as in accordance

with paragraph 2 of Article 36 of the 1961 Convention Articles are accorded to a diplomatic agent, as if in that paragraph the reference to paragraph 1 of that Article were a reference to paragraph 16 of this Schedule.

19. In this Part of this Schedule –

(a) 'representative' means a person who is such a representative to the organisation specified in the relevant Order or such a representative on, or member of, an organ, committee or other subordinate body of that organisation as is mentioned in section 1(3)(a) of this Act;

(b) 'member of the official staff' means a person who accompanies a representative as part of his official staff in his capacity as a representative;

(c) references to the importation, in relation to value added tax, shall include references to anything charged with tax in accordance with section 10 or 15 of the Value Added Tax Act 1994 (acquisitions from other member States and importations from outside the European Community), and 'imported' shall be construed accordingly.

20. A member of the official staff who is recognised by Her Majesty's Government in the United Kingdom as holding a rank equivalent to that of a diplomatic agent shall be entitled to the privileges and immunities set out in Part II of this Schedule to the like extent as, by virtue of the relevant Order, the representative whom he accompanies is entitled to them.

21 (1) Subject to sub-paragraph (2) of this paragraph, a member of the official staff who is not so recognised, and who is employed in the administrative or technical service of the representative whom he accompanies, shall be entitled to the privileges and immunities set out in paragraphs 9 and 13 of this Schedule to the like extent as, by virtue of the relevant Order, that representative is entitled to them.

(2) Such a member of the official staff shall not by virtue of the preceding sub-paragraph be entitled to immunity from any civil proceedings in respect of any cause of action arising otherwise than in the course of his official duties.

(3) Such a member of the official staff shall also be entitled to the exemption set out in paragraph 16 of this Schedule as if he were an officer of the organisation specified in the relevant Order.

22. A member of the official staff who is employed in the domestic service of the representative whom he accompanies shall be entitled to the following privileges and immunities, that is to say –

(a) immunity from suit and legal process in respect of things done or omitted to be done in the course of the performance of official duties, and

(b) the exemptions set out in paragraph 13 of this Schedule,

to the like extent as, by virtue of the relevant Order, that representative is entitled to them, and shall be entitled to exemption from taxes on his emoluments in respect of that employment to the like extent as, by virtue of the relevant Order, that representative is entitled to exemption from taxes on his emoluments as a representative.

23 (1) Persons who are members of the family of a representative and form part of his household shall be entitled to the privileges and immunities set out in Part II of this Schedule to the like extent as, by virtue of the relevant Order, that representative is entitled to them.

(2) Persons who are members of the family and form part of the household of an officer of the organisation specified in the relevant Order, where that officer is the holder (whether permanent, temporary or acting) of an office specified in that Order in accordance with section 1(3)(b) of this Act, shall be entitled to the privileges and immunities set out in Part II of this Schedule to the like extent as, by virtue of the relevant Order, that officer is entitled to them.

(3) Persons who are members of the family and form part of the household of such a member of the official staff as is mentioned in paragraph 20 of this Schedule shall be entitled to the privileges and immunities set out in Part II of this Schedule to the like extent as, by virtue of that paragraph, that member of the official staff is entitled to them.

(4) Persons who are members of the family and form part of the household of such a member of the official staff as is mentioned in paragraph 21 of this Schedule shall be entitled to the privileges and immunities set out in paragraphs 9 and 13 of this Schedule to the like extent as, by virtue of paragraph 21 of this Schedule, that member of the official staff is entitled to them.

PART V

24. In the event of the death of the person in respect of whom the exemptions under this paragraph are conferred, exemptions from –

(a) estate duty leviable on his death under the law of any part of the United Kingdom in respect of movable property which is in the United Kingdom immediately before his death and whose presence in the United Kingdom at that time is due solely to his presence there in the capacity by reference to which the exemptions are conferred.

As amended by the Diplomatic and other Privileges Act 1971, s3; European Communities Act 1972, s4, Schedule 3, Pt IV; Finance Act 1972, s55(5), (7); Social Security Act 1973, ss100, 101, Schedule 27, para 80(a); Customs and Excise Management Act 1979, s177(1), Schedule 4, para 12; International Organisations Act 1981, ss1(1), (2), (3), 2, 3, 5(1), (2), (3), 6(4), Schedule; Local Government Finance Act 1988, s137, Schedule 12, Pt III, para 40; Local Government and Housing Act 1989, s194(1), Schedule II, para 14; Local Government Finance Act 1992, s117(1), Schedule 13, paras 27, 28; Taxation of Chargeable Gains Act 1992, s290(3), Schedule 12; Finance (No 2) Act 1992, s14, Schedule 3, Pt III, para 90; Value Added Tax Act 1994, s100(1), Schedule 14, para 4.

FAMILY LAW REFORM ACT 1969
(1969 c 46)

1 Reduction of age of minority from 21 to 18

(1) As from [1 January 1970] a person shall attain full age on attaining the age of eighteen instead of on attaining the age of twenty-one; and a person shall attain full age on that date if he has then already attained the age of eighteen but not the age of twenty-one.

(2) The foregoing subsection applies for the purposes of any rule of law, and, in the absence of a definition or of any indication of a contrary intention, for the construction of 'full age', 'infant', 'infancy', 'minor', 'minority' and similar expressions in –

(a) any statutory provision, whether passed or made before, on or after the date on which this section comes into force; and

(b) any deed, will or other instrument of whatever nature (not being a statutory provision) made on or after that date.

(3) In the statutory provisions specified in Schedule 1 to this Act for any reference to the age of twenty-one years there shall be substituted a reference to the age of eighteen years; but the amendment by this subsection of the provisions specified in Part II of that Schedule shall be without prejudice to any power of amending or revoking those provisions. ...

ADMINISTRATION OF JUSTICE ACT 1970
(1970 c 31)

44A Interest on judgment debts expressed in currencies other than sterling

(1) Where a judgment is given for a sum expressed in a currency other than sterling and the judgment debt is one to which section 17 of the Judgments Act 1838 applies, the court may order that the interest rate applicable to the debt shall be such a rate as the court thinks fit.

(2) Where the court makes such an order, section 17 of the Judgments Act 1838 shall have effect in relation to the judgment debt as if the rate specified in the order were substituted for the rate specified in that section.

As inserted by the Private International Law (Miscellaneous Provisions) Act 1995, s1(1).

ADMINISTRATION OF ESTATES ACT 1971

(1971 c 25)

1   Recognition in England and Wales of Scottish confirmations and Northern Irish grants of representation

(1) Where a person dies domiciled in Scotland –

(a) a confirmation granted in respect of all or part of his estate and noting his Scottish domicile, and

(b) a certificate of confirmation noting his Scottish domicile and relating to one or more items of his estate,

shall, without being resealed, be treated for the purposes of the law of England and Wales as a grant of representation (in accordance with subsection (2) below) to the executors named in the confirmation or certificate in respect of the property of the deceased of which according to the terms of the confirmation they are executors or, as the case may be, in respect of the item or items of property specified in the certificate of confirmation.

(2) Where by virtue of subsection (1) above a confirmation or certificate of confirmation is treated for the purposes of the law of England and Wales as a grant of representation to the executors named therein then, subject to subsections (3) and (5) below, the grant shall be treated –

(a) as a grant of probate where it appears from the confirmation or certificate that the executors so named are executors nominate; and

(b) in any other case, as a grant of letters of administration.

(3) Section 7 of the Administration of Estates Act 1925 (executor of executor represents original testator) shall not, by virtue of subsection (2)(a) above, apply on the death of an executor named in a confirmation or certificate of confirmation.

(4) Subject to subsection (5) below, where a person dies domiciled in Northern Ireland a grant of probate of his will or letters of administration in respect of his estate (or any part of it) made by the High Court in Northern Ireland and noting his domicile there shall, without being resealed, be treated for the purposes of the law of England and Wales as if it had been originally made by the High Court in England and Wales.

(5) Notwithstanding anything in the preceding provisions of this section, a person who is a personal representative according to the law of England and Wales by virtue only of those provisions may not be required, under section 25 of the Administration of Estates Act 1925, to deliver up his grant to the High Court.

(6) This section applies in relation to confirmations, probates and letters of administration granted before as well as after the commencement of this Act, and in relation to a confirmation, probate or letters of administration granted before the commencement of this Act, this section shall have effect as if it had come into force immediately before the grant was made.

(7) In this section 'confirmation' includes an additional confirmation, and the term 'executors', where used in relation to a confirmation or certificate of confirmation, shall be construed according to the law of Scotland.

2 Recognition in Northern Ireland of English grants of representation and Scottish confirmations

(1) Where a person dies domiciled in England and Wales a grant of probate of his will or letters of administration in respect of his estate (or any part of it) made by the High Court in England and Wales and noting his domicile there shall, without being resealed, be treated for the purposes of the law of Northern Ireland as if it had been originally made by the High Court in Northern Ireland.

(2) Where a person dies domiciled in Scotland –

(a) a confirmation granted in respect of all or part of his estate and noting his Scottish domicile, and

(b) a certificate of confirmation noting his Scottish domicile and relating to one or more items of his estate,

shall, without being resealed, be treated for the purposes of the law of Northern Ireland as a grant of representation (in accordance with subsection (3) below) to the executors named in the confirmation or certificate in respect of the property of the deceased of which according to the terms of the confirmation they are executors or, as the case may be, in respect of the item or items of property specified in the certificate of confirmation.

(3) Where by virtue of subsection (2) above a confirmation or certificate of confirmation is treated for the purposes of the law of Northern Ireland as a grant of representation to the executors named therein then, subject to subsection (4) below, the grant shall be treated –

(a) as a grant of probate where it appears from the confirmation or certificate that the executors so named are executors nominate; and

(b) in any other case, a grant of letters of administration.

(4) Notwithstanding anything in any enactment or rule of law, subsection (3)(a) above shall not operate to entitle an executor of a sole or last surviving executor of a testator, whose will has been proved in Scotland only, to act as the executor of that testator.

(5) This section applies in relation to probates, letters of administration and confirmations granted before as well as after the commencement of this Act, and –

(a) in relation to a probate, letters of administration or confirmation granted, and resealed in Northern Ireland, before the commencement of this Act, this section shall have effect as if it had come into force immediately before the grant was so resealed; and

(b) a probate, letters of administration or confirmation granted but not resealed in Northern Ireland before the commencement of this Act shall, for the purposes of this section, be treated as having been granted at the commencement of this Act.

(6) In this section 'confirmation' includes an additional confirmation, and the term 'executors', where used in relation to a confirmation or certificate of confirmation shall be construed according to the law of Scotland.

3 Recognition in Scotland of English and Northern Irish grants of representation

(1) Where a person dies domiciled in England and Wales or in Northern Ireland a grant of probate or letters of administration

(a) from the High Court in England and Wales and noting his domicile there, or

(b) from the High Court in Northern Ireland and noting his domicile there

shall, without being resealed, be of the like force and effect and have the same operation in relation to property in Scotland as a confirmation given under the seal of office of the Commissariat of Edinburgh to the executor or administrator named in the probate or letters of administration.

(2) This section applies in relation to probate and letters of administration granted before as well as after the commencement of this Act, and in relation to a probate or letters of administration granted before the commencement of this Act, this section shall have effect as if it had come into force immediately before the grant was made.

MAINTENANCE ORDERS (RECIPROCAL ENFORCEMENT) ACT 1972

(1972 c 18)

PART I

RECIPROCAL ENFORCEMENT OF MAINTENANCE ORDERS
MADE IN UNITED KINGDOM OR RECIPROCATING COUNTRY

1   Orders in Council designating reciprocating countries

(1) Her Majesty, if satisfied that, in the event of the benefits
conferred by this Part of this Act being applied to, or to particular
classes of, maintenance orders made by the courts of any country or
territory outside the United Kingdom, similar benefits will in that
country or territory be applied to, or to those classes of, maintenance
orders made by the courts of the United Kingdom, may by Order in
Council designate that country or territory as a reciprocating
country for the purposes of this Part of this Act; and, subject to
subsection (2) below, in this Part of this Act 'reciprocating country'
means a country or territory that is for the time being so designated.

(2) A country or territory may be designated under subsection (1)
above as a reciprocating country either as regards maintenance
orders generally, or as regards maintenance orders other than those
of any specified class, or as regards maintenance orders of one or
more specified classes only; and a country or territory which is for
the time being so designated otherwise than as regards maintenance
orders generally shall for the purposes of this Part of this Act be
taken to be a reciprocating country only as regards maintenance
orders of the class to which the designation extends.

2 Transmission of maintenance order made in United Kingdom for enforcement in reciprocating country

(1) Subject to subsection (2) below, where the payer under a maintenance order made, whether before or after the commencement of this Part of this Act, by a court in the United Kingdom is residing or has assets in a reciprocating country, the payee under the order may apply for the order to be sent to that country for enforcement.

(2) Subsection (1) above shall not have effect in relation to a provisional order or to an order made by virtue of a provision of Part II of this Act.

(3) Every application under this section shall be made in the prescribed manner to the prescribed officer of the court which made the maintenance order to which the application relates.

(4) If, on an application duly made under this section to the prescribed officer of a court in the United Kingdom, that officer is satisfied that the payer under the maintenance order to which the application relates is residing or has assets in a reciprocating country, the following documents, that is to say –

   (a) a certified copy of the maintenance order;

   (b) a certificate signed by that officer certifying that the order is enforceable in the United Kingdom;

   (c) a certificate of arrears so signed;

   (d) a statement giving such information as the officer possesses as to the whereabouts of the payer and the nature and location of his assets in that country;

   (e) a statement giving such information as the officer possesses for facilitating the identification of the payer; and

   (f) where available, a photograph of the payer;

shall be sent by that officer to the Lord Chancellor with a view to their being transmitted by the Lord Chancellor to the responsible authority in the reciprocating country if he is satisfied that the statement relating to the whereabouts of the payer and the nature and location of his assets in that country gives sufficient information to justify that being done.

(5) Nothing in this section shall be taken as affecting any jurisdiction of a court in the United Kingdom with respect to a maintenance order to which this section applies, and any such order may be enforced, varied or revoked accordingly.

3 Power of magistrates' court to make provisional maintenance order against person residing in reciprocating country

(1) Where an application is made to a magistrates' court for a maintenance order against a person residing in a reciprocating country and the court would have jurisdiction to determine the application under the Domestic Proceedings and Magistrates' Courts Act 1978 or the Children Act 1989 if that person –

(a) were residing in England and Wales, and

(b) received reasonable notice of the date of the hearing of the application,

the court shall (subject to subsection (2) below) have jurisdiction to determine the application.

(2) A maintenance order made by virtue of this section shall be a provisional order.

(4) No enactment (or provision made under an enactment) requiring or enabling –

(a) a court to transfer proceedings from a magistrates' court to a county court or the High Court, or

(b) a magistrates' court to refuse to make an order on an application on the ground that any matter in question is one that would be more conveniently dealt with by the High Court.

(5) Where a court makes a maintenance order which is by virtue of this section a provisional order, the following documents, that is to say –

(a) a certified copy of the maintenance order;

(b) a document, authenticated in the prescribed manner, setting out or summarising the evidence given in the proceedings;

(c) a certificate signed by the prescribed officer of the court certifying that the grounds stated in the certificate are the grounds on which the making of the order might have been opposed by the payer under the order;

(d) a statement giving such information as was available to the court as to the whereabouts of the payer;

(e) a statement giving such information as the officer possesses for facilitating the identification of the payer; and

(f) where available, a photograph of the payer;

shall be sent by that officer to the Lord Chancellor with a view to their being transmitted by the Lord Chancellor to the responsible authority in the reciprocating country in which the payer is residing if he is satisfied that the statement relating to the whereabouts of the payer gives sufficient information to justify that being done.

(6) A maintenance order made by virtue of this section which has been confirmed by a competent court in a reciprocating country shall be treated for all purposes as if the magistrates' court which made the order had made it in the form in which it was confirmed and as if the order had never been a provisional order, and subject to section 5 of this Act, any such order may be enforced, varied or revoked accordingly. ...

5 Variation and revocation of maintenance order made in United Kingdom

(1) This section applies to a maintenance order a certified copy of which has been sent to a reciprocating country in pursuance of section 2 of this Act and to a maintenance order made by virtue of section 3 or 4 thereof which has been confirmed by a competent court in such a country.

(2) A court in the United Kingdom having power to vary a maintenance order to which this section applies shall have power to vary that order by a provisional order.

(3) Where the court hearing an application for the variation of a maintenance order to which this section applies proposes to vary it by increasing the rate of the payments under the order then, unless either –

(a) both the payer and the payee under the order appear in the proceedings, or

(b) the applicant appears and the appropriate process has been duly served on the other party,

the order varying the order shall be a provisional order.

(3A) Where subsection (1) of section 60 of the Magistrates' Courts Act 1980 (revocation, variation etc of orders for periodical payment) applies in relation to a maintenance order to which this section applies, that subsection shall have effect as if for the words 'by order on complaint', there were substituted 'on an application being made, by order'.

(4) Where a court in the United Kingdom makes a provisional order varying a maintenance order to which this section applies, the prescribed officer of the court shall send in the prescribed manner to the court in a reciprocating country having power to confirm the provisional order a certified copy of the provisional order together with a document, authenticated in the prescribed manner, setting out or summarising the evidence given in the proceedings.

(5) Where a certified copy of a provisional order made by a court in a reciprocating country, being an order varying or revoking a maintenance order to which this section applies, together with a document, duly authenticated, setting out or summarising the evidence given in the proceedings in which the provisional order was made, is received by the court in the United Kingdom which made the maintenance order, that court may confirm or refuse to confirm the provisional order and, if that order is an order varying the maintenance order, confirm it either without alteration or with such alterations as it thinks reasonable.

(6) For the purpose of determining whether a provisional order should be confirmed under subsection (5) above, the court shall proceed as if an application for the variation or revocation, as the case may be, of the maintenance order in question had been made to it.

(7) Where a maintenance order to which this section applies has been varied by an order (including a provisional order which has been confirmed) made by a court in the United Kingdom or by a competent court in a reciprocating country, the maintenance order shall, as from the date on which under the provisions of the order the variation is to take effect, have effect as varied by that order and, where that order was a provisional order, as if that order had been made in the form in which it was confirmed and as if it had never been a provisional order.

(8) Where a maintenance order to which this section applies has been revoked by an order made by a court in the United Kingdom or by a competent court in a reciprocating country, including a provisional order made by the last-mentioned court which has been confirmed by a court in the United Kingdom, the maintenance order shall, as from the date on which under the provisions of the order the revocation is to take effect, be deemed to have ceased to have effect except as respects any arrears due under the maintenance order at that date.

(9) Where before a maintenance order made by virtue of section 3

or 4 of this Act is confirmed a document, duly authenticated, setting out or summarising evidence taken in a reciprocating country for the purpose of proceedings relating to the confirmation of the order is received by the court in the United Kingdom which made the order, or that court, in compliance with a request made to it by a court in such a country, takes the evidence of a person residing in the United Kingdom for the purpose of such proceedings, the court in the United Kingdom which made the order shall consider that evidence and if, having done so, it appears to it that the order ought not to have been made –

(a) it shall, in such manner as may be prescribed, give to the person on whose application the maintenance order was made an opportunity to consider that evidence, to make representations with respect to it and to adduce further evidence; and

(b) after considering all the evidence and any representations made by that person, it may revoke the maintenance order. ...

6 Registration in United Kingdom court of maintenance order made in reciprocating country

(1) This section applies to a maintenance order made, whether before or after the commencement of this Part of this Act, by a court in a reciprocating country, including such an order made by such a court which has been confirmed by a court in another reciprocating country but excluding a provisional order which has not been confirmed.

(2) Where a certified copy of an order to which this section applies is received by the Lord Chancellor from the responsible authority in a reciprocating country, and it appears to the Lord Chancellor that the payer under the order is residing or has assets in the United Kingdom, he shall send a copy of the order to the prescribed officer of the appropriate court.

(3) Where the prescribed officer of the appropriate court receives from the Lord Chancellor a certified copy of an order to which this section applies, he shall, subject to subsection (4) below, register the order in the prescribed manner in that court.

(4) Before registering an order under this section an officer of a court shall take such steps as he thinks fit for the purpose of ascertaining whether the payer under the order is residing or has assets within the jurisdiction of the court, and if after taking those steps he is satisfied that the payer is not residing and has no assets within the

jurisdiction of the court he shall return the certified copy of the order to the Lord Chancellor with a statement giving such information as he possesses as to the whereabouts of the payer and the nature and location of his assets.

7   Confirmation by United Kingdom court of provisional maintenance order made in reciprocating country

(1) This section applies to a maintenance order made, whether before or after the commencement of this Part of this Act, by a court in a reciprocating country being a provisional order.

(2) Where a certified copy of an order to which this section applies together with –

(a) a document, duly authenticated, setting out or summarising the evidence given in the proceedings in which the order was made; and

(b) a statement of the grounds on which the making of the order might have been opposed by the payer under the order,

is received by the Lord Chancellor from the responsible authority in a reciprocating country, and it appears to the Lord Chancellor that the payer under the order is residing in the United Kingdom, he shall send the copy of the order and documents which accompanied it to the prescribed officer of the appropriate court, and that court shall –

(i) if the payer under the order establishes any grounds on which he might have opposed the making of the order in the proceedings in which the order was made, refuse to confirm the order; and

(ii) in any other case, confirm the order either without alteration or with such alteration as it thinks reasonable.

(3) In any proceedings for the confirmation under this section of a provisional order, the statement received from the court which made the order of the grounds on which the making of the order might have been opposed by the payer under the order shall be conclusive evidence that the payer might have opposed the making of the order on any of those grounds. ...

(5) The prescribed officer of a court having power under this section to confirm a provisional order shall, if the court confirms the order, register the order in the prescribed manner in that court, and shall,

if the court refuses to confirm the order, return the certified copy of the order and the documents which accompanied it to the Secretary of State.

(5A) Where a magistrates' court in England and Wales confirms a provisional order under this section, it shall at the same time exercise one of its powers under subsection (5B) below.

(5B) The powers of the court are –

(a) the power to order that payments under the order be made directly to the clerk of the court or the clerk of any other magistrates' court in England and Wales;

(b) the power to order that payments under the order be made to the clerk of the court, or to the clerk of any other magistrates' court in England and Wales, by such method of payment falling within section 59(6) of the Magistrates' Courts Act 1980 (standing order, etc) as may be specified;

(c) the power to make an attachment of earnings order under the Attachment of Earnings Act 1971 to secure payments under the order.

(5C) In deciding which of the powers under subsection (5B) above it is to exercise, the court shall have regard to any representations made by the payer under the order.

(5D) Subsection (4) of section 59 of the Magistrates' Courts Act 1980 (power of court to require debtor to open account) shall apply for the purposes of subsection (5B) above as it applies for the purposes of that section but as if for paragraph (a) there were substituted –

'(a) the court proposes to exercise its power under paragraph (b) of section 7(5B) of the Maintenance Orders (Reciprocal Enforcement) Act 1972, and'

(6) If notice of the proceedings for the confirmation of the provisional order cannot be duly served on the payer under that order the officer by whom the certified copy of the order was received shall return that copy and the documents which accompanied it to the Secretary of State with a statement giving such information as he possesses as to the whereabouts of the payer. ...

8 Enforcement of maintenance order registered in the United Kingdom court

(1) Subject to subsection (2) below, a registered order may be enforced in the United Kingdom as if it had been made by the

registering court and as if that court had had jurisdiction to make it; and proceedings for or with respect to the enforcement of any such order may be taken accordingly.

(2) Subsection (1) above does not apply to an order which is for the time being registered in the High Court under Part I of the Maintenance Orders Act 1958...

(3) Any person for the time being under an obligation to make payments in pursuance of a registered order shall give notice of any change of address to the clerk of the registering court, and any person failing without reasonable excuse to give such a notice shall be liable on summary conviction to a fine not exceeding level 2 on the standard scale.

(4) An order which by virtue of this section is enforceable by a magistrates' court shall, subject to the modifications of sections 76 and 93 of the Magistrates' Courts Act 1980 specified in subsections (4A) and (4B) below, be enforceable as if it were a magistrates' court maintenance order made by that court.

In this subsection 'magistrates' court maintenance order' has the same meaning as in section 150(1) of the Magistrates' Courts Act 1980. ...

(5) The magistrates' court by which an order is enforceable by virtue of this section, and the officers thereof, shall take all such steps for enforcing or facilitating the enforcement of the order as may be prescribed.

(6) In any proceedings for or with respect to the enforcement of an order which is for the time being registered in any court under this Part of this Act a certificate of arrears sent to the prescribed officer of the court shall be evidence of the facts stated therein.

(7) Subject to subsection (8) below, sums of money payable under a registered order shall be payable in accordance with the order as from the date on which they are required to be paid under the provisions of the order.

(8) The court having power under section 7 of this Act to confirm a provisional order may, if it decides to confirm the order, direct that the sums of money payable under it shall be deemed to have been payable in accordance with the order as from such date, being a date later than the date on which the order was made, as it may specify; and subject to any such direction, a maintenance order registered under the said section 7 shall be treated as if it had been

made in the form in which it was confirmed and as if it had never been a provisional order. ...

9 Variation and revocation of maintenance order registered in United Kingdom court

(1) Subject to the provisions of this section, the registering court –

(a) shall have the like power, on an application made by the payer or payee under a registered order, to vary or revoke the order as if it had been made by the registering court and as if that court had had jurisdiction to make it; and

(b) shall have power to vary or revoke a registered order by a provisional order. ...

(1A) The powers conferred by subsection (1) above are not exercisable in relation to so much of a registered order as provides for the payment of a lump sum.

(1B) The registering court shall not vary or revoke a registered order if neither the payer nor the payee under the order is resident in the United Kingdom.

(2) The registering court shall not vary a registered order otherwise than by a provisional order unless –

(a) both the payer and the payee under the registered order are for the time being residing in the United Kingdom; or

(b) the application is made by the payee under the registered order; or

(c) the variation consists of a reduction in the rate of the payments under the registered order and is made solely on the ground that there has been a change in the financial circumstances of the payer since the registered order was made or, in the case of an order registered under section 7 of this Act, since the registered order was confirmed, and the courts in the reciprocating country in which the maintenance order in question was made do not have power, according to the law in force in that country, to confirm provisional orders varying maintenance orders.

(3) The registering court shall not revoke a registered order otherwise than by a provisional order unless both the payer and the payee under the registered order are for the time being residing in the United Kingdom.

(4) On an application for the revocation of a registered order the registering court shall, unless both the payer and the payee under the registered order are for the time being residing in the United Kingdom, apply the law applied by the reciprocating country in which the registered order was made; but where by virtue of this subsection the registering court is required to apply that law, that court may make a provisional order if it has reason to believe that the ground on which the application is made is a ground on which the order could be revoked according to the law applied by the reciprocating country, notwithstanding that it has not been established that it is such a ground.

(5) Where the registering court makes a provisional order varying or revoking a registered order the prescribed officer of the court shall send in the prescribed manner to the court in the reciprocating country which made the registered order a certified copy of the provisional order together with a document, authenticated in the prescribed manner, setting out or summarising the evidence given in the proceedings.

(6) Where a certified copy of a provisional order made by a court in a reciprocating country, being an order varying a registered order, together with a document, duly authenticated, setting out or summarising the evidence given in the proceedings in which the provisional order was made, is received by the registering court, that court may confirm the order either without alteration or with such alterations as it thinks reasonable or refuse to confirm the order.

(7) For the purpose of determining whether a provisional order should be confirmed under subsection (6) above the court shall proceed as if an application for the variation of the registered order had been made to it.

(8) Where a registered order has been varied by an order (including a provisional order which has been confirmed) made by a court in the United Kingdom or by a competent court in a reciprocating country, the registered order shall, as from the date on which under the provisions of the order the variation is to take effect, have effect as varied by that order and, where that order was a provisional order, as if that order had been made in the form in which it was confirmed and as if it had never been a provisional order.

(9) Where a registered order has been revoked by an order made by a court in the United Kingdom or by a competent court in a reciprocating country, including a provisional order made by the first-mentioned court which has been confirmed by a competent

court in a reciprocating country, the registered order shall, as from the date on which under the provisions of the order the revocation is to take effect, be deemed to have ceased to have effect except as respects any arrears due under the registered order at that date.

(10) The prescribed officer of the registering court shall register in the prescribed manner any order varying a registered order other than a provisional order which is not confirmed. ...

12 Appeals

(1) No appeal shall lie from a provisional order made in pursuance of any provision of this Part of this Act by a court in the United Kingdom.

(2) Where in pursuance of any such provision any such court confirms or refuses to confirm a provisional order made by a court in a reciprocating country, whether a maintenance order or an order varying or revoking a maintenance order, the payer or payee under the maintenance order shall have the like right of appeal (if any) from the confirmation of, or refusal to confirm, the provisional order as he would have if that order were not a provisional order and the court which confirmed or refused to confirm it had made or, as the case may be, refused to make it.

(3) Where in pursuance of any such provision any such court makes, or refuses to make, an order varying or revoking a maintenance order made by a court in a reciprocating country, then, subject to subsection (1) above, the payer or payee under the maintenance order shall have the like right of appeal (if any) from that order or from the refusal to make it as he would have if the maintenance order had been made b y the first-mentioned court.

(4) Nothing in this section (except subsection (1)) shall be construed as affecting any right of appeal conferred by any other enactment.

13 Admissibility of evidence given in reciprocating country

(1) A statement contained in –

(a) a document, duly authenticated, which purports to set out or summarise evidence given in proceedings in a court in a reciprocating country; or

(b) a document, duly authenticated, which purports to set out or summarise evidence taken in such a country for the purpose of proceedings in court in the United Kingdom under this Part of this Act, whether in response to a request made by such a court or otherwise; or

(c) a document, duly authenticated, which purports to have been received in evidence in proceedings in a court in such a country or to be a copy of a document so received,

shall in any proceedings in a court in the United Kingdom relating to a maintenance order to which this Part of this Act applies be admissible as evidence of any fact stated therein to the same extent as oral evidence of that fact is admissible in those proceedings.

(2) A document purporting to set out or summarise evidence given as mentioned in subsection (1)(a) above, or taken as mentioned in subsection (1)(b) above, shall be deemed to be duly authenticated for the purposes of that subsection if the document purports to be certified by the judge, magistrate or other person before whom the evidence was given, or, as the case may be, by whom it was taken, to be the original document containing or recording, or, as the case may be, summarising, that evidence or a true copy of that document.

(3) A document purporting to have been received in evidence as mentioned in subsection (1)(c) above, or to be a copy of a document so received, shall be deemed to be duly authenticated for the purposes of that subsection if the document purports to be certified by a judge, magistrate or officer of the court in question to have been, or to be a true copy of a document which has been, so received.

(4) It shall not be necessary in any such proceedings to prove the signature or official position of the person appearing to have given such a certificate.

(5) Nothing in this section shall prejudice the admission in evidence of any document which is admissible in evidence apart from this section.

14 Obtaining of evidence needed for purpose of certain proceedings

(1) Where for the purpose of any proceedings in a court in a reciprocating country relating to a maintenance order to which this Part of this Act applies a request is made by or on behalf of that court for the taking in the United Kingdom of the evidence of a person residing therein relating to matters specified in the request, such court in the United Kingdom as may be prescribed shall have

power to take that evidence and, after giving notice of the time and place at which the evidence is to be taken to such persons and in such manner as it thinks fit, shall take the evidence in such manner as may be prescribed.

Evidence taken in compliance with such a request shall be sent in the prescribed manner by the prescribed officer of the court to the court in the reciprocating country by or on behalf of which the request was made.

(2) Where any person, not being the payer or the payee under the maintenance order to which the proceedings in question relate, is required by virtue of this section to give evidence before a court in the United Kingdom the court may order that there shall be paid –

(a) if the court is a court in England, Wales or Scotland, out of moneys provided by Parliament; ...

such sums as appear to the court reasonably sufficient to compensate that person for the expense, trouble or loss of time properly incurred in or incidental to his attendance.

(3) Section 97(1), (3) and (4) of the Magistrates' Courts Act 1980 (which provide for compelling the attendance of witnesses etc) shall apply in relation to a magistrates' court having power under subsection (1) above to take the evidence of any person as if the proceedings in the court in a reciprocating country for the purpose of which a request for the taking of the evidence has been made were proceedings in the magistrates' court and had been begun by complaint. ...

(5) A court in the United Kingdom may for the purpose of any proceedings in that court under this Part of this Act relating to a maintenance order to which this Part of this Act applies request a court in a reciprocating country to take or provide evidence relating to such matters as may be specified in the request and may remit the case to that court for that purpose. ...

15   Order, etc made abroad need not be proved

For the purposes of this Part of this Act, unless the contrary is shown –

(a) any order made by a court in a reciprocating country purporting to bear the seal of that court or to be signed by any person in his capacity as a judge, magistrate or officer of the court, shall be deemed without further proof to have been duly sealed or, as the case may be, to have been signed by that person;

(b) the person by whom the order was signed shall be deemed without further proof to have been a judge, magistrate or officer, as the case may be, of that court when he signed it and, in the case of an officer, to have been authorised to sign it; and

(c) a document purporting to be a certified copy of an order made by a court in a reciprocating country shall be deemed without further proof to be such a copy.

16 Payment of sums under orders made abroad: conversion of currency

(1) Payment of sums due under a registered order shall, while the order is registered in a court in England, Wales or Northern Ireland, be made in such manner and to such person as may be prescribed.

(2) Where the sums required to be paid under a registered order are expressed in a currency other than the currency of the United Kingdom, then, as from the relevant date, the order shall be treated as if it were an order requiring the payment of such sums in the currency of the United Kingdom as, on the basis of the rate of exchange prevailing at that date, are equivalent to the sums so required to be paid.

(3) Where the sum specified in any statement, being a statement of the amount of any arrears due under a maintenance order made by a court in a reciprocating country, is expressed in a currency other than the currency of the United Kingdom, that sum shall be deemed to be such sum in the currency of the United Kingdom as, on the basis of the rate of exchange prevailing at the relevant date, is equivalent to the sum so specified.

(4) For the purposes of this section a written certificate purporting to be signed by an officer of any bank in the United Kingdom certifying that a specified rate of exchange prevailed between currencies at a specified date and that at such rate a specified sum in the currency of the United Kingdom is equivalent to a specified sum in another specified currency shall be evidence of the rate of exchange so prevailing on that date and of the equivalent sums in terms of the respective currencies.

(5) In this section 'the relevant date' means –

(a) in relation to a registered order or to a statement of arrears due under a maintenance order made by a court in a reciprocating country, the date on which the order first becomes a registered order or (if earlier) the date on which it is confirmed by a court in the United Kingdom;

(b) in relation to a registered order which has been varied, the date on which the last order varying that order is registered in a court in the United Kingdom or (if earlier) the date on which the last order varying that order is confirmed by such a court. ...

21   Interpretation of Part I

(1) In this Part of this Act –

'affiliation order' means an order (however described) adjudging, finding or declaring a person to be the father of a child, whether or not it also provides for the maintenance of the child;

'the appropriate court' in relation to a person residing or having assets in England and Wales or in Northern Ireland means a magistrates' court, and in relation to a person residing or having assets in Scotland means a sheriff court within the jurisdiction of which that person is residing or has assets;

'certificate of arrears', in relation to a maintenance order, means a certificate certifying that the sum specified in the certificate is to the best of the information or belief of the officer giving the certificate the amount of the arrears due under the order at the date of the certificate or, as the case may be, that to the best of his information or belief there are no arrears due thereunder at that date;

'certified copy', in relation to an order of a court, means a copy of the order certified by the proper officer of the court to be a true copy;

'court' includes any tribunal or person having power to make, confirm, enforce, vary or revoke a maintenance order; ...

'maintenance order' means an order (however described) of any of the following descriptions, that is to say –

(a) an order (including an affiliation order or order consequent upon an affiliation order) which provides for the payment of a lump sum or the making of periodical payments towards the maintenance of any person, being a person whom the person liable to make payments under the order is, according to the law applied in the place where the order was made, liable to maintain; and

(b) an affiliation order or order consequent upon an affiliation order, being an order which provides for the payment by a person adjudged, found or declared to be a child's father of expenses incidental to the child's birth or, where the child has died, of his funeral expenses,

and, in the case of a maintenance order which has been varied, means that order as varied; ...

'payee', in relation to a maintenance order, means the person entitled to the payments for which the order provides;

'payer', in relation to a maintenance order, means the person liable to make payments under the order;

'prescribed', in relation to a magistrates' court in England and Wales or in Northern Ireland, means prescribed by rules made under section 144 of the Magistrates' Courts Act 1980 and in relation to any other court means prescribed by rules of court;

'provisional order' means (according to the context) –

(a) an order made by a court in the United Kingdom which is provisional only and has no effect unless and until confirmed, with or without alteration, by a competent court in a reciprocating country; or

(b) an order made by a court in a reciprocating country which is provisional only and has no effect unless and until confirmed, with or without alteration, by a court in the United Kingdom having power under this Part of this Act to confirm it;

'reciprocating country' has the meaning assigned to it by section 1 of this Act;

'registered order' means a maintenance order which is for the time being registered in a court in the United Kingdom under this Part of this Act;

'registering court', in relation to a registered order, means the court in which that order is for the time being registered under this Part of this Act;

'the responsible authority', in relation to a reciprocating country, means any person who in that country has functions similar to those of the Lord Chancellor under this Part of this Act;

'revoke' and 'revocation' include discharge.

(2) For the purposes of this Part of this Act an order shall be taken to be a maintenance order so far (but only so far) as it relates to the payment of a lump sum or the making of periodical payments as mentioned in paragraph (a) of the definition of 'maintenance order' in subsection (1) above or to the payment by a person adjudged,

found or declared to be a child's father of any such expenses as are mentioned in paragraph (b) of that definition.

(3) Any reference in this Part of this Act to the payment of money for the maintenance of a child shall be construed as including a reference to the payment of money for the child's education.

23 Maintenance order registered in High Court under the Maintenance Orders, etc Act 1920

(1) Where a country or territory, being a country or territory to which at the commencement of section 1 of this Act the Maintenance Orders (Facilities for Enforcement) Act 1920 extended, becomes a reciprocating country, then, if immediately before the order in Council made under section 12 of that Act extending that Act to that country or territory was revoked any maintenance order made by a court in that country or territory was registered in the High Court under section 1 of that Act, the High Court may, on an application by the payer or the payee under the order or of its own motion, transfer the order to such magistrates' court as having regard to the place where the payee is residing and to all the circumstances it thinks most appropriate, with a view to the order being registered in that court under this Part of this Act.

(2) Where the High Court transfers an order to magistrates' court under this section it shall –

(a) cause a certified copy of the order to be sent to the clerk of that court, and

(b) cancel the registration of the order in the High Court.

(3) The clerk of the court who receives a certified copy of an order sent to him under this section shall register the order in the prescribed manner in that court.

(4) On registering a maintenance order in a magistrates' court by virtue of this section the clerk of the court shall, if the order is registered in that court under Part I of the Maintenance Orders Act 1958, cancel that registration. ...

24 Application of Part I to certain orders and proceedings under the Maintenance Orders, etc Act 1920

Where Her Majesty proposes by an Order in Council under section 1 of this Act to designate as a reciprocating country a country or territory to which at the commencement of that section the Maintenance Orders (Facilities for Enforcement) Act 1920 extended, that Order in Council may contain such provisions as Her Majesty considers expedient for the purpose of securing –

(a) that the provisions of this Part of this Act apply, subject to such modifications as may be specified in the Order, to maintenance orders, or maintenance orders of a specified class –

(i) made by a court in England, Wales or Northern Ireland against a person residing or having assets in that country or territory, or

(ii) made by court in that country or territory against a person residing or having assets in England, Wales or Northern Ireland,

being orders to which immediately before the date of the coming into operation of the Order in Council the said Act of 1920 applied, except any order which immediately before that date is registered in the High Court or the High Court of Justice in Northern Ireland under section 1 of that Act;

(b) that any maintenance order, or maintenance order of a specified class, made by a court in that country or territory which has been confirmed by a court in England, Wales or Northern Ireland under section 4 of the said Act of 1920 and is in force immediately before that date is registered under section 7 of this Act;

(c) that any proceedings brought under or by virtue of a provision of the said Act of 1920 in a court in England, Wales or Northern Ireland which are pending at that date, being proceedings affecting a person resident in that country or territory, are continued as if they had been brought under or by virtue of the corresponding provision of this Part of this Act.

PART II

RECIPROCAL ENFORCEMENT OF CLAIMS FOR THE RECOVERY OF MAINTENANCE

25 Convention countries

(1) Her Majesty may by Order in Council declare that any country or territory specified in the Order, being a country or territory outside

the United Kingdom to which the Maintenance Convention extends, is a convention country for the purposes of this Part of this Act.

(2) In this section 'the Maintenance Convention' means the United Nations Convention on the Recovery Abroad of Maintenance done at New York on 20 June 1956.

26 Application by person in United Kingdom for recovery, etc of maintenance in convention country

(1) Where a person in the United Kingdom ('the applicant') claims to be entitled to recover in a convention country maintenance from another person, and that other person is for the time being subject to the jurisdiction of that country, the applicant may apply to the Lord Chancellor, in accordance with the provisions of this section, to have his claim for the recovery of maintenance from that other person transmitted to that country.

(2) Where the applicant seeks to vary any provision made in a convention country for the payment by any other person of maintenance to the applicant, and that other person is for the time being subject to the jurisdiction of that country, the applicant may apply to the Lord Chancellor, in accordance with the provisions of this section, to have his application for the variation of that provision transmitted to that country.

(3) An application to the Lord Chancellor under subsection (1) or (2) above shall be made through the appropriate officer, and that officer shall assist the applicant in completing an application which will comply with the requirements of the law applied by the convention country and shall send the application to the Lord Chancellor, together with such other documents, if any, as are required by that law.

(3A) An application under subsection (1) or (2) above, for the purpose of recovering maintenance from a person in a specified State within the meaning of the Recovery of Maintenance (United States of America) Order 1993, and a certificate signed by a justice of the peace or, where the applicant is residing in Scotland, the sheriff, to the effect that the application sets forth facts from which it may be determined that the respondent owes a duty to maintain the applicant and any other person named in the application and that court in the specified State may obtain jurisdiction of the respondent or his property, shall be registered in the court in the prescribed manner by the appropriate officer or, in Scotland, by the sheriff clerk in the Maintenance Orders (Reciprocal Enforcement) Act 1972 register.

(4) On receiving an application from the appropriate officer the Lord Chancellor shall transmit it, together with any accompanying documents, to the appropriate authority in the convention country, unless he is satisfied that the application is not made in good faith or that it does not comply with the requirements of the law applied by that country.

(5) The Lord Chancellor may request the appropriate officer to obtain from the court of which he is an officer such information relating to the application as may be specified in the request, and it shall be the duty of the court to furnish the Lord Chancellor with the information he requires.

(6) Where the applicant is residing in England and Wales or in Northern Ireland the appropriate officer for the purposes of this section is the clerk of a magistrates' court acting for the petty sessions area or petty sessions district, as the case may be, in which the applicant is residing. ...

27A Applications for recovery of maintenance in England and Wales

(1) This section applies to any application which –

(a) is received by the Lord Chancellor from the appropriate authority in a convention country, and

(b) is an application by a person in that country for the recovery of maintenance from another person who is for the time being residing in England and Wales.

(2) Subject to sections 27B to 28B of this Act, an application to which this section applies shall be treated for the purposes of any enactment as if it were an application for a maintenance order under the relevant Act, made at the time when the application was received by the Lord Chancellor.

(3) In the case of an application for maintenance for a child (or children) alone, the relevant Act is the Children Act 1989.

(4) In any other case, the relevant Act is the Domestic Proceedings and Magistrates' Courts Act 1978.

(5) In subsection (3) above, 'child' means the same as in Schedule 1 to the Children Act 1989.

27B Sending application to the appropriate magistrates' court

(1) On receipt of an application to which section 27A of this Act applies, the Lord Chancellor shall send it, together with any accompanying documents, to the clerk of a magistrates' court acting for the petty sessions area in which the respondent is residing.

(2) Subject to subsection (4) below, if notice of the hearing of the application by a magistrates' court having jurisdiction to hear it cannot be duly served on the respondent, the clerk of the court shall return the application and the accompanying documents to the Lord Chancellor with a statement giving such information as he possesses as to the whereabouts of the respondent.

(3) If the application is returned to the Lord Chancellor under subsection (2) above, then, unless he is satisfied that the respondent is not residing in the United Kingdom, he shall deal with it in accordance with subsection (1) above or section 28C of this Act or send it to the Secretary of State to be dealt with in accordance with section 31 of this Act (as the circumstances of the case require).

(4) If the clerk of a court to whom the application is sent under this section is satisfied that the respondent is residing within the petty sessions area for which another magistrates' court acts, he shall send the application and accompanying documents to the clerk of that other court and shall inform the Lord Chancellor that he has done so.

(5) If the application is sent to the clerk of a court under subsection (4) above, he shall proceed as if it had been sent to him under subsection (1) above.

27C Applications to which section 27A applies: general

(1) This section applies where a magistrates' court makes an order on an application to which section 27A of this Act applies.

(2) Section 59 of the Magistrates' Courts Act 1980 (orders for periodical payment: means of payment) shall not apply.

(3) The court shall, at the same time that it makes the order, exercise one of its powers under subsection (4) below.

(4) Those powers are –

    (a) the power to order that payments under the order be made

directly to the clerk of the court as the clerk of any other magistrates' court in England and Wales;

(b) the power to order that payments under the order be made to the clerk of the court, or to the clerk of any other magistrates' court in England and Wales, by such method of payment falling within section 59(6) of the Magistrates' Courts Act 1980 (standing order, etc) as may be specified;

(c) the power to make an attachment of earnings order under the Attachment of Earnings Act 1971 to secure payments under the order.

(5) In deciding which of the powers under subsection (4) above it is to exercise, the court shall have regard to any representations made by the person liable to make payments under the order.

(6) Subsection (4) of section 59 of the Magistrates' Courts Act 1980 (power of court to require debtor to open account) shall apply for the purposes of subsection (4) above as it applies for the purposes of that section, but as if for paragraph (a) there were substituted –

'(a) the court proposes to exercise its power under paragraph (b) of section 27C(4) of the Maintenance Orders (Reciprocal Enforcement) Act 1972, and'.

(7) The clerk of the court shall register the order in the prescribed manner in the court.

28 Application by spouses under the Domestic Proceedings and Magistrates' Courts Act 1978

(1) The magistrates' court hearing an application which by virtue of section 27A of this Act is to be treated as if it were an application for a maintenance order under the Domestic Proceedings and Magistrates' Courts Act 1978 may make any order on the application which it has power to make under section 2 or 19(1) of that Act.

(2) Part I of that Act shall apply in relation to such an application, and to any order made on such an application, with the following modifications –

(a) sections 6 to 8, 16 to 18, 20ZA, 25 to 27 and 28(2) shall be omitted,

(b) in section 30(1), for the words 'either the applicant or the respondent ordinarily resides' there shall be substituted 'the respondent resides', and

(c) section 32(2) shall be omitted.

(3) Subsections (1) and (2) above do not apply where section 28A of this Act applies.

28A Applications by former spouses under the Domestic Proceedings and Magistrates' Courts Act 1978

(1) This section applies where in the case of any application which by virtue of section 27A of this Act is to be treated as if it were an application for a maintenance order under the Domestic Proceedings and Magistrates' Courts Act 1978 ('the 1978 Act') –

(a) the applicant and respondent were formerly married,

(b) their marriage was dissolved or annulled in a country or territory outside the United Kingdom by a divorce or annulment which is recognised as valid by the law of England and Wales,

(c) an order for the payment of maintenance for the benefit of the applicant or a child of the family has, by reason of the divorce or annulment, been made by a court in a convention country, and

(d) where the order for the payment of maintenance was made by a court of a different country from that in which the divorce or annulment was obtained, either the applicant or the respondent was resident in the convention country whose court made that order at the time that order was applied for.

(2) Any magistrates' court that would have jurisdiction to hear the application under section 30 of the 1978 Act (as modified in accordance with subsection (6) below) if the applicant and the respondent were still married shall have jurisdiction to hear it notwithstanding the dissolution or annulment of the marriage.

(3) If the magistrates' court hearing the application is satisfied that the respondent has failed to comply with the provisions of any order such as is mentioned in subsection (1)(c) above, it may (subject to subsections (4) and (5) below) make any order which it has power to make under section 2 or 19(1) of the 1978 Act.

(4) The court shall not make an order for the making of periodical payments for the benefit of the applicant or any child of the family unless the order made in the convention country provides for the making of periodical payments for the benefit of the applicant or as the case may be, that child.

(5) The court shall not make an order for the payment of a lump sum for the benefit of the applicant or any child of the family unless the order made in the convention country provides for the payment of a lump sum to the applicant or, as the case may be, to that child.

(6) Part I of the 1978 Act shall apply in relation to the application, and to any order made on the application with the following modifications –

(a) section 1 shall be omitted,

(b) for the reference in section 2(1) to any ground mentioned in section 1 of that Act there shall be substituted a reference to non-compliance with any such order as is mentioned in subsection (1)(c) of this section,

(c) for the references in section 3(2) and (3) to the occurrence of the conduct which is alleged as the ground of the application there shall be substituted references to the breakdown of the marriage,

(d) the reference in section 4(2) to the subsequent dissolution or annulment of the marriage of the parties affected by the order shall be omitted,

(e) sections 6 to 8, 16 to 18, 20ZA and 25 to 28 shall be omitted,

(f) in section 30(1), for the words 'either the applicant or the respondent ordinarily resides' there shall be substituted 'the respondent resides', and

(g) section 32(2) shall be omitted.

(7) A divorce or annulment obtained in a country or territory outside the United Kingdom shall be presumed for the purposes of this section to be one the validity of which is recognised by the law of England and Wales, unless the contrary is proved by the respondent.

(8) In this section, 'child of the family' has the meaning given in section 88 of the 1978 Act.

28B Applications under the Children Act 1989

No provision of an order made under Schedule 11 to the Children Act 1989 requiring or enabling a court to transfer proceedings from a magistrates' court to a county court or the High Court shall apply in relation to an application which by virtue of section 27A of this Act is to be treated as if it were an application for a maintenance order under that Act.

33   Enforcement of orders

(1) Subject to subsection (2) below, a registered order which is registered in a court other than the court by which the order was made may be enforced as if it had been made by the registering court and as if that court had had jurisdiction to make it; and proceedings for or with respect to the enforcement of any such order may be taken in accordance with this subsection but not otherwise.

(2) Subsection (1) above does not apply to an order which is for the time being registered in the High Court under Part I of the Maintenance Orders Act 1958 ...

(3) An order which by virtue of subsection (1) above is enforceable by a magistrates' court shall, subject to the modifications of sections 76 and 93 of the Magistrates' Courts Act 1980 (enforcement of sums adjudged to be paid and complaint for arrears) specified in subsection (4A) and (4B) of section 8 of this Act, be enforceable as if it were a magistrates' court maintenance order made by that court.

In this subsection 'magistrates' court maintenance order' has the same meaning as in section 150(1) of the Magistrates' Courts Act 1980.

(3A) Where, by virtue of being registered in the magistrates' court in which it was made, a registered order is enforceable as a magistrates' court maintenance order, sections 76 and 93 of the Magistrates' Courts Act 1980 shall have effect subject to the modifications specified in subsection (4A) and (4B) of section 8 of this Act.

(4) A magistrates' court in which an order is registered under this Part of this Act, and the officers thereof, shall take all such steps for enforcing the order as may be prescribed.

(5) In any proceedings for or with respect to the enforcement of an order which is for the time being registered in any court under this Part of this Act a certificate of arrears sent under section 32 of this Act to the prescribed officer of the court shall be evidence of the facts stated therein.

(6) Part II of the Maintenance Orders Act 1950 (enforcement of certain orders throughout the United Kingdom) shall not apply to a registered order. ...

36 Admissibility of evidence given in convention country

(1) A statement contained in –

(a) a document, duly authenticated, which purports to set out or summarise evidence given in proceedings in a court in a convention country; or

(b) a document, duly authenticated, which purports to set out or summarise evidence taken in such a country for the purpose of proceedings in a court in the United Kingdom under this Part of this Act, whether in response to a request made on behalf of such a court or otherwise; or

(c) a document, duly authenticated, which purports to have been received in evidence in proceedings in a court in such a country, or to be a copy of a document so received,

shall, in any proceedings in a magistrates' court or in, or remitted from, a sheriff court arising out of an application to which section 27A(1) of this Act applies, an application received by the Lord Chancellor as mentioned in section 28C(1) of this Act, an application received by the Secretary of State as mentioned in section 31(1) of this Act or an application made by any person for the variation or revocation of a registered order or in proceedings on appeal from any such proceedings, be admissible as evidence of any fact stated therein to the same extent as oral evidence of that fact is admissible in those proceedings.

(2) A document purporting to set out or summarise evidence given as mentioned in subsection (1)(a) above, or taken as mentioned in subsection (1)(b) above, shall be deemed to be duly authenticated for the purposes of that subsection if the document purports to be certified by the judge, magistrate or other person before whom the evidence was given or, as the case may be, by whom it was taken, to be the original document containing or recording, or, as the case may be, summarising, that evidence or a true copy of that document.

(3) A document purporting to have been received in evidence as mentioned in subsection (1)(c) above, or to be a copy of a document so received, shall be deemed to be duly authenticated for the purposes of that subsection if the document purports to be certified by a judge, magistrate or officer of the court in question to have been, or to be a true copy of a document which has been, so received.

(4) It shall not be necessary in any such proceedings to prove the signature or official position of the person appearing to have given such a certificate.

(5) Nothing in this section shall prejudice the admission in evidence of any document which is admissible in evidence apart from this section.

37 Obtaining of evidence for purpose of proceedings in United Kingdom court

(1) A court in the United Kingdom may for the purpose of any proceedings in that court under this Part of this Act arising out of an application received by the Secretary of State from a convention country request the Secretary of State to make to the appropriate authority or court in the convention country a request for the taking in that country of the evidence of a person residing therein relating to matters connected with the application. ...

38 Taking of evidence at request of court in convention country

(1) Where a request is made to the Secretary of State by or on behalf of a court in a convention country to obtain the evidence of a person residing in the United Kingdom relating to matters connected with an application to which section 26 of this Act applies, the Secretary of State shall request such court, or such officer of a court, as he may determine to take the evidence of that person relating to such matters connected with that application as may be specified in the request. ...

39 Interpretation of Part II

In this Part of this Act – ...

'maintenance order' has the same meaning as in Part I of this Act;

'prescribed' has the same meaning as in Part I of this Act;

'registered order' means an order which is for the time being registered in a court in the United Kingdom under this Part of this Act;

'registering court', in relation to a registered order, means the court in which that order is for the time being registered under this Part of this Act;

'revoke' and 'revocation' include discharge.

PART III

MISCELLANEOUS AND SUPPLEMENTAL

40 Power to apply Act to maintenance orders and applications for recovery of maintenance made in certain countries

Where Her Majesty is satisfied –

(a) that arrangements have been or will be made in a country or territory outside the United Kingdom to ensure that maintenance orders made by courts in the United Kingdom can be enforced in that country or territory or that applications by persons in the United Kingdom for the recovery of maintenance from persons in that country or territory can be entertained by courts in that country or territory; and

(b) that in the interest of reciprocity it is desirable to ensure that maintenance orders made by courts in that country or territory can be enforced in the United Kingdom or, as the case may be, that applications by persons in that country or territory for the recovery of maintenance from persons in the United Kingdom can be entertained by courts in the United Kingdom,

Her Majesty may by Order in Council make provision for applying the provisions of this Act, with such exceptions, adaptations and modifications as may be specified in the Order, to such orders or applications as are referred to in paragraphs (a) and (b) above and to maintenance and other orders made in connection with such applications by courts in the United Kingdom or in that country or territory.

42 Provisional order for maintenance of party to marriage made by magistrates' court to cease to have effect on remarriage of party

(1) Where a magistrates' court has, by virtue of section 3 of this Act, made a provisional maintenance order consisting of, or including, a provision such as is mentioned in section 2(1)(a) of the Domestic Proceedings and Magistrates' Courts Act 1978 (making of periodical payments by husband or wife)... and the order has been confirmed by a competent court in a reciprocating country, then, if after the making of that order the marriage of the parties to the proceedings in which the order was made is dissolved or annulled but the order continues in force, that order or, as the case may be, that provision

thereof shall cease to have effect on the remarriage of the party in whose favour it was made, except in relation to any arrears due under it on the date of such remarriage and shall not be capable of being revived.

(2) For the avoidance of doubt it is hereby declared that references in this section to remarriage include references to a marriage which is by law void or voidable. ...

44 Exclusion of certain enactments relating to evidence

(1) Section 20 of the Family Law Reform Act 1969 (power of court hearing certain proceedings to require use of blood tests to determine paternity) and any corresponding enactment of the Parliament of Northern Ireland shall not apply to any proceedings under this Act, but the foregoing provision is without prejudice to the power of a court to allow the report of any person who has carried out such tests to be given in evidence in those proceedings.

(2) The Evidence (Proceedings in Other Jurisdictions) Act 1975 shall not apply to the taking of evidence in the United Kingdom for the taking of which section 14 or section 38 of this Act provides.

47 Interpretation general

(1) In this Act –

'enactment' includes an enactment of the Parliament of Northern Ireland; ...

(2) References in this Act to a part of the United Kingdom are references to England and Wales, to Scotland, or to Northern Ireland.

(3) Any reference in this Act to the jurisdiction of a court, where the reference is to assets being located or to a person residing within the jurisdiction of a court, shall be construed in relation to a magistrates' court in England and Wales as a reference to the petty sessions area, and in relation to a magistrates' court in Northern Ireland as a reference to the petty sessions district, for which the court acts.

(4) Any reference in this Act to any other enactment is a reference thereto as amended, and includes a reference thereto as extended or applied, by or under any other enactment.

As amended by the Evidence (Proceedings in Other Jurisdictions) Act 1975, s8(1), Schedule 1; Domestic Proceedings and Magistrates' Courts Act 1978, ss54(a)–(f), 60(3), Schedule 2, para 37; Magistrates' Courts Act 1980, s154, Schedule 7, paras 105, 107; Civil Jurisdiction and Judgements Act 1982, s37(1), Schedule 11, Pt III, paras 9–12, 15–18, Schedule 14; Criminal Justice Act 1982, s46; Family Law Reform Act 1987, s33(1), Schedule 2, paras 45, 50; Maintenance Enforcement Act 1991, s10, Schedule 1, paras 12-14, 18; Maintenance Orders (Reciprocal Enforcement) Act 1992, s1(2), Schedule 1, Pt II, paras 6–8, 12, 13, 17, 19; Transfer of Functions (Magistrates' Courts and Family Law Order 1992, art 4(3), (5); Recovery of Maintenance (United States of America) Order 1993, art 3(2).

CIVIL EVIDENCE ACT 1972
(1972 c 30)

4   Evidence of foreign law

(1) It is hereby declared that in civil proceedings a person who is suitably qualified to do so on account of his knowledge or experience is competent to give expert evidence as to the law of any country or territory outside the United Kingdom, or of any part of the United Kingdom other than England and Wales, irrespective of whether he has acted or is entitled to act as a legal practitioner there.

(2) Where any question as to the law of any country or territory outside the United Kingdom, or of any part of the United Kingdom other than England and Wales, with respect to any matter has been determined (whether before or after the passing of this Act) in any such proceedings as are mentioned in subsection (4) below, then in any civil proceedings (not being proceedings before a court which can take judicial notice of the law of that country, territory or part with respect to that matter) –

(a) any finding made or decision given on that question in the first-mentioned proceedings shall, if reported or recorded in citable form, be admissible in evidence for the purpose of proving the law of that country, territory or part with respect to that matter; and

(b) if that finding or decision, as so reported or recorded, is adduced for that purpose, the law of that country, territory or part with respect to that matter shall be taken to be in accordance with that finding or decision unless the contrary is proved:

Provided that paragraph (b) above shall not apply in the case of a finding or decision which conflicts with another finding or decision on the same question adduced by virtue of this subsection in the same proceedings.

(3) Except with the leave of the court, a party to any civil proceedings shall not be permitted to adduce any such finding or decision as is

mentioned in subsection (2) above by virtue of that subsection unless he has in accordance with rules of court given to every other party to the proceedings notice that he intends to do so.

(4) The proceedings referred to in subsection (2) above are the following, whether civil or criminal, namely –

(a) proceedings at first instance in any of the following courts, namely the High Court, the Crown Court, a court of quarter sessions, the Court of Chancery of the county palatine of Lancaster and the Court of Chancery of the county palatine of Durham;

(b) appeals arising out of any such proceedings as are mentioned in paragraph (a) above,

(c) proceedings before the Judicial Committee of the Privy Council on appeal (whether to Her Majesty in Council or to the Judicial Committee as such) from any decision of any court outside the United Kingdom.

(5) For the purposes of this section a finding or decision on any such question as is mentioned in subsection (2) above shall be taken to be reported or recorded in citable form if, but only if, it is reported or recorded in writing in a report, transcript or other document which, if that question had been a question as to the law of England and Wales, could be cited as an authority in legal proceedings in England and Wales.

EUROPEAN COMMUNITIES ACT 1972
(1972 c 68)

2   General implementation of Treaties

(1) All such rights, powers, liabilities, obligations and restrictions from time to time created or arising by or under the Treaties, and all such remedies and procedures from time to time provided for by or under the Treaties, as in accordance with the Treaties are without further enactment to be given legal effect or used in the United Kingdom shall be recognised and available in law, and be enforced, allowed and followed accordingly; and the expression 'enforceable Community right' and similar expressions shall be read as referring to one to which this subsection applies.

(2) Subject to Schedule 2 to this Act, at any time after its passing Her Majesty may by Order in Council, and any designated Minister or department may by regulations, make provision –

(a) for the purpose of implementing any Community obligation of the United Kingdom, or enabling any such obligation to be implemented, or of enabling any rights enjoyed or to be enjoyed by the United Kingdom under or by virtue of the Treaties to be exercised;

(b) for the purpose of dealing with matters arising out of or related to any such obligation or rights or the coming into force, or the operation from time to time, of subsection (1) above;

and in the exercise of any statutory power or duty, including any power to give directions or legislate by means of orders, rules, regulations or other subordinate instrument, the person entrusted with the power or duty may have regard to the objects of the Communities and to any such obligation or rights as aforesaid.

In this subsection 'designated Minister or department' means such Minister of the Crown or government department as may from time to time be designated by Order in Council in relation to any matter or for any purpose, but subject to such restrictions or conditions (if any) as may be specified by the Order in Council. ...

(4) The provision that may be made under subsection (2) above includes, subject to Schedule 2 to this Act, any such provision (of any such extent) as might be made by Act of Parliament, and any enactment passed or to be passed, other than one contained in this Part of this Act, shall be construed and have effect subject to the foregoing provisions of this section; but, except as may be provided by any Act passed after this Act, Schedule 2 shall have effect in connection with the powers conferred by this and the following sections of this Act to make Orders in Council and regulations.

3   Decisions on, and proof of, Treaties and Community Instruments, etc

(1) For the purposes of all legal proceedings any question as to the meaning or effect of any of the Treaties, or as to the validity, meaning or effect of any Community instrument, shall be treated as a question of law and, if not referred to the European Court, be for determination as such in accordance with the principles laid down by and any relevant decision of the European Court or any court attached thereto.

(2) Judicial notice shall be taken of the Treaties, of the Official Journal of the Communities and of any decision of, or expression of opinion by, the European Court or any court attached thereto on any such question as aforesaid; and the Official Journal shall be admissible as evidence of any instrument or other act thereby communicated of any of the Communities or of any Community institution.

(3) Evidence of any instrument issued by a Community institution, including any judgment or order of the European Court or any court attached thereto, or of any document in the custody of a Community institution, or any entry in or extract from such a document, may be given in any legal proceedings by production of a copy certified as a true copy by an official of that institution; and any document purporting to be such a copy shall be received in evidence without proof of the official position or handwriting of the person signing the certificate.

(4) Evidence of any Community instrument may also be given in any legal proceedings –

(a) by production of a copy purporting to be printed by the Queen's Printer;

(b) where the instrument is in the custody of a government

department (including a department of the Government of Northern Ireland), by production of a copy certified on behalf of the department to be a true copy by an officer of the department generally or specially authorised so to do;

and any document purporting to be such a copy as is mentioned in paragraph (b) above of an instrument in the custody of a department shall be received in evidence without proof of the official position or handwriting of the person signing the certificate, or of his authority to do so, or of the document being in the custody of the department. ...

SCHEDULE 2

PROVISIONS AS TO SUBORDINATE LEGISLATION

1 – (1) The powers conferred by section 2(2) of this Act to make provision for the purposes mentioned in section 2(2)(a) and (b) shall not include power –

(a) to make any provision imposing or increasing taxation; or

(b) to make any provision taking effect from a date earlier than that of the making of the instrument containing the provision; or

(c) to confer any power to legislate by means of orders, rules, regulations or other subordinate instrument, other than rules of procedure for any court or tribunal; or

(d) to create any new criminal offence punishable with imprisonment for more than two years or punishable on summary conviction with imprisonment for more than three months or with a fine of more than level 5 on the standard scale (if not calculated on a daily basis) or with a fine of more than £100 a day.

(2) Sub-paragraph (1)(c) above shall not be taken to preclude the modification of a power to legislate conferred otherwise than under section 2(2), or the extension of any such power to purposes of the like nature as those for which it was conferred; and a power to give directions as to matters of administration is not to be regarded as a power to legislate within the meaning of sub-paragraph (1)(c).

2 – (1) Subject to paragraph 3 below, where a provision contained in any section of this Act confers power to make regulations (otherwise than by modification or extension of an existing power), the power shall be exercisable by statutory instrument.

(2) Any statutory instrument containing an Order in Council or

regulations made in the exercise of a power so conferred, if made without a draft having been approved by resolution of each House of Parliament, shall be subject to annulment in pursuance of a resolution of either House.

3 Nothing in paragraph 2 above shall apply to any Order in Council made by the Governor of Northern Ireland or to any regulations made by a Minister or department of the Government of Northern Ireland; but where a provision contained in any section of this Act confers power to make such an Order in Council or regulations, then any Order in Council or regulations made in the exercise of that power, if made without a draft having been approved by resolution of each House of the Parliament of Northern Ireland, shall be subject to negative resolution within the meaning of section 41(6) of the Interpretation Act (Northern Ireland) 1954 as if the Order or regulations were a statutory instrument within the meaning of that Act. ...

As amended by the Criminal Justice Act 1982, ss40, 46; European Communities (Amendment) Act 1986, s2.

MATRIMONIAL CAUSES ACT 1973
(1973 c 18)

1 Divorce on breakdown of marriage

(1) Subject to section 3 below, a petition for divorce may be presented to the court by either party to a marriage on the ground that the marriage has broken down irretrievably.

(2) The court hearing a petition for divorce shall not hold the marriage to have broken down irretrievably unless the petitioner satisfies the court of one or more of the following facts, that is to say –

(a) that the respondent has committed adultery and the petitioner finds it intolerable to live with the respondent;

(b) that the respondent has behaved in such a way that the petitioner cannot reasonably be expected to live with the respondent;

(c) that the respondent has deserted the petitioner for a continuous period of at least two years immediately preceding the presentation of the petition;

(d) that the parties to the marriage have lived apart for a continuous period of at least two years immediately preceding the presentation of the petition (hereafter in this Act referred to as 'two years' separation') and the respondent consents to a decree being granted;

(e) that the parties to the marriage have lived apart for a continuous period of at least five years immediately preceding the presentation of the petition (hereafter in this Act referred to as 'five years' separation').

(3) On a petition for divorce it shall be the duty of the court to inquire, so far as it reasonably can, into the facts alleged by the petitioner and into any facts alleged by the respondent.

(4) If the court is satisfied on the evidence of any such fact as is

mentioned in subsection (2) above, then, unless it is satisfied on all the evidence that the marriage has not broken down irretrievably, it shall, subject to section 5 below, grant a decree of divorce.

(5) Every decree of divorce shall in the first instance be a decree nisi and shall not be made absolute before the expiration of six months from its grant unless the High Court by general order from time to time fixes a shorter period, or unless in any particular case the court in which the proceedings are for the time being pending from time to time by special order fixes a shorter period than the period otherwise applicable for the time being by virtue of this subsection.

11 Grounds on which a marriage is void

A marriage celebrated after 31 July 1971 shall be void on the following grounds only, that is to say –

(a) that it is not a valid marriage under the provisions of the Marriage Acts 1949 to 1986 (that is to say where –

(i) the parties are within the prohibited degrees of relationship;

(ii) either party is under the age of sixteen; or

(iii) the parties have intermarried in disregard of certain requirements as to the formation of marriage);

(b) that at the time of the marriage either party was already lawfully married;

(c) that the parties are not respectively male and female;

(d) in the case of a polygamous marriage entered into outside England and Wales, that either party was at the time of the marriage domiciled in England and Wales.

For the purposes of paragraph (d) of this subsection a marriage is not polygamous if at its inception neither party has any spouse additional to the other.

12 Grounds on which a marriage is voidable

A marriage celebrated after 31 July 1971 shall be voidable on the following grounds only, that is to say –

(a) that the marriage has not been consummated owing to the incapacity of either party to consummate it;

(b) that the marriage has not been consummated owing to the wilful refusal of the respondent to consummate it;

(c) that either party to the marriage did not validly consent to it, whether in consequence of duress, mistake, unsoundness of mind or otherwise;

(d) that at the time of the marriage either party, though capable of giving a valid consent, was suffering (whether continuously or intermittently) from mental disorder within the meaning of the Mental Health Act 1983 of such kind or to such an extent as to be unfitted for marriage;

(e) that at the time of the marriage the respondent was suffering from venereal disease in a communicable form;

(f) that at the time of the marriage the respondent was pregnant by some person other than the petitioner.

13   Bars to relief where marriage is voidable

(1) The court shall not, in proceedings instituted after 31 July 1971, grant a decree of nullity on the ground that a marriage is voidable if the respondent satisfies the court –

(a) that the petitioner, with knowledge that it was open to him to have the marriage avoided, so conducted himself in relation to the respondent as to lead the respondent reasonably to believe that he would not seek to do so; and

(b) that it would be unjust to the respondent to grant the decree.

(2) Without prejudice to subsection (1) above, the court shall not grant a decree of nullity by virtue of section 12 above on the grounds mentioned in paragraph (c), (d), (e) or (f) of that section unless –

(a) it is satisfied that proceedings were instituted within the period of three years from the date of the marriage, or

(b) leave for the institution of proceedings after the expiration of that period has been granted under subsection (4) below.

(3) Without prejudice to subsections (1) and (2) above, the court shall not grant a decree of nullity by virtue of section 12 above on the grounds mentioned in paragraph (e) or (f) of that section unless it is satisfied that the petitioner was at the time of the marriage ignorant of the facts alleged.

(4) In the case of proceedings for the grant of a decree of nullity by virtue of section 12 above on the grounds mentioned in paragraph (c), (d), (e) or (f) of that section, a judge of the court may, on an application made to him, grant leave for the institution of

proceedings after the expiration of the period of three years from the date of the marriage if –

(a) he is satisfied that the petitioner has at some time during that period suffered from mental disorder within the meaning of the Mental Health Act 1983, and

(b) he considers that in all the circumstances of the case it would be just to grant leave for the institution of proceedings.

(5) An application for leave under subsection (4) above may be made after the expiration of the period of three years from the date of the marriage.

14 Marriages governed by foreign law or celebrated abroad under English law

(1) Where, apart from this Act, any matters affecting the validity of a marriage would fall to be determined (in accordance with the rules of private international law) by reference to the law of a country outside England and Wales, nothing in section 11, 12 or 13(1) above shall –

(a) preclude the determination of that matter as aforesaid; or

(b) require the application to the marriage of the grounds or bar there mentioned except so far as applicable in accordance with those rules.

(2) In the case of a marriage which purports to have been celebrated under the Foreign Marriage Acts 1892 to 1947 or has taken place outside England and Wales and purports to be a marriage under common law, section 11 above is without prejudice to any ground on which the marriage may be void under those Acts or, as the case may be, by virtue of the rules governing the celebration of marriages outside England and Wales under common law.

16 Effect of decree of nullity in case of voidable marriage

A decree of nullity granted after 31 July 1971 in respect of a voidable marriage shall operate to annul the marriage only as respects any time after the decree has been made absolute, and the marriage shall, notwithstanding the decree, be treated as if it had existed up to that time.

24 Property adjustment orders in connection with divorce proceedings, etc

(1) On granting a decree of divorce, a decree of nullity of marriage or a decree of judicial separation or at any time thereafter (whether, in the case of a decree of divorce, or of nullity of marriage, before or after the decree is made absolute), the court may make any one or more of the following orders, that is to say –

(a) an order that a party to the marriage shall transfer to the other party, to any child of the family or to such person as may be specified in the order for the benefit of such a child such property as may be so specified, being property to which the first-mentioned party is entitled, either in possession or reversion;

(b) an order that a settlement of such property as may be so specified, being property to which a party to the marriage is so entitled, be made to the satisfaction of the court for the benefit of the other party to the marriage and of the children of the family or either or any of them;

(c) an order varying for the benefit of the parties to the marriage and of the children of the family or either or any of them any ante-nuptial or post-nuptial settlement (including such a settlement made by will or codicil) made on the parties to the marriage;

(d) an order extinguishing or reducing the interest of either of the parties to the marriage under any such settlement;

subject, however, in the case of an order under paragraph (a) above, to the restrictions imposed by section 29(1) and (3) below on the making of orders for a transfer of property in favour of children who have attained the age of eighteen.

(2) The court may make an order under subsection (1)(c) above notwithstanding that there are no children of the family.

(3) Without prejudice to the power to give a direction under section 30 below for the settlement of an instrument by conveyancing counsel, where an order is made under this section on or after granting a decree of divorce or nullity of marriage, neither the order nor any settlement made in pursuance of the order shall take effect unless the decree has been made absolute.

47 Matrimonial relief and declarations of validity in respect of polygamous marriages

(1) A court in England and Wales shall not be precluded from granting matrimonial relief or making a declaration concerning the validity of a marriage by reason only that either party to the marriage is, or has during the substance of the marriage been, married to more than one person.

(2) In this section 'matrimonial relief' means –

(a) any decree under Part I of this Act;

(b) a financial provision order under section 27 above;

(c) an order under section 35 above altering a maintenance agreement;

(d) an order under any provision of this Act which confers a power exercisable in connection with, or in connection with proceedings for, any such decree or order as is mentioned in paragraphs (a) to (c) above;

(dd) an order under Part III of the Matrimonial and Family Proceedings Act 1984;

(e) an order under Part I of the Domestic Proceedings and Magistrates' Courts Act 1978.

(3) In this section 'a declaration concerning the validity of a marriage' means any declaration under Part III of the Family Law Act 1986 involving a determination as to the validity of a marriage.

(4) Provision may be made by rules of court –

(a) for requiring notice of proceedings brought by virtue of this section to be served on any additional spouse of a party to the marriage in question; and

(b) for conferring on any such additional spouse the right to be heard in the proceedings,

in such cases as may be specified in the rules.

As amended by the Domestic Proceedings and Magistrates' Courts Act 1978, s89(2)(a), Schedule 2, para 39; Mental Health Act 1983, s148, Schedule 4, para 34; Matrimonial and Family Proceedings Act 1984, ss2, 46(1), Schedule 1, paras 10, 15; Marriage (Prohibited Degrees of Relationship) Act 1986, s6(4); Family Law Act 1986, s68(1), Schedule 1, para 14; Private International Law (Miscellaneous Provisions) Act 1995, s8(2), Schedule, para 2.

DOMICILE AND MATRIMONIAL PROCEEDINGS ACT 1973
(1973 c 45)

1   Abolition of wife's dependent domicile

(1) Subject to subsection (2) below, the domicile of a married woman as at any time after the coming into force of this section shall, instead of being the same as her husband's by virtue only of marriage, be ascertained by reference to the same factors as in the case of any other individual capable of having an independent domicile.

(2) Where immediately before this section came into force a woman was married and then had her husband's domicile by dependence, she is to be treated as retaining that domicile (as a domicile of choice, if it is not also her domicile of origin) unless and until it is changed by acquisition or revival of another domicile either on or after the coming into force of this section. ...

3   Age at which independent domicile can be acquired

(1) The time at which a person first becomes capable of having an independent domicile shall be when he attains the age of sixteen or marries under that age; and in the case of a person who immediately before 1 January 1974 was incapable of having an independent domicile, but has then attained the age of sixteen or been married, it shall be that date. ...

4   Dependent domicile of child not living with his father

(1) Subsection (2) of this section shall have effect with respect to the dependent domicile of a child as at any time after the coming into force of this section when his father and mother are alive but living apart.

(2) The child's domicile as at that time shall be that of his mother if –

(a) he then has his home with her and has no home with his father; or

(b) he has at any time had her domicile by virtue of paragraph (a) above and has not since had a home with his father.

(3) As at any time after the coming into force of this section, the domicile of a child whose mother is dead shall be that which she last had before she died if at her death he had her domicile by virtue of subsection (2) above and he has not since had a home with his father.

(4) Nothing in this section prejudices any existing rule of law as to the cases in which a child's domicile is regarded as being, by dependence, that of his mother.

(5) In this section, 'child' means a person incapable of having an independent domicile. ...

As amended by the Children Act 1975, s108(1)(b), Schedule 4, Pt I.

ARBITRATION ACT 1975

(1975 c 8)

1 Staying court proceedings where party proves arbitration agreement

(1) If any party to an arbitration agreement to which this section applies, or any person claiming through or under him, commences any legal proceedings in any court against any other party to the agreement, or any person claiming through or under him, in respect of any matter agreed to be referred, any party to the proceedings may at any time after appearance, and before delivering any pleadings or taking any other steps in the proceedings, apply to the court to stay the proceedings; and the court, unless satisfied that the arbitration agreement is null and void, inoperative or incapable of being performed or that there is not in fact any dispute between the parties with regard to the matter agreed to be referred, shall make an order staying the proceedings.

(2) This section applies to any arbitration agreement which is not a domestic arbitration agreement; and neither section 4(1) of the Arbitration Act 1950 nor section 4 of the Arbitration Act (Northern Ireland) 1937 shall apply to an arbitration agreement to which this section applies. ...

(4) In this section 'domestic arbitration agreement' means an arbitration agreement which does not provide, expressly or by implication, for arbitration in a State other than the United Kingdom and to which neither –

(a) an individual who is a national of, or habitually resident in, any State other than the United Kingdom; nor

(b) a body corporate which is incorporated in, or whose central management and control is exercised in, any State other than the United Kingdom;

is a party at the time the proceedings are commenced.

2   Replacement of former provisions

Sections 3 to 6 of this Act shall have effect with respect to the enforcement of Convention awards; and where a Convention award would, but for this section, be also a foreign award within the meaning of Part II of the Arbitration Act 1950, that Part shall not apply to it.

3   Effect of Convention awards

(1) A Convention award shall, subject to the following provisions of this Act, be enforceable –

(a) in England and Wales, either by action or in the same manner as the award of an arbitrator is enforceable by virtue of section 26 of the Arbitration Act 1950;...

(2) Any Convention award which would be enforceable under this Act shall be treated as binding for all purposes on the persons as between whom it was made, and may accordingly be relied on by any of those persons by way of defence, set off or otherwise in any legal proceedings in the United Kingdom; and any reference in this Act to enforcing a Convention award shall be construed as including references to relying on such an award.

4   Evidence

The party seeking to enforce a Convention award must produce –

(a) the duly authenticated original award or a duly certified copy of it; and

(b) the original arbitration agreement or a duly certified copy of it; and

(c) where the award or agreement is in a foreign language, a translation of it certified by an official or sworn translator or by a diplomatic or consular agent.

5   Refusal of enforcement

(1) Enforcement of a Convention award shall not be refused except in the cases mentioned in this section.

(2) Enforcement of a Convention award may be refused if the person against whom it is invoked proves –

(a) that a party to the arbitration agreement was (under the law applicable to him) under some incapacity; or

(b) that the arbitration agreement was not valid under the law to which the parties subjected it or, failing any indication thereon, under the law of the country where the award was made; or

(c) that he was not given proper notice of the appointment of the arbitrator or of the arbitration proceedings or was otherwise unable to present his case; or

(d) (subject to subsection (4) of this section) that the award deals with a difference not contemplated by or not falling within the terms of the submission to arbitration or contains decisions on matters beyond the scope of the submission to arbitration; or

(e) that the composition of the arbitral authority or the arbitral procedure was not in accordance with the agreement of the parties or, failing such agreement, with the law of the country where the arbitration took place; or

(f) that the award has not yet become binding on the parties, or has been set aside or suspended by a competent authority of the country in which, or under the law of which, it was made.

(3) Enforcement of a Convention award may also be refused if the award is in respect of a matter which is not capable of settlement by arbitration, or if it would be contrary to public policy to enforce the award.

(4) A Convention award which contains decisions on matters not submitted to arbitration may be enforced to the extent that it contains decisions on matters submitted to arbitration which can be separated from those on matters not so submitted.

(5) Where an application for the setting aside or suspension of a Convention award has been made to such a competent authority as is mentioned in subsection (2)(f) of this section, the court before which enforcement of the award is sought may, if it thinks fit, adjourn the proceedings and may, on the application of the party seeking to enforce the award, order the other party to give security.

6   Saving

Nothing in this Act shall prejudice any right to enforce or rely on an award otherwise than under this Act or Part II of the Arbitration Act 1950.

7   Interpretation

(1) In this Act –

'arbitration agreement' means an agreement in writing (including an agreement contained in an exchange of letters or telegrams) to submit to arbitration present or future differences capable of settlement by arbitration;

'Convention award' means an award made in pursuance of an arbitration agreement in the territory of a State, other than the United Kingdom, which is a party to the New York Convention; and

'the New York Convention' means the Convention on the Recognition and Enforcement of Foreign Arbitral Awards adopted by the United Nations Conference on International Commercial Arbitration on 10 June 1958.

(2) If Her Majesty by Order in Council declares that any State specified in the Order is a party to the New York Convention the Order shall, while in force, be conclusive evidence that that State is a party to that Convention.

(3) An Order in Council under this section may be varied or revoked by a subsequent Order in Council.

EVIDENCE (PROCEEDINGS IN OTHER JURISDICTIONS) ACT 1975
(1975 c 84)

1   Application to United Kingdom court for assistance in obtaining evidence for civil proceedings in other court

Where an application is made to the High Court, the Court of Session or the High Court of Justice in Northern Ireland for an order for evidence to be obtained in the part of the United Kingdom in which it exercises jurisdiction, and the court is satisfied –

(a) that the application is made in pursuance of a request issued by or on behalf of a court or tribunal ('the requesting court') exercising jurisdiction in any other part of the United Kingdom or in a country or territory outside the United Kingdom; and

(b) that the evidence to which the application relates is to be obtained for the purposes of civil proceedings which either have been instituted before the requesting court or whose institutions before that court is contemplated,

the High Court, Court of Session or High Court of Justice in Northern Ireland, as the case may be, shall have the powers conferred on it by the following provisions of this Act.

2   Power of United Kingdom court to give effect to application for assistance

(1) Subject to the provisions of this section, the High Court, the Court of Session and the High Court of Justice in Northern Ireland shall each have power, on any such application as is mentioned in section 1 above, by order to make such provision for obtaining evidence in the part of the United Kingdom in which it exercises jurisdiction as may appear to the court to be appropriate for the purpose of giving effect to the request in pursuance of which the application is made; and any such order may require a person

specified therein to take such steps as the court consider appropriate for that purpose.

(2) Without prejudice to the generality of subsection (1) above but subject to the provisions of this section, an order under this section may, in particular, make provision –

(a) for the examination of witnesses, either orally or in writing;

(b) for the production of documents;

(c) for the inspection, photographing, preservation, custody or detention of any property;

(d) for the taking of samples of any property and the carrying out of any experiments on or with any property;

(e) for the medical examination of any person;

(f) without prejudice to paragraph (e) above, for the taking and testing of samples of blood from any person.

(3) An order under this section shall not require any particular steps to be taken unless they are steps which can be required to be taken by way of obtaining evidence for the purposes of civil proceedings in the court making the order (whether or not proceedings of the same description as those to which the application for the order relates); but this subsection shall not preclude the making of an order requiring a person to give testimony (either orally or in writing) otherwise than on oath where this is asked for by the requesting court.

(4) An order under this section shall not require a person –

(a) to state what documents relevant to the proceedings to which the application for the order relates are or have been in his possession, custody or power; or

(b) to produce any documents other than particular documents specified in the order as being documents appearing to the court making the order to be, or to be likely to be, in his possession, custody or power.

(5) A person who, by virtue of an order under this section, is required to attend at any place shall be entitled to the like conduct money and payment for expenses and loss of time as on attendance as a witness in civil proceedings before the court making the order.

3   Privilege of witnesses

(1) A person shall not be compelled by virtue of an order under section 2 above to give any evidence which he could not be compelled to give –

> (a) in civil proceedings in the part of the United Kingdom in which the court that made the order exercises jurisdiction; or
>
> (b) subject to subsection (2) below, in civil proceedings in the country or territory in which the requesting court exercises jurisdiction.

(2) Subsection (1)(b) above shall not apply unless the claim of the person in question to be exempt from giving the evidence is either –

> (a) supported by a statement contained in the request (whether it is so supported unconditionally or subject to conditions that are fulfilled); or
>
> (b) conceded by the applicant for the orders;

and where such a claim made by any person is not supported or conceded as aforesaid he may (subject to the other provisions of this section) be required to give the evidence to which the claim relates but that evidence shall not be transmitted to the requesting court if that court, on the matter being referred to it, upholds the claim.

(3) Without prejudice to subsection (1) above, a person shall not be compelled by virtue of an order under section 2 above to give any evidence if his doing so would be prejudicial to the security of the United Kingdom; and a certificate signed by or on behalf of the Secretary of State to the effect that it would be so prejudicial for that person to do so shall be conclusive evidence of that fact.

(4) In this section references to giving evidence include references to answering any question and to producing any document and the reference in subsection (2) above to the transmission of evidence given by a person shall be construed accordingly.

6   Power of United Kingdom court to assist in obtaining evidence for international proceedings

(1) Her Majesty may by Order in Council direct that, subject to such exceptions, adaptations or modifications as may be specified in the Order, the provisions of sections 1 to 3 above shall have effect in relation to international proceedings of any description specified in the order.

(2) An Order in Council under this section may direct that section 1(4) of the Perjury Act 1911 ... shall have effect in relation to international proceedings to which the Order applies as it has effect in relation to a judicial proceeding in a tribunal of a foreign state.

(3) In this section 'international proceedings' means proceedings before the International Court of Justice or any other court, tribunal, commission, body or authority (whether consisting of one or more persons) which, in pursuance of any international agreement or any resolution of the General Assembly of the United Nations, exercises any jurisdiction or performs any functions of a judicial nature or by way of arbitration, conciliation or inquiry or is appointed (whether permanently or temporarily) for the purpose of exercising any jurisdiction or performing any such functions.

7 Rules of court

The power to make rules of court under section 84 of the Supreme Court Act 1981 ... shall include power to make rules of court –

(a) as to the manner in which any such application as is mentioned in section 1 above is to be made;

(b) subject to the provisions of this Act, as to the circumstances in which an order can be made under section 2 above; and

(c) as to the manner in which any such reference as it mentioned in section 8(2) above is to be made;

and any such rules may include such incidental, supplementary and consequential provision as the authority making the rules may consider necessary or expedient.

9 Interpretation

(1) In this Act –

'civil proceedings', in relation to the requesting court, means proceedings in any civil or commercial matter;

'requesting court' has the meaning given in section 1 above;

'property' includes any land, chattel or other corporeal property of any description;

'request' includes any commission, order or other process issued by or on behalf of the requesting court. ...

As amended by the Supreme Court Act 1981, s152(1), Schedule 5.

LEGITIMACY ACT 1976
(1976 c 31)

1 Legitimacy of children of certain void marriages

(1) The child of a void marriage, whenever born, shall, subject to subsection (2) below and Schedule 1 to this Act, be treated as the legitimate child of his parents if at the time of the insemination resulting in the birth or, where there was no such insemination, the child's conception (or at the time of the celebration of the marriage if later) both or either of the parties reasonably believed that the marriage was valid.

(2) This section only applies where the father of the child was domiciled in England and Wales at the time of the birth or, if he died before the birth, was so domiciled immediately before his death.

(3) It is hereby declared for the avoidance of doubt that subsection (1) above applies notwithstanding that the belief that the marriage was valid was due to a mistake as to law.

(4) In relation to a child born after the coming into force of section 28 of the Family Law Reform Act 1987, it shall be presumed for the purposes of subsection (1) above, unless the contrary is shown, that one of the parties to the void marriage reasonably believed at the time of the insemination resulting in the birth or, where there was no such insemination, the child's conception (or at the time of the celebration of the marriage if later) that the marriage was valid.

2 Legitimation by subsequent marriage of parents

Subject to the following provisions of this Act, where the parents of an illegitimate person marry one another, the marriage shall, if the father of the illegitimate person is at the date of marriage domiciled in England and Wales, render that person, if living, legitimate from the date of the marriage.

3   Legitimation by extraneous law

Subject to the following provisions of this Act, where the parents of an illegitimate person marry one another and the father of the illegitimate person is not at the time of the marriage domiciled in England and Wales but is domiciled in a country by the law of which the illegitimate person becomes legitimated by virtue of such subsequent marriage, that person, if living, shall in England and Wales be recognised as having been so legitimated from the date of the marriage notwithstanding that, at the time of his birth, his father was domiciled in a country the law of which did not permit legitimation by subsequent marriage.

4   Legitimation of adopted child

(1) Section 39 of the Adoption Act 1976 does not prevent an adopted child being legitimated under section 2 or 3 above if either natural parent is the sole adoptive parent.

(2) Where an adopted child (with a sole adoptive parent) is legitimated –

(a) subsection (2) of the said section 39 shall not apply after the legitimation to the natural relationship with the other natural parent, and

(b) revocation of the adoption order in consequence of the legitimation shall not affect sections 39, 41 or 42 of the Adoption Act 1976 as it applies to any instrument made before the date of legitimation.

5   Rights of legitimated persons and others to take interests in property

(1) Subject to any contrary indication, the rules of construction contained in this section apply to any instrument other than an existing instrument, so far as the instrument contains a disposition of property.

(2) For the purposes of this section, provisions of the law of intestate succession applicable to the estate of a deceased person shall be treated as if contained in an instrument executed by him (while in full capacity) immediately before his death.

(3) A legitimated person, and any other person, shall be entitled to take any interest as if the legitimated person had been born legitimate.

(4) A disposition which depends on the date of birth of a child or children of the parent or parents shall be construed as if –

(a) a legitimated child had been born on the date of legitimation,

(b) two or more legitimated children legitimated on the same date had been born on that date in the order of their actual births,

but this does not affect any reference to the age of a child.

(5) Examples of phrases in wills on which subsection (4) above can operate are –

1. Children of A 'living at my death or born afterwards'.

2. Children of A 'living at my death or born afterwards before any one of such children for the time being in existence attains a vested interest, and who attain the age of 21 years'.

3. As in example 1 or 2, but referring to grandchildren of A, instead of children of A.

4. A for life 'until he has a child' and then to his child or children.

Note. Subsection (4) above will not affect the reference to the age of 21 years in example 2.

(6) If an illegitimate person or a person adopted by one of his natural parents dies, or has died before the commencement of this Act, and –

(a) after his death his parents marry or have married; and

(b) the deceased would, if living at the time of the marriage, have become a legitimated person,

this section shall apply for the construction of the instrument so far as it relates to the taking of interests by, or in succession to, his spouse, children and remoter issue as if he had been legitimated by virtue of the marriage.

(7) In this section 'instrument' includes a private Act settling property, but not any other enactment.

8   Personal rights and obligations

A legitimated person shall have the same rights, and shall be under the same obligations in respect of the maintenance and support of himself or of any other person, as if he had been born legitimate, and, subject to the provisions of this Act, the provisions of any Act relating to claims for damages, compensation, allowance, benefit or otherwise by or in respect of a legitimate child shall apply in like manner in the case of a legitimated person.

9   Re-registration of birth of legitimated person

(1) It shall be the duty of the parents of a legitimated person or, in cases where re-registration can be effected on information furnished by one parent and one of the parents is dead, of the surviving parent to furnish to the Registrar General information with a view to obtaining the re-registration of the birth of that person within three months after the date of the marriage by virtue of which he was legitimated.

(2) The failure of the parents or either of them to furnish information as required by subsection (1) above in respect of any legitimated person shall not affect the legitimation of that person.

(3) This section does not apply in relation to a person who was legitimated otherwise than by virtue of the subsequent marriage of his parents.

(4) Any parent who fails to give information as required by this section shall be liable on summary conviction to a fine not exceeding level 1 on the standard scale.

As amended by the Adoption Act 1976, s73(2), Schedule 3, para 23; Criminal Justice Act 1982, ss38, 46; Family Law Reform Act 1987, s28.

ADOPTION ACT 1976
(1976 c 36)

6   Duty to promote welfare of child

In reaching any decision relating to the adoption of a child a court or adoption agency shall have regard to all the circumstances, first consideration being given to the need to safeguard and promote the welfare of the child throughout his childhood; and shall so far as practicable ascertain the wishes and feelings of the child regarding the decision and give due consideration to them, having regard to his age and understanding.

12   Adoption orders

(1) An adoption order is an order giving parental responsibility for a child to the adopters, made on their application by an authorised court.

(2) The order does not affect parental responsibility so far as it relates to any period before the making of the order.

(3) The making of an adoption order operates to extinguish –

(a) the parental responsibility which any person has for the child immediately before the making of the order;

(aa) any order under the Children Act 1989;

(b) any duty arising by virtue of an agreement or the order of a court to make payments, so far as the payments are in respect of the child's maintenance or upbringing for any period after the making of the order.

(4) Subsection (3)(b) does not apply to a duty arising by virtue of an agreement –

(a) which constitutes a trust, or

(b) which expressly provides that the duty is not to be extinguished by the making of an adoption order.

(5) An adoption order may not be made in relation to a child who is or has been married.

(6) An adoption order may contain such terms and conditions as the court thinks fit.

(7) An adoption order may be made notwithstanding that the child is already an adopted child.

14 Adoption by married couple

(1) An adoption order shall not be made on the application of more than one person except in the circumstances specified in subsections (1A) and (1B).

(1A) An adoption order may be made on the application of a married couple where both the husband and the wife have attained the age of 21 years.

(1B) An adoption order may be made on the application of a married couple where –

    (a) the husband or the wife –

        (i) is the father or mother of the child; and

        (ii) has attained the age of 18 years; and

    (b) his or her spouse has attained the age of 21 years.

(2) An adoption order shall not be made on the application of a married couple unless –

    (a) at least one of them is domiciled in a part of the United Kingdom, or in the Channel Islands or the Isle of Man, or

    (b) the application is for a Convention adoption order and section 17 is complied with.

15 Adoption by one person

(1) An adoption order may be made on the application of one person where he has attained the age of 21 years and –

    (a) is not married, or

    (b) is married and the court is satisfied that –

        (i) his spouse cannot be found, or

        (ii) the spouses have separated and are living apart, and the separation is likely to be permanent, or

(iii) his spouse is by reason of ill-health, whether physical or mental, incapable of making an application for an adoption order.

(2) An adoption order shall not be made on the application of one person unless –

(a) he is domiciled in a part of the United Kingdom, or in the Channel Islands or the Isle of Man, or

(b) the application is for a Convention adoption order and section 17 is complied with.

(3) An adoption order shall not be made on the application of the mother or father of the child alone unless the court is satisfied that –

(a) the other natural parent is dead or cannot be found or, by virtue of section 28 of the Human Fertilisation and Embryology Act 1990, there is no other parent, or

(b) there is some other reason justifying the exclusion of the other natural parent,

and where such an order is made the reason justifying the exclusion of the other natural parent shall be recorded by the court.

16 Parental agreement

(1) An adoption order shall not be made unless –

(a) the child is free for adoption by virtue of an order made –

(i) in England and Wales, under section 18; or ...

(b) in the case of each parent or guardian of the child the court is satisfied that –

(i) he freely, and with full understanding of what is involved, agrees unconditionally to the making of an adoption order (whether or not he knows the identity of the applicants); or

(ii) his agreement to the making of the adoption order should be dispensed with on a ground specified in subsection (2).

(2) The grounds mentioned in subsection (1)(b)(ii) are that the parent or guardian –

(a) cannot be found or is incapable of giving agreement;

(b) is withholding his agreement unreasonably;

(c) has persistently failed without reasonable cause to discharge his parental responsibility for the child;

(d) has abandoned or neglected the child;

(e) has persistently ill-treated the child;

(f) has seriously ill-treated the child (subject to subsection (5)).

(3) Subsection (1) does not apply in any case where the child is not a United Kingdom national and the application for the adoption order is for a Convention adoption order.

(4) Agreement is ineffective for the purposes of subsection (1)(b)(i) if given by the mother less than six weeks after the child's birth.

(5) Subsection (2)(f) does not apply unless (because of the ill-treatment or for other reasons) the rehabilitation of the child within the household of the parent or guardian is unlikely.

17   Convention adoption orders

(1) An adoption order shall be made as a Convention adoption order if the application is for a Convention adoption order and the following conditions are satisfied both at the time of the application and when the order is made.

(2) The child –

(a) must be a United Kingdom national or a national of a Convention country, and

(b) must habitually reside in British territory or a Convention country.

(3) The applicant or applicants and the child must not all be United Kingdom nationals living in British territory.

(4) If the application is by a married couple, either –

(a) each must be a United Kingdom national or a national of a Convention country, and both must habitually reside in Great Britain, or

(b) both must be United Kingdom nationals, and each must habitually reside in British territory or a Convention country,

and if the applicants are nationals of the same Convention country the adoption must not be prohibited by a specified provision (as defined in subsection (8)) of the internal law of that country.

(5) If the application is by one person, either –

(a) he must be a national of a Convention country, and must habitually reside in Great Britain, or

(b) he must be a United Kingdom national and must habitually reside in British territory or a Convention country,

and if he is a national of a Convention country the adoption must not be prohibited by a specified provision (as defined in subsection (8)) of the internal law of that country.

(6) If the child is not a United Kingdom national the order shall not be made –

(a) except in accordance with the provisions, if any, relating to consents and consultations of the internal law relating to adoption of the Convention country of which the child is a national, and

(b) unless the court is satisfied that each person who consents to the order in accordance with that internal law does so with full understanding of what is involved.

(7) The reference to consents and consultations in subsection (6) does not include a reference to consent by and consultation with the applicant and members of the applicant's family (including his or her spouse), and for the purposes of subsection (6) consents may be proved in the manner prescribed by rules and the court shall be treated as the authority by whom, under the law mentioned in subsection (6), consents may be dispensed with and the adoption in question may be effected; and where the provisions there mentioned require the attendance before that authority of any person who does not reside in Great Britain, that requirement shall be treated as satisfied for the purposes of subsection (6) if –

(a) that person has been given a reasonable opportunity of communicating his opinion on the adoption in question to the proper officer or clerk of the court, or to an appropriate authority of the country in question, for transmission to the court; and

(b) where he has availed himself of that opportunity, his opinion has been transmitted to the court.

(8) In subsections (4) and (5) 'specified provision' means a provision specified in an order of the Secretary of State as one notified to the Government of the United Kingdom in pursuance of the provisions of the Convention which relate to prohibitions on an adoption contained in the national law of the Convention country in question.

38 Meaning of 'adoption' in Part IV [ss38–49]

(1) In this part 'adoption' means adoption –

(a) by an adoption order;

(b) by an order made under the Children Act 1975, the Adoption Act 1958, the Adoption Act 1950 or any enactment repealed by the Adoption Act 1950;

(c) by an order made in Scotland, Northern Ireland, the Isle of Man or in any of the Channel Islands;

(d) which is an overseas adoption; or

(e) which is an adoption recognised by the law of England and Wales and effected under the law of any other country,

and cognate expressions shall be construed accordingly.

(2) The definition of adoption includes, where the context admits, an adoption effected before the passing of the Children Act 1975, and the date of an adoption effected by an order is the date of the making of the order.

39 Status conferred by adoption

(1) An adopted child shall be treated in law –

(a) where the adopters are a married couple, as if he had been born as a child of the marriage (whether or not he was in fact born after the marriage was solemnised);

(b) in any other case, as if he had been born to the adopter in wedlock (but not as a child of any actual marriage of the adopter).

(2) An adopted child shall, subject to subsection (3), be treated in law as if he were not the child of any person other than the adopters or adopter.

(3) In the case of a child adopted by one of its natural parents as sole adoptive parent, subsection (2) has no effect as respects entitlement to property depending on relationship to that parent, or as respects anything else depending on that relationship.

(4) It is hereby declared that this section prevents an adopted child from being illegitimate.

(5) This section has effect –

(a) in the case of an adoption before 1 January 1976, from that date, and

(b) in the case of any other adoption, from the date of the adoption.

(6) Subject to the provisions of this Part, this section –

(a) applies for the construction of enactments or instruments passed or made before the adoption or later, and so applies subject to any contrary indication; and

(b) has effect as respects things done, or events occurring, after the adoption, or after 31 December 1975, whichever is the later.

42 Rules of construction for instruments concerning property

(1) Subject to any contrary indication, the rules of construction contained in this section apply to any instrument, other than an existing instrument, so far as it contains a disposition of property.

(2) In applying section 39(1) to a disposition which depends on the date of birth of a child or children of the adoptive parent or parents, the disposition shall be construed as if –

(a) the adopted child had been born on the date of adoption,

(b) two or more children adopted on the same date had been born on that date in the order of their actual births,

but this does not affect any reference to the age of a child.

(3) Examples of phrases in wills on which subsection (2) can operate are –

1. Children of A 'living at my death or born afterwards'.

2. Children of A 'living at my death or born afterwards before any one of such children for the time being in existence attains a vested interest and who attain the age of 21 years'.

3. As in example 1 or 2, but referring to grandchildren of A instead of children of A.

4. A for life 'until he has a child', and then to his child or children.

Note. Subsection (2) will not affect the reference to the age of 21 years in example 2.

(4) Section 39(2) does not prejudice any interest vested in possession

in the adopted child before the adoption, or any interest expectant (whether immediately or not) upon an interest so vested.

(5) Where it is necessary to determine for the purposes of a disposition of property effected by an instrument whether a woman can have a child, it shall be presumed that once a woman has attained the age of 55 years she will not adopt a child after execution of the instrument, and, notwithstanding section 39, if she does so that child shall not be treated as her child or as the child of her spouse (if any) for the purposes of the instrument.

(6) In this section, 'instrument' includes a private Act settling property, but not any other enactment.

46   Meaning of 'disposition'

(1) In this Part, unless the context otherwise requires –

'disposition' includes the conferring of a power of appointment and any other disposition of an interest in or right over property;

'power of appointment' includes any discretionary power to transfer a beneficial interest in property without the furnishing of valuable consideration.

(2) This Part applies to an oral disposition as if contained in an instrument made when the disposition was made.

(3) For the purposes of this Part, the death of the testator is the date at which a will or codicil is to be regarded as made.

(4) For the purposes of this Part, provisions of the law of intestate succession applicable to the estate of a deceased person shall be treated as if contained in an instrument executed by him (while of full capacity) immediately before his death.

(5) It is hereby declared that references in this Part to dispositions of property include references to a disposition by the creation of an entailed interest.

47   Miscellaneous enactments

(1) Section 39 does not apply for the purposes of the table of kindred and affinity in Schedule 1 to the Marriage Act 1949 or sections 10 and 11 (incest) of the Sexual Offences Act 1956.

(2) Section 39 does not apply for the purposes of any provision of –

(a) the British Nationality Act 1981,

(b) the Immigration Act 1971,

(c) any instrument having effect under an enactment within paragraph (a) or (b), or

(d) any other provision of the law for the time being in force which determines British citizenship, British Dependent Territories citizenship, the status of a British National (Overseas) or British Overseas citizenship.

52   Revocation of adoptions on legitimation

(1) Where any person adopted by his father or mother alone has subsequently become a legitimated person on the marriage of his father and mother, the court by which the adoption order was made may, on the application of any of the parties concerned, revoke that order.

(2) Where any person legitimated by virtue of section 1 of the Legitimacy Act 1959 had been adopted by his father and mother before the commencement of that Act, the court by which the adoption order was made may, on the application of any of the parties concerned, revoke that order.

(3) Where a person adopted by his father or mother alone by virtue of a regulated adoption has subsequently become a legitimated person on the marriage of his father and mother, the High Court may, upon an application under this subsection by the parties concerned, by order revoke the adoption.

(4) In relation to an adoption order made by a magistrates' court, the reference in subsections (1) and (2) to the court by which the order was made includes a reference to a court acting for the same petty sessions area.

53   Annulment, etc of overseas adoptions

(1) The High Court may, upon an application under this subsection, by order annul a regulated adoption, or an adoption effected by a Convention adoption order –

(a) on the ground that at the relevant time the adoption was prohibited by a notified provision, if under the internal law then in force in the country of which the adopter was then a national or the adopters were then nationals the adoption could have been impugned on that ground;

(b) on the ground that at the relevant time the adoption contravened provisions relating to consents of the internal law relating to adoption of the country of which the adopted person was then a national, if under that law the adoption could then have been impugned on that ground;

(c) on any other ground on which the adoption can be impugned under the law for the time being in force in the country in which the adoption was effected.

(2) The High Court may, upon an application under this subsection –

(a) order that an overseas adoption or a determination shall cease to be valid in Great Britain on the ground that the adoption or determination is contrary to public policy or that the authority which purported to authorise the adoption or make the determination was not competent to entertain the case;

(b) decide the extent, if any, to which a determination has been affected by a subsequent determination.

(3) Any court in Great Britain may, in any proceedings in that court, decide that an overseas adoption or a determination shall, for the purposes of those proceedings, be treated as invalid in Great Britain on either of the grounds mentioned in subsection (2).

(4) An order or decision of the Court of Session on an application under subsection (3) of section 6 of the Adoption Act 1968 shall be recognised and have effect as if it were an order or decision of the High Court on an application under subsection (3) of this section.

(5) Except as provided by this section and section 52(3) the validity of an overseas adoption or a determination shall not be impugned in England and Wales in proceedings in any court.

54 Provisions supplementary to ss52(3) and 53

(1) Any application for an order under section 52(3) or 53 or a decision under section 53(3) shall be made in the prescribed manner and within such period, if any, as may be prescribed.

(2) No application shall be made under section 52(3) or section 53(1) in respect of an adoption unless immediately before the application is made the person adopted or the adopter habitually resides in England and Wales or, as the case may be, both adopters habitually reside there.

(3) In deciding in pursuance of section 53 whether such an authority

as is mentioned in section 59 was competent to entertain a particular case, a court shall be bound by any finding of fact made by the authority and stated by the authority to be so made for the purpose of determining whether the authority was competent to entertain the case.

(4) In section 53 –

'determination' means such a determination as is mentioned in section 59 of this Act;

'notified provision' means a provision specified in an order of the Secretary of State as one in respect of which a notification to or by the Government of the United Kingdom was in force at the relevant time in pursuance of the provisions of the Convention relating to prohibitions contained in the national law of the adopter; and

'relevant time' means the time when the adoption in question purported to take effect under the law of the country in which it purports to have been effected.

55 Adoption of children abroad

(1) Where on an application made in relation to a child by a person who is not domiciled in England and Wales or Scotland or Northern Ireland an authorised court is satisfied that he intends to adopt the child under the law of or within the country in which the applicant is domiciled, the court may, subject to the following provisions of this section, make an order giving him parental responsibility for the child.

(2) The provisions of Part II relating to adoption orders, except sections 12(1), 14((2), 15(2), 17 to 21 and 25, shall apply in relation to orders under this section as they apply in relation to adoption orders subject to the modification that in section 13(1) for '19' and '13' there are substituted '32' and '26' respectively.

(3) Sections 50 and 51 and paragraphs 1 and 2(1) of Schedule 1 shall apply in relation to an order under this section as they apply in relation to an adoption order except that any entry in the Registers of Births, or the Adopted Children Register which is required to be marked in consequence of the making of an order under this section shall, in lieu of being marked with the word 'Adopted' or 'Re-adopted' (with or without the addition of the words '(Scotland)' or '(Northern Ireland)'), be marked with the words 'Proposed foreign adoption' or 'Proposed foreign re-adoption', as the case may require.

62 Courts

(1) In this Act, 'authorised court', as respects an application for an order relating to a child, shall be construed as follows.

(2) Subject to subsections (4) to (6), if the child is in England and Wales when the application is made, the following are authorised courts –

(a) the High Court;

(b) the county court within whose district the child is, and, in the case of an application for an order freeing a child for adoption, any county court within whose district a parent or guardian of the child is;

(c) any other county court prescribed by rules made under section 75 of the County Courts Act 1984;

(d) a magistrates' court within whose area the child is, and, in the case of an application for an order freeing the child for adoption, a magistrates' court within whose area a parent or guardian of the child is.

(3) If, in the case of an application for an adoption order or for an order freeing a child for adoption, the child is not in Great Britain when the application is made, the High Court is the authorised court.

(4) In the case of an application for a Convention adoption order, paragraphs (b), (c) and (d) of subsection (2) do not apply.

(6) In the case of an order under section 55, paragraph (d) of subsection (2) does not apply.

(7) Any court to which the proceedings on an application are transferred under any enactment is, as regards the transferred proceedings, an authorised court if it is not an authorised court under the preceding provisions of this section.

70 Nationality

(1) If the Secretary of State by order declares that a description of persons specified in the order has, in pursuance of the Convention, been notified to the Government of the United Kingdom as the description of persons who are deemed to possess the nationality of a particular Convention country, persons of that description shall, subject to the following provisions of this section, be treated for the purposes of this Act as nationals of that country.

(2) Subject to section 54(3) and subsection (3) of this section, where it appears to the court in any proceedings under this Act, or to any court by which a decision in pursuance of section 53(3) falls to be given, that a person is or was at a particular time a national of two or more countries, then –

(a) if it appears to the said court that he is or was then a United Kingdom national, he shall be treated for the purposes of those proceedings or that decision as if he were or had then been a United Kingdom national only;

(b) if, in a case not falling within paragraph (a), it appears to the said court that one only of those countries is or was then a Convention country, he shall be treated for those purposes as if he were or had then been a national of that country only;

(c) if, in a case not falling within paragraph (a), it appears to the said court that two or more of those countries are or were then Convention countries, he shall be treated for those purposes as if he were or had then been a national of such one only of those Convention countries as the said court considers is the country with which he is or was then most closely connected;

(d) in any other case, he shall be treated for those purposes as if he were or had then been a national of such one only of those countries as the said court considers is the country with which he is or was then most closely connected.

(3) A court in which proceedings are brought in pursuance of section 17, 52(3) or 53 shall be entitled to disregard the provisions of subsection (2) in so far as it appears to that court appropriate to do so for the purposes of those proceedings; but nothing in this subsection shall be construed as prejudicing the provisions of section 54(3).

(4) Where, after such inquiries as the court in question considers appropriate, it appears to the court in any proceedings under this Act, or to any court by which such a decision as aforesaid falls to be given, that a person has no nationality or no ascertainable nationality, he shall be treated for the purposes of those proceedings or that decision as a national of the country in which he resides or, where that country is one of two or more countries having the same law of nationality, as a national of those countries.

71 Internal law of a country

(1) In this Act 'internal law' in relation to any country means the law

applicable in a case where no question arises as to the law in force in any other country.

(2) In any case where the internal law of a country falls to be ascertained for the purposes of this Act by any court and there are in force in that country two or more systems of internal law, the relevant system shall be ascertained in accordance with any rule in force throughout that country indicating which of the systems is relevant in the case in question or, if there is no such rule, shall be the system appearing to that court to be most closely connected with the case.

72 Interpretation

(1) In this Act, unless the context otherwise requires – ...

'authorised court' shall be construed in accordance with section 62; ...

'British territory' means, for the purposes of any provision of this Act, any of the following countries, that is to say, Great Britain, Northern Ireland, the Channel Islands, the Isle of Man and a colony, being a country designated for the purposes of that provision by order of the Secretary of State or, if no country is so designated, any of those countries;

'child', except where used to express a relationship, means a person who has not attained the age of 18 years;

'the Convention' means the Convention relating to the adoption of children concluded at the Hague on 15 November 1965 and signed on behalf of the United Kingdom on that date;

'Convention adoption order' means an adoption order made in accordance with section 17(1);

'Convention country' means any country outside British territory, being a country for the time being designated by an order of the Secretary of State as a country in which, in his opinion, the Convention is in force; ...

'overseas adoption' has the meaning assigned by subsection (2); ...

'regulated adoption' means an overseas adoption of a description designated by an order under subsection (2) as that of an adoption regulated by the Convention;

'United Kingdom national' means, for the purposes of any provision of this Act, a citizen of the United Kingdom and colonies satisfying such conditions, if any, as the Secretary of State may by order specify for the purposes of that provision; ...

(2) In this Act 'overseas adoption' means an adoption of such a description as the Secretary of State may by order specify, being a description of adoptions of children appearing to him to be effected under the law of any country outside Great Britain; and an order under this subsection may contain provision as to the manner in which evidence of an overseas adoption may be given. ...

As amended by the Domestic Proceedings and Magistrates' Courts Act 1978, s74(2); British Nationality Act 1981, s52(6), (8), Schedules 7, 9; Matrimonial and Family Proceedings Act 1984, s46(1), Schedule 1, para 20(a)(b); Hong Kong (British Nationality) Order 1986, art 8, Schedule; Children Act 1989, ss88(1), 108(7), Schedule 10, Pt I, paras 3, 5, 22, Schedule 15; Human Fertilisation and Embryology Act 1990, s49(5), Schedule 4, para 4.

UNFAIR CONTRACT TERMS ACT 1977
(1977 c 50)

26 International supply contracts

(1) The limits imposed by this Act on the extent to which a person may exclude or restrict liability by reference to a contract term do not apply to liability arising under such a contract as is described in sub-section (3) below.

(2) The terms of such a contract are not subject to any requirement of reasonableness under section 3 or 4 ...

(3) Subject to sub-section (4), that description of contract is one whose characteristics are the following –

(a) either it is a contract of sale of goods or it is one under or in pursuance of which the possession or ownership of goods passes; and

(b) it is made by parties whose places of business (or, if they have none, habitual residences) are in the territories of different States (the Channel Islands and the Isle of Man being treated for this purpose as different States from the United Kingdom).

(4) A contract falls within sub-section (3) above only if either –

(a) the goods in question are, at the time of the conclusion of the contract, in the course of carriage, or will be carried, from the territory of one State to the territory of another; or

(b) the acts constituting the offer and acceptance have been done in the territories of different States; or

(c) the contract provides for the goods to be delivered to the territory of a State other than that within whose territory those acts were done.

27 Choice of law clauses

(1) Where the law applicable to a contract is the law of any part of the United Kingdom only by choice of the parties (and apart from that choice would be the law of some country outside the United Kingdom) sections 2 to 7 [avoidance of liability for negligence, breach of contract, etc; liability arising from sale or supply of goods] ... of this Act do not operate as part of the law applicable to the contract.

(2) This Act has effect notwithstanding any contract term which applies or purports to apply the law of some country outside the United Kingdom, where (either or both) –

(a) the term appears to the court, or arbitrator or arbiter to have been imposed wholly or mainly for the purpose of enabling the party imposing it to evade the operation of this Act; or

(b) in the making of the contract one of the parties dealt as consumer, and he was then habitually resident in the United Kingdom, and the essential steps necessary for the making of the contract were taken there, whether by him or by others on his behalf ...

As amended by the Contracts (Applicable Law) Act 1990, s5, Schedule 4, para 4.

EMPLOYMENT PROTECTION
(CONSOLIDATION) ACT 1978
(1978 c 44)

141 Employment outside Great Britain

(1) Sections 1 to 4 and 49 to 51 do not apply in relation to employment during any period when the employee is engaged in work wholly or mainly outside Great Britain unless –

(a) the employee ordinarily works in Great Britain and the work outside Great Britain is for the same employer, or

(b) the law which governs his contract of employment is the law of England and Wales or of Scotland.

(2) Sections 8 and 53 and Parts II, III and V do not apply to employment where under his contract of employment the employee ordinarily works outside Great Britain.

(2A) Part VII does not apply to employment where under his contract of employment the employee ordinarily works outside the territory of the Member States of the European Communities and of Austria, Finland, Iceland, Norway and Sweden.

(3) An employee shall not be entitled to a redudnacy payment if on the relevant date he is outside Great Britain, unless under his contract of employment he ordinarily worked in Great Britain.

(4) An employee who under his contract of employment ordinarily works outside Great Britain shall not be entitled to a redundancy payment unless on the relevant date he is in Great Britain in accordance with instructions given to him by his employer.

(5) For the purposes of subsection (2), a person employed to work on board a ship registered in the United Kingdom (not being a ship registered at a port outside Great Britain) shall, unless –

(a) the employment is wholly outside Great Britain, or

(b) he is not ordinarily resident in Great Britain.

be regarded as a person who under his contract ordinarily works in Great Britain.

153 Interpretation

(5) For the purposes of this Act it is immaterial whether the law which (apart from this Act) governs any person's employment is the law of the United Kingdom, or of a part of the United Kingdom, or not.

As amended by the Employer (Excluded Classes) Regulations 1983; Trade Union Reform and Employment Rights Act 1993, s49(2), Schedule 8, para 22; Insolvency of Employer (Excluded Classes) Regulations 1995, regs 3, 5.

DOMESTIC PROCEEDINGS AND MAGISTRATES' COURTS ACT 1978

(1978 c 22)

1 Grounds of application for financial provision

Either party to a marriage may apply to a magistrates' court for an order under section 2 of this Act on the ground that the other party to the marriage –

(a) has failed to provide reasonable maintenance for the applicant; or

(b) has failed to provide, or to make a proper contribution towards, reasonable maintenance for any child of the family; or

(c) has behaved in such a way that the applicant cannot reasonably be expected to live with the respondent; or

(d) has deserted the applicant.

2 Powers of court to make orders for financial provision

(1) Where on an application for an order under this section the applicant satisfies the court of any ground mentioned in section 1 of this Act, the court may, subject to the provisions of this Part of this Act, make any one or more of the following orders, that is to say –

(a) an order that the respondent shall make to the applicant such periodical payments, and for such term, as may be specified in the order;

(b) an order that the respondent shall pay to the applicant such lump sum as may be so specified;

(c) an order that the respondent shall make to the applicant for the benefit of a child of the family to whom the application relates, or to such a child, such periodical payments, and for such term, as may be so specified;

(d) an order that the respondent shall pay to the applicant for the benefit of a child of the family to whom the application relates, or to such a child, such lump sum as may be so specified.

(2) Without prejudice to the generality of subsection (1)(b) or (d) above, an order under this section for the payment of a lump sum may be made for the purpose of enabling any liability or expenses reasonably incurred in maintaining the applicant, or any child of the family to whom the application relates, before the making of the order to be met.

(3) The amount of any lump sum required to be paid by an order under this section shall not exceed £1,000 or such larger amount as the Lord Chancellor may from time to time by order fix for the purposes of this subsection. Any order made by the Lord Chancellor under this subsection shall be made by statutory instrument and shall be subject to annulment in pursuance of a resolution of either House of Parliament.

3 Matters to which court is to have regard in exercising its powers under s2

(1) Where an application is made for an order under section 2 of this Act, it shall be the duty of the court, in deciding whether to exercise its powers under that section and, if so, in what manner, to have regard to all the circumstances of the case, first consideration being given to the welfare while a minor of any child of the family who has not attained the age of eighteen.

(2) As regards the exercise of its powers under subsection (1)(a) or (b) of section 2, the court shall in particular have regard to the following matters –

(a) the income, earning capacity, property and other financial resources which each of the parties to the marriage has or is likely to have in the foreseeable future, including in the case of earning capacity any increase in that capacity which it would in the opinion of the court be reasonable to expect a party to the marriage to take steps to acquire;

(b) the financial needs, obligations and responsibilities which each of the parties to the marriage has or is likely to have in the foreseeable future;

(c) the standard of living enjoyed by the parties to the marriage before the occurrence of the conduct which is alleged as the ground of the application;

(d) the age of each party to the marriage and the duration of the marriage;

(e) any physical or mental disability of either of the parties to the marriage;

(f) the contributions which each of the parties has made or is likely in the foreseeable future to make to the welfare of the family, including any contribution by looking after the home or caring for the family;

(g) the conduct of each of the parties, if that conduct is such that it would in the opinion of the court be inequitable to disregard it.

(3) As regards the exercise of its powers under subsection (1)(c) or (d) of section 2, the court shall in particular have regard to the following matters –

(a) the financial needs of the child;

(b) the income, earning capacity (if any), property and other financial resources of the child;

(c) any physical or mental disability of the child;

(d) the standard of living enjoyed by the family before the occurrence of the conduct which is alleged as the ground of the application;

(e) the manner in which the child was being and in which the parties to the marriage expected him to be educated or trained;

(f) the matters mentioned in relation to the parties to the marriage in paragraphs (a) and (b) of subsection (2) above.

(4) As regards the exercise of its powers under section 2 in favour of a child of the family who is not the child of the respondent, the court shall also have regard –

(a) to whether the respondent had assumed any responsibility for the child's maintenance and, if he did, to the extent to which, and the basis on which, he assumed that responsibility and to the length of time during which he discharged that responsibility;

(b) to whether in assuming and discharging that responsibility the respondent did so knowing that the child was not his own child;

(c) to the liability of any other person to maintain the child.

4 Duration of orders for financial provisions for a party to a marriage

(1) The term to be specified in any order made under section 2(1)(a) of this Act shall be such term as the court thinks fit except that the term shall not begin earlier than the date of the making of the application for the order and shall not extend beyond the death of either of the parties to the marriage.

(2) Where an order is made under the said section 2(1)(a) and the marriage of the parties affected by the order is subsequently dissolved or annulled but the order continues in force, the order shall, notwithstanding anything in it, cease to have effect on the remarriage of the party in whose favour it was made, except in relation to any arrears due under the order on the date of the remarriage.

As amended by the Matrimonial and Family Proceedings Act 1984, ss9, 46(1), Schedule 1, para 21; Transfer of Functions (Magistrates' Courts and Family Law) Order 1992, art 3(2), Schedule 2.

STATE IMMUNITY ACT 1978
(1978 c 33)

PART I

PROCEEDINGS IN UNITED KINGDOM BY OR AGAINST OTHER STATES

1   General immunity from jurisdiction

(1) A State is immune from the jurisdiction of the courts of the United Kingdom except as provided in the following provisions of this Part of this Act.

(2) A court shall give effect to the immunity conferred by this section even though the State does not appear in the proceedings in question.

2   Submission to jurisdiction

(1) A State is not immune as respects proceedings in respect of which it has submitted to the jurisdiction of the courts of the United Kingdom.

(2) A State may submit after the dispute giving rise to the proceedings has arisen or by a prior written agreement; but a provision in any agreement that it is to be governed by the law of the United Kingdom is not to be regarded as a submission.

(3) A State is deemed to have submitted –

(a) if it has instituted the proceedings; or

(b) subject to subsection (4) and (5) below, if it has intervened or taken any step in the proceedings.

(4) Subsection (3)(b) above does not apply to intervention or for any step taken for the purpose only of –

(a) claiming immunity; or

(b) asserting an interest in property in circumstances such that the State would have been entitled to immunity if the proceedings had been brought against it.

(5) Subsection (3)(b) above does not apply to any step taken by the State in ignorance of the facts entitling it to immunity if those facts could not reasonably have been ascertained and immunity is claimed as soon as reasonably practicable.

(6) A submission in respect of any proceedings extends to any appeal but not to any counter-claim unless it arises out of the same legal relationship or facts as the claim.

(7) The head of a State's diplomatic mission in the United Kingdom, or the person for the time being performing his functions, shall be deemed to have authority to submit on behalf of the State in respect of any proceedings; and any person who has entered into a contract on behalf of and with the authority of a State shall be deemed to have authority to submit on its behalf in respect of proceedings arising out of the contract.

3 Commercial transactions and contracts to be performed in United Kingdom

(1) A State is not immune as respects proceedings relating to –

(a) a commercial transaction entered into by the State; or

(b) an obligation of the State which by virtue of a contract (whether a commercial transaction or not) falls to be performed wholly or partly in the United Kingdom.

(2) This section does not apply if the parties to the dispute are States or have otherwise agreed in writing; and subsection (1)(b) above does not apply if the contract (not being a commercial transaction) was made in the territory of the State concerned and the obligation in question is governed by its administrative law.

(3) In this section 'commercial transaction' means –

(a) any contract for the supply of goods or services;

(b) any loan or other transaction for the provision of finance and any guarantee or indemnity in respect of any such transaction or of any other financial obligation; and

(c) any other transaction or activity (whether of a commercial, industrial, financial, professional or other similar character) into which a State enters or in which it engages otherwise than in the exercise of sovereign authority;

but neither paragraph of subsection (1) above applies to a contract of employment between a State and an individual.

4 Contracts of employment

(1) A State is not immune as respects proceedings relating to a contract of employment between the State and an individual where the contract was made in the United Kingdom or the work is to be wholly or partly performed there.

(2) Subject to subsections (3) and (4) below, this section does not apply if –

(a) at the time when the proceedings are brought the individual is a national of the State concerned; or

(b) at the time when the contract was made the individual was neither a national of the United Kingdom nor habitually resident there; or

(c) the parties to the contract have otherwise agreed in writing.

(3) Where the work is for an office, agency or establishment maintained by the State in the United Kingdom for commercial purposes, subsection (2)(a) and (b) above do not exclude the application of this section unless the individual was, at the time when the contract was made, habitually resident in that State.

(4) Subsection (2)(c) above does not exclude the application of this section where the law of the United Kingdom requires the proceedings to be brought before a court of the United Kingdom.

(5) In subsection (2)(b) above 'national of the United Kingdom' means:

(a) a British citizen, a British Dependent Territories citizen, a British National (Overseas) or a British Overseas citizen; or

(b) a person who under the British Nationality Act 1981 is a British subject; or

(c) a British protected person (within the meaning of that Act).

(6) In this section 'proceedings relating to a contract of employment' includes proceedings between the parties to such a contract in respect of any statutory rights or duties to which they are entitled or subject as employer or employee.

5   Personal injuries and damage to property

A State is not immune as respects proceedings in respect of –

(a) death or personal injury; or

(b) damage to or loss of tangible property,

caused by an act or omission in the United Kingdom.

6   Ownership, possession and use of property

(1) A State is not immune as respects proceedings relating to –

(a) any interest of the State in, or its possession or use of, immovable property in the United Kingdom; or

(b) any obligation of the State arising out of its interest in, or its possession or use of, any such property.

(2) A State is not immune as respects proceedings relating to any interest of the State in movable or immovable property, being an interest arising by way of succession, gift or bona vacantia.

(3) The fact that a State has or claims an interest in any property shall not preclude any court from exercising in respect of it any jurisdiction relating to the estates of deceased persons or persons of unsound mind or to insolvency, the winding up of companies or the administration of trusts.

(4) A court may entertain proceedings against a person other than a State notwithstanding that the proceedings relate to property –

(a) which is in the possession of a State; or

(b) in which a State claims an interest,

if the State would not have been immune had the proceedings been brought against it or, in a case within paragraph (b) above, if the claim is neither admitted nor supported by prima facie evidence.

7   Patents, trade-marks, etc

A State is not immune as respects proceedings relating to –

(a) any patent, trade-mark, design or plant breeders' rights belonging to the State and registered or protected in the United Kingdom or for which the State has applied in the United Kingdom;

(b) an alleged infringement by the State in the United Kingdom of any patent, trade-mark, design, plant breeders' rights or copyright; or

(c) the right to use a trade or business name in the United Kingdom.

8   Membership of bodies corporate, etc

(1) A State is not immune as respects proceedings relating to its membership of a body corporate, an unincorporated body or a partnership which –

(a) has members other than States; and

(b) is incorporated or constituted under the law of the United Kingdom or is controlled from or has its principal place of business in the United Kingdom,

being proceedings arising between the State and the body or its other members or, as the case may be, between the State and the other partners.

(2) This section does not apply if provision to the contrary has been made by an agreement in writing between the parties to the dispute or by the constitution or other instrument establishing or regulating the body or partnership in question.

9   Arbitrations

(1) Where a State has agreed in writing to submit a dispute which has arisen, or may arise, to arbitration, the State is not immune as respects proceedings in the courts of the United Kingdom which relate to the arbitration.

(2) This section has the effect subject to any contrary provision in the arbitration agreement and does not apply to any arbitration agreement between States.

10   Ships used for commercial purposes

(1) This section applies to –

(a) Admiralty proceedings; and

(b) proceedings on any claim which could be made the subject of Admiralty proceedings.

(2) A State is not immune as respects –

(a) an action in rem against a ship belonging to that State; or

(b) an action in personam for enforcing a claim in connection with such a ship,

if, at the time when the cause of action arose, the ship was in use or intended for use for commercial purposes.

(3) Where an action in rem is brought against a ship belonging to a State for enforcing a claim in connection with another ship belonging to that State, subsection (2)(a) above does not apply as respects the first-mentioned ship unless, at the time when the cause of action relating to the other ship arose, both ships were in use or intended for use for commercial purposes.

(4) A State is not immune as respects –

(a) an action in rem against a cargo belonging to that State if both the cargo and the ship carrying it were, at the time when the cause of action arose, in use or intended for use for commercial purposes; or

(b) an action in personam for enforcing a claim in connection with such a cargo if the ship carrying it was then in use or intended for use as aforesaid.

(5) In the foregoing provisions references to a ship or cargo belonging to a State include references to a ship or cargo in its possession or control or in which it claims an interest; and, subject to subsection (4) above, subsection (2) above applies to property other than a ship as it applies to a ship.

(6) Sections 3 to 5 above do not apply to proceedings of the kind described in subsection (1) above if the State in question is a party to the Brussels Convention and the claim relates to the operation of a ship owned or operated by that State, the carriage of cargo or passengers on any such ship or the carriage of cargo owned by that State on any other ship.

14   States entitled to immunities and privileges

(1) The immunities and privileges conferred by this Part of this Act apply to any foreign or commonwealth State other than the United Kingdom; and references to a State include references to –

(a) the sovereign or other head of that State in his public capacity;

(b) the government of that State; and

(c) any department of that government,

but not to any entity (hereafter referred to as a 'separate entity') which is distinct from the executive organs of the government of the State and capable of suing or being sued.

(2) A separate entity is immune from the jurisdiction of the courts of the United Kingdom if, and only if –

(a) the proceedings relate to anything done by it in the exercise of sovereign authority; and

(b) the circumstances are such that a State (or, in the case of proceedings to which section 10 above applies, a State which is not a party to the Brussels Convention) would have been so immune.

(3) If a separate entity (not being a State's central bank or other monetary authority) submits to the jurisdiction in respect of proceedings in the case of which it is entitled to immunity by virtue of subsection (2) above, subsections (1) to (4) of section 13 above shall apply to it in respect of those proceedings as if references to a State were references to that entity.

(4) Property of a State's central bank or their monetary authority shall not be regarded for the purposes of subsection (4) of section 13 above as in use or intended for use for commercial purposes; and where any such bank or authority is a separate entity subsections (1) to (3) of that section shall apply to it as if references to a State were references to the bank or authority.

(5) Section 12 above applies to proceedings against the constituent territories of a federal State; and Her Majesty may by Order in Council provide for the other provisions of this Part of this Act to apply to any such constituent territory specified in the Order as they apply to a State.

(6) Where the provisions of this Part of this Act do not apply to a constituent territory by virtue of any such Order subsections (2) and (3) above shall apply to it as if it were a separate entity.

15 Restriction and extension of immunities and privileges

(1) If it appears to Her Majesty that the immunities and privileges conferred by this Part of this Act in relation to any State –

(a) exceed those accorded by the law of that State in relation to the United Kingdom; or

(b) are less than those required by any treaty, convention or other international agreement to which that State and the United Kingdom are parties,

Her Majesty may by Order in Council provide for restricting or, as the case may be, extending those immunities and privileges to such extent as appears to Her Majesty to be appropriate.

(2) Any statutory instrument containing an Order under this section shall be subject to annulment in pursuance of a resolution of either House of Parliament.

16 Excluded matters

(1) This Part of this Act does not affect any immunity or privilege conferred by the Diplomatic Privileges Act 1964 or the Consular Regulations Act 1968; and –

(a) section 4 above does not apply to proceedings concerning the employment of the members of a mission within the meaning of the Convention scheduled to the said Act of 1964 or of the members of a consular post within the meaning of the Convention scheduled to the said Act of 1968;

(b) section 6(1) above does not apply to proceedings concerning a State's title to or its possession of property used for the purposes of a diplomatic mission.

(2) This Part of this Act does not apply to proceedings relating to anything done by or in relation to the armed forces of a State while present in the United Kingdom and, in particular, has effect subject to the Visiting Forces Act 1952.

(3) This Part of this Act does not apply to proceedings to which section 17(6) of the Nuclear Installations Act 1965 applies.

(4) This Part of this Act does not apply to criminal proceedings.

(5) This Part of this Act does not apply to any proceedings relating to taxation other than those mentioned in section 11 above.

17 Interpretation of Part I

(1) In this Part of this Act –

'the Brussels Convention' means the International Convention for the Unification of Certain Rules Concerning the Immunity of State-owned Ships signed in Brussels on 10 April 1926;

'commercial purposes' means purposes of such transactions or activities as are mentioned in section 3(3) above;

'ship' includes hovercraft.

(2) In sections 2(2) and 13(3) above references to an agreement include references to a treaty, convention or other international agreement.

(3) For the purposes of sections 3 to 8 above the territory of the United Kingdom shall be deemed to include any dependent territory in respect of which the United Kingdom is a party to the European Convention on State Immunity.

(4) In sections 3(1), 4(1), 5 and 16(2) above references to the United Kingdom include references to its territorial waters and any area designated under section 1(7) of the Continental Shelf Act 1964. ...

PART II

JUDGMENTS AGAINST UNITED KINGDOM IN CONVENTION STATES

18   Recognition of judgments against United Kingdom

(1) This section applies to any judgment given against the United Kingdom by a court in another State party to the European Convention on State Immunity, being a judgment –

(a) given in proceedings in which the United Kingdom was not entitled to immunity by virtue of provisions corresponding to those of sections 2 to 11 above; and

(b) which is final, that is to say, which is not or is no longer subject to appeal or, if given in default of appearance, liable to be set aside.

(2) Subject to section 19 below, a judgment to which this section applies shall be recognised in any court in the United Kingdom as conclusive between the parties thereto in all proceedings founded on the same cause of action and may be relied on by way of defence or counterclaim in such proceedings.

(3) Subsection (2) above (but not section 19 below) shall have effect

also in relation to any settlement entered into by the United Kingdom before a court in another State party to the Convention which under the law of that State is treated as equivalent to a judgment.

(4) In this section references to a court in a State party to the Convention include references to a court in any territory in respect of which it is a party.

19 Exceptions to recognition

(1) A court need not give effect to section 18 above in the case of a judgment –

(a) if to do so would be manifestly contrary to public policy or if any party to the proceedings in which the judgment was given had no adequate opportunity to present his case; or

(b) if the judgment was given without provisions corresponding to those of section 12 above having been complied with and the United Kingdom has not entered an appearance or applied to have the judgment set aside.

(2) A court need not give effect to section 18 above in the case of a judgment –

(a) if proceedings between the same parties, based on the same facts and having the same purpose –

(i) are pending before a court in the United Kingdom and were the first to be instituted; or

(ii) are pending before a court in another State party to the Convention, were the first to be instituted and may result in a judgment to which that section will apply; or

(b) if the result of the judgment is inconsistent with the result of another judgment given in proceedings between the same parties and –

(i) the other judgment is by a court in the United Kingdom and either those proceedings were the first to be instituted or the judgment of that court was given before the first-mentioned judgment became final within the meaning of subsection (1)(b) of section 18 above; or

(ii) the other judgment is by a court in another State party to the Convention and that section has already become applicable to it.

(3) Where the judgment was given against the United Kingdom in proceedings in respect of which the United Kingdom was not entitled to immunity by virtue of a provision corresponding to section 6(2) above, a court need not give effect to section 18 above in respect of the judgment if the court that gave the judgment –

(a) would not have had jurisdiction in the matter if it had applied rules of jurisdiction corresponding to those applicable to such matters in the United Kingdom; or

(b) applied a law other than that indicated by the United Kingdom rules of private international law and would have reached a different conclusion if it had applied the law so indicated.

(4) In subsection (2) above references to a court in the United kingdom include references to a court in any dependent territory in respect of which the United Kingdom is a party to the Convention, and references to a court in another State party to the Convention include references to a court in any territory in respect of which it is a party.

PART III

MISCELLANEOUS AND SUPPLEMENTARY

20 Heads of State

(1) Subject to the provisions of this section and to any necessary modifications, the Diplomatic Privileges Act 1964 shall apply to –

(a) a sovereign or other head of State;

(b) members of his family forming part of his household; and

(c) his private servants,

as it applies to the head of a diplomatic mission, to members of his family forming part of his household and to his private servants.

(2) The immunities and privileges conferred by virtue of subsection (1)(a) and (b) above shall not be subject to the restrictions by reference to nationality or residence mentioned in Article 37(1) or 38 in Schedule 1 to the said Act of 1964.

(3) Subject to any direction to the contrary by the Secretary of State, a person on whom immunities and privileges are conferred by virtue

of subsection (1) above shall be entitled to the exemption conferred by section 8(3) of the Immigration Act 1971.

(4) Except as respects value added tax and duties of customs or excise, this section does not affect any question whether a person is exempt from, or immune as respects proceedings relating to, taxation.

(5) This section applies to the sovereign or other head of any State on which immunities and privileges are conferred by Part I of this Act and is without prejudice to the application of that Part to any such sovereign or head of State in his public capacity.

21 Evidence by certificate

A certificate by or on behalf of the Secretary of State shall be conclusive evidence on any question –

(a) whether any country is a State for the purposes of Part I of this Act, whether any territory is a constituent territory of a federal State for those purposes or as to the person or persons to be regarded for those purposes as the head or government of a State;

(b) whether a State is a party to the Brussels Convention mentioned in Part I of this Act;

(c) whether a State is a party to the European Convention on State Immunity, whether it has made a declaration under Article 24 of that Convention or as to the territories in respect of which the United Kingdom or any other State is a party;

(d) whether, and if so when, a document has been served or received as mentioned in section 12(1) or (5) above.

22 General interpretation

(1) In this Act 'court' includes any tribunal or body exercising judicial functions; and references to the courts or law of the United Kingdom include references to the courts or law of any part of the United Kingdom.

(2) In this Act references to entry of appearance and judgments in default of appearance include references to any corresponding procedures.

(3) In this Act 'the European Convention on State Immunity' means the Convention of that name signed in Basle on 16 May 1972.

(4) In this Act 'dependent territory' means –

(a) any of the Channel Islands;

(b) the Isle of Man;

(c) any colony other than one for whose external relations a country other than the United Kingdom is responsible; or

(d) any country or territory outside Her Majesty's dominions in which Her Majesty has jurisdiction in right of the government of the United Kingdom.

(5) Any powers conferred by this Act to make an Order in Council includes power to vary or revoke a previous order.

As amended by the British Nationality Act 1981, s52(6), Schedule 7; Hong Kong (British Nationality) Order 1986, art 8, Schedule 1.

ARBITRATION ACT 1979
(1979 c 42)

1 Judicial review of arbitration awards

(1) In the Arbitration Act 1950 (in this Act referred to as 'the principal Act') section 21 (statement of case for a decision of the High Court) shall cease to have effect and, without prejudice to the right of appeal conferred by subsection (2) below, the High Court shall not have jurisdiction to set aside or remit an award on an arbitration agreement on the ground of errors of fact or law on the face of the award.

(2) Subject to subsection (3) below, an appeal shall lie to the High Court on any question of law arising out of an award made on an arbitration agreement; and on the determination of such an appeal the High Court may by order –

(a) confirm, vary or set aside the award; or

(b) remit the award to the reconsideration of the arbitrator or umpire together with the court's opinion on the question of law which was the subject of the appeal;

and where the award is remitted under paragraph (b) above the arbitrator or umpire shall, unless the order otherwise directs, make his award within three months after the date of the order.

(3) An appeal under this section may be brought by any of the parties to the reference –

(a) with the consent of all the other parties to the reference; or

(b) subject to section 3 below, with the leave of the court.

(4) The High Court shall not grant leave under subsection (3)(b) above unless it considers that, having regard to all the circumstances, the determination of the question of law concerned could substantially affect the rights of one or more of the parties to the arbitration agreement; and the court may make any leave which it gives conditional upon the applicant complying with such conditions as it considers appropriate.

(5) Subject to subsection (6) below, if an award is made and, on an application made by any of the parties to the reference, –

(a) with the consent of all the other parties to the reference, or

(b) subject to section 3 below, with the leave of the court,

it appears to the High Court that the award does not or does not sufficiently set out the reasons for the award, the court may order the arbitrator or umpire concerned to state the reasons for his award in sufficient detail to enable the court, should an appeal be brought under this section, to consider any question of law arising out of the award.

(6) In any case where an award is made without any reason being given, the High Court shall not make an order under subsection (5) above unless it is satisfied –

(a) that before the award was made one of the parties to the reference gave notice to the arbitrator or umpire concerned that a reasoned award would be required; or

(b) that there is some special reason why such a notice was not given.

(6A) Unless the High Court gives leave, no appeal shall lie to the Court of Appeal from a decision of the High Court:

(a) to grant or refuse leave under subsection (3)(b) or (5)(b) above; or

(b) to make or not to make an order under subsection (5) above.

(7) No appeal shall lie to the Court of Appeal from a decision of the High Court on an appeal under this section unless –

(a) the High Court or the Court of Appeal gives leave; and

(b) it is certified by the High Court that the question of law to which its decision relates either is one of general public importance or is one which for some other special reason should be considered by the Court of Appeal.

(8) Where the award of an arbiter or umpire is varied on appeal, the award as varied shall have effect (except for the purposes of this section) as if it were the award of the arbitrator or umpire.

2 Determination of preliminary point of law by court

(1) Subject to subsection (2) and section 3 below, on an application to the High Court made by any of the parties to a reference –

(a) with the consent of an arbitrator who has entered on the reference or, if an umpire has entered on the reference, with his consent, or

(b) with the consent of all the other parties,

the High Court shall have jurisdiction to determine any question of law arising in the course of the reference.

(2) The High Court shall not entertain an application under subsection (1)(a) above with respect to any question of law unless it is satisfied that –

(a) the determination of the application might produce substantial savings in costs to the parties; and

(b) the question of law is one in respect of which leave to appeal would be likely to be given under section 1(3)(b) above.

(2A) Unless the High Court gives leave, no appeal shall lie to the Court of Appeal from a decision of the High Court to entertain or not to entertain an application under subsection (1)(a) above.

(3) A decision of the High Court under subsection (1) above shall be deemed to be a judgment of the court within the meaning of section 16 of the Supreme Court Act 1981 (appeals to the Court of Appeal), but no appeal shall lie from such a decision unless –

(a) the High Court or the Court of Appeal gives leave; and

(b) it is certified by the High Court that the question of law to which its decision relates either is one of general public importance or is one which for some other special reason should be considered by the Court of Appeal.

3   Exclusion agreements affecting rights under ss1 and 2

(1) Subject to the following provisions of this section and section 4 below –

(a) the High Court shall not, under section 1(3)(b) above, grant leave to appeal with respect to a question of law arising out of an award, and

(b) the High Court shall not, under section 1(5)(b) above, grant leave to make an application with respect to an award, and

(c) no application may be made under section 2(1)(a) above with respect to a question of law, if the parties to the reference in question have entered into an agreement in writing (in this section referred to as an 'exclusion agreement') which excludes the right of appeal under section 1 above in relation to that award or, in a case falling within paragraph (c) above, in relation to an award to which the determination of the question of law is material.

(2) An exclusion agreement may be expressed so as to relate to a particular award, to awards under a particular reference or to any other description of awards, whether arising out of the same reference or not; and an agreement may be an exclusion agreement for the purposes of this section whether it is entered into before or after the passing of this Act and whether or not it forms part of an arbitration agreement.

(3) In any case where –

(a) an arbitration agreement, other than a domestic arbitration agreement, provides for disputes between the parties to be referred to arbitration, and

(b) a dispute to which the agreement relates involves the question whether a party has been guilty of fraud, and

(c) the parties have entered into an exclusion agreement which is applicable to any award made on the reference of that dispute,

then, except in so far as the exclusion agreement otherwise provides, the High Court shall not exercise its powers under section 24(2) of the principal Act (to take steps necessary to enable the question to be determined by the High Court) in relation to that dispute.

(4) Except as provided by subsection (1) above, sections 1 and 2 above shall have effect notwithstanding anything in any agreement purporting –

(a) to prohibit or restrict access to the High Court; or

(b) to restrict the jurisdiction of that court; or

(c) to prohibit or restrict the making of a reasoned award.

(5) An exclusion agreement shall be of no effect in relation to an award made on, or a question of law arising in the course of a reference under, a statutory arbitration, that is to say, such an arbitration as is referred to in subsection (1) of section 31 of the principal Act.

(6) An exclusion agreement shall be of no effect in relation to an award made on, or a question of law arising in the course of a

reference under, an arbitration agreement which is a domestic arbitration agreement unless the exclusion agreement is entered into after the commencement of the arbitration in which the award is made or, as the case may be, in which the question of law arises.

(7) In this section 'domestic arbitration agreement' means an arbitration agreement which does not provide, expressly or by implication, for arbitration in a State other than the United Kingdom and to which neither –

(a) an individual who is a national of, or habitually resident in, any State other than the United Kingdom, nor

(b) a body corporate which is incorporated in, or whose central management and control is exercised in, any State other than the United Kingdom,

is a party at the time the arbitration agreement is entered into.

4   Exclusion agreements not to apply in certain cases

(1) Subject to subsection (3) below, if an arbitration award or a question of law arising in the course of a reference relates, in whole or in part, to –

(a) a question or claim falling within the Admiralty jurisdiction of the High Court, or

(b) a dispute arising out of a contract of insurance, or

(c) a dispute arising out of a commodity contract,

an exclusion agreement shall have no effect in relation to the award or question unless either –

(i) the exclusion agreement is entered into after the commencement of the arbitration in which the award is made or, as the case may be, in which the question of law arises, or

(ii) the award or question relates to a contract which is expressed to be governed by a law other than the law of England and Wales.

(2) In subsection (1)(c) above 'commodity contract' means a contract –

(a) for the sale of goods regularly dealt with on a commodity market or exchange in England or Wales which is specified for the purposes of this section by an order made by the Secretary of State; and

(b) of a description so specified.

(3) The Secretary of State may by order provide that subsection (1) above –

(a) shall cease to have effect; or

(b) subject to such conditions as may be specified in the order, shall not apply to any exclusion agreement made in relation to an arbitration award of a description so specified;

and an order under this subsection may contain such supplementary, incidental and transitional provisions as appear to the Secretary of State to be necessary or expedient.

(4) The power to make an order under subsection (2) or subsection (3) above shall be exercisable by statutory instrument which shall be subject to annulment in pursuance of a resolution of either House of Parliament.

(5) In this section 'exclusion agreement' has the same meaning as in section 3 above.

5   Interlocutory orders

(1) If any party to a reference under an arbitration agreement fails within the time specified in the order or, if no time is so specified, within a reasonable time to comply with an order made by the arbitrator or umpire in the course of the reference, then, on the application of the arbitrator or umpire or of any party to the reference, the High Court may make an order extending the powers of the arbitrator or umpire as mentioned in subsection (2) below.

(2) If an order is made by the High Court under this section, the arbitrator or umpire shall have power, to the extent and subject to any conditions specified in that order, to continue with the reference in default of appearance or of any other act by one of the parties in like manner as a judge of the High Court might continue with proceedings in that court where a party fails to comply with an order of that court or a requirement of rules of court.

(3) Section 4(5) of the Administration of Justice Act 1970 (jurisdiction of the High Court to be exercisable by the Court of Appeal in relation to judge-arbitrators and judge-umpires) shall not apply in relation to the power of the High Court to make an order under this section, but in the case of a reference to a judge-arbitrator or judge-umpire that power shall be exercisable as in the case of

other reference to arbitration and also by the judge-arbitrator or judge-umpire himself.

(4) Anything done by a judge-arbitrator or judge-umpire in the exercise of the power conferred by subsection (3) above shall be done by him in his capacity as judge of the High Court and have effect as if done by that court.

(5) The preceding provisions of this section have effect notwithstanding anything in any agreement but do not derogate from any powers conferred on an arbitrator or umpire, whether by an arbitration agreement or otherwise.

(6) In this section 'judge-arbitrator' and 'judge-umpire' have the same meaning as in Schedule 3 to the Administration of Justice Act 1970.

7 Application and interpretation of certain provisions of Part I of principal Act

(1) References in the following provisions of Part I of the principal Act to that Part of that Act shall have effect as if the preceding provisions of this Act were included in that Part, namely –

    (a) section 14 (interim awards);

    (b) section 28 (terms as to costs of orders);

    (c) section 30 (Crown to be bound);

    (d) section 31 (application to statutory arbitration); and

    (e) section 32 (meaning of 'arbitration agreement').

(2) Subsections (2) and (3) of section 29 of the principal Act shall apply to determine when an arbitration is deemed to be commenced for the purposes of this Act.

(3) For the avoidance of doubt, it is hereby declared that the reference in subsection (1) of section 31 of the principal Act (statutory arbitrations) to arbitration under any other Act does not extend to arbitration under section 64 of the County Courts Act 1984 (cases in which proceedings are to be or may be referred to arbitration) and accordingly nothing in this Act or in Part I of the principal Act applies to arbitration under the said section 64.

As amended by the Supreme Court Act 1981, s148(2), (3), (4), 152(1), Schedule 5; County Courts Act 1984, s148(1), Schedule 2, para 70.

PROTECTION OF TRADING INTERESTS ACT 1980
(1980 c 11)

1 Overseas measures affecting United Kingdom trading interests

(1) If it appears to the Secretary of State –

(a) that measures have been or are proposed to be taken by or under the law of any overseas country for regulating or controlling international trade; and

(b) that those measures, in so far as they apply or would apply to things done or to be done outside the territorial jurisdiction of that country by persons carrying on business in the United Kingdom, are damaging or threaten to damage the trading interests of the United Kingdom,

the Secretary of State may by order direct that this section shall apply to those measures either generally or in their applications to such cases as may be specified in the order.

(2) The Secretary of State may by order make provision for requiring, or enabling the Secretary of State to require, a person in the United Kingdom who carries on business there to give notice to the Secretary of State of any requirement or prohibition imposed or threatened to be imposed on that person pursuant to any measures in so far as this section applies to them by virtue of an order under subsection (1) above.

(3) The Secretary of State may give to any person in the United Kingdom who carries on business there such directions for prohibiting compliance with any such requirement or prohibition as aforesaid as he considers appropriate for avoiding damage to the trading interests of the United Kingdom.

(4) The power of the Secretary of State to make orders under subsection (1) or (2) above shall be exercisable by statutory

instrument subject to annulment in pursuance of a resolution of either House of Parliament.

(5) Directions under subsection (3) above may be either general or special and may prohibit compliance with any requirement or prohibition either absolutely or in such cases or subject to such conditions as to consent or otherwise as may be specified in the directions; and general directions under that subsection shall be published in such manner as appears to the Secretary of State to be appropriate.

(6) In this section 'trade' includes any activity carried on in the course of a business of any description and 'trading interests' shall be construed accordingly.

2   Documents and information required by overseas courts and authorities

(1) If it appears to the Secretary of State –

(a) that a requirement has been or may be imposed on a person or persons in the United Kingdom to produce to any court, tribunal or authority of an overseas country any commercial document which is not within the territorial jurisdiction of that country or to furnish any commercial information to any such court, tribunal or authority; or

(b) that any such authority has imposed or may impose a requirement on a person or persons in the United Kingdom to publish any such document or information,

the Secretary of State may, if it appears to him that the requirement is inadmissible by virtue of subsection (2) or (3) below, give directions for prohibiting compliance with the requirement.

(2) A requirement such as is mentioned in subsection (1)(a) or (b) above is inadmissible –

(a) if it infringes the jurisdiction of the United Kingdom or is otherwise prejudicial to the sovereignty of the United Kingdom; or

(b) if compliance with the requirement would be prejudicial to the security of the United Kingdom or to the relations of the government of the United Kingdom with the government of any other country.

(3) A requirement such as is mentioned in subsection (1)(a) above is also inadmissible –

(a) if it is made otherwise than for the purposes of civil or criminal proceedings which have been instituted in the overseas country; or

(b) if it requires a person to state what documents relevant to any such proceedings are or have been in his possession, custody or power or to produce for the purposes of any such proceedings any documents other than particular documents specified in the requirement.

(4) Directions under subsection (1) above may be either general or special and may prohibit compliance with any requirement either absolutely or in such cases or subject to such conditions as to consent or otherwise as may be specified in the directions; and general directions under that subsection shall be published in such manner as appears to the Secretary of State to be appropriate.

(5) For the purposes of this section the making of a request or demand shall be treated as the imposition of a requirement if it is made in circumstances in which a requirement to the same effect could be or could have been imposed; and

(a) any request or demand for the supply of a document or information which, pursuant to the requirement of any court, tribunal or authority of an overseas country, is addressed to a person in the United Kingdom; or

(b) any requirement imposed by such a court, tribunal or authority to produce or furnish any document or information to a person specified in the requirement,

shall be treated as a requirement to produce or furnish that document or information to that court, tribunal or authority.

(6) In this section 'commercial document' and 'commercial information' mean respectively a document or information relating to a business of any description and 'document' includes any record or device by means of which material is recorded or stored.

3   Offences under ss1 and 2

(1) Subject to subsection (2) below, any person who without reasonable excuse fails to comply with any requirement imposed under subsection (2) of section 1 above or knowingly contravenes any

directions given under subsection (3) of that section or section 2(1) above shall be guilty of an offence and liable –

(a) on conviction on indictment, to a fine;

(b) on summary conviction, to a fine not exceeding the statutory maximum.

(2) A person who is neither a citizen of the United Kingdom and Colonies nor a body corporate incorporated in the United Kingdom shall not be guilty of an offence under subsection (1) above by reason of anything done or omitted outside the United Kingdom in contravention of directions under section 1(3) or 2(1) above.

(3) No proceedings for an offence under subsection (1) above shall be instituted in England, Wales or Northern Ireland except by the Secretary of State or with the consent of the Attorney General or, as the case may be, the Attorney General for Northern Ireland.

(4) Proceedings against any person for an offence under this section may be taken before the appropriate court in the United Kingdom having jurisdiction in the place where that person is for the time being.

4 Restriction of Evidence (Proceedings in Other Jurisdictions) Act 1975

A court in the United Kingdom shall not make an order under section 2 of the Evidence (Proceedings in Other Jurisdictions) Act 1975 for giving effect to a request issued by or on behalf of a court or tribunal of an overseas country if it is shown that the request infringes the jurisdiction of the United Kingdom or is otherwise prejudicial to the sovereignty of the United Kingdom; and a certificate signed by or on behalf of the Secretary of State to the effect that it infringes that jurisdiction or is so prejudicial shall be conclusive evidence of that fact.

5 Restriction on enforcement of certain overseas judgments

(1) A judgment to which this section applies shall not be registered under Part II of the Administration of Justice Act 1920 or Part I of the Foreign Judgments (Reciprocal Enforcement) Act 1933 and no court in the United Kingdom shall entertain proceedings at common law for the recovery of any sum payable under such a judgment.

(2) This section applies to any judgment given by a court of an overseas country, being –

(a) a judgment for multiple damages within the meaning of subsection (3) below;

(b) a judgment based on a provision or rule of law specified or described in an order under subsection (4) below and given after the coming into force of the order; or

(c) a judgment on a claim for contribution in respect of damages awarded by a judgment falling within paragraph (a) or (b) above.

(3) In subsection (2)(a) above a judgment for multiple damages means a judgment for an amount arrived at by doubling, trebling or otherwise multiplying a sum assessed as compensation for the loss or damage sustained by the person in whose favour the judgment is given.

(4) The Secretary of State may for the purposes of subsection (2)(b) above make an order in respect of any provision or rule of law which appears to him to be concerned with the prohibition or regulation of agreements, arrangements or practices designed to restrain, distort or restrict competition in the carrying on of business of any description or to be otherwise concerned with the promotion of such competition as aforesaid.

(5) The power of the Secretary of State to make orders under subsection (4) above shall be exercisable by statutory instrument subject to annulment in pursuance of a resolution of either House of Parliament.

(6) Subsection (2)(a) above applies to a judgment given before the date of the passing of this Act as well as to a judgment given on or after that date but this section does not affect any judgment which has been registered before that date under the provisions mentioned in subsection (1) above or in respect of which such proceedings as are there mentioned have been finally determined before that date.

6   Recovery of awards of multiple damages

(1) This section applies where a court of an overseas country has given a judgment for multiple damages within the meaning of section 5(3) above against –

(a) a citizen of the United Kingdom and Colonies; or

(b) a body corporate incorporated in the United Kingdom or in a territory outside the United Kingdom for whose international relations Her Majesty's Government in the United Kingdom are responsible; or

(c) a person carrying on business in the United Kingdom (in this section referred to as a 'qualifying defendant') and an amount on account of the damages has been paid by the qualifying defendant either to the party in whose favour the judgment was given or to another party who is entitled as against the qualifying defendant to contribution in respect of the damages.

(2) Subject to subsection (3) and (4) below, the qualifying defendant shall be entitled to recover from the party in whose favour the judgment was given so much of the amount referred to in subsection (1) above as exceeds the part attributable to compensation; and that part shall be taken to be such part of the amount as bears to the whole of it the same proportion as the sum assessed by the court that gave the judgment as compensation for the loss or damage sustained by that party bears to the whole of the damages awarded to that party.

(3) Subsection (2) above does not apply where the qualifying defendant is an individual who was ordinarily resident in the overseas country at the time when the proceedings in which the judgment was given were instituted or a body corporate which had its principal place of business there at that time.

(4) Subsection (2) above does not apply where the qualifying defendant carried on business in the overseas country and the proceedings in which the judgment was given were concerned with activities exclusively carried on in that country.

(5) A court in the United Kingdom may entertain proceedings on a claim under this section notwithstanding that the person against whom the proceedings are brought is not within the jurisdiction of the court.

(6) The reference in subsection (1) above to an amount paid by the qualifying defendant includes a reference to an amount obtained by execution against his property or against the property of a company which (directly or indirectly) is wholly owned by him; and references in that subsection and subsection (2) above to the party in whose favour the judgment was given or to a party entitled to contribution include references to any person in whom the rights of any such party have become vested by succession or assignment or otherwise.

(7) This section shall, with the necessary modifications, apply also in relation to any order which is made by a tribunal or authority of an overseas country and would, if that tribunal or authority were a court, be a judgment for multiple damages within the meaning of section 5(3) above.

(8) This section does not apply to any judgment given or order made before the passing of this Act.

7 Enforcement of overseas judgment under provision corresponding to s6

(1) If it appears to Her Majesty that the law of an overseas country provides or will provide for the enforcement in that country of judgments given under section 6 above, Her Majesty may by Order in Council provide for the enforcement in the United Kingdom of judgments of any description specified in the Order which are given under any provision of the law of that country relating to the recovery of sums paid or obtained pursuant to a judgment for multiple damages within the meaning of section 5(3) above, whether or not that provision corresponds to section 6 above.

(1A) Such an Order in Council may, as respects judgments to which it relates –

(a) make different provisions for different descriptions of judgment; and

(b) impose conditions or restrictions on the enforcement of judgments of any description.

(2) An Order under this section may apply, with or without modification, any of the provisions of the Foreign Judgments (Reciprocal Enforcement) Act 1933.

8 Short title, interpretation, repeals and extent ...

(2) In this Act 'overseas country' means any country or territory outside the United Kingdom other than one for whose international relations Her Majesty's Government in the United Kingdom are responsible.

(3) References in this Act to the law or a court, tribunal or authority of an overseas country include, in the case of a federal state, references to the law or a court, tribunal or authority of any constituent part of that country.

(4) References in this Act to a claim for, or to entitlement to, contribution are references to a claim or entitlement based on an enactment or rule of law. ...

(8) Her Majesty may by Order in Council direct that this Act shall extend with such exceptions, adaptations and modifications, if any, as may be specified in the Order to any territory outside the United Kingdom, being a territory for the international relations of which Her Majesty's Government in the United Kingdom are responsible.

As amended by the Shipping Contracts and Commercial Documents Act 1964; Magistrates' Courts Act 1980, s154(3), Schedule 9; Civil Jurisdiction and Judgments Act 1982, s38; Statute Law (Repeals) Act 1993, s1(1), Schedule 1, Pt XIV.

MAGISTRATES' COURTS ACT 1980

(1980 c 43)

59 Orders for periodical payment: means of payment

(1) In any case where a magistrates' court orders money to be paid periodically by one person (in this section referred to as 'the debtor') to another (in this section referred to as 'the creditor'), then –

    (a) if the order is a qualifying maintenance order, the court shall at the same time exercise one of its powers under paragraphs (a) to (d) of subsection (3) below;

    (b) if the order is not a maintenance order, the court shall at the same time exercise one of its powers under paragraphs (a) and (b) of that subsection.

(2) For the purposes of this section a maintenance order is a 'qualifying maintenance order' if, at the time it is made, the debtor is ordinarily resident in England and Wales.

(3) The powers of the court are –

    (a) the power to order that payments under the order be made directly by the debtor to the creditor;

    (b) the power to order that payments under the order be made to the clerk of the court or to the clerk of any other magistrates' court;

    (c) the power to order that payments under the order be made by the debtor to the creditor by such method of payment falling within subsection (6) below as may be specified;

    (cc) the power to order that payments under the order be made in accordance with arrangements made by the Secretary of State for their collection;

    (d) the power to make an attachment of earnings order under the Attachment of Earnings Act 1971 to secure payments under the order.

(3A) No order made by a magistrates' court under paragraphs (a) to

(d) of subsection (3) above (other than one made under paragraph (cc)) shall have effect at any time when the Secretary of State is arranging for the collection of payments under the qualifying maintenance order concerned.

(4) In any case where –

(a) the court proposes to exercise its power under paragraph (c) of subsection (3) above, and

(b) having given the debtor an opportunity of opening an account from which payment under the order may be made in accordance with the method of payment proposed to be ordered under that paragraph, the court is satisfied that the debtor has failed, without reasonable excuse, to open such an account,

the court in exercising its power under that paragraph may order that the debtor open such an account.

(5) In deciding, in the case of a maintenance order, which of the powers under paragraphs (a) to (d) of subsection (3) above (other than paragraph (cc)) it is to exercise, the court having (if practicable) given them an opportunity to make representations shall have regard to any representations made –

(a) by the debtor,

(b) by the creditor, and

(c) if the person who applied for the maintenance order is a person other than the creditor, by that other person.

(6) The methods of payment referred to in subsection (3)(c) above are the following, that is to say –

(a) payment by standing order; or

(b) payment by any other method which requires one person to give his authority for payments of a specific amount to be made from an account of his to an account of another's on specific dates during the period for which the authority is in force and without the need for any further authority from him.

(7) Where the maintenance order is an order –

(a) under the Guardianship of Minors Act 1971 and 1973,

(b) under Part I of the Domestic Proceedings and Magistrates' Courts Act 1978, or

(c) under, or having effect as if made under, Schedule 1 to the Children Act 1989, and the court does not propose to exercise its power under paragraph (c), (cc) or (d) of subsection (3) above, the court shall, unless upon representations expressly made in that behalf by the person who applied for the maintenance order it is satisfied that it is undesirable to do so, exercise its power under paragraph (b) of that subsection.

(8) The Lord Chancellor may by regulations confer on magistrates' courts, in addition to their powers under paragraphs (a) to (d) of subsection (3) above, the power (the 'additional power') to order that payments under a qualifying maintenance order be made by the debtor to the creditor or the clerk of the magistrates' court (as the regulations may provide) by such method of payment as may be specified in the regulations.

(9) Any reference in any enactment to paragraphs (a) to (d) of subsection (3) above (but not a reference to any specific paragraph of that subsection) shall be taken to include a reference to the additional power, and the reference in subsection (10) below to the additional power shall be construed accordingly.

(10) Regulations under subsection (8) above may make provisions for any enactment concerning, or connected with, payments under maintenance orders to apply, with or without modifications, in relation to the additional power.

(11) The power of the Lord Chancellor to make regulations under subsection (8) above shall be exercisable by statutory instrument and any such statutory instrument shall be subject to annulment in pursuance of a resolution of either House of Parliament.

(12) For the purposes of this section –

(a) the reference in subsection (1) above to money paid periodically by one person to another includes, in the case of a maintenance order, a reference to a lump sum paid by instalments by one person to another; and

(b) references to arrangements made by the Secretary of State for the collection of payments are to arrangements made by him under section 30 of the Child Support Act 1991 and regulations made under that section.

60 Revocation, variation, etc of orders for periodical payment

(1) Where a magistrates' court has made an order for money to be paid periodically by one person to another, the court may, by order on complaint, revoke, revive or vary the order.

(2) The power under subsection (1) above to vary an order shall include power to suspend the operation of any provision of the order temporarily and to revive the operation of any provision so suspended.

(3) Where the order mentioned in subsection (1) above is a maintenance order, the power under that subsection to vary the order shall include power, if the court is satisfied that payment has not been made in accordance with the order, to exercise one of its powers under paragraphs (a) to (d) of section 59(3) above.

(4) In any case where –

(a) a magistrates' court has made a maintenance order, and

(b) payments under the order are required to be made by any method of payment falling within section 59(6) above,

an interested party may apply in writing to the clerk of the court for the order to be varied as mentioned in subsection (5) below.

(5) Subject to subsection (8) below, where an application has been made under subsection (4) above, the clerk, after giving written notice (by post or otherwise) of the application to any other interested party and allowing that party, within the period of 14 days beginning with the date of the giving of that notice, an opportunity to make written representations, may vary the order to provide that payments under the order shall be made to the clerk.

(6) The clerk may proceed with an application under subsection (4) above notwithstanding that any such interested party as is referred to in subsection (5) above has not received written notice of the application.

(7) In subsections (4) to (6) above 'interested party', in relation to a maintenance order, means –

(a) the debtor;

(b) the creditor; and

(c) if the person who applied for the maintenance order is a person other than the creditor, that other person.

(8) Where an application has been made under subsection (4) above, the clerk may, if he considers it inappropriate to exercise his power under subsection (5) above, refer the matter to the court which may vary the order by exercising one of its powers under paragraphs (a) to (d) of section 59(3) above.

(9) Subsections (4), (5) and (7) of section 59 above shall apply for the purposes of subsections (3) and (8) above as they apply for the purpose of that section.

(10) None of the powers of the court, or of the clerk of the court, conferred by subsections (3) to (9) above shall be exercisable in relation to a maintenance order which is not a qualifying maintenance order (within the meaning of section 59 above).

(11) For the purposes of this section –

(a) 'creditor' and 'debtor' have the same meaning as they have in section 59 above; and

(b) the reference in subsection (1) above to money paid periodically by one person to another includes, in the case of a maintenance order, a reference to a lump sum paid by instalments by one person to another.

As amended by the Maintenance Enforcement Act 1991, ss2, 4; Transfer of Functions (Magistrates' Courts and Family Law) Order 1992, art 3(2), Schedule 2; Child Support Act 1991 (Consequential Amendments) Order 1994, art 3(1)-(6).

LIMITATION ACT 1980
(1980 c 58)

ORDINARY TIME LIMITS FOR DIFFERENT CLASSES
OF ACTION

1   Time limits under Part I subject to extension or exclusion under Part II

(1) This Part of this Act gives the ordinary time limits for bringing actions of the various classes mentioned in the following provisions of this Part.

(2) The ordinary time limits given in this Part of this Act are subject to extension or exclusion in accordance with the provisions of Part II of this Act.

2   Time limit for actions founded on tort

An action founded on tort shall not be brought after the expiration of six years from the date on which the cause of action accrued.

3   Time limit in case of successive conversions and extinction of title of owner of converted goods

(1) Where any cause of action in respect of the conversion of a chattel has accrued to any person and, before he recovers possession of the chattel, a further conversion takes place, no action shall be brought in respect of the further conversion after the expiration of six years from the accrual of the cause of action in respect of the original conversion.

(2) Where any such cause of action has accrued to any person and the period prescribed for bringing that action has expired and he has not during that period recovered possession of the chattel, the title of that person to the chattel shall be extinguished.

4   Special time limit in case of theft

(1) The right of any person from whom a chattel is stolen to bring an action in respect of the theft shall not be subject to the time limits under sections 2 and 3(1) of this Act, but if his title to the chattel is extinguished under section 3(2) of this Act he may not bring an action in respect of a theft preceding the loss of his title, unless the theft in question preceded the conversion from which time began to run for the purposes of section 3(2).

(2) Subsection (1) above shall apply to any conversion related to the theft of a chattel as it applies to the theft of a chattel; and, except as provided below, every conversion following the theft of a chattel before the person from whom it is stolen recovers possession of it shall be regarded for the purposes of this section as related to the theft. If anyone purchases the stolen chattel in good faith neither the purchase nor any conversion following it shall be regarded as related to the theft.

(3) Any cause of action accruing in respect of the theft or any conversion related to the theft of a chattel to any person from whom the chattel is stolen shall be disregarded for the purpose of applying section 3(1) or (2) of this Act to his case.

(4) Where in any action brought in respect of the conversion of a chattel it is proved that the chattel was stolen from the plaintiff or anyone through whom he claims it shall be presumed that any conversion following the theft is related to the theft unless the contrary is shown.

(5) In this section 'theft' includes –

(a) any conduct outside England and Wales which would be theft if committed in England and Wales; and

(b) obtaining any chattel (in England and Wales or elsewhere) in the circumstances described in section 15(1) of the Theft Act 1968 (obtaining by deception) or by blackmail within the meaning of section 21 of that Act;

and references in this section to a chattel being 'stolen' shall be construed accordingly.

CIVIL JURISDICTION AND JUDGMENTS ACT 1982

(1982 c 27)

PART I

IMPLEMENTATION OF THE CONVENTIONS

1 Interpretation of references to the Conventions and Contracting States

(1) In this Act –

'the 1968 Convention' means the Convention on jurisdiction and the enforcement of judgments in civil and commercial matters (including the Protocol annexed to that Convention), signed at Brussels in 27 September 1968;

'the 1971 Protocol' means the Protocol on the interpretation of the 1968 Convention by the European Court, signed at Luxembourg on 3 June 1971;

'the Accession Convention' means the Convention on the accession to the 1968 Convention and the 1971 Protocol of Denmark, the Republic of Ireland and the United Kingdom, signed at Luxembourg on 9 October 1978;

'the 1982 Accession Convention' means the Convention on the accession of the Hellenic Republic to the 1968 Convention and the 1971 Protocol, with the adjustments made to them by the Accession Convention, signed at Luxembourg on 25 October 1982;

'the 1989 Accession Convention' means the Convention on the accession of the Kingdom of Spain and the Portuguese Republic to the 1968 Convention and the 1971 Protocol, with the adjustments made to them by the Accession Convention and the 1982 Accession Convention, signed at Donostia – San Sebastian on 26 May 1989;

'the Brussels Conventions' means the 1968 Convention, the 1971

Protocol, the Accession Convention, the 1982 Accession
Convention and the 1989 Accession Convention;

'the Lugano Convention' means the Convention on jurisdiction
and the enforcement of judgments in civil and commercial
matters (including the Protocols annexed to that Convention)
opened for signature at Lugano on 16 September 1988 and
signed by the United Kingdom on 18 September 1989.

(2) In this Act, unless the context otherwise requires –

(a) references to, or to any provision of, the 1968 Convention or
the 1971 Protocol are references to that Convention, Protocol or
provision as amended by the Accession Convention, the 1982
Accession Convention and the 1989 Accession Convention;

(b) any reference in any provision to a numbered Article without
more is a reference –

(i) to the Article so numbered of the 1968 Convention, in so
far as the provision applies in relation to that Convention; and

(ii) to the Article so numbered of the Lugano Convention, in
so far as the provision applies in relation to that Convention,

and any reference to a sub-division of a numbered Article shall
be construed accordingly.

(3) In this Act:

'Contracting State', without more, in any provision means:

(a) in the application of the provision in relation to the Brussels
Conventions, a Brussels Contracting State; and

(b) in the application of the provision in relation to the Lugano
Convention, a Lugano Contracting State;

'Brussels Contracting State' means

(a) one of the original parties to the 1968 Convention (Belgium,
the Federal Republic of Germany, France, Italy, Luxembourg
and the Netherlands); or

(b) one of the parties acceding to that Convention under the
Accession Convention (Denmark, the Republic of Ireland and
the United Kingdom), or under the 1982 Accession Convention
(the Hellenic Republic), or under the 1989 Accession
Convention (Spain and Portugal), being a state in respect of
which the Accession Convention has entered into force in
accordance with Article 39 of that Convention, or being a state
in respect of which the 1982 Accession Convention has entered
into force in accordance with Article 15 of that convention, or
being a state in respect of which the 1989 Accession

Convention has entered into force in accordance with Article 32 of that Convention, as the case might be;

'Lugano Contracting State' means one of the original parties to the Lugano Convention, that is to say –

Austria, Belgium, Denmark, Finland, France, the Federal Republic of Germany, the Hellenic Republic, Iceland, the Republic of Ireland, Italy, Luxembourg, the Netherlands, Norway, Portugal, Spain, Sweden, Switzerland and the United Kingdom,

being a State in relation to which that Convention has taken effect in accordance with paragraph 3 or 4 of Article 61.

2   The Brussels Conventions to have the force of law

(1) The Brussels Conventions shall have the force of law in the United Kingdom, and judicial notice shall be taken of them.

(2) For convenience of reference there are set out in Schedules 1, 2, 3, 3A and 3B respectively the English texts of –

(a) the 1968 Convention as amended by Titles II and III of the Accession Convention, by Titles II and III of the 1982 Accession Convention and by Titles II and III of, and Annex I(d) to, the 1989 Accession Convention;

(b) the 1971 Protocol as amended by Title IV of the Accession Convention, by Title IV of the 1982 Accession Convention and by Title IV of the 1989 Accession Convention;

(c) Titles V and VI of the Accession Convention (transitional and final provisions) as amended by Title V of the 1989 Accession Convention;

(d) Titles V and VI of the 1982 Accession Convention (transitional and final provisions); and

(e) Titles VI and VII of the 1989 Accession Convention (transitional and final provisions),

being texts prepared from the authentic English texts referred to in Articles 37 and 41 of the Accession Convention, in Article 17 of the 1982 Accession Convention and in Article 34 of the 1989 Accession Convention.

3   Interpretation of the Brussels Conventions

(1) Any question as to the meaning or effect of any provision of the Brussels Conventions shall, if not referred to the European Court

in accordance with the 1971 Protocol, be determined in accordance with the principles laid down by any relevant decision of the European Court.

(2) Judicial notice shall be taken of any decision of, or expression of opinion by, the European Court on any such question.

(3) Without prejudice to the generality of subsection (1), the following reports (which are reproduced in the Official Journal of the Communities), namely –

> (a) the reports by Mr P Jenard on the 1968 Convention and the 1971 Protocol;
>
> (b) the report by Professor Peter Schlosser on the Accession Convention;
>
> (c) the report by Professor Demetrios I Evrigenis and Professor KD Kerameus on the 1982 Accession Convention; and
>
> (d) the report by Mr Martinho de Almeida Cruz, Mr Manuel Desantes Real and Mr P Jenard on the 1989 Accession Convention,

may be considered in ascertaining the meaning or effect of any provision of the Brussels Conventions and shall be given such weight as is appropriate in the circumstances.

3A   The Lugano Convention to have the force of law

(1) The Lugano Convention shall have the force of law in the United Kingdom, and judicial notice shall be taken of it.

(2) For convenience of reference there is set out in Schedule 3C the English text of the Lugano Convention.

3B   Interpretation of the Lugano Convention

(1) In determining any question as to the meaning or effect of a provision of the Lugano Convention, a court in the United Kingdom shall, in accordance with Protocol No 2 to that Convention, take account of any principles laid down in any relevant decision delivered by a court of any other Lugano Contracting State concerning provisions of the Convention.

(2) Without prejudice to any practice of the courts as to the matters which may be considered apart from this section the report on the Lugano Convention by Mr P Jenard and Mr G Moller (which is

reproduced in the Official Journal of the Communities of 28 July 1990) may be considered in ascertaining the meaning or effect of any provision of the Convention and shall be given such weight as is appropriate in the circumstances.

4 Enforcement of judgments other than maintenance orders

(1) A judgment other than a maintenance order, which is the subject of an application under Article 31 of the 1968 Convention or of the Lugano Convention for its enforcement in any part of the United Kingdom shall, to the extent that its enforcement is authorised by the appropriate court, be registered in the prescribed manner in that court.

In this subsection 'the appropriate court' means the court to which the application is made in pursuance of Article 32 (that is to say, the High Court or the Court of Session).

(2) Where a judgment is registered under this section, the reasonable costs or expenses of and incidental to its registration shall be recoverable as if they were sums recoverable under the judgment.

(3) A judgment registered under this section shall, for the purposes of its enforcement, be of the same force and effect, the registering court shall have in relation to its enforcement the same powers, and proceedings for or with respect to its enforcement may be taken, as if the judgment had been originally given by the registering court and had (where relevant) been entered.

(4) Subsection (3) is subject to Article 39 (restriction on enforcement where appeal pending or time for appeal unexpired), to section 7 and to any provision made by rules of court as to the manner in which and conditions subject to which a judgment registered under this section may be enforced.

5 Recognition and enforcement of maintenance orders

(1) The function of transmitting to the appropriate court an application under Article 31 of the 1968 Convention or of the Lugano Convention for the recognition or enforcement in the United Kingdom of a maintenance order shall be discharged –

(a) as respects England and Wales and Northern Ireland, by the Lord Chancellor;

(b) as respects Scotland, by the Secretary of State.

In this subsection 'the appropriate court' means the magistrates' court or sheriff court having jurisdiction in the matter in accordance with the second paragraph of Article 32.

(2) Such an application shall be determined in the first instance by the prescribed officer of that court.

(3) Where on such an application the enforcement of the order is authorised to any extent, the order shall to that extent be registered in the prescribed manner in that court.

(4) A maintenance order registered under this section shall for the purposes of its enforcement be of the same force and effect, the registering court shall have in relation to its enforcement the same powers, and proceedings for or with respect to its enforcement may be taken, as if the order had been originally made by the registering court.

(5) Subsection (4) is subject to Article 39 (restriction on enforcement where appeal pending or time for appeal unexpired), to section 7 and to any provision made by rules of court as to the manner in which and conditions subject to which an order registered under this section may be enforced.

(5A) A maintenance order which by virtue of this section is enforceable by a magistrates' court in England and Wales shall, subject to the modifications of sections 76 and 93 of the Magistrates' Courts Act 1980 specified in subsections (5B) and (5C) below, be enforceable in the same manner as a magistrates' court maintenance order made by that court.

In this subsection 'magistrates' court maintenance order' has the same meaning as in section 150(1) of the Magistrates' Courts Act 1980.

(5B) Section 76 (enforcement of sums adjudged to be paid) shall have effect as if for subsections (4) to (6) there were substituted the following subsections –

'(4) Where proceedings are brought for the enforcement of a magistrates' court maintenance order under this section, the court may vary the order by exercising one of its powers under subsection (5) below.

(5) The powers of the court are –

(a) the power to order that payments under the order be made

directly to the clerk of the court or the clerk of any other magistrates' court;

(b) the power to order that payments under the order be made to the clerk of the court, or to the clerk of any other magistrates' court, by such method of payment falling within section 59(6) above (standing order, etc) as may be specified;

(c) the power to make an attachment of earnings order under the Attachment of Earnings Act 1971 to secure payments under the order.

(6) In deciding which of the powers under subsection (5) above it is to exercise, the court shall have regard to any representations made by the debtor (within the meaning of section 59 above).

(7) Subsection (4) of section 59 above (power of court to require debtor to open account) shall apply for the purposes of subsection (5) above as it applies for the purposes of that section but as if for paragraph (a) there were substituted –

'(a) the court proposes to exercise its power under paragraph (b) of section 76(5) below, and'

(5C) In section 93 (complaint for arrears), subsection (6) (court not to impose imprisonment in certain circumstances) shall have effect as if for paragraph (b) there were substituted –

'(b) if the court is of the opinion that it is appropriate –

(i) to make an attachment of earnings order; or

(ii) to exercise its power under paragraph (b) of section 76(5) above.'...

(7) The payer under a maintenance order registered under this section in a magistrates' court in England and Wales or Northern Ireland shall give notice of any change of address to the clerk of that court.

A person who without reasonable excuse fails to comply with this subsection shall be guilty of an offence and liable on summary conviction to a fine not exceeding level 2 on the standard scale.

6   Appeals under Article 37, second paragraph, and Article 41

(1) The single further appeal on a point of law referred to in the 1968 Convention and the Lugano Convention in Article 37, second paragraph and Article 41 in relation to the recognition or enforcement of a judgment other than a maintenance order lies –

(a) in England and Wales or Northern Ireland, to the Court of Appeal or to the House of Lords in accordance with Part II of the Administration of Justice Act 1969 (appeals direct from the High Court to the House of Lords);

(b) in Scotland, to the Inner House of the Court of Session.

(2) Paragraph (a) of subsection (1) has effect notwithstanding section 15(2) of the Administration of Justice Act 1969 (exclusion of direct appeal to the House of Lords in cases where no appeal to that House lies from a decision of the Court of Appeal).

(3) The single further appeal on a point of law referred to in each of those Conventions in Article 37, second paragraph and Article 41 in relation to the recognition or enforcement of a maintenance order lies –

(a) in England and Wales, to the High Court by way of case stated in accordance with section 111 of the Magistrates' Courts Act 1980; ...

7 Interest on registered judgments

(1) Subject to subsection (4), where in connection with an application for registration of a judgment under section 4 or 5 the applicant shows –

(a) that the judgment provides for the payment of a sum of money; and

(b) that in accordance with the law of the Contracting State in which the judgment was given interest on that sum is recoverable under the judgment from a particular date or time,

the rate of interest and the date or time from which it is so recoverable shall be registered with the judgment and, subject to any provisions made under subsection (2), the debt resulting, apart from section 4(2), from the registration of the judgment shall carry interest in accordance with the registered particulars.

(2) Provision may be made by rules of court as to the manner in which and the periods of reference to which any interest payable by virtue of subsection (1) is to be calculated and paid, including provision for such interest to cease to accrue as from a prescribed date.

(3) Costs or expenses recoverable by virtue of section 4(2) shall carry interest as if they were the subject of an order for the payment of

costs or expenses made by the registering court on the date of registration.

(4) Interest or arrears of sums payable under a maintenance order registered under section 5 in a magistrates' court in England and Wales or Northern Ireland shall not be recoverable in that court, but without prejudice to the operation in relation to any such order of section 2A of the Maintenance Orders Act 1958 or section 11A of the Maintenance and Affiliation Orders Act (Northern Ireland) 1966 (which enable interest to be recovered if the order is re-registered for enforcement in the High Court).

(5) Except as mentioned in subsection (4), debts under judgments registered under section 4 or 5 shall carry interest only as provided by this section.

8 Currency of payment under registered maintenance orders

(1) Sums payable in the United Kingdom under a maintenance order by virtue of its registration under section 5, including any arrears so payable, shall be paid in the currency of the United Kingdom.

(2) Where the order is expressed in any other currency, the amounts shall be converted on the basis of the exchange rate prevailing on the date of registration of the order.

(3) For the purposes of this section, a written certificate purporting to be signed by an officer of any bank in the United Kingdom and stating the exchange rate prevailing on a specified date shall be evidence, and in Scotland sufficient evidence, of the facts stated.

9 Provisions supplementary to Title VII of 1968 Convention

(1) The provisions of Title VII of the 1968 Convention and, apart from Article 54B, of Title VII of the Lugano Convention (relationship between the Convention in question and other conventions to which Contracting States are or may become parties) shall have effect in relation to –

(a) any statutory provision, whenever passed or made, implementing any such other convention in the United Kingdom; and

(b) any rule of law so far as it has the effect of so implementing any such other convention,

as they have effect in relation to that other convention itself.

(1A) Any question arising as to whether it is the Lugano Convention or any of the Brussels Conventions which applies in the circumstances of a particular case falls to be determined in accordance with the provisions of Article 54B of the Lugano Convention.

(2) Her Majesty may by Order in Council declare a provision of a convention entered into by the United Kingdom to be a provision whereby the United Kingdom assumed an obligation of a kind provided for in Article 59 (which allows a Contracting State to agree with a third State to withhold recognition in certain cases from a judgment given by a court in another Contracting State which took jurisdiction on one of the grounds mentioned in the second paragraph of Article 3).

10 Allocation within United Kingdom of jurisdiction with respect to trusts and consumer contracts

(1) The provisions of this section have effect for the purpose of allocating within the United Kingdom jurisdiction in certain proceedings in respect of which the 1968 Convention or the Lugano Convention confers jurisdiction on the courts of the United Kingdom generally and to which section 16 does not apply.

(2) Any proceedings which by virtue of Article 5(6) (trusts) are brought in the United Kingdom shall be brought in the courts of the part of the United Kingdom in which the trust is domiciled.

(3) Any proceedings which by virtue of the first paragraph of Article 14 (consumer contracts) are brought in the United Kingdom by a consumer on the ground that he is himself domiciled there shall be brought in the courts of the part of the United Kingdom in which he is domiciled.

11 Proof and admissibility of certain judgments and related documents

(1) For the purposes of the 1968 Convention or the Lugano Convention –

(a) a document, duly authenticated, which purports to be a copy of a judgment given by a court of a Contracting State other than the United Kingdom shall without further proof be deemed to be a true copy, unless the contrary is shown; and

(b) the original or a copy of any such document as is mentioned in Article 46(2) or 47 (supporting documents to be produced by a party seeking recognition or enforcement of a judgment) shall be evidence, and in Scotland sufficient evidence, of any matter to which it relates.

(2) A document purporting to be a copy of a judgment given by any such court as is mentioned in subsection (1)(a) is duly authenticated for the purposes of this section if it purports –

(a) to bear the seal of that court; or

(b) to be certified by any person in his capacity as a judge or officer of that court to be a true copy of a judgment given by that court.

(3) Nothing in this section shall prejudice the admission in evidence of any document which is admissible apart from this section.

12 Provision for issue of copies of, and certificates in connection with, United Kingdom judgments

Rules of court may make provision for enabling any interested party wishing to secure under the 1968 Convention or the Lugano Convention the recognition or enforcement in another Contracting State of a judgment given by a court in the United Kingdom to obtain, subject to any conditions specified in the rules –

(a) a copy of the judgment; and

(b) a certificate giving particulars relating to the judgment and the proceedings in which it was given.

13 Modifications to cover authentic instruments and court settlements

(1) Her Majesty may by Order in Council provide that –

(a) any provision of this Act relating to the recognition or enforcement in the United Kingdom or elsewhere of judgments to which the 1968 Convention or the Lugano Convention applies; and

(b) any other statutory provision, whenever passed or made, so relating, shall apply, with such modifications as may be specified in the Order, in relation to documents and settlements within Title IV of the 1968 Convention or, as the case may be, Title IV of the Lugano Convention (authentic instruments and court settlements enforceable in the same manner as judgments) as if they were judgments to which the Convention in question applies.

(2) An Order in Council under this section may make different provision in relation to different descriptions of documents and settlements.

(3) Any Order in Council under this section shall be subject to annulment in pursuance of a resolution of either House of Parliament.

14 Modifications consequential on revision of the Convention

(1) If at any time it appears to Her Majesty in Council that Her Majesty's Government in the United Kingdom have agreed to a revision of the Lugano Convention or any of the Brussels Conventions, including in particular any revision connected with the accession of the Lugano Convention or the 1968 Convention of one or more further states, Her Majesty may by order in Council make such modifications of this Act or any other statutory provision, whenever passed or made, as Her Majesty considers appropriate in consequence of the revision.

(2) An Order in Council under this section shall not be made unless a draft of the Order has been laid before Parliament and approved by a resolution of each House of Parliament.

(3) In this section 'revision' means an omission from, addition to or alteration of the Lugano Convention or any of the Brussels Conventions and includes replacement of the Lugano Convention or any of the Brussels Conventions to any extent by another convention, protocol or other description of international agreement.

15 Interpretation of Part I and consequential amendments

(1) In this Part, unless the context otherwise requires –

'judgment' has the meaning given by Article 25;

'maintenance order' means a maintenance judgment within the meaning of the 1968 Convention or, as the case may be, Title IV of the Lugano Convention;

'payer', in relation to a maintenance order, means the person liable to make the payments for which the order provides;

'prescribed' means prescribed by rules of court.

(2) References in this Part to a judgment registered under section 4 or 5 include, to the extent of its registration, references to a judgment so registered to a limited extent only.

(3) Anything authorised or required by the 1968 Convention, the Lugano Convention or this Part to be done by, to or before a particular magistrates' court may be done by, to or before any magistrates' court acting for the same petty sessions area ... as that court.

(4) The enactments specified in Part 1 of Schedule 12 shall have effect with the amendments specified there, being amendments consequential on this Part.

PART II

JURISDICTION, AND RECOGNITION AND ENFORCEMENT OF JUDGMENTS, WITHIN UNITED KINGDOM

16   Allocation within United Kingdom of jurisdiction in certain civil proceedings

(1) The provisions set out in Schedule 4 (which contains a modified version of Title II of the 1968 Convention) shall have effect for determining, for each part of the United Kingdom, whether the courts of law of that part, or any particular court of law in that part, have or has jurisdiction in proceedings where –

(a) the subject-matter of the proceedings is within the scope of the 1968 Convention as determined by Article 1 (whether or not that or any other Convention has effect in relation to the proceedings); and

(b) the defendants or defender is domiciled in the United Kingdom or the proceedings are of a kind mentioned in Article 16 of the 1968 Convention (exclusive jurisdiction regardless of domicile).

(2) In Schedule 4 modification of Title II of the 1968 Convention are indicated as follows –

(a) modifications by way of omission are indicated by dots; and

(b) within each Article words resulting from modifications by way of addition or substitution are printed in heavy type.

(3) In determining any question as to the meaning or effect of any provision contained in Schedule 4 –

(a) regard shall be had to any relevant principles laid down by the European Court in connection with Title II of the 1968 Convention and to any relevant decision of that court as to the meaning or effect of any provision of that Title; and

(b) without prejudice to the generality of paragraph (a), the reports mentioned in section 3(3) may be considered and shall, so far as relevant, be given such weight as is appropriate in the circumstances.

(4) The provisions of this section and Schedule 4 shall have effect subject to the 1968 Convention and the Lugano Convention and to the provisions of section 17.

(5) In section 15(1)(a) of the Maintenance Orders Act 1950 (domestic proceedings in which initial process may be served in another part of the United Kingdom), after sub-paragraph (v) there shall be added –

'(vi) Article 5(2) of Schedule 4 to the Civil Jurisdiction and Judgments Act 1982; or'.

17 Exclusion of certain proceedings from Schedule 4

(1) Schedule 4 shall not apply to proceedings of any description listed in Schedule 5 or to proceedings in Scotland under any enactment which confers jurisdiction on a Scottish court in respect of a specific subject-matter on specific grounds.

(2) Her Majesty may by Order in Council –

(a) add to the list in Schedule 5 any description of proceedings in any part of the United Kingdom; and

(b) remove from that list any description of proceedings in any part of the United Kingdom (whether included in the list as originally enacted or added by virtue of this subsection).

(3) An Order in Council under subsection (2) –

(a) may make different provisions for different descriptions of proceedings, for the same description of proceedings in different courts or for different parts of the United Kingdom; and

(b) may contain such transitional and other incidental provisions as appear to Her Majesty to be appropriate.

(4) An Order in Council under subsection (2) shall not be made unless a draft of the Order has been laid before Parliament and approved by a resolution of each House of Parliament.

18 Enforcement of United Kingdom judgments in other parts of United Kingdom

(1) In relation to any judgment to which this section applies –

(a) Schedule 6 shall have effect for the purpose of enabling any money provisions contained in the judgment to be enforced in a part of the United Kingdom other than the part in which the judgment was given; and

(b) Schedule 7 shall have effect for the purpose of enabling any non-money provisions so contained to be enforced.

(2) In this section 'judgment' means any of the following (references to the giving of a judgment being construed accordingly) –

(a) any judgment or order (by whatever named called) given or made by a court of law in the United Kingdom;

(b) any judgment or order not within paragraph (a) which has been entered in England and Wales or Northern Ireland in the High Court or county court;

(c) any document which in Scotland has been registered for execution in the Books of Council and Session or in the sheriff court books kept for any sheriffdom;

(d) any award or order made by a tribunal in any part of the United Kingdom which is enforceable in that part without an order of a court of law;

(e) an arbitration award which has become enforceable in the part of the United Kingdom in which it was given in the same manner as a judgment given by a court of law in that part;

and, subject to the following provisions of this section, this section applies to all such judgments.

(3) Subject to subsection (4), this section does not apply to –

(a) a judgment given in proceedings in a magistrates' court in England and Wales or Northern Ireland;

(b) a judgment given in proceedings other than civil proceedings;

(ba) a judgment given in the exercise of jurisdiction in relation to insolvency law, within the meaning of section 426 of the Insolvency Act 1986;

(c) a judgment given in proceedings relating to – ...

(iii) the obtaining of title to administer the estate of a deceased person.

(4) This section applies, whatever the nature of the proceedings in which it is made, to –

(a) a decree issued under section 13 of the Court of Exchequer (Scotland) Act 1856 (recovery of certain rent-charges and penalties by process of the Court of Session);

(b) an order which is enforceable in the same manner as a judgment of the High Court in England and Wales by virtue of section 16 of the Contempt of Court Act 1981 or section 140 of the Supreme Court Act 1981 (which relate to fines for contempt of court and forfeiture of recognisances).

(4A) This section does not apply as respects ... the enforcement in England and Wales of orders made by the Court of Session under or for the purposes of Part I of the Criminal Justice (Scotland) Act 1987.

(5) This section does not apply to so much of any judgment as –

(a) is an order to which section 16 of the Maintenance Orders Act 1950 applies (and is therefore an order for whose enforcement in another part of the United Kingdom provision is made by Part II of that Act);

(b) concerns that status or legal capacity of an individual;

(c) relates to the management of the affairs of a person not capable of managing his own affairs;

(d) is a provisional (including protective) measure other than an order for the making of an interim payment;

and except where otherwise stated references to a judgment to which this section applies are to such a judgment exclusive of any such provisions.

(6) The following are within subsection (5)(b), but without prejudice to the generality of that provision –

(a) a decree of judicial separation or of separation;

(b) any order which is a Part I order for the purposes of the Family Law Act 1986.

(7) This section does not apply to a judgment of a court outside the United Kingdom which falls to be treated for the purposes of its

enforcement as a judgment of a court of law in the United Kingdom by virtue of registration under Part II of the Administration of Justice Act 1920, Part I of the Foreign Judgments (Reciprocal Enforcement) Act 1933, Part I of the Maintenance Orders (Reciprocal Enforcement) Act 1972 or section 4 or 5 of this Act.

(8) A judgment to which this section applies, other than a judgment within paragraph (e) of subsection (2), shall not be enforced in another part of the United Kingdom except by way of registration under Schedule 6 or 7.

19 Recognition of United Kingdom judgments in other parts of United Kingdom

(1) A judgment to which this section applies given in one part of the United Kingdom shall not be refused recognition in another part of the United Kingdom solely on the ground that, in relation to that judgment, the court which gave it was not a court of competent jurisdiction according to the rules of private international law in force in that other part.

(2) Subject to subsection (3), this section applies to any judgment to which section 18 applies.

(3) This section does not apply to –

(a) the documents mentioned in paragraph (c) of the definition of 'judgment' in section 18(2);

(b) the awards and orders mentioned in paragraphs (d) and (e) of that definition;

(c) the decrees and orders referred to in section 18(4).

PART IV

MISCELLANEOUS PROVISIONS

24 Interim relief and protective measures in cases of doubtful jurisdiction

(1) Any power of a court in England and Wales or Northern Ireland to grant interim relief pending trial or pending the determination of an appeal shall extend to a case where –

(a) the issue to be tried, or which is the subject of the appeal, relates to the jurisdiction of the court to entertain the proceedings; or

(b) the proceedings involve the reference of any matter to the European Court under the 1971 Protocol. ...

(3) Subsections (1) and (2) shall not be construed as restricting any power to grant relief of protective measures which a court may have apart from this section.

25 Interim relief in England and Wales and Northern Ireland in the absence of substantive proceedings

(1) The High Court in England and Wales or Northern Ireland shall have power to grant interim relief where –

(a) proceedings have been or are to be commenced in a Brussels or Lugano Contracting State other than the United Kingdom or in a part of the United Kingdom other than that in which the High Court in question exercises jurisdiction; and

(b) they are or will be proceedings whose subject-matter is within the scope of the 1968 Convention as determined by Article 1 (whether or not that or any other Convention has effect in relation to the proceedings).

(2) On an application for any interim relief under subsection (1) the court may refuse to grant that relief if, in the opinion of the court, the fact that the court has no jurisdiction apart from this section in relation to the subject-matter of the proceedings in question makes it inexpedient for the court to grant it.

(3) Her Majesty may by Order in Council extend the power to grant interim relief conferred by subsection (1) so as to make it exercisable in relation to proceedings of any of the following descriptions, namely –

(a) proceedings commenced or to be commended otherwise than in a Brussels or Lugano Contracting State;

(b) proceedings whose subject-matter is not within the scope of the 1968 Convention as determined by Article 1;

(c) arbitration proceedings.

(4) An Order in Council under subsection (3) –

(a) may confer power to grant only specified descriptions of interim relief;

(b) may make different provision for different classes of proceedings, for proceedings pending in different countries or courts outside the United Kingdom or in different parts of the United Kingdom, and for other different circumstances; and

(c) may impose conditions or restrictions on the exercise of any power conferred by the Order.

(5) An Order in Council under subsection (3) which confers power to grant interim relief in relation to arbitration proceedings may provide for the repeal of any provision of section 12(6) of the Arbitration Act 1950 or section 21(1) of the Arbitration Act (Northern Ireland) 1937 to the extent that it is superseded by the provisions of the Order.

(6) Any Order in Council under subsection (3) shall be subject to annulment in pursuance of a resolution of either House of Parliament.

(7) In this section 'interim relief', in relation to the High Court in England and Wales or Northern Ireland, means interim relief of any kind which that court has power to grant in proceedings relating to matters within its jurisdiction, other than –

(a) a warrant for the arrest of property; or

(b) provision for obtaining evidence.

26 Security in Admiralty proceedings in England and Wales or Northern Ireland in case of stay, etc

(1) Where in England and Wales or Northern Ireland a court stays or dismisses Admiralty proceedings on the ground that the dispute in question should be submitted to arbitration or to the determination of the courts of another part of the United Kingdom or of an overseas country, the court may, if in those proceedings property has been arrested or bail or other security has been given to prevent or obtain release from arrest –

(a) order that the property arrested be retained as security for the satisfaction of any award or judgment which –

(i) is given in respect of the dispute in the arbitration or legal proceedings in favour of which those proceedings are stayed or dismissed; and

(ii) is enforceable in England and Wales or, as the case may be, in Northern Ireland; or

(b) order that the stay or dismissal of those proceedings be conditional on the provision of equivalent security for the satisfaction of any such award or judgment.

(2) Where a court makes an order under subsection (1), it may attach such conditions to the order as it thinks fit, in particular conditions with respect to the institution or prosecution of the relevant arbitration or legal proceedings.

(3) Subject to any provision made by rules of court and to any necessary modifications, the same law and practice shall apply in relation to property retained in pursuance of an order made by a court under subsection (1) as would apply if it were held for the purposes of proceedings in that court.

30 Proceedings in England and Wales or Northern Ireland for torts to immovable property

(1) The jurisdiction of any court in England and Wales or Northern Ireland to entertain proceedings for trespass to, or any other tort affecting, immovable property shall extend to cases in which the property in question is situated outside that part of the United Kingdom unless the proceedings are principally concerned with a question of the title to, or the right to possession of, that property.

(2) Subsection (1) has effect subject to the 1968 Convention and the Lugano Convention and to the provisions set out in Schedule 4.

31 Overseas judgments given against states, etc

(1) A judgment given by a court of an overseas country against a state other than the United Kingdom or the state to which that court belongs shall be recognised and enforced in the United Kingdom if, and only if –

(a) it would be so recognised and enforced if it had not been given against a state; and

(b) that court would have had jurisdiction in the matter if it had applied rules corresponding to those applicable to such matters in the United Kingdom in accordance with sections 2 to 11 of the State Immunity Act 1978.

(2) References in subsection (1) to a judgment given against a state include references to judgments of any of the following descriptions given in relation to a state –

(a) judgments against the government, or a department of the government, of the state but not (except as mentioned in paragraph (c)) judgments against an entity which is distinct from the executive organs of government;

(b) judgments against the sovereign or head of state in his public capacity;

(c) judgments against any such separate entity as is mentioned in paragraph (a) given in proceedings relating to anything done by it in the exercise of the sovereign authority of the state.

(3) Nothing in subsection (1) shall affect the recognition or enforcement in the United Kingdom of a judgment to which Part I of the Foreign Judgments (Reciprocal Enforcement) Act 1933 applies by virtue of section 4 of the Carriage of Goods by Road Act 1965, section 17(4) of the Nuclear Installations Act 1965, section 13(3) of the Merchant Shipping (Oil Pollution) Act 1971, section 6 of the International Transport Conventions Act 1983 or section 5 of the Carriage of Passengers by Road Act 1974.

(4) Sections 12, 13 and 14(3) and (4) of the State Immunity Act 1978 (service of process and procedural privileges) shall apply to proceedings for the recognition or enforcement in the United Kingdom of a judgment given by a court of an overseas country (whether or not that judgment is within subsection (1) of this section) as they apply to other proceedings.

(5) In this section 'state', in the case of a federal state, includes any of its constituent territories.

32 Overseas judgments given in proceedings brought in breach of agreement for settlement of disputes

(1) Subject to the following provisions of this section, a judgment given by a court of an overseas country in any proceedings shall not be recognised or enforced in the United Kingdom if –

(a) the bringing of those proceedings in that court was contrary to an agreement under which the dispute in question was to be settled otherwise than by proceedings in the courts of that country; and

(b) those proceedings were not brought in that court by, or with the agreement of, the person against whom the judgment was given; and

(c) that person did not counterclaim in the proceedings or otherwise submit to the jurisdiction of that court.

(2) Subsection (1) does not apply where the agreement referred to in paragraph (a) of that subsection was illegal, void or unenforceable or was incapable of being performed for reasons not attributable to

the fault of the party bringing the proceedings in which the judgment was given.

(3) In determining whether a judgment given by a court of an overseas country should be recognised or enforced in the United Kingdom, a court in the United Kingdom shall not be bound by any decision of the overseas court relating to any of the matters mentioned in subsection (1) or (2).

(4) Nothing in subsection (1) shall affect the recognition or enforcement in the United Kingdom of –

(a) a judgment which is required to be recognised or enforced there under the 1968 Convention or the Lugano Convention;

(b) a judgment to which Part I of the Foreign Judgments (Reciprocal Enforcement) Act 1933 applies by virtue of section 4 of the Carriage of Goods by Road Act 1965, section 17(4) of the Nuclear Installations Act 1965, section 13(3) of the Merchant Shipping (Oil Pollution) Act 1971, section 6 of the International Transport Conventions Act 1983, section 5 of the Carriage of Passengers by Road Act 1974 or section 6(4) of the Merchant Shipping Act 1974.

33 Certain steps not to amount to submission to jurisdiction of overseas court

(1) For the purposes of determining whether a judgment given by a court of an overseas country should be recognised or enforced in England and Wales or Northern Ireland, the person against whom the judgment was given shall not be regarded as having submitted to the jurisdiction of the court by reason only of the fact that he appeared (conditionally or otherwise) in the proceedings for all or any one or more of the following purposes, namely –

(a) to contest the jurisdiction of the court;

(b) to ask the court to dismiss or stay the proceedings on the ground that the dispute in question should be submitted to arbitration or to the determination of the courts of another country;

(c) to protect, or obtain the release of, property seized or threatened with seizure in the proceedings.

(2) Nothing in this section shall affect the recognition or enforcement in England and Wales or Northern Ireland of a judgment which is

required to be recognised or enforced there under the 1968 Convention or the Lugano Convention.

34 Certain judgments a bar to further proceedings on the same cause of action

No proceedings may be brought by a person in England and Wales or Northern Ireland on a cause of action in respect of which a judgment has been given in his favour in proceedings between the same parties, or their privies, in a court in another part of the United Kingdom or in a court of an overseas country, unless that judgment is not enforceable or entitled to recognition in England and Wales or, as the case may be, in Northern Ireland.

35 Minor amendments relating to overseas judgments

(1) The Foreign Judgments (Reciprocal Enforcement) Act 1933 shall have effect with the amendments specified in Schedule 10, being amendments whose main purpose is to enable Part I of that Act to be applied to judgments of courts other than superior courts, to judgments providing for interim payments and to certain arbitration awards. ...

37 Minor amendments relating to maintenance orders

(1) The enactments specified in Schedule II shall have effect with the amendments specified there, being amendments whose main purpose is as follows –

Part I – to extend certain enforcement provisions to lump sum maintenance orders;

Part II – to provide for the recovery of interest according to the law of the country of origin in the case of maintenance orders made in other jurisdictions and registered in the High Court.

Part III – to extend the Maintenance Orders (Reciprocal Enforcement) Act 1972 to cases where the payer under a maintenance order is not resident within the jurisdiction but has assets there.

39 Application of provisions corresponding to 1968 Convention in relation to certain territories

(1) Her Majesty may by Order in Council make provision corresponding to the provision made by the 1968 Convention as

between the Contracting States to that Convention, with such modifications as appear to Her Majesty to be appropriate, for regulating, as between the United Kingdom and any of the territories mentioned in subsection (2), the jurisdiction of courts and the recognition and enforcement of judgments.

(2) The territories referred to in subsection (1) are –

(a) the Isle of Man;

(b) any of the Channel Islands;

(c) any colony.

(3) An Order in Council under this section may contain such supplementary and incidental provisions as appear to Her Majesty to be necessary or expedient, including in particular provisions corresponding to or applying any of the provisions of Part I with such modifications as may be specified in the Order.

(4) Any Order in Council under this section shall be subject to annulment in pursuance of a resolution of either House of Parliament.

PART V

SUPPLEMENTARY AND GENERAL PROVISIONS

41 Domicile of individuals

(1) Subject to Article 52 (which contains provisions for determining whether a party is domiciled in a Contracting State), the following provisions of this section determine, for the purposes of the 1968 Convention, the Lugano Convention and this Act, whether an individual is domiciled in the United Kingdom or in a particular part of, or place in, the United Kingdom or in a state other than a Contracting State.

(2) An individual is domiciled in the United Kingdom if and only if –

(a) he is resident in the United Kingdom; and

(b) the nature and circumstances of his residence indicate that he has a substantial connection with the United Kingdom.

(3) Subject to subsection (5), an individual is domiciled in a particular part of the United Kingdom if and only if –

(a) he is resident in that part; and

(b) the nature and circumstances of his residence indicate that he has a substantial connection with that part.

(4) An individual is domiciled in a particular place in the United Kingdom if and only if he –

(a) is domiciled in the part of the United Kingdom in which that part is situated; and

(b) is resident in that place.

(5) An individual who is domiciled in the United Kingdom but in whose case the requirements of subsection (3)(b) are not satisfied in relation to any particular part of the United Kingdom shall be treated as domiciled in the part of the United Kingdom in which he is resident.

(6) In the case of an individual who –

(a) is resident in the United Kingdom, or in a particular part of the United Kingdom; and

(b) has been so resident for the last three months or more,

the requirements of subsection (2)(b) or, as the case may be, subsection (3)(b) shall be presumed to be fulfilled unless the contrary is proved.

(7) An individual is domiciled in a state other than a Contracting State if and only if –

(a) he is resident in that state; and

(b) the nature and circumstances of his residence indicate that he has a substantial connection with that state.

42 Domicile and seat of corporation of association

(1) For the purposes of this Act the seat of a corporation or association (as determined by this section) shall be treated as its domicile.

(2) The following provisions of this section determine where a corporation or association has its seat –

(a) for the purpose of Article 53 (which for the purposes of the 1968 Convention or, as the case may be, the Lugano Convention equates the domicile of such a body with its seat); and

(b) for the purposes of this Act other than the provisions mentioned in section 43(1)(b) and (c).

(3) A corporation or association has its seat in the United Kingdom if and only if –

(a) it was incorporated or formed under the law of a part of the United Kingdom and has its registered office or some other official address in the United Kingdom; or

(b) its central management and control is exercised in the United Kingdom.

(4) A corporation or association has its seat in a particular part of the United Kingdom if and only if it has its seat in the United Kingdom and –

(a) it has its registered office or some other official address in that part; or

(b) its central management and control is exercised in that part; or

(c) it has a place of business in that part.

(5) A corporation or association has its seat in a particular place in the United Kingdom if and only if it has its seat in the part of the United Kingdom in which that place is situated and –

(a) it has its registered office or some other official address in that place; or

(b) its central management and control is exercised in that place; or

(c) it has a place of business in that place.

(6) Subject to subsection (7), a corporation or association has its seat in a state other than the United Kingdom if and only if –

(a) it was incorporated or formed under the law of that state and has its registered office or some other official address there; or

(b) its central management and control is exercised in that state.

(7) A corporation or association shall not be regarded as having its seat in a Contracting State other than the United Kingdom if it is shown that the courts of that state would not regard it as having its seat there.

(8) In this section –

'business' includes any activity carried on by a corporation or association, and 'place of business' shall be construed accordingly;

'official address', in relation to a corporation or association, means an address which it is required by law to register, notify or maintain for the purpose of receiving notices or other communications.

43   Seat of corporation or association for purposes of Article 16(2) and related provisions

(1) The following provisions of this section determine where a corporation or association has its seat for the purposes of –

(a) Article 16(2) of the 1968 Convention or of the Lugano Convention (which confers exclusive jurisdiction over proceedings relating to the formation or dissolution of such bodies, or to the decisions of their organs);

(b) Articles 5A and 16(2) in Schedule 4; and

(c) Rules 2(12) and 4(1)(b) in Schedule 8.

(2) A corporation or association has its seat in the United Kingdom if and only if –

(a) it was incorporated or formed under the law of a part of the United Kingdom; or

(b) its central management and control is exercised in the United Kingdom.

(3) A corporation or association has its seat in a particular part of the United Kingdom if and only if it has its seat in the United Kingdom and –

(a) subject to subsection (5), it was incorporated or formed under the law of that part; or

(b) being incorporated or formed under the laws of a state other than the United Kingdom, its central management and control is exercised in that part.

(4) A corporation or association has its seat in a particular place in Scotland if and only if it has its seat in Scotland and –

(a) it has its registered office or some other official address in that place; or

(b) it has no registered office or other official address in Scotland, but its central management and control is exercised in that place.

(5) A corporation or association incorporated or formed under –

(a) an enactment forming part of the law or more than one part of the United Kingdom; or

(b) an instrument having effect in the domestic law of more than one part of the United Kingdom,

shall, if it has a registered office, be taken to have its seat in the part of the United Kingdom in which that office is situated, and not in any other part of the United Kingdom.

(6) Subject to subsection (7), a corporation or association has its seat in a Contracting State other than the United Kingdom if and only if –

(a) it was incorporated or formed under the law of that State; or

(b) its central management and control is exercised in that state.

(7) A corporation or association shall not be regarded as having its seat in a Contracting State other than the United Kingdom if –

(a) it has its seat in the United Kingdom by virtue of subsection (2)(a); or

(b) it is shown that the courts of that other state would not regard it for the purposes of Article 16(2) as having its seat there.

(8) In this section 'official address' has the same meaning as in section 42.

44 Persons deemed to be domiciled in the United Kingdom for certain purposes

(1) This section applies to –

(a) proceedings within Section 3 of Title II of the 1968 Convention or Section 3 of Title II of the Lugano Convention (insurance contracts), and

(b) proceedings within Section 4 of Title II of either of those Conventions (consumer contracts).

(2) A person who, for the purposes of proceedings to which this section applies arising out of the operations of a branch, agency or other establishment in the United Kingdom, is deemed for the

purposes of the 1968 Convention or, as the case may be, of the Lugano Convention to be domiciled in the United Kingdom by virtue of –

(a) Article 8, second paragraph (insurers); or

(b) Article 13, second paragraph (suppliers of goods, services or credit to consumers),

shall, for the purposes of those proceedings, be treated for the purposes of this Act as so domiciled and as domiciled in the part of the United Kingdom in which the branch, agency or establishment in question is situated.

45 Domicile of trusts

(1) The following provisions of this section determine, for the purposes of the 1968 Convention, the Lugano Convention and this Act, where a trust is domiciled.

(2) A trust is domiciled in the United Kingdom if and only if it is by virtue of subsection (3) domiciled in a part of the United Kingdom.

(3) A trust is domiciled in a part of the United Kingdom if and only if the system of law of that part is the system of law with which the trust has its closest and most real connection.

46 Domicile and seat of the Crown

(1) For the purposes of this Act the seat of the Crown (as determined by this section) shall be treated as its domicile.

(2) The following provisions of this section determine where the Crown has its seat –

(a) for the purposes of the 1968 Convention and the Lugano Convention (in each of which Article 53 equates the domicile of a legal person with its seat); and

(b) for the purposes of this Act.

(3) Subject to the provisions of any Order in Council for the time being in force under subsection (4) –

(a) the Crown in right of Her Majesty's government in the United Kingdom has its seat in every part of, and every place in, the United Kingdom; and

(b) the Crown in right of Her Majesty's government in Northern Ireland has its seat in, and in every place in, Northern Ireland.

(4) Her Majesty may by Order in Council provide that, in the case of proceedings of any specified description against the Crown in right of Her Majesty's government in the United Kingdom, the Crown shall be treated for the purposes of the 1968 Convention, the Lugano Convention and this Act as having its seat in, and in every place in, a specified part of the United Kingdom and not in any other part of the United Kingdom.

(5) An Order in Council under subsection (4) may frame a description of proceedings in any way, and in particular may do so by reference to the government department or officer of the Crown against which or against whom they fall to be instituted.

(6) Any Order in Council made under this section shall be subject to annulment in pursuance of a resolution of either House of Parliament.

(7) Nothing in this section applies to the Crown otherwise than in right of Her Majesty's government in the United Kingdom or Her Majesty's government in Northern Ireland.

47 Modifications occasioned by decisions of European Court as to meaning or effect of Conventions

(1) Her Majesty may by Order in Council –

(a) make such provision as Her Majesty considers appropriate for the purpose of bringing the law of any part of the United Kingdom into accord with the Brussels Conventions as affected by any principle laid down by the European Court in connection with the Brussels Conventions or by any decision of that court as to the meaning or effect of any provision of the Brussels Conventions; or

(b) make such modifications of Schedule 4 or Schedule 8, or of any other statutory provision affected by any provision of either of those Schedules, as Her Majesty considers appropriate in view of any principle laid down by the European Court in connection with Title II of the 1968 Convention or of any decision of that court as to the meaning or effect of any provision of that Title.

(2) The provision which may be made by virtue of paragraph (a) of subsection (1) includes such modifications of this Act or any other

statutory provision, whenever passed or made, as Her Majesty considers appropriate for the purpose mentioned in that paragraph.

(3) The modifications which may be made by virtue of paragraph (b) of subsection (1) include modifications designed to produce divergence between any provision of Schedule 4 or Schedule 8 and a corresponding provision of Title II of the 1968 Convention as affected by any such principle or decision as is mentioned in that paragraph.

(4) An Order in Council under this section shall not be made unless a draft of the Order has been laid before Parliament and approved by a resolution of each House of Parliament.

48   Matters for which rules of court may provide

(1) Rules of court may make provisions for regulating the procedure to be followed in any court in connection with any provision of this Act, the Lugano Convention or the Brussels Conventions.

(2) Rules of court may make provision as to the manner in which and the conditions subject to which a certificate or judgment registered in any court under any provision of this Act may be enforced, including provision for enabling the court or, in Northern Ireland the Enforcement of Judgments Office, subject to any conditions specified in the rules, to give directions about such matters.

(3) Without prejudice to the generality of subsections (1) and (2), the power to make rules of court for magistrates' courts, and in Northern Ireland the power to make Judgment Enforcement Rules, shall include power to make such provision as the rule-making authority considers necessary or expedient for the purposes of the provisions of the Lugano Convention, the Brussels Convention and this Act relating to maintenance proceedings and the recognition and enforcement of maintenance orders, and shall in particular include power to make provisions as to any of the following matters –

(a) authorising the service in another Contracting State of process issued by or for the purposes of a magistrates' court and the service and execution in England and Wales or Northern Ireland of process issued in another Contracting State;

(b) requesting courts in other parts of the United Kingdom or in other Contracting States to take evidence there for the purposes of proceedings in England and Wales or Northern Ireland;

(c) the taking of evidence in England and Wales or Northern Ireland in response to similar requests received from such courts;

(d) the circumstances in which and the conditions subject to which any powers conferred under paragraphs (a) to (c) are to be exercised;

(e) the admission in evidence, subject to such conditions as may be prescribed in the rules, of statements contained in documents purporting to be made or authenticated by a court in another part of the United Kingdom or in another Contracting State, or by a judge or official of such a court, which purport –

(i) to set out or summarise evidence given in proceedings in that court or to be documents received in evidence in such proceedings or copies of such documents; or

(ii) to set out or summarise evidence taken for the purposes of proceedings in England and Wales or Northern Ireland, whether or not in response to any such request as is mentioned in paragraph (b); or

(iii) to record information relating to the payments made under an order of that court;

(f) the circumstances and manner in which a magistrates' court may or must vary or revoke a maintenance order registered in that court, cancel the registration of, or refrain from enforcing, such an order or transmit such an order for enforcement in another part of the United Kingdom;

(g) the cases and manner in which courts in other parts of the United Kingdom or in other Contracting States are to be informed of orders made, or other things done, by or for the purposes of a magistrates' court;

(h) the circumstances and manner in which a magistrates' court may communicate for other purposes with such courts;

(i) the giving of notice of such matters as may be prescribed in the rules to such persons as may be so prescribed and the manner in which such notice is to be given.

(4) Nothing in this section shall be taken as derogating from the generality of any power to make rules of court conferred by any other enactment.

49 Saving for powers to stay, sist, strike out or dismiss proceedings

Nothing in this Act shall prevent any court in the United Kingdom from staying, sisting, striking out or dismissing any proceedings before it, on the ground of forum non conveniens or otherwise, where to do so is not inconsistent with the 1968 Convention or, as the case may be, the Lugano Convention.

50 Interpretation: general

In this Act, unless the context otherwise requires –

'the Accession Convention', 'the 1982 Accession Convention' and 'the 1989 Accession Convention' have the meaning given by section 1(1);

'Article' and references to sub-divisions of numbered Articles are to be construed in accordance with section 1(2)(b);

'association' means an unincorporated body of persons;

'Brussels Contracting State' has the meaning given by section 1(3);

'Brussels Conventions' has the meaning given by section 1(1);

'Contracting State' has the meaning given by section 1(3);

'the 1968 Convention' has the meaning given by section 1(1), and references to that Convention and to provisions of it are to be construed in accordance with section 1(2)(a);

'corporation' means a body corporate, and includes a partnership subsisting under the law of Scotland;

'court', without more, includes a tribunal;

'court of law', in relation to the United Kingdom, means any of the following courts, namely –

(a) the House of Lords,

(b) in England and Wales or Northern Ireland, the Court of Appeal, the High Court, the Crown Court, a county court and a magistrates' court,

(c) in Scotland, the Court of Session and a sheriff court;

'the Crown' is to be construed in accordance with section 51(2);

'enactment' includes an enactment comprised in Northern Ireland legislation;

'judgment', subject to sections 15(1) and 18(2) and to paragraph 1 of Schedules 6 and 7, means any judgment or order (by whatever name called) given or made by a court in any civil proceedings;

'Lugano Contracting State' has the meaning given by section 1(3);

'the Lugano Convention' has the meaning given by section 1(1);

'magistrates' court', in relation to Northern Ireland, means a court of summary jurisdiction;

'modifications' includes additions, omissions and alterations;

'overseas country' means any country or territory outside the United Kingdom;

'part of the United Kingdom' means England and Wales, Scotland or Northern Ireland;

'the 1971 Protocol' has the meaning given by section 1(1), and references to that Protocol and to provisions of it are to be construed in accordance with section 1(2)(a);

'rules of court', in relation to any court, means rules, orders or regulations made by the authority having power to make rules, orders or regulations regulating the procedure of that court, and includes –

(a) in Scotland, Acts of Sederunt;

(b) in Northern Ireland, Judgment Enforcement Rules;

'statutory provision' means any provision contained in an Act, or in any Northern Ireland legislation, or in –

(a) subordinate legislation (as defined in section 21(1) of the Interpretation Act 1978); or

(b) any instrument of a legislative character made under any Northern Ireland legislation;

'tribunal' –

(a) means a tribunal of any description other than a court of law;

(b) in relation to an overseas country, includes, as regards matters relating to maintenance within the meaning of the 1968 Convention, any authority having power to give, enforce, vary or revoke a maintenance order.

51 Application to Crown

(1) This Act binds the Crown.

(2) In this section and elsewhere in this Act references to the Crown

do not include references to Her Majesty in Her private capacity or to Her Majesty in right to Her Duchy of Lancaster or to the Duke of Cornwall.

52 Extent

(1) This Act extends to Northern Ireland.

(2) Without prejudice to the power conferred by section 39, Her Majesty may by Order in Council direct that all or any of the provisions of this Act apart from that section shall extend, subject to such modifications as may be specified in the Order, to any of the following territories, that is to say –

  (a) the Isle of Man;
  (b) any of the Channel Islands;
  (c) any colony.

SCHEDULE 1

CONVENTION ON JURISDICTION AND THE ENFORCEMENT OF JUDGMENTS IN CIVIL AND COMMERCIAL MATTERS

Preamble

The High Contracting Parties to the Treaty establishing the European Economic Community.

Desiring to implement the provisions of Article 220 of that Treaty by virtue of which they undertook to secure the simplification of formalities governing the reciprocal recognition and enforcement of judgments of courts or tribunals;

Anxious to strengthen in the Community the legal protection of persons therein established;

Considering that it is necessary for this purpose to determine the international jurisdiction of their courts, to facilitate recognition and to introduce an expeditious procedure for securing the enforcement of judgments, authentic instruments and court settlements;

Have decided to conclude this Convention and to this end have designated as their Plenipotentiaries: ...

Who, meeting within the Council, having exchanged their Full Powers, found in good and due form.

Have agreed as follows:

TITLE I

SCOPE

ARTICLE 1

This Convention shall apply in civil and commercial matters whatever the nature of the court or tribunal. It shall not extend, in particular, to revenue, customs or administrative matters.

The Convention shall not apply to:

(1) the status or legal capacity of natural persons, rights in property arising out of a matrimonial relationship, wills and succession;

(2) bankruptcy, proceedings relating to the winding-up of insolvent companies or other legal persons, judicial arrangements, compositions and analogous proceedings;

(3) social security;

(4) arbitration.

TITLE II

JURISDICTION

Section 1

ARTICLE 2

Subject to the provisions of this Convention, persons domiciled in a Contracting State shall, whatever their nationality, be sued in the courts of that State.

Persons who are not nationals of the State in which they are domiciled shall be governed by the rules of jurisdiction applicable to nationals of that State.

ARTICLE 3

Persons domiciled in a Contracting State may be sued in the courts of another Contracting State only by virtue of the rules set out in Sections 2 to 6 of this Title.

In particular the following provisions shall not be applicable as against them: ...

– in the United Kingdom the rules which enable jurisdiction to be founded on:

(a) the document instituting the proceedings having been served on the defendant during his temporary presence in the United Kingdom; or

(b) the presence within the United Kingdom of property belonging to the defendant; or

(c) the seizure by the plaintiff of property situated in the United Kingdom.

ARTICLE 4

If the defendant is not domiciled in a Contracting State, the jurisdiction of the courts of each Contracting State shall, subject to the provisions of Article 16, be determined by the law of that State.

As against such a defendant, any person domiciled in a Contracting State may, whatever his nationality, avail himself in that State of the rules of jurisdiction there in force, and in particular those specified in the second paragraph of Article 3, in the same way as the nationals of that State.

Section 2

ARTICLE 5

A person domiciled in a Contracting State may, in another Contracting State, be sued:

(1) in matters relating to a contract, in the courts for the place of performance of the obligation in question; in matters relating to individual contracts of employment, this place is that where the employee habitually carried out his work, or if the employee does not habitually carry out his work in any one country, the employer may

also be sued in the courts for the place where the business which engaged the employee was or is now situated;

(2) in matters relating to maintenance, in the courts for the place where the maintenance creditor is domiciled or habitually resident or, if the matter is ancillary to proceedings concerning the status of a person, in the court which, according to its own law, has jurisdiction to entertain those proceedings, unless that jurisdiction is based solely on the nationality of one of the parties;

(3) in matters relating to tort, delict or quasi-delict, in the courts for the place where the harmful event occurred;

(4) as regards a civil claim for damages or restitution which is based on an act giving rise to criminal proceedings, in the court seised of those proceedings, to the extent that that court has jurisdiction under its own law to entertain civil proceedings;

(5) as regards a dispute arising out of the operations of a branch, agency or other establishment, in the courts for the place in which the branch, agency or other establishment is situated;

(6) as settlor, trustee or beneficiary of a trust created by the operation of a statute, or by a written instrument, or created orally and evidenced in writing, in the courts of the Contracting State in which the trust is domiciled;

(7) as regards a dispute concerning the payment of remuneration claimed in respect of the salvage of a cargo or freight, in the court under the authority of which the cargo or freight in question:

(a) has been arrested to secure such payment, or

(b) could have been so arrested, but bail or other security has been given;

provided that his provision shall apply only if it is claimed that the defendant has an interest in the cargo or freight or had such an interest at the time of salvage.

ARTICLE 6

A person domiciled in a Contracting State may also be sued:

(1) where he is one of a number of defendants, in the courts for the place where any one of them is domiciled;

(2) as a third party in an action on a warranty or guarantee or in any other third party proceedings, in the court seised of the

original proceedings, unless these were instituted solely with the object of removing him from the jurisdiction of the court which would be competent in his case;

(3) on a counterclaim arising from the same contract or facts on which the original claim was based, in the court in which the original claim is pending;

(4) in matters relating to a contract, if the action may be combined with an action against the same defendant in matters relating to rights in rem in immovable property, in the court of the Contracting State in which the property is situated.

ARTICLE 6A

Where by virtue of this convention a court of a Contracting State has jurisdiction in actions relating to liability arising from the use or operation of a ship, that a court, or any other court substituted for this purpose by the internal law of that State, shall also have jurisdiction over claims for limitation of such liability.

Section 3

ARTICLE 7

In matters relating to insurance, jurisdiction shall be determined by this Section, without prejudice to the provisions of Articles 4 and 5(5).

ARTICLE 8

An insurer domiciled in a Contracting State may be sued:

(1) in the courts of the State where he is domiciled, or

(2) in another Contracting State, in the courts for the place where the policy-holder is domiciled, or

(3) if he is a co-insurer, in the courts of a Contracting State in which proceedings are brought against the leading insurer.

An insurer who is not domiciled in a Contracting State but has a branch, agency or other establishment in one of the Contracting States shall, in disputes arising out of the operations of the branch, agency or establishment, be deemed to be domiciled in that State.

ARTICLE 9

In respect of liability insurance or insurance of immovable property, the insurer may in addition be sued in the courts for the place where the harmful event occurred. The same applies if movable and immovable property are covered by the same insurance policy and both are adversely affected by the same contingency.

ARTICLE 10

In respect of liability insurance, the insurer may also, if the law of the court permits it, be joined in proceedings which the injured party has brought against the insured.

The provisions of Articles 7, 8 and 9 shall apply to actions brought by the injured party directly against the insurer, where such direct actions are permitted.

If the law governing such direct actions provides that the policy-holder or the insured may be joined as a party to the action, the same court shall have jurisdiction over them.

ARTICLE 11

Without prejudice to the provisions of the third paragraph of Article 10, an insurer may bring proceedings only in the courts of the Contracting State in which the defendant is domiciled, irrespective of whether he is the policy-holder, the insured or a beneficiary.

The provisions of this Section shall not affect the right to bring a counterclaim in the court in which, in accordance with this Section, the original claim is pending.

ARTICLE 12

The provisions of this Section may be departed from only by an agreement on jurisdiction:

(1) which is entered into after the dispute has arisen, or

(2) which allows the policy-holder, the insured or a beneficiary to bring proceedings in courts other than those indicated in this Section, or

(3) which is concluded between a policy-holder and an insurer, both of whom are at the time of conclusion of the contract domiciled or habitually resident in the same Contracting State, and which has the effect of conferring jurisdiction on the courts of that State even if the harmful event were to occur abroad, provided that such an agreement is not contrary to the law of that State, or

(4) which is concluded with a policy-holder who is not domiciled in a Contracting State, except in so far as the insurance is compulsory or relates to immovable property in a Contracting State, or

(5) which relates to a contract of insurance in so far as it covers one or more of the risks set out in Article 12A.

ARTICLE 12A

The following are the risks referred to in Article 12(5):

(1) Any loss of or damage to

(a) seagoing ships, installations situated offshore or on the high seas, or aircraft, arising from perils which relate to their use for commercial purposes,

(b) goods in transit other than passengers' baggage where the transit consists of or includes carriage by such ships or aircraft;

(2) Any liability, other than for bodily injury to passengers or loss of or damage to their baggage,

(a) arising out of the use or operation of ships, installations or aircraft as referred to in (1)(a) above in so far as the law of the Contracting State in which such aircraft are registered does not prohibit agreements on jurisdiction regarding insurance of such risks,

(b) for loss or damage caused by goods in transit as described in (1)(b) above;

(3) Any financial loss connected with the use or operation of ships, installations or aircraft as referred to in (1)(a) above, in particular loss of freight or charter hire;

(4) Any risk or interest connected with any of those referred to in (1) to (3) above.

Section 4

ARTICLE 13

In proceedings concerning a contract concluded by a person for a purpose which can be regarded as being outside his trade or profession, hereinafter called the 'consumer', jurisdiction shall be determined by this Section, without prejudice to the provisions of Articles 4 and 5(5), if it is:

(1) a contract for the sale of goods on instalment credit terms, or

(2) a contract for a loan repayable by instalments, or for any other form of credit, made to finance the sale of goods, or

(3) any other contract for the supply of goods or a contract for the supply of services and

(a) in the State of the consumer's domicile the conclusion of the contract was preceded by a specific invitation addressed to him or by advertising, and

(b) the consumer took in that State the steps necessary for the conclusion of the contract.

Where a consumer enters into a contract with a party who is not domiciled in a Contracting State but has a branch, agency or other establishment in one of the Contracting States, that party shall, in disputes arising out of the operations of the branch, agency or establishment, be deemed to be domiciled in that State.

This Section shall not apply to contracts of transport.

ARTICLE 14

A consumer may bring proceedings against the other party to a contract either in the courts of the Contracting State in which that party is domiciled or in the courts of the Contracting State in which he is himself domiciled.

Proceedings may be brought against a consumer by the other party to the contract only in the courts of the Contracting State in which the consumer is domiciled.

These provisions shall not affect the right to bring a counter-claim in the court in which, in accordance with this Section, the original claim is pending.

ARTICLE 15

The provisions of this Section may be departed from only by an agreement:

(1) which is entered into after the dispute has arisen, or

(2) which allows the consumer to bring proceedings in courts other than those indicated in this Section, or

(3) which is entered into by the consumer and the other party to the contract, both of whom are at the time of conclusion of the contract domiciled or habitually resident in the same Contracting State, and which confers jurisdiction on the courts of that State, provided that such an agreement is not contrary to the law of that State.

Section 5

ARTICLE 16

The following courts shall have exclusive jurisdiction, regardless of domicile:

(1) (a) in proceedings which have as their object rights in rem in immovable property or tenancies of immovable property, the court of the Contracting State in which the property is situated;

(b) however, in proceedings which have as their object tenancies of immovable property concluded for temporary private use for a maximum period of six consecutive months, the courts of the Contracting State in which the defendant is domiciled shall also have jurisdiction, provided that the landlord and the tenant are natural persons and are domiciled in the same Contracting State;

(2) in proceedings which have as their object the validity of the constitution, the nullity of the dissolution of companies or other legal persons or associations of natural or legal persons, or the decisions of their organs, the courts of the Contracting State in which the company, legal person or association has its seat;

(3) in proceedings which have as their object the validity of entries in public registers, the courts of the Contracting State in which the register is kept;

(4) in proceedings concerned with the registration or validity of

patents, trademarks, designs, or other similar rights required to be deposited or registered, the courts of the Contracting State in which the deposit or registration has been applied for, has taken place or is under the terms of an international convention deemed to have taken place;

(5) in proceedings concerned with the enforcement of judgments, the courts of the Contracting State in which the judgment has been or is to be enforced.

Section 6

ARTICLE 17

If the parties, one or more of whom is domiciled in a Contracting State, have agreed that a court or the courts of a Contracting State are to have jurisdiction to settle any disputes which have arisen or which may arise in connection with a particular legal relationship, that court or those courts shall have exclusive jurisdiction. Such an agreement conferring jurisdiction shall be either –

(a) in writing or evidenced in writing, or

(b) in a form which accords with practices which the parties have established between themselves, or

(c) in international trade or commerce, in a form which accords with a usage of which the parties are or ought to have been aware and which in such trade or commerce is widely known to, and regularly observed by, parties to contracts of the type involved in the particular trade or commerce concerned.

Where such an agreement is concluded by parties, none of whom is domiciled in a Contracting State, the courts of other Contracting States shall have no jurisdiction over their disputes unless the court or courts chosen have declined jurisdiction.

The court or courts of a Contracting State on which a trust instrument has conferred jurisdiction shall have exclusive jurisdiction in any proceedings brought against a settlor, trustee or beneficiary, if relations between these persons or their rights or obligations under the trust are involved.

Agreements or provisions of a trust instrument conferring jurisdiction shall have no legal force if they are contrary to the provisions of Articles 12 or 15, of if the courts whose jurisdiction they purport to exclude have exclusive jurisdiction by virtue of Article 16.

If an agreement conferring jurisdiction was concluded for the benefit of only one of the parties, that party shall retain the right to bring proceedings in any other court which has jurisdiction by virtue of the Convention.

In matters relating to individual contracts of employment an agreement conferring jurisdiction shall have legal force only if it is entered into after the dispute has arisen or if the employee invokes it to seise courts other than those for the defendant's domicile or those specified in Article 5(1).

ARTICLE 18

Apart from jurisdiction derived from other provisions of this Convention, a court of a Contracting State before whom a defendant enters an appearance shall have jurisdiction. This rule shall not apply where appearance was entered solely to contest the jurisdiction, or where another court has exclusive jurisdiction by virtue of Article 16.

Section 7

ARTICLE 19

Where a court of a Contracting State is seised of a claim which is principally concerned with a matter over which the courts of another Contracting State have exclusive jurisdiction by virtue of Article 16, it shall declare of its own motion that it has no jurisdiction.

ARTICLE 20

Where a defendant domiciled in one Contracting State is sued in a court of another Contracting State and does not enter an appearance, the court shall declare of its own motion that it has no jurisdiction unless its jurisdiction is derived from the provision of this Convention.

The court shall stay the proceedings so long as it is not shown that the defendant has been able to receive the document instituting the proceedings or an equivalent document in sufficient time to enable him to arrange for his defence, or that all necessary steps have been taken to this end.

The provisions of the foregoing paragraph shall be replaced by those of Article 15 of the Hague Convention of 15 November 1965 on the Service Abroad of Judicial and Extrajudicial Documents in Civil or Commercial Matters, if the document instituting the proceedings or notice thereof had to be transmitted abroad in accordance with that Convention.

Section 8

ARTICLE 21

Where proceedings involving the same cause of action and between the same parties are brought in the courts of different Contracting States, any court other than the court first seised shall of its own motion stay its proceedings until such time as the jurisdiction of the court first seised is established.

Where the jurisdiction of the court first seised is established, any court other than the court first seised shall decline jurisdiction in favour of that court.

ARTICLE 22

Where related actions are brought in the courts of different Contracting States, any court other than the court first seised may, while the actions are pending at first instance, stay its proceedings.

A court other than the court first seised may also, on the application of one of the parties, decline jurisdiction if the law of that court permits the consolidation of related actions and the court first seised has jurisdiction over both actions.

For the purposes of this Article, actions are deemed to be related where they are so closely connected that it is expedient to hear and determine them together to avoid the risk of irreconcilable judgments resulting from separate proceedings.

ARTICLE 23

Where actions come within the exclusive jurisdiction of several courts, any court other than the court first seised shall decline jurisdiction in favour of that court.

Section 9

ARTICLE 24

Application may be made to the courts of a Contracting State for such provisional, including protective, measures as may be available under the law of that State, even if, under this Convention, the courts of another Contracting State have jurisdiction as to the substance of the matter.

TITLE III

RECOGNITION AND ENFORCEMENT

ARTICLE 25

For the purposes of this Convention, 'judgment' means any judgment given by a court or tribunal of a Contracting State, whatever the judgment may be called, including a decree, order, decision or writ of execution, as well as the determination of costs or expenses by an officer of the court.

Section 1

ARTICLE 26

A judgment given in a Contracting State shall be recognised in the other Contracting States without any special procedure being required.

Any interested party who raises the recognition of a judgment as the principal issue in a dispute may, in accordance with the procedures provided for in Sections 2 and 3 of this Title, apply for a decision that the judgment be recognised.

If the outcome of proceedings in a court of a Contracting State depends on the determination of an incidental question of recognition that court shall have jurisdiction over that question.

ARTICLE 27

A judgment shall not be recognised:

(1) if such recognition is contrary to public policy in the State in which recognition is sought;

(2) where it was given in default of appearance, if the defendant was not duly served with the document which instituted the proceedings or with an equivalent document in sufficient time to enable him to arrange for his defence;

(3) if the judgment is irreconcilable with a judgment given in a dispute between the same parties in the State in which recognition is sought;

(4) if the court of the State in which the judgment was given, in order to arrive at its judgment, has decided a preliminary question concerning the status or legal capacity of natural persons, rights in property arising out of a matrimonial relationship, wills or succession in a way that conflicts with a rule of the private international law of the State in which the recognition is sought, unless the same result would have been reached by the application of the rules of private international law of that State;

(5) if the judgment is irreconcilable with an earlier judgment given in a non-Contracting State involving the same cause of action and between the same parties, provided that this latter judgment fulfils the conditions necessary for its recognition in the State addressed.

ARTICLE 28

Moreover, a judgment shall not be recognised if it conflicts with the provisions of Sections 3, 4 or 5 of Title II, or in a case provided for in Article 59.

In its examination of the grounds of jurisdiction referred to in the foregoing paragraph, the court or authority applied to shall be bound by the findings of fact on which the court of the State in which the judgment was given based its jurisdiction.

Subject to the provisions of the first paragraph, the jurisdiction of the court of the State in which the judgment was given may not be reviewed; the test of public policy referred to in Article 27(1) may not be applied to the rules relating to jurisdiction.

ARTICLE 29

Under no circumstances may a foreign judgment be reviewed as to its substance.

ARTICLE 30

A court of a Contracting State in which recognition is sought of a judgment given in another Contracting State may stay the proceedings if an ordinary appeal against the judgment has been lodged.

A court of a Contracting State in which recognition is sought of a judgment given in Ireland or the United Kingdom may stay the proceedings if enforcement is suspended in the State of origin, by reason of an appeal.

Section 2

ARTICLE 31

A judgment given in a Contracting State and enforceable in that State shall be enforced in another Contracting State when, on the application of any interested party, it has been declared enforceable there.

However, in the United Kingdom, such a judgment shall be enforced in England and Wales, in Scotland, or in Northern Ireland when, on the application of any interested party, it has been registered for enforcement in that part of the United Kingdom.

ARTICLE 32

(1) The application shall be submitted: ...

– in the United Kingdom –

(a) in England and Wales, to the High Court of Justice, or in the case of a maintenance judgment to the Magistrates' Court on transmission by the Secretary of State; ...

(2) The jurisdiction of local courts shall be determined by reference to the place of domicile of the party against whom enforcement is sought. If he is not domiciled in the State in which enforcement is

sought, it shall be determined by reference to the place of enforcement.

ARTICLE 33

The procedure for making the application shall be governed by the law of the State in which enforcement is sought.

The applicant must give an address for service of process within the area of jurisdiction of the court applied to. However, if the law of the State in which enforcement is sought does not provide for the furnishing of such an address, the applicant shall appoint a representative ad litem.

The documents referred to in Articles 46 and 47 shall be attached to the application.

ARTICLE 34

The court applied to shall give its decision without delay; the party against whom enforcement is sought shall not at this stage of the proceedings be entitled to make any submissions on the application.

The application may be refused only for one of the reasons specified in Articles 27 and 28.

Under no circumstances may the foreign judgment be reviewed as to its substance.

ARTICLE 35

The appropriate officer of the court shall without delay bring the decision given on the application to the notice of the applicant in accordance with the procedure laid down by the law of the State in which enforcement is sought.

ARTICLE 36

If enforcement is authorised, the party against whom enforcement is sought may appeal against the decision within one month of service thereof.

If that party is domiciled in a Contracting State other than that in which the decision authorising enforcement was given, the time for appealing shall be two months and shall run from the date of service, either on him in person or at his residence. No extension of time may be granted on account of distance.

ARTICLE 37

(1) An appeal against the decision authorising enforcement shall be lodged in accordance with the rules governing procedure in contentious matters: ...

> (1) in England and Wales, with the High Court of Justice, or in the case of a maintenance judgment with the Magistrates' Court; ...

(2) The judgment given on the appeal may be contested only: ...

– in the United Kingdom, by a single further appeal on a point of law.

ARTICLE 38

The court with which the appeal under the first paragraph of Article 37(1) is lodged may, on the application of the appellant, stay the proceedings if an ordinary appeal has been lodged against the judgment in the State or origin or if the time for such an appeal has not yet expired; in the latter case, the court may specify the time within which such an appeal is to be lodged.

Where the judgment was given in Ireland or the United Kingdom any form of appeal available in the State of origin shall be treated as an ordinary appeal for the purposes of the first paragraph.

The court may also make enforcement conditional on the provision of such security as it shall determine.

ARTICLE 39

During the time specified for an appeal pursuant to Article 36 and until any such appeal has been determined, no measures of enforcement may be take other than protective measures taken against the property of the party against whom enforcement is sought.

The decision authorising enforcement shall carry with it the power to proceed to any such protective measures.

ARTICLE 40

(1) If the application for enforcement is refused, the applicant may appeal – ...

– in the United Kingdom –

    (a) in England and Wales, to the High Court of Justice, or in the case of a maintenance judgment to the Magistrates' Court; ...

(2) The party against whom enforcement is sought shall be summoned to appear before the appellate court. If he fails to appear, the provisions of the second and third paragraphs of Article 20 shall apply even where he is not domiciled in any of the Contracting States.

ARTICLE 41

A judgment given on an appeal provided for in Article 40 may be contested only: ...

– in the United Kingdom, by a single further appeal on a point of law.

ARTICLE 42

Where a foreign judgment has been given in respect of several matters and enforcement cannot be authorised for all of them, the court shall authorise enforcement for one or more of them.

An applicant may request partial enforcement of a judgment.

ARTICLE 43

A foreign judgment which orders a periodic payment by way of a penalty shall be enforceable in the State in which enforcement is sought only if the amount of the payment has been finally determined by the courts of the State of origin.

ARTICLE 44

An applicant who, in the State in which the judgment was given, has benefited from complete or partial legal aid or exemption from costs or expenses, shall be entitled, in the procedures provided for in Articles 32 to 35, to benefit from the most favourable legal aid or the most extensive exemption from costs or expenses provided for by the law of the State addressed.

An applicant who requests the enforcement of a decision given by an administrative authority in Denmark in respect of a maintenance order may, in the State addressed, claim the benefits referred to in the first paragraph if he presents a statement from the Danish Ministry of Justice to the effect that he fulfils the economic requirements to qualify for the grant of complete or partial legal aid or exemption from costs or expenses.

ARTICLE 45

No security, bond or deposit, however described, shall be required of a party who in one Contracting State applies for enforcement of a judgment given in another Contracting State on the ground that he is a foreign national or that he is not domiciled or resident in the State in which enforcement is sought.

Section 3

ARTICLE 46

A party seeking recognition or applying for enforcement of a judgment shall produce:

(1) a copy of the judgment which satisfies the conditions necessary to establish its authenticity;

(2) in the case of a judgment given in default, the original or a certified true copy of the document which establishes that the party in default was served with the document instituting the proceedings or with an equivalent document.

ARTICLE 47

A party applying for enforcement shall also produce:

(1) documents which establish that, according to the law of the State of origin the judgment is enforceable and has been served;

(2) where appropriate, a document showing that the applicant is in receipt of legal aid in the State of origin.

ARTICLE 48

If the documents specified in Article 46(2) and Article 47(2) are not produced, the court may specify a time for their production, accept equivalent documents or, if it considers that it has sufficient information before it, dispense with their production.

If the court so requires, a translation of the documents shall be produced; the translation shall be certified by a person qualified to do so in one of the Contracting States.

ARTICLE 49

No legalisation or other similar formality shall be required in respect of the documents referred to in Articles 46 or 47 or the second paragraph of Article 48, or in respect of a document appointing a representative ad litem.

TITLE IV

AUTHENTIC INSTRUMENTS AND COURT SETTLEMENTS

ARTICLE 50

A document which has been formally drawn up or registered as an authentic instrument and is enforceable in one Contracting State shall, in another Contracting State, be declared enforceable there, on application made in accordance with the procedures provided for in Article 31 et seq. The application may be refused only if enforcement of the instrument is contrary to public policy in the State addressed.

The instrument produced must satisfy the conditions necessary to establish its authenticity in the State of origin.

The provisions of Section 3 of Title III shall apply as appropriate.

ARTICLE 51

A settlement which has been approved by a court in the course of proceedings and is enforceable in the State in which it was concluded shall be enforceable in the State addressed under the same conditions as authentic instruments.

TITLE V

GENERAL PROVISIONS

ARTICLE 52

In order to determine whether a party is domiciled in the Contracting State whose courts are seised of the matter, the court shall apply its internal law.

If a party is not domiciled in the State whose courts are seised of the matter, then, in order to determine whether the party is domiciled in another Contracting State, the court shall apply the law of that State.

ARTICLE 53

For the purposes of this Convention, the seat of a company or other legal person or association of natural or legal persons shall be treated as its domicile. However, in order to determine that seat, the court shall apply its rules of private international law.

In order to determine whether a trust is domiciled in the Contracting State whose courts are seised of the matter, the court shall apply its rules of private international law.

TITLE VI

TRANSITIONAL PROVISIONS

ARTICLE 54

The provisions of this Convention shall apply only to legal proceedings instituted and to documents formally drawn up or registered as authentic instruments after its entry into force in the

State of origin and, where recognition or enforcement of a judgment or authentic instruments is sought, in the State addressed.

However, judgments given after the date of entry into force of this Convention between the State of origin and the State addressed in proceedings instituted before that date shall be recognised and enforced in accordance with the provisions of Title III if jurisdiction was founded upon rules which accorded with those provided for either in Title II of this Convention or in a convention concluded between the State of origin and the State addressed which was in force when the proceedings were instituted.

If the parties to a dispute concerning a contract had agreed in writing before 1 June 1988 for Ireland or before 1 January 1987 for the United Kingdom that the contract was to be governed by the law of Ireland or of a part of the United Kingdom, the courts of Ireland or of that part of the United Kingdom shall retain the right to exercise jurisdiction in the dispute...

TITLE VII

RELATIONSHIP TO OTHER CONVENTIONS

ARTICLE 55

Subject to the provisions of the second paragraph of Article 54, and of Article 56, this Convention shall, for the States which are parties to it, supersede the following conventions concluded between two or more of them: ...

– the Convention between the United Kingdom and the French Republic providing for the Reciprocal Enforcement of Judgments in Civil and Commercial Matters, with Protocol, signed at Paris on 18 January 1934;

– the Convention between the United Kingdom and the Kingdom of Belgium providing for the Reciprocal Enforcement of Judgments in Civil and Commercial Matters, with Protocol, signed at Brussels on 2 May 1934; ...

– the Convention between the United Kingdom and the Federal Republic of Germany for the Reciprocal Recognition and Enforcement of Judgments in Civil and Commercial Matters, signed at Bonn on 14 July 1960; ...

– the Convention between the United Kingdom and the Republic of Italy for the Reciprocal Recognition and Enforcement of Judgments in Civil and Commercial Matters, signed at Rome on 7 February 1964, with amending Protocol signed at Rome on 14 July 1970;

– the Convention between the United Kingdom and the Kingdom of the Netherlands providing for the Reciprocal Recognition and Enforcement of Judgments in Civil Matters, signed at The Hague on 17 November 1967. ...

ARTICLE 56

The Treaty and the conventions referred to in Article 55 shall continue to have effect in relation to matters to which this Convention does not apply.

They shall continue to have effect in respect of judgments given and documents formally drawn up or registered as authentic instruments before the entry into force of this Convention.

ARTICLE 57

(1) This Convention shall not affect any conventions to which the Contracting States are or will be parties and which in relation to particular matters, govern jurisdiction or the recognition or enforcement of judgments.

(2) With a view to its uniform interpretation, paragraph 1 shall be applied in the following manner –

(a) this Convention shall not prevent a court of a Contracting State which is a party to a convention on a particular matter from assuming jurisdiction in accordance with that Convention, even where the defendant is domiciled in another Contracting State which is not a party to that Convention. The court hearing the action shall, in any event, apply Article 20 of this Convention;

(b) judgments given in a Contracting State by a court in the exercise of jurisdiction provided for in a convention on a particular matter shall be recognised and enforced in the other Contracting State in accordance with this Convention.

Where a convention on a particular matter to which both the State of origin and the State addressed are parties lays down conditions for the recognition or enforcement of judgments, those conditions shall apply. In any event, the provisions of this

Convention which concern the procedure for recognition and enforcement of judgments may be applied.

(3) This Convention shall not affect the application of provisions which, in relation to particular matters, govern jurisdiction or the recognition or enforcement of judgments and which are or will be contained in acts of the institutions of the European Communities or in national laws harmonised in implementation of such acts.

ARTICLE 58

Until such time as the Convention on jurisdiction and the enforcement of judgments in civil and commercial matters, signed at Lugano on 16 September 1988, takes effect with regard to France and the Swiss Confederation, this convention shall not affect the rights granted to Swiss nationals by the Convention between France and the Swiss Confederation on Jurisdiction and the Enforcement of Judgments in Civil Matters, signed at Paris on 15 June 1869.

ARTICLE 59

This Convention shall not prevent a Contracting State from assuming, in a convention on the recognition and enforcement of judgments, an obligation towards a third State not to recognise judgments given in other Contracting States against defendants domiciled or habitually resident in the third State where, in cases provided for in Article 4, the judgment could only be founded on a ground of jurisdiction specified in the second paragraph of Article 3.

However, a Contracting State may not assume an obligation towards a third State not to recognise a judgment given in another Contracting State by a court basing its jurisdiction on the presence within that State of property belonging to the defendant, or the seizure by the plaintiff of property situated there:

(1) if the action is brought to assert or declare proprietary or possessory rights in that property, seeks to obtain authority to dispose of it, or arises from another issue relating to such property, or,

(2) if the property constitutes the security for a debt which is the subject-matter of the action.

TITLE VIII

FINAL PROVISIONS

ARTICLE 61

This Convention shall be ratified by the signatory States. The instruments of ratification shall be deposited with the Secretary-General of the Council of the European Communities.

ARTICLE 62

This convention shall enter into force on the first day of the third month following the deposit of the instrument of ratification by the last signatory State to take this step.

ARTICLE 63

The Contracting States recognise that any State which becomes a member of the European Economic Community shall be required to accept this Convention as a basis for the negotiations between the Contracting States and that State necessary to ensure the implementation of the last paragraph of Article 220 of the Treaty establishing the European Economic Community.

The necessary adjustments may be the subject of a special convention between the Contracting States of the one part and the new Member State of the other part.

ARTICLE 64

The Secretary-General of the Council of the European Communities shall notify the signatory States of:

(a) the deposit of each instrument of ratification;

(b) the date of entry into force of this Convention;

(d) any declaration received pursuant to Article IV of the Protocol;

(e) any communication made pursuant to Article VI of the Protocol.

ARTICLE 65

The Protocol annexed to this Convention by common accord of the Contracting States shall form an integral part thereof.

ARTICLE 66

This convention is concluded for an unlimited period.

ARTICLE 67

Any Contracting State may request the revision of this Convention. In this event, a revision conference shall be convened by the President of the Council of the European Communities.

ARTICLE 68

This convention, drawn up in a single original in the Dutch, French, German and Italian languages, all four texts being equally authentic, shall be deposited in the archives of the Secretariat of the Council of the European Communities. The Secretary-General shall transmit a certified copy to the Government of each signatory State. ...

SCHEDULE 2

TEXT OF 1971 PROTOCOL, AS AMENDED

ARTICLE 1

The Court of Justice of the European Communities shall have jurisdiction to give rulings on the interpretation of the Convention on Jurisdiction and the Enforcement of Judgments in Civil and Commercial Matters and of the Protocol annexed to that Convention signed at Brussels on 27 September 1968, and also on the interpretation of the present Protocol.

The Court of Justice of the European Communities shall also have jurisdiction to give rulings on the interpretation of the Convention on the Accession of the Kingdom of Denmark, Ireland and the United Kingdom of Great Britain and Northern Ireland to the Convention of 27 September 1968 and to this Protocol.

The Court of Justice of the European Communities shall also have jurisdiction to give rulings on the interpretation of the Convention on the accession of the Kingdom of Spain and the Portuguese Republic to the Convention of 27 September 1968 and to this Protocol, as adjusted by the 1978 Convention and the 1982 Convention.

ARTICLE 2

The following courts may request the Court of Justice to give preliminary rulings on questions of interpretation: ...

– in the United Kingdom: the House of Lords and courts to which application has been made under the second paragraph of Article 37 or under Article 41 of the Convention;

(2) the courts of the contracting States when they are sitting in an appellate capacity;

(3) in the cases provided for in Article 37 of the Convention, the courts referred to in that Article.

ARTICLE 3

(1) Where a question of interpretation of the Convention or of one of the other instruments referred to in Article 1 is raised in a case pending before one of the courts listed in Article 2(1) that court shall, if it considers that a decision on the question is necessary to enable it to give judgment, request the Court of Justice to give a ruling thereon.

(2) Where such a question is raised before any court referred to in Article 2(2) or (3), that court may, under the conditions laid down in paragraph (1), request the Court of Justice to give a ruling thereon.

ARTICLE 4

(1) The competent authority of a Contracting State may request the Court of Justice to give a ruling on a question of interpretation of the Convention or of one of the other instruments referred to in Article 1 if judgments given by courts of that State conflict with the interpretation given either by the Court of Justice or in a judgment of one of the courts of another Contracting State referred to in article 2(1) or (2). The provisions of this paragraph shall apply only to judgments which have become res judicata.

(2) The interpretation given by the Court of Justice in response to such a request shall not affect the judgments which gave rise to the request for interpretation.

(3) The Procurators-General of the Courts of Cassation of the Contracting States, or any other authority designated by a Contracting State, shall be entitled to request the Court of Justice for a ruling on interpretation in accordance with paragraph (1).

(4) The Registrar of the Court of Justice shall give notice of the request to the Contracting States, to the Commission and to the Council of the European Communities; they shall then be entitled within two months of the notification to submit statements of case or written observations to the Court.

(5) No fees shall be levied or any costs or expenses awarded in respect of the proceedings provided for in this Article.

ARTICLE 5

(1) Except where this Protocol otherwise provides, the provisions of the Treaty establishing the European Economic Community and those of the Protocol on the Statute of the Court of Justice annexed thereto, which are applicable when the Court is requested to give a preliminary ruling, shall also apply to any proceedings for the interpretation of the Convention and the other instruments referred to in Article 1.

(2) The Rules of Procedure of the Court of Justice shall, if necessary, be adjusted and supplemented in accordance with Article 188 of the Treaty establishing the European Economic Community.

ARTICLE 7

This Protocol shall be ratified by the signatory States. The instruments of ratification shall be deposited with the Secretary-General of the Council of the European Communities.

ARTICLE 8

This Protocol shall enter into force on the first day of the third month following the deposit of the instrument of ratification by the last signatory State to take this step; provided that it shall at the earliest enter into force at the same time as the Convention of 27

September 1968 on Jurisdiction and the Enforcement of Judgments in Civil and Commercial Matters.

ARTICLE 9

The Contracting States recognise that any State which becomes a member of the European Economic Community, and to which Article 63 of the Convention on Jurisdiction and the Enforcement of Judgments in Civil and Commercial Matters applies, must accept the provisions of this Protocol, subject to such adjustments as may be required.

ARTICLE 10

The Secretary-General of the Council of the European Communities shall notify the signatory States of:

(a) the deposit of each instrument of ratification;

(b) the date of entry into force of this Protocol;

(c) any designation received pursuant to Article 4(3).

ARTICLE 11

The Contracting States shall communicate to the Secretary-General of the Council of the European Communities the texts of any provisions of their laws which necessitate an amendment to the list of courts in Article 2(1).

ARTICLE 12

This Protocol is concluded for an unlimited period.

ARTICLE 13

Any Contracting State may request the revision of this Protocol. In this event, a revision conference shall be convened by the President of the Council of the European Communities.

ARTICLE 14

This Protocol, drawn up in a single original in the Dutch, French, German and Italian languages, all four texts being equally authentic, shall be deposited in the archives of the Secretariat of the Council of the European Communities. The Secretary-General shall transmit a certified copy to the Government of each signatory State.

SCHEDULE 3C

TEXT OF THE LUGANO CONVENTION ...

CONVENTION ON JURISDICTION AND THE ENFORCEMENT OF JUDGMENTS IN CIVIL AND COMMERCIAL MATTERS

Preamble

The High Contracting Parties to this Convention,

Anxious to strengthen in their territories the legal protection of persons therein established,

Considering that it is necessary for this purpose to determine the international jurisdiction of their courts, to facilitate recognition and to introduce an expeditious procedure for securing the enforcement of judgments, authentic instruments and court settlements,

Aware of the links between them, which have been sanctioned in the economic field by the free trade agreements concluded between the European Economic Community and the States members of the European Free Trade Association,

Taking into account the Brussels Convention of 27 September 1968 on jurisdiction and the enforcement of judgments in civil and commercial matters, as amended by the Accession Conventions under the successive enlargements of the European Communities,

Persuaded that the extension of the principles of that Convention to the States parties to this instrument will strengthen legal and economic cooperation in Europe.

Desiring to ensure as uniform an interpretation as possible of this instrument,

Have in this spirit decided to conclude this Convention and

Have agreed as follows:

TITLE I

SCOPE

ARTICLE 1

This Convention shall apply in civil and commercial matters whatever the nature of the court or tribunal. It shall not extend, in particular, to revenue, customs or administrative matters.

The Convention shall not apply to

1. the status or legal capacity of natural persons, rights in property arising out of matrimonial relationship, wills and succession;

2. bankruptcy, proceedings relating to the winding-up of insolvent companies or other legal persons, judicial arrangements, compositions and analogous proceedings;

3. social security;

4. arbitration.

TITLE II

JURISDICTION

Section 1

ARTICLE 2

Subject to the provisions of this Convention, persons domiciled in a Contracting State shall, whatever their nationality, be sued in the courts of that State.

Persons who are not nationals of the State in which they are domiciled shall be governed by the rules of jurisdiction applicable to nationals of that State.

ARTICLE 3

Persons domiciled in a Contracting State may be sued in the courts of another Contracting State only by virtue of the rules set out in Sections 2 to 6 of this Title.

In particular the following provisions shall not be applicable as against them: ...

– in the United Kingdom: the rules which enable jurisdiction to be founded on:

(a) the document instituting the proceedings having been served on the defendant during his temporary presence in the United Kingdom; or

(b) the presence within the United Kingdom of property belonging to the defendant; or

(c) the seizure by the plaintiff of property situated in the United Kingdom.

ARTICLE 4

If the defendant is not domiciled in a Contracting State, the jurisdiction of the courts of each Contracting State shall, subject to the provisions of Article 16, be determined by the law of that State.

As against such a defendant, any person domiciled in a Contracting State may, whatever his nationality, avail himself in that State of the rules of jurisdiction there in force, and in particular those specified in the second paragraph of Article 3, in the same way as the nationals of that State.

Section 2

ARTICLE 5

A person domiciled in a Contracting State may, in another Contracting State, be sued:

1. in matters relating to a contract, in the courts for the place of performance of the obligation in question; in matters relating to individual contracts of employment, this place is that where the employee habitually carries out his work, or if the employee does not

habitually carry out his work in any one country, this place shall be the place of business through which he was engaged;

2. in matters relating to maintenance, in the courts for the place where the maintenance creditor is domiciled or habitually resident or, if the matter is ancillary to proceedings concerning the status of a person, in the court which, according to its own law, has jurisdiction to entertain those proceedings, unless that jurisdiction is based solely on the nationality of one of the parties;

3. in matters relating to tort, delict or quasi-delict, in the courts for the place where the harmful event occurred;

4. as regards a civil claim for damages or restitution which is based on an act giving rise to criminal proceedings, in the court seised of those proceedings, to the extent that that court has jurisdiction under its own law to entertain civil proceedings;

5. as regards a dispute arising out of the operations of a branch, agency or other establishment, in the courts for the place in which the branch, agency or other establishment is situated;

6. in his capacity as settlor, trustee or beneficiary of a trust created by the operation of a statute, or by a written instrument, or created orally and evidenced in writing, in the courts of the Contracting State in which the trust is domiciled;

7. as regards a dispute concerning the payment of remuneration claimed in respect of the salvage of a cargo or freight, in the court under the authority of which the cargo or freight in question:

(a) has been arrested to secure such payment, or

(b) could have been so arrested, but bail or other security has been given;

provided that this provision shall apply only if it is claimed that the defendant has an interest in the cargo or freight or had such an interest at the time of salvage.

ARTICLE 6

A person domiciled in a Contracting State may also be sued:

1. where he is one of a number of defendants, in the courts for the place where any one of them is domiciled;

2. as a third party in an action on a warranty or guarantee or in any other third party proceedings, in the court seised of the original proceedings, unless these were instituted solely with the object of removing him from the jurisdiction of the court which would be competent in his case;

3. on a counterclaim arising from the same contract or facts on which the original claim was based, in the court in which the original claim is pending;

4. in matters relating to a contract, if the action may be combined with an action against the same defendant in matters relating to rights in rem in immovable property, in the court of the Contracting State in which the property is situated.

ARTICLE 6A

Where by virtue of this Convention a court of a Contracting State has jurisdiction in actions relating to liability arising from the use or operation of a ship, that court, or any other court substituted for this purpose by the internal law of that State, shall also have jurisdiction over claims for limitation of such liability.

Section 3

ARTICLE 7

In matters relating to insurance, jurisdiction shall be determined by this Section, without prejudice to the provisions of Articles 4 and 5(5).

ARTICLE 8

An insurer domiciled in a Contracting State may be sued:

1. in the courts of the State where he is domiciled; or

2. in another Contracting State, in the courts for the place where the policy-holder is domiciled; or

3. if he is a co-insurer, in the courts of a Contracting State in which proceedings are brought against the leading insurer.

An insurer who is not domiciled in a Contracting State but has a branch, agency or other establishment in one of the Contracting States shall, in disputes arising out of the operations of the branch, agency or establishment, be deemed to be domiciled in that State.

ARTICLE 9

In respect of liability insurance or insurance of immovable property, the insurer may in addition be sued in the courts for the place where the harmful event occurred. The same applies if movable and immovable property are covered by the same insurance policy and both are adversely affected by the same contingency.

ARTICLE 10

In respect of liability insurance, the insurer may also, if the law of the court permits it, be joined in proceedings which the injured party has brought against the insured.

The provisions of Articles 7, 8 and 9 shall apply to actions brought by the injured party directly against the insurer, where such direct actions are permitted.

If the law governing such direct actions provides that the policy-holder or the insured may be joined as a party to the action, the same court shall have jurisdiction over them.

ARTICLE 11

Without prejudice to the provisions of the third paragraph of Article 10, an insurer may bring proceedings only in the courts of the Contracting State in which the defendant is domiciled, irrespective of whether he is the policy-holder, the insured or a beneficiary.

The provisions of this Section shall not affect the right to bring a counterclaim in the courts in which, in accordance with this Section, the original claim is pending.

ARTICLE 12

The provisions of this Section may be departed from only by an agreement on jurisdiction:

1. which is entered into after the dispute has arisen; or

2. which allows the policy-holder, the insured or a beneficiary to bring proceedings in courts other than those indicated in this Section; or

3. which is concluded between a policy-holder and an insurer, both of whom are at the time of conclusion of the contract domiciled or habitually resident in the same Contracting State, and which has the effect of conferring jurisdiction on the courts of that State even if the harmful event were to occur abroad, provided that such an agreement is not contrary to the law of the State; or

4. which is concluded with a policy-holder who is not domiciled in a Contracting State, except in so far as the insurance is compulsory or relates to immovable property in a Contracting State; or

5. which relates to a contract of insurance in so far as it covers one or more of the risks set out in Article 12A.

ARTICLE 12A

The following are the risks referred to in Article 12(5):

1. any loss of or damage to:

(a) sea-going ships, installations situated offshore or on the high seas, or aircraft, arising from perils which relate to their use for commercial purposes;

(b) goods in transit other than passengers' baggage where the transit consists of or includes carriage by such ships or aircraft;

2. any liability, other than for bodily injury to passengers or loss of or damage to their baggage;

(a) arising out of the use or operation of ships, installations or aircraft as referred to in (1)(a) above in so far as the law of the Contracting State in which such aircraft are registered does not prohibit agreements on jurisdiction regarding insurance of such risks;

(b) for loss or damage caused by goods in transit as described in (1)(b) above;

3. any financial loss connected with the use or operation of ships, installations or aircraft as referred to in (1)(a) above, in particular loss of freight or charter-hire;

4. any risk or interest connected with any of those referred to in (1) to (3) above.

Section 4

ARTICLE 13

In proceedings concerning a contract concluded by a person for a purpose which can be regarded as being outside his trade or profession, hereinafter called 'the consumer', jurisdiction shall be determined by this Section, without prejudice to the provisions of Articles 4 and 5(5), if it is:

1. a contract for the sale of goods on instalment credit terms; or

2. a contract for a loan repayable by instalments, or for any other form of credit, made to finance the sale of goods; or

3. any other contract for the supply of goods or a contract for the supply of services, and

(a) in the State of the consumer's domicile the conclusion of the contract was preceded by a specific invitation addressed to him or by advertising, and

(b) the consumer took in that State the steps necessary for the conclusion of the contract.

Where a consumer enters into a contract with a party who is not domiciled in a Contracting State but has a branch, agency or other establishment in one of the Contracting States, that party shall, in disputes arising out of the operations of the branch, agency or establishment, be deemed to be domiciled in that State.

This Section shall not apply to contracts of transport.

ARTICLE 14

A consumer may bring proceedings against the other party to a contract either in the courts of the Contracting State in which that party is domiciled or in the courts of the Contracting State in which he is himself domiciled.

Proceedings may be brought against a consumer by the other party to the contract only in the courts of the Contracting State in which the consumer is domiciled.

These provisions shall not affect the right to bring a counterclaim in the court in which, in accordance with this Section, the original claim is pending.

ARTICLE 15

The provisions of this Section may be departed from only by an agreement:

1. which is entered into after the dispute has arisen; or

2. which allows the consumer to bring proceedings in courts other than those indicated in this Section; or

3. which is entered into by the consumer and the other party to the contract, both of whom are at the time of conclusion of the contract domiciled or habitually resident in the same Contracting State, and which confers jurisdiction on the courts of that State, provided that such an agreement is not contrary to the law of that State.

Section 5

ARTICLE 16

The following courts shall have exclusive jurisdiction, regardless of domicile:

1. (a) in proceedings which have as their object rights in rem in immovable property or tenancies of immovable property, the courts of the Contracting State in which the property is situated;

    (b) however, in proceedings which have as their object tenancies of immovable property concluded for temporary private use for a maximum period of six consecutive months, the courts of the Contracting State in which the defendant is domiciled shall also have jurisdiction, provided that the tenant is a natural person and neither party is domiciled in the Contracting State in which the property is situated;

2. in proceedings which have as their object the validity of the constitution, the nullity or the dissolution of companies or other legal persons or associations of natural or legal persons, or the decision of their organs, the courts of the Contracting State in which the company, legal persons or association has its seat;

3. in proceedings which have as their object the validity of entries in public registers, the courts of the Contracting State in which the register is kept;

4. in proceedings concerned with the registration or validity of patents, trade marks, designs, or other similar rights required to be

deposited or registered, the courts of the Contracting State in which the deposit or registration has been applied for, has taken place or is under the terms of an international convention deemed to have taken place;

5. in proceedings concerned with the enforcement of judgments, the courts of the Contracting State in which the judgment has been or is to be enforced.

Section 6

ARTICLE 17

1. If the parties, one or more of whom is domiciled in a Contracting State, have agreed that a court or the courts of a Contracting State are to have jurisdiction to settle any disputes which have arisen or which may arise in connection with a particular legal relationship, that court or those courts shall have exclusive jurisdiction. Such an agreement conferring jurisdiction shall be either:

(a) in writing or evidenced in writing, or

(b) in a form which accords with practices which the parties have established between themselves, or

(c) in international trade or commerce, in a form which accords with a usage of which the parties are or ought to have been aware and which in such trade or commerce is widely known to, and regularly observed by, parties to contracts of the type involved in the particular trade or commerce concerned.

Where such an agreement is concluded by parties, none of whom is domiciled in a Contracting State, the courts of other Contracting States shall have no jurisdiction over their disputes unless the court or courts chosen have declined jurisdiction.

2. The court or courts of a Contracting State on which a trust instrument has conferred jurisdiction shall have exclusive jurisdiction in any proceedings brought against a settlor, trustee or beneficiary, if relations between these persons or their rights or obligations under the trust are involved.

3. Agreements or provisions of a trust instrument conferring jurisdiction shall have no legal force if they are contrary to the provisions of Article 12 or 15, or if the courts whose jurisdiction they purport to exclude have exclusive jurisdiction by virtue of Article 16.

4. If an agreement conferring jurisdiction was concluded for the benefit of only one of the parties, that party shall retain the right to bring proceedings in any other court which has jurisdiction by virtue of this Convention.

5. In matters relating to individual contracts of employment an agreement conferring jurisdiction shall have legal force only if it is entered into after the dispute has arisen.

ARTICLE 18

Apart from jurisdiction derived from other provisions of this Convention, a court of a Contracting State before whom a defendant enters an appearance shall have jurisdiction.. This rule shall not apply where appearance was entered solely to contest the jurisdiction, or where another court has exclusive jurisdiction by virtue of Article 16.

Section 7

ARTICLE 19

Where a court of a Contracting State is seised of a claim which is principally concerned with a matter over which the courts of another Contracting State have exclusive jurisdiction by virtue of Article 16, it shall declare of its own motion that it has no jurisdiction.

ARTICLE 20

Where a defendant domiciled in one Contracting State is sued in a court of another Contracting State and does not enter an appearance, the court shall declare of its own motion that it has no jurisdiction unless its jurisdiction is derived from the provisions of this Convention.

The court shall stay the proceedings so long as it is not shown that the defendant has been able to receive the document instituting the proceedings or an equivalent document in sufficient time to enable him to arrange for his defence, or that all necessary steps have been taken to this end.

The provisions of the foregoing paragraph shall be replaced by those of Article 15 of the Hague Convention of 15 November 1965 on the service abroad of judicial and extrajudicial documents in civil or commercial matters, if the document instituting the proceedings or notice thereof had to be transmitted abroad in accordance with that Convention.

Section 8

ARTICLE 21

Where proceedings involving the same cause of action and between the same parties are brought in the courts of different Contracting States any court other than the court first seised shall of its own motion stay its proceedings until such time as the jurisdiction of the court first seised is established.

Where the jurisdiction of the court first seised is established, any court other than the court first seised shall decline jurisdiction in favour of that court.

ARTICLE 22

Where related actions are brought in the courts of different Contracting States, any court other than the court first seised may, while the actions are pending at first instance, stay its proceedings.

A court other than the court first seised may also, on the application of one of the parties, decline jurisdiction if the law of that court permits the consolidation of related actions and the court first seised has jurisdiction over both actions.

For the purposes of this Article, actions are deemed to be related where they are so closely connected that it is expedient to hear and determine them together to avoid the risk of irreconcilable judgments resulting from separate proceedings.

ARTICLE 23

Where actions come within the exclusive jurisdiction of several courts, any court other than the court first seised shall decline jurisdiction in favour of that court.

Section 9

Article 24

Application may be made to the courts of a Contracting State for such provisional, including protective, measures as may be available under the law of that State, even if, under this Convention, the courts of another Contracting State have jurisdiction as to the substance of the matter.

TITLE III

RECOGNITION AND ENFORCEMENT

ARTICLE 25

For the purposes of this Convention, 'judgment' means any judgment given by a court or tribunal of a Contracting State, whatever the judgment may be called, including a decree, order, decision or writ of execution, as well as the determination of costs or expenses by an officer of the court.

Section 1

ARTICLE 26

A judgment given in a Contracting State shall be recognised in the other Contracting States without any special procedure being required.

Any interested party who raises the recognition of a judgment as the principal issue in the dispute may, in accordance with the procedures provided for in Sections 2 and 3 of this Title, apply for a decision that the judgment be recognised.

If the outcome of proceedings in a court of a Contracting State depends on the determination of an incidental question of recognition that court shall have jurisdiction over that question.

ARTICLE 27

A judgment shall not be recognised:

1. if such recognition is contrary to public policy in the State in which recognition is sought;

2. where it was given in default of appearance, if the defendant was not duly served with the document which instituted the proceedings or with an equivalent documents in sufficient time to enable him to arrange for his defence;

3. if the judgment is irreconcilable with a judgment given in a dispute between the same parties in the State in which recognition is sought;

4. if the court of the State of origin, in order to arrive at its judgment, has decided a preliminary question concerning the status or legal capacity of natural persons, rights in property arising out of a matrimonial relationship, wills or succession in a way that conflicts with a rule of the private international law of the State in which the recognition is sought, unless the same result would have been reached by the application of the rules of private international law of that State;

5. if the judgment is irreconcilable with an earlier judgment given in a non-contracting State involving the same cause of action and between the same parties, provided that this latter judgment fulfils the conditions necessary for its recognition in the State addressed.

ARTICLE 28

Moreover, a judgment shall not be recognised if it conflicts with the provisions of Section 3, 4 or 5 of Title II or in a case provided for in Article 59.

A judgment may furthermore be refused recognition in any case provided for in Article 54B(3) or 57(4).

In its examination of the grounds of jurisdiction referred to in the foregoing paragraphs, the court or authority applied to shall be bound by the findings of fact on which the court of the State of origin based its jurisdiction.

Subject to the provisions of the first and second paragraphs, the jurisdiction of the court of the State of origin may not be reviewed;

the test of public policy referred to in Article 27(1) may not be applied to the rules relating to jurisdiction.

ARTICLE 29

Under no circumstances may a foreign judgment be reviewed as to its substance.

ARTICLE 30

A court of a Contracting State in which recognition is sought of a judgment given in another Contracting State may stay the proceedings if an ordinary appeal against the judgment has been lodged.

A court of a Contracting State in which recognition is sought of a judgment given in Ireland or the United Kingdom may stay the proceedings if enforcement is suspended in the State of origin by reason of an appeal.

Section 2

ARTICLE 31

A judgment given in a Contracting State and enforceable in that State shall be enforced in another Contracting State when, on the application of any interested party, it has been declared enforceable there.

However, in the United Kingdom, such a judgment shall be enforced in England and Wales, in Scotland, or in Northern Ireland when, on the application of any interested party, it has been registered for enforcement in that part of the United Kingdom.

ARTICLE 32

1. The application shall be submitted: ...

– in the United Kingdom:

> (a) in England and Wales, to the High Court of Justice, or in the case of a maintenance judgment to the Magistrates' Court on transmission by the Secretary of State; ...

2. The jurisdiction of local courts shall be determined by reference to the place of domicile of the party against whom enforcement is sought. If he is not domiciled in the State in which enforcement is sought, it shall be determined by reference to the place of enforcement.

ARTICLE 33

The procedure for making the application shall be governed by the law of the State in which enforcement is sought.

The applicant must give an address for service of process within the area of jurisdiction of the court applied to. However, if the law of the State in which enforcement is sought does not provide for the furnishing of such an address, the applicant shall appoint a representative ad litem.

The documents referred to in Articles 46 and 47 shall be attached to the application.

ARTICLE 34

The court applied to shall give its decision without delay; the party against whom enforcement is sought shall not at this stage of the proceedings be entitled to make any submissions on the application.

The application may be refused only for one of the reasons specified in Articles 27 and 28.

Under no circumstances may the foreign judgment be reviewed as to its substance.

ARTICLE 35

The appropriate officer of the court shall without delay bring the decision given on the application to the notice of the applicant in accordance with the procedure laid down by the law of the State in which enforcement is sought.

ARTICLE 36

If enforcement is authorised, the party against whom enforcement is sought may appeal against the decision within one month of service thereof.

If that party is domiciled in a Contracting State other than that in which the decision authorising enforcement was given, the time for appealing shall be two months and shall run from the date of service, either on him in person or at his residence. No extension of time may be granted on account of distance.

ARTICLE 37

1. An appeal against the decision authorising enforcement shall be lodged in accordance with the rules governing procedure in contentious matters: ...

– in the United Kingdom:

    (a) in England and Wales, with the High Court of Justice, or in the case of a maintenance judgment with the Magistrates' Court: ...

2. The judgment given on the appeal may be contested only: ...

– in the United Kingdom, by a single further appeal on a point of law.

ARTICLE 38

The court with which the appeal under the first paragraph of Article 37 is lodged may, on the application of the appellant, stay the proceedings if an ordinary appeal has been lodged against the judgment in the State of origin or if the time for such an appeal has not yet expired; in the latter case, the court may specify the time within which such an appeal is to be lodged.

Where the judgment was given in Ireland or the United Kingdom, any form of appeal available in the State of origin shall be treated as an ordinary appeal for the purposes of the first paragraph.

The court may also make enforcement conditional on the provision of such security as it shall determine.

ARTICLE 39

During the time specified for an appeal pursuant to Article 36 and until any such appeal has been determined, no measures of enforcement may be taken other than protective measures taken against the property of the party against whom enforcement is sought.

The decision authorising enforcement shall carry with it the power to proceed to any such protective measures.

ARTICLE 40

1. If the application for enforcement is refused, the applicant may appeal: ...

– in the United Kingdom

> (a) in England and Wales, to the High Court of Justice, or in the case of a maintenance judgment to the Magistrates' Court; ...

2. The party against whom enforcement is sought shall be summoned to appear before the appellate court. If he fails to appear, the provisions of the second and third paragraphs of Article 20 shall apply even where he is not domiciled in any of the Contracting States.

ARTICLE 41

A judgment given on an appeal provided for in Article 40 may be contested only: ...

– in the United Kingdom, by a single further appeal on a point of law.

ARTICLE 42

Where a foreign judgment has been given in respect of several matters and enforcement cannot be authorised for all of them, the court shall authorise enforcement for one or more of them.

An applicant may request partial enforcement of a judgment.

ARTICLE 43

A foreign judgment which orders a periodic payment by way of a penalty shall be enforceable in the State in which enforcement is sought only if the amount of the payment has been finally determined by the courts of the State of origin.

ARTICLE 44

An applicant who, in the state of origin, has benefited from complete or partial legal aid or exemption from costs or expenses, shall be entitled, in the procedures provided for in Articles 32 to 35, to benefit from the most favourable legal aid or the most extensive exemption from costs or expenses provided for by the law of the State addressed.

However, an applicant who requests the enforcement of a decision given by an administrative authority in Denmark or in Iceland in respect of a maintenance order may, in the State addressed, claim the benefits referred to in the first paragraph if he presents a statement from, respectively, the Danish Ministry of Justice or the Icelandic Ministry of Justice to the effect that he fulfils the economic requirements to qualify for the grant of complete or partial legal aid or exemption from costs or expenses.

ARTICLE 45

No security, bond or deposit, however described, shall be required of a party who in one Contracting State applies for enforcement of a judgment given in another Contracting State on the ground that he is a foreign national or that he is not domiciled or resident in the State in which enforcement is sought.

Section 3

ARTICLE 46

A party seeking recognition or applying for enforcement of a judgment shall produce:

1. a copy of the judgment which satisfies the conditions necessary to establish its authenticity;

2. in the case of a judgment given in default, the original or a certified true copy of the document which establishes that the party in default was served with the document instituting the proceedings or with an equivalent document.

ARTICLE 47

A party applying for enforcement shall also produce:

1. documents which establish that, according to the law of the State of origin, the judgment is enforceable and has been served;

2. where appropriate, a document showing that the applicant is in receipt of legal aid in the State of origin.

ARTICLE 48

If the documents specified in Article 46(2) and Article 47(2) are not produced, the court may specify a time for their production, accept equivalent documents or, if it considers that it has sufficient information before it, dispense with their production.

If the court so requires, a translation of the documents shall be produced; the translation shall be certified by a person qualified to do so in one of the Contracting States.

ARTICLE 49

No legislation or other similar formality shall be required in respect of the documents referred to in Article 46 or 47 or the second paragraph of Article 48, or in respect of a document appointing a representative ad litem.

TITLE IV

AUTHENTIC INSTRUMENTS AND COURT SETTLEMENTS

ARTICLE 50

A document which has been formally drawn up or registered as an authentic instrument and is enforceable in one Contracting State shall, in another Contracting State, be declared enforceable there, on application made in accordance with the procedures provided for in Articles 31 et seq. The application may be refused only if enforcement of the instrument is contrary to public policy in the State addressed.

The instrument produced must satisfy the conditions necessary to establish its authenticity in the State of origin.

The provisions of Section 3 of Title III shall apply as appropriate.

ARTICLE 51

A settlement which has been approved by a court in the course of proceedings and is enforceable in the State in which it was concluded shall be enforceable in the State addressed under the same conditions as authentic instruments.

TITLE V

GENERAL PROVISIONS

ARTICLE 52

In order to determine whether a party is domiciled in the Contracting State whose courts are seised of a matter, the court shall apply its internal law.

If a party is not domiciled in the State whose courts are seised of the matter, then, in order to determine whether the party is domiciled in another Contracting State, the court shall apply the law of that State.

ARTICLE 53

For the purposes of this Convention, the seat of a company or other legal person or association of natural or legal persons shall be treated as its domicile. However, in order to determine that seat, the court shall apply its rules of private international law.

In order to determine whether a trust is domiciled in the Contracting State whose courts are seised of the matter, the court shall apply its rules of private international law.

TITLE VI

TRANSITIONAL PROVISIONS

ARTICLE 54

The provisions of this Convention shall apply only to legal proceedings instituted and to documents formally drawn up or registered as authentic instruments after its entry into force in the State of origin and, where recognition or enforcement of a judgment or authentic instrument is sought, in the State addressed.

However, judgments given after the date of entry into force of this Convention between the State of origin and the State addressed in proceedings instituted before that date shall be recognised and enforced in accordance with the provisions of Title III if jurisdiction was founded upon rules which accorded with those provided for either in Title II of this Convention or in a convention concluded between the State of origin and the State addressed which was in force when the proceedings were instituted.

If the parties to a dispute concerning a contract had agreed in writing before the entry into force of this Convention that the contract was to be governed by the law of Ireland or of a part of the United Kingdom, the courts of Ireland or of that part of the United Kingdom shall retain the right to exercise jurisdiction in the dispute.
...

TITLE VII

RELATIONSHIP TO THE BRUSSELS CONVENTION AND TO OTHER CONVENTIONS

ARTICLE 54B

1. This Convention shall not prejudice the application by the Member States of the European Communities of the Convention on Jurisdiction and the Enforcement of Judgments in Civil and Commercial Matters, signed at Brussels on 27 September 1968 and of the Protocol on interpretation of that Convention by the Court of Justice, signed at Luxembourg on 3 June 1971, as amended by the Convention of Accession to the said Convention and the said Protocol by the States acceding to the European Communities, all of these Conventions and the Protocol being hereinafter referred to as the 'Brussels Convention'.

2. However, this Convention shall in any event be applied:

(a) in matters of jurisdiction, where the defendant is domiciled in the territory of a Contracting State which is not a member of the European Communities, or where Article 16 or 17 of this Convention confers a jurisdiction on the courts of such a Contracting State;

(b) in relation to a lis pendens or to related actions as provided for in Articles 21 and 22, when proceedings are instituted in a Contracting State which is not a member of the European Communities and in a Contracting State which is a member of the European Communities;

(c) in matters of recognition and enforcement, where either the State of origin or the State addressed is not a member of the European Communities.

3. In addition to the grounds provided for in Title III recognition or enforcement may be refused if the ground of jurisdiction on which the judgment has been based differs from that resulting from this Convention and recognition or enforcement is sought against a party who is domiciled in a Contracting State which is not a member of the European Communities, unless the judgment may otherwise be recognised or enforced under any rule of law in the State addressed.

ARTICLE 55

Subject to the provisions of the second paragraph of Article 54 and of Article 56, this Convention shall, for the States which are parties to it, supersede the following conventions concluded between two or more of them: ...

– the Convention between Norway and the United Kingdom providing for the reciprocal recognition and enforcement of judgments in civil matters, signed at London on 12 June 1961.

– the Convention between the United Kingdom and Austria providing for the reciprocal recognition and enforcement of judgments in civil and commercial matters, signed at Vienna on 14 July 1961, with amending Protocol signed at London on 6 March 1970.

ARTICLE 56

The Treaty and the conventions referred to in Article 55 shall continue to have effect in relation to matters to which this Convention does not apply.

They shall continue to have effect in respect of judgments given and documents formally drawn up or registered as authentic instruments before the entry into force of this Convention.

ARTICLE 57

1. This Convention shall not affect any conventions to which the Contracting States are or will be parties and which, in relation to particular matters, govern jurisdiction or the recognition or enforcement of judgments.

2. This Convention shall not prevent a court of a Contracting State which is party to a convention referred to in the first paragraph from assuming jurisdiction in accordance with that convention, even where the defendant is domiciled in a Contracting State which is not a party to that convention. The court hearing the act in shall, in any event, apply Article 20 of this Convention.

3. Judgments given in a Contracting State by a court in the exercise of jurisdiction provided for in a convention referred to in the first paragraph shall be recognised and enforced in the other Contracting States in accordance with Title III of this Convention.

4. In addition to the grounds provided for in Title III, recognition or enforcement may be refused if the State addressed is not a contracting party to a convention referred to in the first paragraph and the person against whom recognition or enforcement is sought is domiciled in that State, unless the judgment may otherwise be recognised or enforced under any rule of law in the State addressed.

5. Where a convention referred to in the first paragraph to which both the State of origin and the State addressed are parties lays down conditions for the recognition or enforcement of judgments, those conditions shall apply. In any event, the provisions of this Convention which concern the procedures for recognition and enforcement of judgments may be applied.

ARTICLE 59

This Convention shall not prevent a Contracting State from assuming, in a convention on the recognition and enforcement of judgments, an obligation towards a third State not to recognise judgments given in other Contracting States against defendants domiciled or habitually resident in the third State where, in cases provided for in Article 4, the judgment could only be founded on a ground of jurisdiction specified in the second paragraph of Article 3.

However, a Contracting State may not assume an obligation towards a third State not to recognise a judgment given in another Contracting State by a court basing its jurisdiction on the presence within that State of property belonging to the defendant, or the seizure by the plaintiff of property situated there:

1. if the action is brought to assert or declare proprietary or possessory rights in that property, seeks to obtain authority to dispose of it, or arises from another issue relating to such property, or

2. if the property constitutes the security for a debt which is the subject-matter of the action.

TITLE VIII

FINAL PROVISIONS

ARTICLE 60

The following may be parties to this Convention:

(a) States which, at the time of the opening of this Convention for signature, are members of the European Communities or of the European Free Trade Association;

(b) States which, after the opening of this Convention for signature, become members of the European Communities or of the European Free Trade Association;

(c) States invited to accede in accordance with Article 62(1)(b).

ARTICLE 61

1. This Convention shall be opened for signature by the States members of the European Communities or the European Free Trade Association.

2. The Convention shall be submitted for ratification by the signatory States. The instruments of ratification shall be deposited with the Swiss Federal Council.

3. The Convention shall enter into force on the first day of the third month following the date on which two States, of which one is a member of the European Communities and the other a member of the European Free Trade Association, deposit their instruments of ratification.

4. The Convention shall take effect in relation to any other signatory State on the first day of the third month following the deposit of its instrument of ratification.

ARTICLE 62

1. After entering into force this Convention shall be open to accession by:

(a) the States referred to in Article 60(b);

(b) other States which have been invited to accede upon a request made by one of the Contracting States to the depository State. The depository State shall invite the State concerned to accede only if, after having communicated the contents of the communications that this State intends to make in accordance with Article 63, it has obtained the unanimous agreement of the signatory States and the Contracting States referred to in Article 60(a) and (b).

2. If an acceding State wishes to furnish details for the purposes of Protocol No 1, negotiations shall be entered into to that end. A negotiating conference shall be convened by the Swiss Federal Council.

3. In respect of an acceding State, the Convention shall take effect on the first day of the third month following the deposit of its instrument of accession.

4. However, in respect of an acceding State referred to in paragraph 1(a) or (b), the Convention shall take effect only in relations between the acceding State and the Contracting States which have not made any objections to the accession before the first day of the third month following the deposit of the instrument of accession.

ARTICLE 63

Each acceding State shall, when depositing its instrument of accession, communicate the information required for the application of Articles 3, 32, 37, 40, 41 and 55 of this Convention and furnish, if need be, the details prescribed during the negotiations for the purposes of Protocol No 1.

ARTICLE 64

1. This Convention is concluded for an initial period of five years from the date of its entry into force in accordance with Article 61(3), even in the case of States which ratify it or accede to it after that date.

2. At the end of the initial five-year period, the Convention shall be automatically renewed from year to year.

3. Upon the expiry of the initial five-year period, any Contracting State may, at any time, denounce the Convention by sending a notification to the Swiss Federal Council.

4. The denunciation shall take effect at the end of the calendar year following the expiry of a period of six months from the date of receipt by the Swiss Federal Council of the notification of denunciation.

ARTICLE 65

The following are annexed to this Convention:

– a Protocol No 1, on certain questions of jurisdiction, procedure and enforcement,

– a Protocol No 2, on the uniform interpretation of the Convention,

– a Protocol No 3, on the application of Article 57.

These Protocols shall form an integral part of the Convention.

ARTICLE 66

Any Contracting State may request the revision of this Convention. To that end, the Swiss Federal Council shall issue invitations to a revision conference within a period of six months from the date of the request for revision.

ARTICLE 67

The Swiss Federal Council shall notify the States represented at the Diplomatic Conference of Lugano and the States who have later acceded to the Convention of:

(a) the deposit of each instrument of ratification or accession;

(b) the dates of entry into force of this Convention in respect of the Contracting States;

(c) any denunciation received pursuant to Article 64;

(d) any declaration received pursuant to Article 1a of Protocol No 1;

(e) any declaration received pursuant to Article 1b of Protocol No 1;

(f) any declaration received pursuant to Article IV of Protocol No 1;

(g) any communication made pursuant to Article VI of Protocol No 1.

ARTICLE 68

This Convention, drawn up in a single original in the Danish, Dutch, English, Finnish, French, German, Greek, Icelandic, Irish, Italian, Norwegian, Portuguese, Spanish and Swedish languages, all fourteen texts being equally authentic, shall be deposited in the archives of the Swiss Federal Council. The Swiss Federal Council shall transmit a certified copy to the Government of each State represented at the Diplomatic Conference of Lugano and to the Government of each acceding State.

PROTOCOL No 2 ON THE UNIFORM INTERPRETATION OF THE CONVENTION

Preamble

The High Contracting Parties,

Having regard to Article 65 of this Convention,

Considering the substantial link between this Convention and the Brussels Convention,

Considering that the Court of Justice of the European Communities by virtue of the Protocol of 3 June 1971 has jurisdiction to give rulings on the interpretation of the provisions of the Brussels Convention,

Being aware of the rulings delivered by the Court of Justice of the European Communities on the interpretation of the Brussels Convention up to the time of signature of this Convention,

Considering that the negotiations which led to the conclusion of the Convention were based on the Brussels Convention in the light of these rulings,

Desiring to prevent, in full deference to the independence of the courts, divergent interpretations and to arrive at as uniform an interpretation as possible of the provisions of the Convention, and of these provisions and those of the Brussels Convention which are substantially reproduced in this Convention,

Have agreed as follows:

ARTICLE 1

The courts of each Contracting State shall, when applying and interpreting the provisions of the Convention, pay due account to the principles laid down by any relevant decision delivered by courts of the other Contracting States concerning provisions of this Convention.

ARTICLE 2

1. The Contracting Parties agree to set up a system of exchange of information concerning judgments delivered pursuant to this Convention as well as relevant judgments under the Brussels Convention. This system shall comprise:

– transmission to a central body by the competent authorities of judgments delivered by courts of last instance and the Court of Justice of the European Communities as well as judgments of particular importance which have become final and have been delivered pursuant to this Convention or the Brussels Convention,

– classification of these judgments by the central body including, as far as necessary, the drawing-up and publication of translations and abstracts,

– communication by the central body of the relevant documents to the competent national authorities of all signatories and acceding States to the Convention and to the Commission of the European Communities.

2. The central body is the Registrar of the Court of Justice of the European Communities.

ARTICLE 3

1. A Standing Committee shall be set up for the purposes of this Protocol.

2. The Committee shall be composed of representatives appointed by each signatory and acceding State.

3. The European Communities (Commission, Court of Justice and General Secretariat of the Council) and the European Free Trade Association may attend the meetings as observers.

ARTICLE 4

1. At the request of a Contracting Party, the depository of the Convention shall convene meetings of the Committee for the purpose of exchanging views on the functioning of the Convention and in particular on:

– the development of the case-law as communicated under the first paragraph first indent of Article 2,

– the application of Article 57 of the Convention.

2. The Committee, in the light of these exchanges, may also examine the appropriateness of starting on particular topics a revision of the Convention and make recommendations.

SCHEDULE 4

TITLE II OF 1968 CONVENTION AS MODIFIED FOR ALLOCATION OF JURISDICTION WITHIN UK

TITLE II

JURISDICTION

[As to the use of the dots and heavy type, see s16(2) of the Act, above]

Section 1

ARTICLE 2

Subject to the provisions of this **Title**, persons domiciled in a **part of the United Kingdom** shall be sued in the courts of that **part**.

ARTICLE 3

Persons domiciled in a **part of the United Kingdom** may be sued in the courts of another **part of the United Kingdom** only by virtue of the rules set out in Sections **2, 4, 5 and 6** of this Title.

Section 2

ARTICLE 5

A person domiciled in a **part of the United Kingdom** may, in another **part of the United Kingdom**, be sued:

(1) in matters relating to a contract, in the courts for the place of performance of the obligation in question; in matters relating to individual contracts of employment, this place is that where the employee habitually carries out his work or if the employee does not habitually carry out his work in any one country, the employer may also be sued in the courts for the place where the business which engaged the employee was or is now situated;

(2) in matters relating to maintenance, in the courts for the place where the maintenance creditor is domiciled or habitually resident or, if the matter is ancillary to proceedings concerning the status of a person, in the court which, according to its own law, has

jurisdiction to entertain those proceedings, unless that jurisdiction is based solely on the nationality of one of the parties;

(3) in matters relating to tort, delict or quasi-delict, in the courts for the place where the harmful event occurred **or in the case of a threatened wrong is likely to occur**;

(4) as regards a civil claim for damages or restitution which is based on an act giving rise to criminal proceedings, in the court seised of those proceedings, to the extent that that court has jurisdiction under its own law to entertain civil proceedings;

(5) as regards a dispute arising out of the operations of a branch, agency or other establishment, in the courts for the place in which the branch, agency or other establishment is situated;

(6) in his capacity as a settlor, trustee or beneficiary of a trust created by the operation of a statute, or by a written instrument, or created orally and evidenced in writing, in the courts of the **part of the United Kingdom** in which the trust is domiciled;

(7) as regards a dispute concerning the payment of remuneration claimed in respect of the salvage of a cargo or freight, in the court under the authority of which the cargo or freight in question

   (a) has been arrested to secure such payment, or
   (b) could have been so arrested, but bail or other security has been given;

provided that this provisions shall apply only if it is claimed that the defendant has an interest in the cargo or freight or had such an interest at the time of salvage;

(8) in proceedings –

   (a) concerning a debt secured on immovable property; or
   (b) which are brought to assert, declare or determine proprietary or possessory rights, or rights of security, in or over movable property, or to obtain authority to dispose of movable property,

in the courts of the part of the United Kingdom in which the property is situated.

ARTICLE 5A

Proceedings which have as their object a decision of an organ of a company or other legal person or of an association

of natural or legal persons may, without prejudice to the other provisions of this Title, be brought in the courts of the part of the United Kingdom in which that company, legal person or association has its seat.

ARTICLE 6

A person domiciled in a **part of the United Kingdom** may, **in another part of the United Kingdom**, also be sued:

(1) where he is one of a number of defendants, in the courts for the place where any one of them is domiciled;

(2) as a third party in an action on a warranty or guarantee or in any other third party proceedings, in the court seised of the original proceedings, unless these were instituted solely with the object of removing him from the jurisdiction of the court which would be competent in his case;

(3) on a counterclaim arising from the same contract or facts on which the original claim was based, in the court in which the original claim is pending.

(4) in matters relating to a contract, if the action may be combined with an action against the same defendant in matters relating to rights in rem in immovable property, in the court of the **part of the United Kingdom** in which the property is situated.

ARTICLE 6A

Where by virtue of this **Title** a court of a **part of the United Kingdom** has jurisdiction in actions relating to liability arising from the use or operation of a ship, that court, or any other court substituted for this purpose by the internal law of that **part**, shall also have jurisdiction over claims for limitation of such liability.

Section 4

ARTICLE 13

In proceedings concerning a contract concluded by a person for a purpose which can be regarded as being outside his trade or profession, hereinafter called 'the consumer', jurisdiction shall be determined by this Section, without prejudice to the provisions of Articles 5(5) **and (8)(b),** if it is:

(1) a contract for the sale of goods on instalment credit terms, or

(2) a contract for a loan repayable by instalments, or for any other form of credit, made to finance the sale of goods, or

(3) any other contract for the supply of goods or a contract for the supply of services and the consumer took in **the part of the United Kingdom in which he is domiciled** the steps necessary for the conclusion of the contract.

This Section shall not apply to contracts of transport **or insurance.**

ARTICLE 14

A consumer may bring proceedings against the other party to a contract either in the courts of the **part of the United Kingdom** in which that party is domiciled or in the courts of the **part of the United Kingdom** in which he is himself domiciled.

Proceedings may be brought against a consumer by the other party to the contract only in the courts of the **part of the United Kingdom** in which the consumer is domiciled.

These provisions shall not affect the right to bring a counterclaim in the court in which, in accordance with this Section, the original claim is pending.

ARTICLE 15

The provisions of this Section may be departed from only by an agreement:

(1) which is entered into after the dispute has arisen, or

(2) which allows the consumer to bring proceedings in courts other than those indicated in this Section, or

(3) which is entered into by the consumer and the other party to the contract, both of whom are at the time of conclusion of the contract domiciled or habitually resident in the same **part of the United Kingdom,** and which confers jurisdiction on the courts of that **part**, provided that such an agreement is not contrary to the law of that **part.**

Section 5

ARTICLE 16

The following courts shall have exclusive jurisdiction, regardless of domicile:

(1) (a) in proceedings which have as their object rights in rem in immovable property or tenancies of immovable property, the courts of the **part of the United Kingdom** in which the property is situated;

(b) however, in proceedings which have as their object tenancies of immovable property concluded for temporary private use for a maximum period of six consecutive months, the courts of the **part of the United Kingdom** in which the defendant is domiciled shall also have jurisdiction, provided that the landlord and the tenant are natural persons and are domiciled in the same part of the United Kingdom.

(2) in proceedings which have as their object the validity of the constitution, the nullity or the dissolution of companies or other legal persons or associations of natural or legal persons, the courts of the **part of the United Kingdom** in which the company, legal person or association has its seat;

(3) in proceedings which have as their object the validity of entries in public registers, the courts of the **part of the United Kingdom** in which the register is kept;

(5) in proceedings concerned with the enforcement of judgments, the courts of the **part of the United Kingdom** in which the judgments has been or is to be enforced.

Section 6

ARTICLE 17

If the parties have agreed that a court or the courts of a **part of the United Kingdom** are to have jurisdiction to settle any disputes which have arisen or which may arise in connection with a particular legal relationship, **and, apart from this Schedule, the agreement would be effective to confer jurisdiction under the law of that part**, that court or those courts shall have jurisdiction.

The court or courts of a **part of the United Kingdom** on which a trust instrument has conferred jurisdiction shall have jurisdiction in any proceedings brought against a settlor, trustee or beneficiary, if relations between these persons or their rights or obligations under the trust are involved.

Agreements or provisions of a trust instrument conferring jurisdiction shall have no legal force if they are contrary to the provisions of Article 15, or if the courts whose jurisdiction they purport to exclude have exclusive jurisdiction by virtue of Article 16.

In matters relating to individual contracts of employment an agreement conferring jurisdiction shall have legal force only if it is entered into after the dispute has arisen or if the employee invokes it to seise courts other than those for the defendant's domicile or those specified in Article 5(1).

ARTICLE 18

Apart from jurisdiction derived from other provisions of this **Title**, a court of a **part of the United Kingdom** before whom a defendant enters an appearance shall have jurisdiction. This rule shall not apply where appearance was entered solely to contest the jurisdiction, or where another court has exclusive jurisdiction by virtue of Article 16.

Section 7

ARTICLE 19

Where a court of a **part of the United Kingdom** is seised of a claim which is principally concerned with a matter over which the courts of another **part of the United Kingdom** have exclusive jurisdiction by virtue of Article 16, it shall declare of its own motion that it has no jurisdiction.

ARTICLE 20

Where a defendant domiciled in one **part of the United Kingdom** is sued in a court of another **part of the United Kingdom** and does not enter an appearance, the court shall declare of its own motion that it has no jurisdiction unless its jurisdiction is derived from the provisions of this **Title**.

The court shall stay the proceedings so long as it is not shown that the defendant has been able to receive the document instituting the proceedings or an equivalent document in sufficient time to enable him to arrange for his defence, or that all necessary steps have been taken to this end.

Section 9

ARTICLE 24

Application may be made to the courts of a **part of the United Kingdom** for such provisional, including protective, measures as may be available under the law of that **part**, even if, under this **Title**, the courts of another **part of the United Kingdom** have jurisdiction as to the substance of the matter.

SCHEDULE 5

PROCEEDINGS EXCLUDED FROM SCHEDULE 4

1. Proceedings for the winding up of a company under the Insolvency Act 1986 or the Insolvency (Northern Ireland) Order 1989, or proceedings relating to a company as respects which jurisdiction is conferred on the court having winding up jurisdiction under either of those Acts.

2. Proceedings concerned with the registration or validity of patents, trade marks, designs or other similar rights required to be deposited or registered.

3. Proceedings under section 6 of the Protection of Trading Interests Act 1980 (recovery of sums paid or obtained pursuant to a judgment for multiple damages).

4. Proceedings on appeal from, or for review of, decisions of tribunals

5. Proceedings for, or otherwise relating to, an order under any of the following provisions –

   (a) paragraph 23 of Schedule 2 to the Children Act 1989 ... (contributions in respect of children in care, etc);

   (b) section 49 or 50 of the Child Care Act 1980 ... (applications for, or for variation of, affiliation orders in respect of children in care, etc);

(c) section 43 of the National Assistance Act 1948, section 18 of the Supplementary Benefits Act 1976, section 106 of the Social Security Administration Act 1992 ... (recovery of cost of assistance or benefit from person liable to maintain the assisted person);

(d) section 44 of the National Assistance Act 1948, section 19 of the Supplementary Benefits Act 1976 ... (applications for, or for variation of, affiliation orders in respect of children for whom assistance or benefit provided).

6. Proceedings brought in any court in pursuance of –

(a) any statutory provisions which, in the case of any convention to which Article 57 applies (conventions relating to specific matters which override the general rules in the 1969 Convention), implements the convention or makes provision with respect to jurisdiction in any field to which the convention relates; and

(b) any rule of law so far as it has the effect of implementing any such convention. ...

8. Proceedings for the rectification of the register of aircraft mortgages kept by the Civil Aviation Authority.

9. Proceedings brought in any court in pursuance of an order under section 23 of the Oil and Gas (Enterprise) Act 1982.

Proceedings such as are mentioned in section 188 of the Financial Services Act 1986.

SCHEDULE 6

ENFORCEMENT OF UNITED KINGDOM JUDGMENTS (MONEY PROVISIONS)

1. In this Schedule –

'judgment' means any judgment to which section 18 applies and references to the giving of a judgment shall be construed accordingly;

'money provision' means a provision for the payment of one or more sums of money;

'prescribed' means prescribed by rules of court.

2. (1) Any interested party who wishes to secure the enforcement in another part of the United Kingdom of any money provisions contained in a judgment may apply for a certificate under this Schedule.

(2) The application shall be made in the prescribed manner to the proper officer of the original court, that is to say –

(a) in relation to a judgment within paragraph (a) of the definition of 'judgment' in section 18(2), the court by which the judgment or order was given or made;

(b) in relation to a judgment within paragraph (b) of that definition, the court in which the judgment or order is entered;

(c) in relation to a judgment within paragraph (c) of that definition, the court in whose books the document is registered;

(d) in relation to a judgment within paragraph (d) of that definition, the tribunal by which the award or order was made;

(e) in relation to a judgment within paragraph (e) of that definition, the court which gave the judgment or made the order by virtue of which the award has become enforceable as mentioned in that paragraph.

3. A certificate shall not be issued under this Schedule in respect of a judgment unless under the law of the part of the United Kingdom in which the judgment was given –

(a) either –

(i) the time for bringing an appeal against the judgment has expired, no such appeal having been brought within that time; or

(ii) such an appeal having been brought within that time, that appeal has been finally disposed of; and

(b) enforcement of the judgment is not for the time being stayed or suspended, and the time available for its enforcement has not expired.

4. (1) Subject to paragraph 3, on an application under paragraph 2 the proper officer shall issue to the applicant a certificate in the prescribed form –

(a) stating the sum or aggregate of the sums (including any costs or expenses) payable under the money provision contained in the judgment, the rate of interest, if any, payable thereon and the date or time from which any such interest began to accrue;

(b) stating that the conditions specified in paragraph 3(a) and (b) are satisfied in relation to the judgment; and

(c) containing such other particulars as may be prescribed.

(2) More than one certificate may be issued under this Schedule (simultaneously or at different times) in respect of the same judgment. ...

6. (1) A certificate registered under this Schedule shall, for the purposes of its enforcement, be of the same force and effect, the registering court shall have in respect to its enforcement the same powers, and proceedings for or with respect to its enforcement may be taken, as if the certificate had been a judgment originally given in the registering court and had (where relevant) been entered.

(2) Sub-paragraph (1) is subject to the following provisions of this Schedule and to any provision made by rules of court as to the manner in which and the conditions subject to which a certificate registered under this Schedule may be enforced. ...

10. Where a certificate has been registered under this Schedule, the registering court –

(a) shall set aside the registration if, on an application made by any interested party, it is satisfied that the registration was contrary to the provisions of this Schedule;

(b) may set aside the registration if, on an application so made, it is satisfied that the matter in dispute in the proceedings in which the judgment in question was given had previously been the subject of a judgment by another court or tribunal having jurisdiction in the matter.

SCHEDULE 7

ENFORCEMENT OF UNITED KINGDOM JUDGMENTS (NON-MONEY PROVISIONS)

1. In this Schedule –

'judgment' means any judgment to which section 18 applies and references to the giving of a judgment shall be construed accordingly;

'non-money provision' means a provision for any relief or remedy not requiring payment of a sum of money;

'prescribed' means prescribed by rules of court.

2. (1) Any interested party who wishes to secure the enforcement in another part of the United Kingdom of any non-money provisions contained in a judgment may apply for a certified copy of the judgment.

(2) The application shall be made in the prescribed manner to the proper officer of the original court, that is to say –

(a) in relation to a judgment within paragraph (a) of the definition of 'judgment' in section 18(2), the court by which the judgment or order was given or made;

(b) in relation to a judgment within paragraph (b) of that definition, the court in which the judgment or order is entered;

(c) in relation to a judgment within paragraph (c) of that definition, the court in whose books the document is registered;

(d) in relation to a judgment within paragraph (d) of that definition, the tribunal by which the award or order was made;

(e) in relation to a judgment within paragraph (e) of that definition, the court which gave the judgment or made the order by virtue of which the award has become enforceable as mentioned in that paragraph.

3. A certified copy of a judgment shall not be issued under this Schedule unless under the law of the part of the United Kingdom in which the judgment was given –

(a) either –

(i) the time for bringing an appeal against the judgment has expired, no such appeal having been brought within that time; or

(ii) such an appeal having been brought within that time, that appeal has been finally disposed of; and

(b) enforcement of the judgment is not for the time being stayed or suspended, and the time available for its enforcement has not expired.

4. (1) Subject to paragraph 3, on an application under paragraph 2 the proper officer shall issue to the applicant –

(a) a certified copy of the judgment (including any money provisions or expected provisions which it may contain); and

(b) a certificate stating that the conditions specified in paragraph 3(a) and (b) are satisfied in relation to the judgment.

(2) In sub-paragraph (1)(a) 'excepted provision' means any provision

of a judgment which is excepted from the application of section 18 by subsection (5) of that section.

(3) There may be issued under this Schedule (simultaneously or at different times) –

(a) more than one certified copy of the same judgment; and

(b) more than one certificate in respect of the same judgment.

6. (1) The non-money provisions contained in a judgment registered under this Schedule shall, for the purposes of their enforcement, be of the same force and effect, the registering court shall have in relation to their enforcement the same powers, and proceedings for or with respect to their enforcement may be taken, as if the judgment containing them had been originally given in the registering court and had (where relevant) been entered.

(2) Sub-paragraph (1) is subject to the following provisions of this Schedule and to any provision made by rules of court as to the manner in which and conditions subject to which the non-money provisions contained in a judgment registered under this Schedule may be enforced.

9. Where a judgment has been registered under this Schedule, the registering court –

(a) shall set aside the registration if, on an application made by an interested party, it is satisfied that the registration was contrary to the provisions of this Schedule;

(b) may set aside the registration if, on an application so made, it is satisfied that the matter in dispute in the proceedings in which the judgment was given had previously been the subject of a judgment by another court or tribunal having jurisdiction in the matter.

As amended by the Criminal Justice Act 1982, s46; Oil and Gas (Enterprise) Act 1982, s37(1), Schedule 3, para 42; International Transport Conventions Act 1983, s11(2); Insolvency Act 1986, s439(2), Schedule 14; Family Law Reform Act 1987, s33(1), Schedule 2, para 89; Criminal Justice (Scotland) Act 1987, s45(3); Children Act 1989, s108(5), Schedule 13, para 47; Civil Jurisdiction and Judgments Act 1982 (Amendment) Order 1989, arts 3–8; Insolvency (Northern Ireland) Order 1989; Companies Act 1989, s200(2); Courts and Legal Services Act 1990, s116, Schedule 16, para 41; Civil Jurisdiction and Judgments Act 1982 (Amendment) Order 1990, arts 3–7, 9, 10, 11, 12(1)–(4), Schedules 2, 3; Civil Jurisdiction and Judgments Act 1991, ss1(1), (2), (3), 2, 3, Schedules 1, 2, paras 1–25; Maintenance Enforcement Act 1991, s10, Schedule 1, para 21; Social Security (Consequential Provisions) Act 1992, s4, Schedule 2, para 62; Transfer of Functions (Magistrates' Courts and Family Law) Order 1992, art 4(6), (7); Civil Jurisdiction and Judgments Act 1982 (Amendment) Order 1993, art 2.

FOREIGN LIMITATION PERIODS ACT
1984
(1984 c 16)

1 Application of foreign limitation law

(1) Subject to the following provisions of this Act, where in any action or proceedings in a court in England and Wales the law of any other country falls (in accordance with rules of private international law applicable by any such court) to be taken into account in the determination of any matter –

(a) the law of that other country relating to limitation shall apply in respect of that matter for the purposes of the action or proceedings; and

(b) except where that matter falls within subsection (2) below, the law of England and Wales relating to limitation shall not so apply.

(2) A matter falls within this subsection if it is a matter in the determination of which both the law of England and Wales and the law of some other country fall to be taken into account.

(3) The law of England and Wales shall determine for the purposes of any law applicable by virtue of subsection (1)(a) above whether, and the time at which, proceedings have been commenced in respect of any matter; and, accordingly, section 35 of the Limitation Act 1980 (new claims in pending proceedings) shall apply in relation to time limits applicable by virtue of subsection (1)(a) above as it applies in relation to time limits under that Act.

(4) A court in England and Wales, in exercising in pursuance of subsection (1)(a) above any discretion conferred by the law of any other country, shall so far as practicable exercise that discretion in the manner in which it is exercised in comparable cases by the courts of that other country.

(5) In this section 'law', in relation to any country, shall not include

rules of private international law applicable by the courts of that country or, in the case of England and Wales, this Act.

2   Exceptions to s1

(1) In any case in which the application of section 1 above would to any extent conflict (whether under subsection (2) below or otherwise) with public policy, that section shall not apply to the extent that its application would so conflict.

(2) The application of section 1 above in relation to any action or proceedings shall conflict with public policy to the extent that its application would cause undue hardship to a person who is, or might be made, a party to the action or proceedings.

(3) Where, under a law applicable by virtue of section 1(1)(a) above for the purposes of any action or proceedings, a limitation period is or may be extended or interrupted in respect of the absence of a party to the action or proceedings from any specified jurisdiction or country, so much of that law as provides for the extension or interruption shall be disregarded for those purposes.

3   Foreign judgments on limitation points

Where a court in any country outside England and Wales has determined any matter wholly or partly by reference to the law of that or any other country (including England and Wales) relating to limitation, then, for the purposes of the law relating to the effect to be given n England and Wales to that determination, that court shall, to the extent that it has so determined the matter, be deemed to have determined it on its merits.

4   Meaning of law relating to limitation

(1) Subject to subsection (3) below, references in this Act to the law of any country (including England and Wales) relating to limitation shall, in relation to any matter, be construed as references to so much of the relevant law of that country as (in any manner) makes provision with respect to a limitation period applicable to the bringing of proceedings in respect to that matter in the courts of that country and shall include –

(a) references to so much of that law as relates to, and to the effect of, the application, extension, reduction or interruption of that period; and

(b) a reference, where under that law there is no limitation period which is so applicable, to the rule that such proceedings may be brought within an indefinite period.

(2) In subsection (1) above 'relevant law', in relation to any country, means the procedural and substantive law applicable, apart from any rules of private international law, by the courts of that country.

(3) References in this Act to the law of England and Wales relating to limitation shall not include the rules by virtue of which a court may, in the exercise of any discretion, refuse equitable relief on the grounds of acquiescence or otherwise; but, in applying those rules to a case in relation to which the law of any country outside England and Wales is applicable by virtue of section 1(1)(a) above (not being a law that provides for a limitation period that has expired), a court in England and Wales shall have regard, in particular, to the provisions of the law that is so applicable.

5   Application of Act to arbitrations

The references to any other limitation enactment in section 34 of the Limitation Act 1980 (application of limitation enactments to arbitration) include references to sections 1, 2 and 4 of this Act; and, accordingly, in subsection (5) of the said section 34, the reference to the time prescribed by a limitation enactment has effect for the purposes of any case to which section 1 above applies as a reference to the limitation period (if any) applicable by virtue of section 1 above.

6   Application to Crown

(1) This Act applies in relation to any action or proceedings by or against the Crown as it applies in relation to actions and proceedings to which the Crown is not a party.

(2) For the purposes of this section references to an action or proceedings by or against the Crown include references to –

(a) any action or proceedings by or against Her Majesty in right of the Duchy of Lancaster;

(b) any action or proceedings by or against any Government department or any officer of the Crown as such or any person acting on behalf of the Crown;

(c) any action or proceedings by or against the Duke of Cornwall.

COUNTY COURTS ACT 1984
(1984 c 28)

74 Interest on judgment debts, etc

(1) The Lord Chancellor may by order made with the concurrence of the Treasury provide that any sums to which this subsection applies shall carry interest at such rate and between such times as may be prescribed by the order.

(2) The sums to which subsection (1) applies are –

(a) sums payable under judgments or orders given or made in a county court, including sums payable by instalments; and

(b) sums which by virtue of any enactment are, if the county court so orders, recoverable as if payable under an order of that court, and in respect of which the county court has so ordered. ...

(5A) The power conferred by subsection (1) includes power to make provision enabling a county court to order that the rate of interest applicable to a sum expressed in a currency other than sterling shall be such rate as the court thinks fit (instead of the rate otherwise applicable).

As amended by the Private International Law (Miscellaneous Provisions) Act 1995, s2.

MATRIMONIAL AND FAMILY PROCEEDINGS ACT 1984

(1984 c 42)

12 Applications for financial relief after overseas divorce, etc

(1) Where –

(a) a marriage has been dissolved or annulled, or the parties to a marriage have been legally separated, by means of judicial or other proceedings in an overseas country, and

(b) the divorce, annulment or legal separation is entitled to be recognised as valid in England and Wales,

either party to the marriage may apply to the court in the manner prescribed by rules of court for an order for financial relief under this Part of this Act.

(2) If after a marriage has been dissolved or annulled in an overseas country one of the parties to the marriage remarries that party shall not be entitled to make an application in relation to that marriage.

(3) For the avoidance of doubt it is hereby declared that the reference in subsection (2) above to remarriage includes a reference to a marriage which is by law void or voidable. ...

13 Leave of the court required for applications for financial relief

(1) No application for an order for financial relief shall be made under this Part of this Act unless the leave of the court has been obtained in accordance with rules of court; and the court shall not grant leave unless it considers that there is substantial ground for the making of an application for such an order.

(2) The court may grant leave under this section notwithstanding that an order has been made by a court in a country outside England

and Wales requiring the other party to the marriage to make any payment or transfer any property to the applicant or a child of the family.

(3) Leave under this section may be granted subject to such conditions as the court thinks fit.

14   Interim orders for maintenance

(1) Where leave is granted under section 13 above for the making of an application for an order for financial relief and it appears to the court that the applicant or any child of the family is in immediate need of financial assistance, the court may make an interim order for maintenance, that is to say, an order requiring the other party to the marriage to make to the applicant or to the child such periodical payments, and for such term, being a term beginning not earlier than the date of the grant of leave and ending with the date of the determination of the application for an order for financial relief, as the court thinks reasonable.

(2) If it appears to the court that the court has jurisdiction to entertain the application for an order for financial relief by reason only of paragraph (c) of section 15(1) below the court shall not make an interim order under this section.

(3) An interim order under subsection (1) above may be made subject to such conditions as the court thinks fit.

15   Jurisdiction of the court

(1) Subject to subsection (2) below, the court shall have jurisdiction to entertain an application for an order for financial relief if any of the following jurisdictional requirements are satisfied, that is to say –

> (a) either of the parties to the marriage was domiciled in England and Wales on the date of the application for leave under section 13 above or was so domiciled on the date on which the divorce annulment or legal separation obtained in the overseas country took effect in that country; or

> (b) either of the parties to the marriage was habitually resident in England and Wales throughout the period of one year ending with the date of the application for leave or was so resident throughout the period of one year ending with the date on which

the divorce, annulment or legal separation obtained in the overseas country took effect in that country; or

(c) either or both of the parties to the marriage had at the date of the application for leave a beneficial interest in possession in a dwelling-house situated in England or Wales which was at some time during the marriage a matrimonial home of the parties to the marriage.

(2) Where the jurisdiction of the court to entertain proceedings under this Part of this Act would fall to be determined by reference to the jurisdictional requirements imposed by virtue of Part I of the Civil Jurisdiction and Judgment Act 1982 (implementation of certain European conventions) then –

(a) satisfaction of the requirements of subsection (1) above shall not obviate the need to satisfy the requirements imposed by virtue of Part I of that Act; and

(b) satisfaction of the requirements imposed by virtue of Part I of that Act shall obviate the need to satisfy the requirements of subsection (1) above;

and the court shall entertain or not entertain the proceedings accordingly.

16 Duty of the court to consider whether England and Wales is appropriate venue for application

(1) Before making an order for financial relief the court shall consider whether in all the circumstances of the case it would be appropriate for such an order to be made by a court in England and Wales, and if the court is not satisfied that it would be appropriate, the court shall dismiss the application.

(2) The court shall in particular have regard to the following matters –

(a) the connection which the parties to the marriage have with England and Wales;

(b) the connection which those parties have with the country in which the marriage was dissolved or annulled or in which they were legally separated;

(c) the connection which those parties have with any other country outside England and Wales;

(d) any financial benefit which the applicant or a child of the family has received, or is likely to receive, in consequence of the divorce, annulment or legal separation, by virtue of any agreement or the operation of the law of a country outside England and Wales;

(e) in a case where an order has been made by a court in a country outside England and Wales requiring the other party to the marriage to make any payment or transfer any property for the benefit of the applicant or a child of the family, the financial relief given by the order and the extent to which the order has been complied with or is likely to be complied with;

(f) any right which the applicant has, or has had, to apply for financial relief from the other party to the marriage under the law of any country outside England and Wales and if the applicant has omitted to exercise that right the reason for that omission;

(g) the availability in England and Wales of any property in respect of which an order under this Part of this Act in favour of the applicant could be made;

(h) the extent to which any order made under this Part of this Act is likely to be enforceable;

(i) the length of time which has elapsed since the date of the divorce, annulment or legal separation.

COMPANIES ACT 1985
(1985 c 6)

690A Branch registration under the Eleventh Company Law Directive (89/666/EEC)

(1) This section applies to any limited company which –

(a) is incorporated outside the United Kingdom and Gibraltar, and

(b) has a branch in Great Britain.

(2) Schedule 21A to this Act (Branch registration under the Eleventh Company Law Directive (89/666/EEC)) shall have effect in relation to any company to which this section applies.

690B Scope of ss691 and 692

Sections 691 and 692 shall not apply to any limited company which –

(a) is incorporated outside the United Kingdom and Gibraltar, and

(b) has a branch in the United Kingdom.

691 Documents to be delivered to registrar

(1) When a company incorporated outside Great Britain establishes a place of business in Great Britain, it shall within one month of doing so deliver to the registrar of companies for registration –

(a) a certified copy of the charter, statutes or memorandum and articles of the company or other instrument constituting or defining the company's constitution, and, if the instrument is not written in the English language, a certified translation of it; and

(b) a return in the prescribed form containing –

(i) a list of the company's directors and secretary, containing the particulars specified in the next subsection,

(ii) a list of the names and addresses of some one or more persons resident in Great Britain authorised to accept on the company's behalf service of process and any notices required to be served on it,

(iii) a list of the documents delivered in compliance with paragraph (a) of this subsection, and

(iv) a statutory declaration (made by a director or secretary of the company or by any person whose name and address are given in the list required by sub-paragraph (ii)), stating the date on which the company's place of business in Great Britain was established. ...

692 Registration of altered particulars

(1) If any alteration is made in –

(a) the charter, statutes, or memorandum and articles of an oversea company or any such instrument as is mentioned above, or

(b) the directors or secretary of an oversea company or the particulars contained in the list of the directors and secretary, or

(c) the names or addresses of the persons authorised to accept service on behalf of an oversea company,

the company shall, within the time specified below, deliver to the registrar of companies for registration a return containing the prescribed particulars of the alteration.

(2) If any change is made in the corporate name of an oversea company, the company shall, within the time specified below, deliver to the registrar of companies for registration a return containing the prescribed particulars of the change.

(3) The time for delivery of the returns required by subsections (1) and (2) is –

(a) in the case of an alteration to which subsection (1)(c) applies, 21 days after the making of the alteration, and

(b) otherwise, 21 days after the date on which notice of the alteration or change in question could have been received in Great Britain in due course of post (if despatched with due diligence).

692A Change in registration regime

(1) Where a company ceases to be a company to which section 690A applies, and, immediately after ceasing to be such a company –

(a) continues to have in Great Britain a place of business which it had immediately before ceasing to be such a company, and

(b) does not have a branch in Northern Ireland,

it shall be treated for the purposes of section 691 as having established the place of business on the date when it ceased to be a company to which section 690A applies.

(2) Where a limited company incorporated outside the United Kingdom and Gibraltar –

(a) ceases to have a branch in Northern Ireland, and

(b) both immediately before and immediately after ceasing to do so, has a place of business, but not a branch, in Great Britain,

it shall be treated for the purposes of section 691 as having established the place of business on the date when it ceased to have a branch in Northern Ireland.

(3) Where a company –

(a) becomes a company to which section 690A applies,

(b) immediately after becoming such a company, has in a part of Great Britain an established place of business but no branch, and

(c) immediately before becoming such a company, had an established place of business in that part,

sections 691 and 692 shall, in relation to that part, continue to apply to the company (notwithstanding section 690B) until such time as it gives notice to the registrar for that part that it is a company to which that section applies. ...

693 Obligation to state name and other particulars

(1) Every oversea company shall –

(a) in every prospectus inviting subscriptions for its shares or debentures in Great Britain, state the country in which the company is incorporated,

(b) conspicuously exhibit on every place where it carries on business in Great Britain the company's name and the country in which it is incorporated,

(c) cause the company's name and the country in which it is incorporated to be stated in legible characters in all bill-heads and letter paper, and in all notices and other official publications of the company, and

(d) if the liability of the members of the company is limited, cause notice of that fact to be stated in legible characters in every such prospectus as above mentioned and in all bill-heads, letter paper, notices and other official publications of the company in Great Britain, and to be affixed on every place where it carries on its business.

(2) Every company to which section 690A applies shall, in the case of each branch of the company registered under paragraph 1 of Schedule 21A, cause the following particulars to be stated in legible characters in all letter paper and order forms used in carrying on the business of the branch –

(a) the place of registration of the branch, and

(b) the registered number of the branch.

(3) Every company to which section 690A applies, which is not incorporated in a Member State and which is required by the law of the country in which it is incorporated to be registered shall, in the case of each branch of the company registered under paragraph 1 of Schedule 21A, cause the following particulars to be stated in legible characters in all letter paper and order forms used in carrying on the business of the branch –

(a) the identity of the registry in which the company is registered in its country of incorporation, and

(b) the number with which it is registered.

(4) Every company to which section 690A applies and which is not incorporated in a Member State shall, in the case of each branch of the company registered under paragraph 1 of Schedule 21A, cause

the following particulars to be stated in legible characters in all letter paper and order forms used in carrying on the business of the branch -•

(a) the legal form of the company,

(b) the location of its head office, and

(c) if applicable, the fact that it is being wound up.

694 Regulation of oversea companies in respect of their names

(1) If it appears to the Secretary of State that the corporate name of an oversea company is a name by which the company, had it been formed under this Act, would on the relevant date (determined in accordance with subsection (3A) and (3B)) have been precluded from being registered by section 26 either –

(a) because it falls within subsection (1) of that section, or

(b) if it falls within subsection (2) of that section, because the Secretary of State would not approve the company's being registered with that name,

the Secretary of State may serve a notice on the company, stating why the name would not have been registered.

(2) If the corporate name of an oversea company is in the Secretary of State's opinion too like a name appearing on the relevant date in the index of names kept by the registrar of companies under section 714 or which should have appeared in that index on that date, or is the same as a name which should have so appeared, the Secretary of State may serve a notice on the company specifying the name in the index which the company's name is too like or which is the same as the company's name.

(3) No notice shall be served on a company under subsection (1) or (2) later than 12 months after the relevant date.

(3A) For the purposes of subsections (1) to (3), the relevant date, in relation to a company, is the date on which it has complied with paragraph 1 of Schedule 21A or section 691(1) or, if there is more than one such date, the first date on which it has complied with that paragraph or that subsection since becoming an oversea company.

(3B) But where the company's corporate name has changed since that date ascertained in accordance with subsection (3A), the relevant date is the date on which the company has, in respect of the change or, if more than one, the latest change, complied with paragraph 7(1) of Schedule 21A or section 692(2), as the case may be.

(4) An oversea company on which a notice is served under subsection (1) or (2) –

(a) may deliver to the registrar of companies for registration a statement in the prescribed form specifying a name approved by the Secretary of State other than its corporate name under which it proposes to carry on business in Great Britain, and

(b) may, after that name has been registered, at any time deliver to the registrar for registration a statement in the prescribed form specifying a name approved by the Secretary of State (other than its corporate name) in substitution for the name previously registered.

(5) The name by which an oversea company is for the time being registered under subsection (4) is, for all purposes of the law applying in Great Britain (including this Act and the Business Names Act 1985), deemed to be the company's corporate name; but –

(a) this does not affect references to the corporate name in this section, or any rights or obligations of the company, or render defective any legal proceedings by or against the company, and

(b) any legal proceedings that might have been continued or commenced against the company by its corporate name or its name previously registered under this section may be continued or commenced against it by its name for the time being so registered.

(6) An oversea company on which a notice is served under subsection (1) or (2) shall not at any time after the expiration of 2 months from the service of that notice (or such longer period as may be specified in that notice) carry on business in Great Britain under its corporate name.

Nothing in this subsection, or in section 697(2) (which imposes penalties for its contravention) invalidates any transaction entered into by the company.

(7) The Secretary of State may withdraw a notice served under subsection (1) or (2) at any time before the end of the period mentioned in subsection (6); and that subsection does not apply to a company served with a notice which has been withdrawn.

694A Service of documents: companies to which s690A applies

(1) This section applies to any company to which section 690A applies.

(2) Any process or notice required to be served on a company to which this section applies in respect of the carrying on of the business of a branch registered by it under paragraph 1 of Schedule 21A is sufficiently served if –

(a) addressed to any person whose name has, in respect of the branch, been delivered to the registrar as a person falling within paragraph 3(e) of that Schedule, and

(b) left at or sent by post to the address for that person which has been so delivered.

(3) Where –

(a) a company to which this section applies makes default, in respect of a branch, in delivering to the registrar the particulars mentioned in paragraph 3(e) of Schedule 21A, or

(b) all the persons whose names have, in respect of a branch, been delivered to the registrar as persons falling within paragraph 3(e) of that Schedule are dead or have ceased to reside in Great Britain, or refuse to accept service on the company's behalf, or for any reason cannot be served,

a document may be served on the company in respect of the carrying on of the business of the branch by leaving it at, or sending it by post to, any place of business established by the company in Great Britain.

(4) Where a company to which this section applies has more than one branch in Great Britain, any notice or process required to be served on the company which is not required to be served in respect of the carrying on of the business of one branch rather than another shall be treated for the purposes of this section as required to be served in respect of the carrying on of the business of each of its branches.

695 Service of documents on oversea company

(1) Any process or notice required to be served on an oversea company to which section 691 applies is sufficiently served if addressed to any person whose name has been delivered to the

registrar under preceding sections of this Part and left at or sent by post to the address which has been so delivered.

(2) However –

(a) where such a company makes default in delivering to the registrar the name and address of a person resident in Great Britain who is authorised to accept on behalf of the company service of process or notices, or

(b) if at any time all the persons whose names and addresses have been so delivered are dead or have ceased so to reside, or refuse to accept service on the company's behalf, or for any reason cannot be served,

a document may be served on the company by leaving it at, or sending it by post to, any place of business established by the company in Great Britain.

695A Registrar to whom documents to be delivered: companies to which s690A applies

(1)References to the registrar, in relation to a company to which section 690A applies (except references to Schedule 21C) shall be construed in accordance with the following provisions.

(2) The documents which a company is required to deliver to the registrar shall be delivered –

(a) to the registrar for England and Wales, if required to be delivered in respect of a branch in England and Wales, and

(b) to the registrar for Scotland, if required to be delivered in respect of a branch in Scotland.

(3) If a company closes a branch in a part of Great Britain, it shall forthwith give notice of that fact to the registrar for that part; and from the date on which notice is so given it is no longer obliged to deliver documents to that registrar in respect of that branch.

(4) In subsection (3) above, the reference to closing a branch in either part of Great Britain includes a reference to a branch ceasing to be situated in that part on becoming situated elsewhere.

696 Office where documents to be filed

(1) Any document which an oversea company to which section 691 applies is required to deliver to the registrar of companies shall be

delivered to the registrar at the registration office in England and Wales or Scotland, according to where the company has established a place of business.

(2) If the company has established a place of business both in England and Wales and in Scotland, the document shall be delivered at the registration office both in England and Wales and in Scotland.

(3) References in this Part (except references to Schedule 21C) to the registrar of companies, in relation to a company to which section 691 applies, are to be construed in accordance with the above subsections.

(4) If an oversea company to which section 691 applies ceased to have a place of business in either part of Great Britain, it shall forthwith give notice of that fact to the registrar of companies for that part; and as from the date on which notice is so given the obligation of the company to deliver any document to the registrar ceases.

697 Penalties for non-compliance

(1) If an oversea company fails to comply with any of sections 691 to 693 and 696, the company, and every officer or agent of the company who knowingly and wilfully authorises or permits the default, is liable to a fine and, in the case of a continuing offence, to a daily default fine for continued contravention.

(2) If an oversea company contravenes section 694(6), the company and every officer or agent of it who knowingly and wilfully authorises or permits the contravention is guilty of an offence and liable to a fine and, for continued contravention, to a daily default fine.

(3) If an oversea company fails to comply with section 695A or Schedule 21A, the company, and every officer or agent of the company who knowingly and wilfully authorises or permits the default, is liable to a fine and, in the case of a continuing offence, to a daily default fine for continued contravention.

698 Definitions

(1) For purposes of this Chapter –

    'certified' means certified in the prescribed manner to be a true copy or a correct translation;

'director', in relation to an oversea company, includes shadow director; and

'secretary' includes any person occupying the position of secretary by whatever name called.

(2) For the purposes of this Part (except section 699A and Schedule 21C):

(a) where a branch comprises places of business in more than one part of the United Kingdom, the branch shall be treated as being situated in that part of the United Kingdom where its principal place of business is situated; and

(b) 'branch' means a branch within the meaning of the Council Directive concerning disclosure requirements in respect of branches opened in a Member State by certain types of company governed by the law of another State (the Eleventh Company Law Directive, 89/666/EEC).

725 Service of documents

(1) A document may be served on a company by leaving it at, or sending it by post to, the company's registered office.

(2) Where a company registered in Scotland carried on business in England and Wales, the process of any court in England and Wales may be served on the company by leaving it at, or sending it by post to, the company's principal place of business in England and Wales, addressed to the manager or other head officer in England and Wales of the company.

(3) Where process is served on a company under subsection (2), the person issuing out the process shall send a copy of it by post to the company's registered office.

NB For the partial repeal of s693(1) in certain circumstances, see the Financial Services Act 1986, s212(3), Schedule 17, Pt I.

As amended by the Overseas Companies and Credit and Financial Institutions (Branch Disclosure) Regulations 1992, regs 3(1), 4, 5, Schedule 2, Pt I, paras 1, 2, 4, 6–13, Schedule 4, paras 1–3.

CHILD ABDUCTION AND CUSTODY ACT 1985

(1985 c 60)

PART I

INTERNATIONAL CHILD ABDUCTION

1   The Hague Convention

(1) In this Part of this Act 'the Convention' means the Convention on the Civil Aspects of International Child Abduction which was signed at The Hague on 25 October 1980.

(2) Subject to the provisions of this Part of this Act, the provisions of that Convention set out in Schedule 1 to this Act shall have the force of law in the United Kingdom.

2   Contracting States

(1) For the purposes of the Convention as it has effect under this Part of this Act the Contracting States other than the United Kingdom shall be those for the time being specified by an Order in Council under this section.

(2) An Order in Council under this section shall specify the date of the coming into force of the Convention as between the United Kingdom and any State specified in the Order; and, except where the Order otherwise provides, the Convention shall apply as between the United Kingdom and that State only in relation to wrongful removals or retentions occurring on or after that date.

(3) Where the Convention applies, or applies only, to a particular territory or particular territories specified in a declaration made by a Contracting State under Article 39 or 40 of the Convention references to that State in subsections (1) and (2) above shall be construed as references to that territory or those territories.

3   Central Authorities

(1) Subject to subsection (2) below, the functions under the Convention of a Central Authority shall be discharged –

(a) in England and Wales and in Northern Ireland by the Lord Chancellor; and

(b) in Scotland by the Secretary of State.

(2) Any application made under the Convention by or on behalf of a person outside the United Kingdom may be addressed to the Lord Chancellor as the Central Authority in the United Kingdom.

(3) Where any such application relates to a function to be discharged under subsection (1) above by the Secretary of State it shall be transmitted by the Lord Chancellor to the Secretary of State and where such an application is addressed to the Secretary of State but relates to a function to be discharged under subsection (1) above by the Lord Chancellor the Secretary of State shall transmit it to the Lord Chancellor.

4   Judicial authorities

The courts having jurisdiction to entertain applications under the Convention shall be –

(a) in England and Wales or in Northern Ireland the High Court;

(b) in Scotland the Court of Session.

5   Interim powers

Where an application has been made to a court in the United Kingdom under the Convention, the court may, at any time before the application is determined, give such interim directions as it thinks fit for the purpose of securing the welfare of the child concerned or of preventing changes in the circumstances relevant to the determination of the application.

6   Reports

Where the Lord Chancellor or the Secretary of State is requested to provide information relating to a child under Article 7(d) of the Convention he may –

(a) request a local authority or a probation officer to make a report to him in writing with respect to any matter which appears to him to be relevant;

(b) request the Department of Health and Social Services for Northern Ireland to arrange for a suitably qualified person to make such a report to him;

(c) request any court to which a written report relating to the child has been made to send him a copy of the report;

and such a request shall be duly complied with.

7 Proof of documents and evidence

(1) For the purposes of Article 14 of the Convention a decision or determination of a judicial or administrative authority outside the United Kingdom may be proved by a duly authenticated copy of the decision or determination; and any document purporting to be such a copy shall be deemed to be a true copy unless the contrary is shown.

(2) For the purposes of subsection (1) above a copy is duly authenticated if it bears the seal, or is signed by a judge or officer, of the authority in question.

(3) For the purposes of Articles 14 and 30 of the Convention any such document as is mentioned in Article 8 of the Convention, or a certified copy of any such document, shall be sufficient evidence of anything stated in it.

8 Declarations by United Kingdom courts

The High Court or Court of Session may, on an application made for the purposes of Article 15 of the Convention by any person appearing to the court to have an interest in the matter, make a declaration or declarator that the removal of any child from, or his retention outside, the United Kingdom was wrongful within the meaning of Article 3 of the Convention.

9 Suspension of court's powers in cases of wrongful removal

The reference in Article 16 of the Convention to deciding on the merits of rights of custody shall be construed as a reference to –

(a) making, varying or revoking a custody order, or a supervision order under section 31 of the Children Act 1989 ...

(aa) enforcing under section 29 of the Family Law Act 1986 a custody order within the meaning of Chapter V of Part I of that Act.

(b) registering or enforcing a decision under Part II of this Act; ...

11 Cost of applications

The United Kingdom having made such a reservation as is mentioned in the third paragraph of Article 26 of the Convention, the costs mentioned in that paragraph shall not be borne by any Minister or other authority in the United Kingdom except so far as they fall to be so borne by virtue of the grant of legal aid or legal advice and assistance under Part III or IV of the Legal Aid Act 1988...

PART II

RECOGNITION AND ENFORCEMENT OF CUSTODY DECISIONS

12 The European Convention

(1) In this Part of this Act 'the Convention' means the European Convention on Recognition and Enforcement of Decisions concerning Custody of Children and on the Restoration of Custody of Children which was signed in Luxembourg on 20 May 1980.

(2) Subject to the provisions of this Part of this Act, the provisions of that Convention set out in Schedule 2 to this Act (which include Articles 9 and 10 as they have effect in consequence of a reservation made by the United Kingdom under Article 17) shall have the force of law in the United Kingdom.

13 Contracting States

(1) For the purposes of the Convention as it has effect under this Part of this Act the Contracting States other than the United Kingdom shall be those for the time being specified by an Order in Council under this section.

(2) An Order in Council under this section shall specify the date of the coming into force of the Convention as between the United Kingdom and any State specified in the Order.

(3) Where the Convention applies, or applies only, to a particular territory or particular territories specified by a Contracting State under Article 24 or 25 of the Convention references to that State in subsections (1) and (2) above shall be construed as references to that territory or those territories.

14 Central Authorities

(1) Subject to subsection (2) below, the functions under the Convention of a Central Authority shall be discharged –

    (a) in England and Wales and in Northern Ireland by the Lord Chancellor; and

    (b) in Scotland by the Secretary of State.

(2) Any application made under the Convention by or on behalf of a person outside the United Kingdom may be addressed to the Lord Chancellor as the Central Authority in the United Kingdom.

(3) Where any such application relates to a function to be discharged under subsection (1) above by the Secretary of State it shall be transmitted by the Lord Chancellor to the Secretary of State and where such an application is addressed to the Secretary of State but relates to a function to be discharged under subsection (1) above by the Lord Chancellor the Secretary of State shall transmit it to the Lord Chancellor.

15 Recognition of decisions

(1) Articles 7 and 12 of the Convention shall have effect in accordance with this section.

(2) A decision to which either of those Articles applies which was made in a Contracting State other than the United Kingdom shall be recognised in each part of the United Kingdom as if made by a court having jurisdiction to make it in that part but –

    (a) the appropriate court in any part of the United Kingdom may, on the application of any person appearing to it to have an interest in the matter, declare on any of the grounds specified in Article 9 or 10 of the Convention that the decision is not to be recognised in any part of the United Kingdom; and

    (b) the decision shall not be enforceable in any part of the United Kingdom unless registered in the appropriate court under section 16 below.

(3) The references in Article 9(1)(c) of the Convention to the removal of the child are to his improper removal within the meaning of the Convention.

16 Registration of decisions

(1) A person on whom any rights are conferred by a decision relating to custody made by an authority in a Contracting State other than the United Kingdom may make an application for the registration of the decision in an appropriate court in the United Kingdom.

(2) The Central Authority in the United Kingdom shall assist such a person in making such an application if a request for such assistance is made by him or on his behalf by the Central Authority of the Contracting State in question.

(3) An application under subsection (1) above or a request under subsection (2) above shall be treated as a request for enforcement for the purposes of Articles 10 and 13 of the Convention.

(4) The High Court or Court of Session shall refuse to register a decision if –

(a) the court is of the opinion that on any of the grounds specified in Article 9 or 10 of the Convention the decision should not be recognised in any part of the United Kingdom;

(b) the court is of the opinion that the decision is not enforceable in the Contracting State where it was made and is not a decision to which Article 12 of the Convention applies; or

(c) an application in respect of the child under Part I of this Act is pending.

(5) Where the Lord Chancellor is requested to assist in making an application under this section to the Court of Session he shall transmit the request to the Secretary of State and the Secretary of State shall transmit to the Lord Chancellor any such request to assist in making an application to the High Court.

(6) In this section 'decision relating to custody' has the same meaning as in the Convention.

17 Variation and revocation of registered decisions

(1) Where a decision which has been registered under section 16 above is varied or revoked by an authority in the Contracting State

in which it was made, the person on whose behalf the application for registration of the decision was made shall notify the court in which the decision is registered of the variation or revocation.

(2) Where a court is notified under subsection (1) above of the revocation of a decision, it shall –

(a) cancel the registration, and

(b) notify such persons as may be prescribed by rules of court of the cancellation.

(3) Where a court is notified under subsection (1) above of the variation of a decision, it shall –

(a) notify such persons as may be prescribed by rules of court of the variation; and

(b) subject to any conditions which may be so prescribed, vary the registration.

(4) The court in which the decision is registered under section 16 above may also, on the application of any person appearing to the court to have an interest in the matter, cancel or vary the registration if it is satisfied that the decision has been revoked or, as the case may be, varied by an authority in the Contracting State in which it was made.

18   Enforcement of decisions

Where a decision relating to custody has been registered under section 16 above, the court in which it is registered shall have the same powers for the purpose of enforcing the decision as if it had been made by that court; and proceedings for or with respect to enforcement may be taken accordingly.

19   Interim powers

Where an application has been made to a court for the registration of a decision under section 16 above or for the enforcement of such a decision, the court may, at any time before the application is determined, give such interim directions as it thinks fit for the purpose of securing the welfare of the child concerned or of preventing changes in the circumstances relevant to the determination of the application or, in the case of an application for registration, to the determination of any subsequent application for the enforcement of the decision.

20   Suspension of court's powers

(1) Where it appears to any court in which such proceedings as are mentioned in subsection (2) below are pending in respect of a child that –

(a) an application has been made for the registration of a decision in respect of the child under section 16 above (other than a decision mentioned in subsection (3) below) or that such a decision is registered; and

(b) the decision was made in proceedings commenced before the proceedings which are pending,

the powers of the court with respect to the child in those proceedings shall be restricted as mentioned in subsection (2) below unless, in the case of an application for registration, the application is refused.

(2) Where subsection (1) above applies the court shall not –

(a) in the case of custody proceedings, make, vary or revoke any custody order, or a supervision order under section 31 of the Children Act 1989 ...

(aa) in the case of proceedings under section 29 of the Family Law Act 1986 for the enforcement of a custody order within the meaning of Chapter V of Part I of that Act, enforce that order.

(2A) Where it appears to the Secretary of State:

(a) that an application has been made for the registration of a decision in respect of a child under section 16 above (other than a decision mentioned in subsection (3) below); or

(b) that such a decision is registered,

the Secretary of State shall not make, vary or revoke any custody order in respect of the child unless, in the case of an application for registration, the application is refused.

(3) The decision referred to in subsection (1) or (2A) above is a decision which is only a decision relating to custody within the meaning of section 16 of this Act by virtue of being a decision relating to rights of access.

(4) Paragraph (b) of Article 10(2) of the Convention shall be construed as referring to custody proceedings within the meaning of this Act...

21 Reports

Where the Lord Chancellor or the Secretary of State is requested to make enquiries about a child under Article 15(1)(b) of the Convention he may –

(a) request a local authority or a probation officer to make a report to him in writing with respect to any matter relating to the child concerned which appears to him to be relevant;

(b) request the Department of Health and Social Services for Northern Ireland to arrange for a suitably qualified person to make such a report to him;

(c) request any court to which a written report relating to the child has been made to send him a copy of the report;

and any such request shall be duly complied with.

22 Proof of documents and evidence

(1) In any proceedings under this Part of this Act a decision of an authority outside the United Kingdom may be proved by a duly authenticated copy of the decision; and any document purporting to be such a copy shall be deemed to be a true copy unless the contrary is shown.

(2) for the purposes of subsection (1) above a copy is duly authenticated if it bears the seal, or is signed by a judge or officer, of the authority in question.

(3) In any proceedings under this Part of this Act any such document as is mentioned in Article 13 of the Convention, or a certified copy of any such document, shall be sufficient evidence of anything stated in it.

23 Decisions of United Kingdom courts

(1) Where a person on whom any rights are conferred by a decision relating to custody made by a court in the United Kingdom makes an application to the Lord Chancellor or the Secretary of State under Article 4 of the Convention with a view to securing its recognition or enforcement in another Contracting State, the Lord Chancellor or the Secretary of State may require the court which made the decision to furnish him with all or any of the documents referred to in Article 13(1)(b), (c) and (d) of the Convention.

(2) Where in any custody proceedings a court in the United Kingdom makes a decision relating to a child who has been removed from the United Kingdom, the court may also, on an application made by any person for the purposes of Article 12 of the Convention, declare the removal to have been unlawful if it is satisfied that the applicant has an interest in the matter and that the child has been taken from or sent or kept out of the United Kingdom without the consent of the person (or, if more than one, all the persons) having the right to determine the child's place of residence under the law of the part of the United Kingdom in which the child was habitually resident.

(3) In this section 'decision relating to custody' has the same meaning as in the Convention.

PART III

SUPPLEMENTARY

24A Power to order disclosure of child's whereabouts

(1) Where –

(a) in proceedings for the return of a child under Part I of this Act; or

(b) on an application for the recognition, registration or enforcement of a decision in respect of a child under Part II of this Act,

there is not available to the court adequate information as to where the child is, the court may order any person who it has reason to believe may have relevant information to disclose it to the court.

(2) A person shall not be excused from complying with an order under subsection (1) above by reason that to do so may incriminate him or his spouse of an offence; but a statement or admission made in compliance with such an order shall not be admissible in evidence against either of them in proceedings for any offence other than perjury.

25 Termination of existing custody orders, etc

(1) Where –

(a) an order is made for the return of a child under Part I of this Act; or

(b) a decision with respect to a child (other than a decision mentioned in subsection (2) below) is recognised under section 16 of this Act,

any custody order relating to him shall cease to have effect.

(2) The decision referred to in subsection (1)(b) above is a decision which is only a decision relating to custody within the meaning of section 16 of this Act by virtue of being a decision relating to rights of access. ...

27 Interpretation

(1) In this Act 'custody order' means (unless the contrary intention appears) any such order or authorisation as is mentioned in Schedule 3 to this Act and 'custody proceedings' means proceedings in which an order within paragraphs 1, 2, 5, 6, 8 or 9 of that Schedule may be made, varied or revoked.

(2) For the purposes of this Act 'part of the United Kingdom' means England and Wales, Scotland or Northern Ireland and 'the appropriate court', in relation to England and Wales or Northern Ireland means the High Court and, in relation to Scotland, the Court of Session.

(3) In this Act 'local authority' means –

(a) in relation to England and Wales, the council of a non-metropolitan county, a metropolitan district, a London borough or the Common Council of the City of London; ...

(4) In this Act a decision relating to rights of access in England and Wales means a decision as to the contact which a child may, or may not have, with any person.

28 Application as respects British Islands and colonies

(1) Her Majesty may by Order in Council direct that any of the provisions of this Act specified in the Order shall extend, subject to such modifications as may be specified in the Order, to –

(a) the Isle of Man,

(b) any of the Channel Islands, and

(c) any colony.

(2) Her Majesty may by Order in Council direct that this Act shall have effect in the United Kingdom as if any reference in this Act, or in any amendment made by this Act, to any order which may be made, or any proceedings which may be brought or any other thing which may be done in, or in any part of, the United Kingdom included a reference to any corresponding order which may be made or, as the case may be, proceedings which may be brought or other thing which may be done in any of the territories mentioned in subsection (1) above.

(3) An Order in Council under this section may make such consequential incidental and supplementary provision as Her Majesty considers appropriate.

(4) An Order in Council under this section shall be subject to annulment in pursuance of a resolution of either House of Parliament.

SCHEDULE 1

CONVENTION ON THE CIVIL ASPECTS OF INTERNATIONAL CHILD ABDUCTION

CHAPTER I – SCOPE OF THE CONVENTION

ARTICLE 3

The removal or the retention of a child is to be considered wrongful where –

(a) it is in breach of rights of custody attributed to a person, an institution or any other body, either jointly or alone, under the law of the State in which the child was habitually resident immediately before the removal or retention; and

(b) at the time of removal or retention those rights were actually exercised, either jointly or alone, or would have been so exercised but for the removal or retention.

The rights of custody mentioned in sub-paragraph (a) above may arise in particular by operation of law or by reason of a judicial or administrative decision, or by reason of an agreement having legal effect under the law of that State.

ARTICLE 4

The Convention shall apply to any child who was habitually resident in a Contracting State immediately before any breach of custody or access rights. The Convention shall cease to apply when the child attains the age of sixteen years.

ARTICLE 5

For the purposes of this Convention –

(a) 'rights of custody' shall include rights relating to the care of the person of the child and, in particular, the right to determine the child's place of residence;

(b) 'rights of access' shall include the right to take a child for a limited period of time to a place other than the child's habitual residence.

CHAPTER II – CENTRAL AUTHORITIES

ARTICLE 7

Central Authorities shall cooperate with each other and promote cooperation amongst the competent authorities in their respective States to secure the prompt return of children and to achieve the other objects of this Convention.

In particular, either directly or through any intermediary, they shall take all appropriate measures –

(a) to discover the whereabouts of a child who has been wrongfully removed or retained;

(b) to prevent further harm to the child or prejudice to interested parties by taking or causing to be taken provisional measures;

(c) to secure the voluntary return of the child or to bring about an amicable resolution of the issues;

(d) to exchange, where desirable, information relating to the social background of the child;

(e) to provide information of a general character as to the law of their State in connection with the application of the Convention;

(f) to initiate or facilitate the institution of judicial or administrative proceedings with a view to obtaining the return of the child and in a proper case, to make arrangements for organising or securing the effective exercise of rights of access;

(g) where the circumstances so require, to provide or facilitate the provision of legal aid and advice, including the participation of legal counsel and advisers;

(h) to provide such administrative arrangements as may be necessary and appropriate to secure the safe return of the child;

(i) to keep each other informed with respect to the operation of this Convention and, as far as possible, to eliminate any obstacles to its application.

CHAPTER III – RETURN OF CHILDREN

ARTICLE 8

Any person, institution, or other body claiming that a child has been removed or retained in breach of custody rights may apply either to the Central Authority of the child's habitual residence or to the Central Authority of any other Contracting State for assistance in securing the return of the child.

The application shall contain –

(a) information concerning the identity of the applicant, of the child and of the person alleged to have removed or retained the child;

(b) where available, the date of birth of the child;

(c) the grounds on which the applicant's claim for return of the child is based;

(d) all available information relating to the whereabouts of the child and the identity of the person with whom the child is presumed to be.

The application may be accompanied or supplemented by –

(e) an authenticated copy of any relevant decision or agreement;

(f) a certificate or an affidavit emanating from a Central Authority, or other competent authority of the State of the child's habitual residence, or from a qualified person, concerning the relevant law of that State;

(g) any other relevant document.

ARTICLE 9

If the Central Authority which receives an application referred to in Article 8 has reason to believe that the child is in another Contracting State, it shall directly and without delay transmit the application to the Central Authority of that Contracting State and inform the requesting Central Authority, or the applicant, as the case may be.

ARTICLE 10

The Central Authority of the State where the child is shall take or cause to be taken all appropriate measures in order to obtain the voluntary return of the child.

ARTICLE 11

The judicial or administrative authorities of Contracting States shall act expeditiously in proceedings for the return of children.

If the judicial or administrative authority concerned has not reached a decision within six weeks from the date of commencement of the proceedings, the applicant or the Central Authority of the requested State, on its own initiative or if asked by the Central Authority of the requesting State, shall have the right to request a statement of the reasons for the delay. If a reply is received by the Central Authority of the requested State, that Authority shall transmit the reply to the Central Authority of the requesting State, or to the applicant, as the case may be.

ARTICLE 12

Where a child has been wrongfully removed or retained in terms of Article 3 and, at the date of the commencement of the proceedings before the judicial or administrative authority of the Contracting State where the child is, a period of less than one year has elapsed from the date of the wrongful removal or retention, the authority concerned shall order the return of the child forthwith.

The judicial or administrative authority, even where the proceedings have been commenced after the expiration of the period of one year referred to in the preceding paragraph, shall also order the return of the child, unless it is demonstrated that the child is now settled in its new environment.

Where the judicial or administrative authority in the requested state has reason to believe that the child has been taken to another State, it may stay the proceedings or dismiss the application for the return of the child.

ARTICLE 13

Notwithstanding the provisions of the preceding Article, the judicial or administrative authority of the requested State is not bound to order the return of the child if the person, institution or other body which opposes its return establishes that –

(a) the person, institution or other body having the care of the person of the child was not actually exercising the custody rights at the time of removal or retention, or had consented to or subsequently acquiesced in the removal or retention; or

(b) there is a grave risk that his or her return would expose the child to physical or psychological harm or otherwise place the child in an intolerable situation.

The judicial or administrative authority may also refuse to order the return of the child if it finds that the child objects to being returned and has attained an age and degree of maturity at which it is appropriate to take account of its views.

In considering the circumstances referred to in this Article, the judicial and administrative authorities shall take into account the information relating to the social background of the child provided by the Central Authority or other competent authority of the child's habitual residence.

ARTICLE 14

In ascertaining whether there has been a wrongful removal or retention within the meaning of Article 3, the judicial or administrative authorities of the requested State may take notice directly of the law of, and of judicial or administrative decisions, formally recognised or not in the State of the habitual residence of the child, without recourse to the specific procedures for the proof of that law or for the recognition of foreign decisions which would otherwise be applicable.

ARTICLE 15

The judicial or administrative authorities of a Contracting State may, prior to the making of an order for the return of the child, request that the applicant obtain from the authorities of the State of the habitual residence of the child a decision or other determination that the removal or retention was wrongful within the meaning of Article 3 of the Convention, where such a decision or determination may be obtained in that State. The Central Authorities of the Contracting States shall so far as practicable assist applicants to obtain such a decision or determination.

ARTICLE 16

After receiving notice of a wrongful removal or retention of a child in the sense of Article 3, the judicial or administrative authorities of the Contracting State to which the child has been removed or in which it has been retained shall not decide on the merits of rights of custody until it has been determined that the child is not to be returned under this Convention or unless an application under this Convention is not lodged within a reasonable time following receipt of the notice.

ARTICLE 17

The sole fact that a decision relating to custody has been given in or is entitled to recognition in the requested State shall not be a ground for refusing to return a child under this Convention, but the judicial or administrative authorities of the requested State may take account of the reasons for that decision in applying this Convention.

ARTICLE 18

The provisions of this Chapter do not limit the power of a judicial or administrative authority to order the return of the child at any time.

ARTICLE 19

A decision under this Convention concerning the return of the child shall not be taken to be a determination on the merits of any custody issue.

CHAPTER IV – RIGHTS OF ACCESS

ARTICLE 21

An application to make arrangements for organising or securing the effective exercise of rights of access may be presented to the Central Authorities of the Contracting States in the same way as an application for the return of a child.

The Central Authorities are bound by the obligations of cooperation which are set forth in Article 7 to promote the peaceful enjoyment of access rights and the fulfilment of any conditions to which the exercise of those rights may be subject. The Central Authorities shall take steps to remove, as far as possible, all obstacles to the exercise of such rights. The Central Authorities, either directly or through intermediaries, may initiate or assist in the institution of proceedings with a view to organising or protecting these rights and securing respect for the conditions to which the exercise of these rights may be subject.

CHAPTER V – GENERAL PROVISIONS

ARTICLE 22

No security, bond or deposit, however described, shall be required to guarantee the payment of costs and expenses in the judicial or administrative proceedings falling within the scope of this Convention.

ARTICLE 24

Any application, communication or other document sent to the Central Authority of the requested State shall be in the original language, and shall be accompanied by a translation into the official language or one of the official languages of the requested State or, where that is not feasible, a translation into French or English.

ARTICLE 26

Each Central Authority shall bear its own costs in applying this Convention.

Central Authorities and other public services of Contracting States shall not impose any charges in relation to applications submitted under this Convention. In particular, they may not require any payment from the applicant towards the costs and expenses of the proceedings or, where applicable, those arising from the participation of legal counsel or advisers. However, they may require the payment of the expenses incurred or to be incurred in implementing the return of the child.

However, a Contracting State may, by making a reservation in accordance with Article 42, declare that it shall not be bound to assume any costs referred to in the preceding paragraph resulting from the participation of legal counsel or advisers or from court proceedings, except insofar as those costs may be covered by its system of legal aid and advice.

Upon ordering the return of a child or issuing an order concerning rights of access under this Convention, the judicial or administrative authorities may, where appropriate, direct the person who removed or retained the child, or who prevented the exercise of rights of access, to pay necessary expenses incurred by or on behalf of the applicant, including travel expenses, any costs incurred or payments made for locating the child, the costs of legal representation of the applicant, and those of returning the child.

ARTICLE 27

When it is manifest that the requirements of this Convention are not fulfilled or that the application is otherwise not well founded, a Central Authority is not bound to accept the application. In that case, the Central Authority shall forthwith inform the applicant or the Central Authority through which the application was submitted, as the case may be, of its reasons.

ARTICLE 28

A Central Authority may require that the application be accompanied by a written authorisation empowering it to act on behalf of the applicant, or to designate a representative so to act.

ARTICLE 29

This Convention shall not preclude any person, institution or body who claims that there has been a breach of custody or access rights within the meaning of Article 3 or 21 from applying directly to the judicial or administrative authorities of a Contracting State, whether or not under the provisions of this Convention.

ARTICLE 30

Any application submitted to the Central Authorities or directly to the judicial or administrative authorities of a Contracting State in accordance with the terms of this Convention, together with documents and any other information appended thereto or provided by a Central Authority, shall be admissible in the courts or administrative authorities of the Contracting States.

ARTICLE 31

In relation to a State which in matters of custody of children has two or more systems of law applicable in different territorial units –

(a) any reference to habitual residence in that State shall be construed as referring to habitual residence in a territorial unit of that State;

(b) any reference to the law of the State of habitual residence shall be construed as referring to the law of the territorial unit in that State where the child habitually resides.

ARTICLE 32

In relation to a State which in matters of custody of children has two or more systems of law applicable to different categories of persons, any reference to the law of that State shall be construed as referring to the legal system specified by the law of that State.

SCHEDULE 2

EUROPEAN CONVENTION ON RECOGNITION AND ENFORCEMENT OF DECISIONS CONCERNING CUSTODY OF CHILDREN

ARTICLE 1

For the purposes of this Convention:

(a) 'child' means a person of any nationality, so long as he is under 16 years of age and has not the right to decide on his own place of residence under the law of his habitual residence, the law of his nationality or the internal law of the State addressed;

(b) 'authority' means a judicial or administrative authority;

(c) 'decision relating to custody' means a decision of an authority in so far as it relates to the care of the person of the child, including the right to decide on the place of his residence, or to the right of access to him.

(d) 'improper removal' means the removal of a child across an international frontier in breach of a decision relating to his custody which has been given in a Contracting State and which is enforceable in such a State; 'improper removal' also includes:

(i) the failure to return a child across an international frontier at the end of a period of the exercise of the right of access to this child or at the end of any other temporary stay in a territory other than that where the custody is exercised;

(ii) a removal which is subsequently declared unlawful within the meaning of Article 12.

ARTICLE 4

(1) Any person who has obtained in a Contracting State a decision relating to the custody of a child and who wishes to have that decision recognised or enforced in another Contracting State may submit an application for this purpose to the central authority in any Contracting State.

(2) The application shall be accompanied by the documents mentioned in Article 13.

(3) The central authority receiving the application, if it is not the central authority in the State addressed, shall send the documents directly and without delay to that central authority.

(4) The central authority receiving the application may refuse to intervene where it is manifestly clear that the conditions laid down in this Convention are not satisfied.

(5) The central authority receiving the application shall keep the applicant informed without delay of the progress of his application.

ARTICLE 5

(1) The central authority in the State addressed shall take or cause to be taken without delay all steps which it considers to be appropriate, if necessary by instituting proceedings before its competent authorities, in order:

(a) to discover the whereabouts of the child;

(b) to avoid, in particular by any necessary provisional measures, prejudice to the interests of the child or of the applicant;

(c) to secure the recognition or enforcement of the decision;

(d) to secure the delivery of the child to the applicant where enforcement is granted;

(e) to inform the requesting authority of the measures taken and their results.

(2) Where the central authority in the State addressed has reason to believe that the child is in the territory of another Contracting State it shall send the documents directly and without delay to the central authority of that State.

(3) With the exception of the cost of repatriation, each Contracting State undertakes not to claim any payment from an applicant in respect of any measures taken under paragraph (1) of this Article by the central authority of that State on the applicant's behalf, including the costs of proceedings and, where applicable, the costs incurred by the assistance of a lawyer.

(4) If recognition or enforcement is refused, and if the central authority of the State addressed considers that it should comply with a request by the applicant to bring in that State proceedings concerning the substance of the case, that authority shall use its best endeavours to secure the representation of the applicant in the proceedings under conditions no less favourable than those available to a person who is resident in and a national of that State and for this purpose it may, in particular, institute proceedings before its competent authorities.

ARTICLE 7

A decision relating to custody given in a Contracting State shall be recognised and, where it is enforceable in the State of origin, made enforceable in every other Contracting State.

ARTICLE 9

(1) Recognition and enforcement may be refused if:

(a) in the case of a decision given in the absence of the defendant or his legal representative, the defendant was not duly served with the documents which instituted the proceedings or an equivalent document in sufficient time to enable him to arrange his defence; but such a failure to effect service cannot constitute a ground for refusing recognition or enforcement where service was not effected because the defendant had concealed his whereabouts from the person who instituted the proceedings in the State of origin;

(b) in the case of a decision given in the absence of the defendant or his legal representative, the competence of the authority giving the decision was not founded:

(i) on the habitual residence of the defendant; or

(ii) on the last common habitual residence of the child's parents, at least one parent being still habitually there, or

(iii) on the habitual residence of the child;

(c) the decision is incompatible with a decision relating to custody which became enforceable in the State addressed before the removal of the child, unless the child has had his habitual residence in the territory of the requesting State for one year before his removal.

(3) In no circumstances may the foreign decision be reviewed as to its substance.

ARTICLE 10

(1) Recognition and enforcement may also be refused on any of the following grounds:

(a) if it is found that the effects of the decision are manifestly incompatible with the fundamental principles of the law relating to the family and children in the State addressed;

(b) if it is found that by reason of a change in the circumstances including the passage of time but not including a mere change in the residence of the child after an improper removal, the effects of the original decision are manifestly no longer in accordance with the welfare of the child;

(c) if at the time when the proceedings were instituted in the State of origin:

(i) the child was a national of the State addressed or was habitually resident there and no such connection existed with the State of origin;

(ii) the child was a national both of the State of origin and of the State addressed and was habitually resident in the State addressed;

(d) if the decision is incompatible with a decision given in the State addressed or enforceable in that State after being given in a third State, pursuant to proceedings begun before the submission of the request for recognition or enforcement, and if the refusal is in accordance with the welfare of the child.

(2) Proceedings for recognition or enforcement may be adjourned on any of the following grounds:

(a) if an ordinary form of review of the original decision has been commenced;

(b) if proceedings relating to the custody of the child, commenced before the proceedings in the State of origin were instituted, are pending in the State addressed;

(c) if another decision concerning the custody of the child is the subject of proceedings for enforcement or of any other proceedings concerning the recognition of the decision.

ARTICLE 11

(1) Decisions on rights of access and provisions of decision relating to custody which deal with the rights of access shall be recognised and enforced subject to the same conditions as other decisions relating to custody.

(2) However, the competent authority of the State addressed may fix the conditions for the implementation and exercise of the right of access taking into account, in particular, undertakings given by the parties on this matter.

(3) Where no decision on the right of access has been taken or where recognition or enforcement of the decision relating to custody is refused, the central authority of the State addressed may apply to its competent authorities for a decision on the right of access if the person claiming a right of access so requests.

ARTICLE 12

Where, at the time of the removal of a child across an international frontier, there is no enforceable decision given in a Contracting State relating to his custody, the provisions of this Convention shall apply to any subsequent decision, relating to the custody of that child and declaring the removal to be unlawful, given in a Contracting State at the request of any interested person.

ARTICLE 13

(1) A request for recognition or enforcement in another Contracting State of a decision relating to custody shall be accompanied by:

(a) a document authorising the central authority of the State addressed to act on behalf of the applicant or to designate another representative for that purpose;

(b) a copy of the decision which satisfies the necessary conditions of authenticity;

(c) in the case of a decision given in the absence of the defendant or his legal representative, a document which establishes that the defendant was duly served with the document which instituted the proceedings or an equivalent document;

(d) if applicable, any document which establishes that, in accordance with the law of the State of origin, the decision is enforceable;

(e) if possible, a statement indicating the whereabouts or likely whereabouts of the child in the State addressed;

(f) proposals as to how the custody of the child should be restored.

ARTICLE 15

(1) Before reaching a decision under paragraph (1)(b) of Article 10, the authority concerned in the State addressed:

(a) shall ascertain the child's views unless this is impracticable having regard in particular to his age and understanding; and

(b) may request that any appropriate enquiries be carried out.

(2) The cost of enquiries in any Contracting State shall be met by the authorities of the State where they are carried out.

Requests for enquiries and the results of enquiries may be sent to the authority concerned through the central authorities.

ARTICLE 26

(1) In relation to a State which has in matters of custody two or more systems of law of territorial application:

(a) reference to the law of a person's habitual residence or to the law of a person's nationality shall be construed as referring to the system of law determined by the rules in force in that State or, if there are no such rules, to the system of law with which the person concerned is most closely connected.

(b) reference to the State of origin or to the State addressed shall be construed as referring, as the case may be, to the territorial unit where the decision was given or to the territorial unit where recognition or enforcement of the decision or restoration of custody is requested.

(2) Paragraph (1)(a) of this Article also applies mutatis mutandis to States which have in matters of custody two or more systems of law of personal application.

SCHEDULE 3

CUSTODY ORDERS

PART I

ENGLAND AND WALES

1. The following are the orders referred to in section 27(1) of this Act –

(a) a care order under the Children Act 1989 (as defined by section 31(11) of that Act, read with section 105(1) and Schedule 14);

(b) a residence order (as defined by section 8 of the Act of 1989); and

(c) any order made by a court in England and Wales under any of the following enactments:

(i) section 9(1), 10(1)(a) or 11(a) of the Guardianship of Minors Act 1971;

(ii) section 42(1) or (2) or 43(1) of the Matrimonial Causes Act 1973;

(iii) section 2(2)(b), (4)(b) or (5) of the Guardianship Act 1973 as applied by section 34(5) of the Children Act 1975;

(iv) section 8(2)(a), 10(1) or 19(1)(ii) of the Domestic Proceedings and Magistrates' Courts Act 1978;

(v) section 26(1)(b) of the Adoption Act 1976.

2. An order made by the High Court in the exercise of its jurisdiction relating to wardship so far as it gives the care and control of a child to any person.

3. An order made by the Secretary of State under section 25(1) of the Children and Young Persons Act 1969 (except where the order superseded was made under section 74(1)(a) or (b) or 78(1) of the Children and Young Persons Act (Northern Ireland) 1968 or was made under section 97(2)(a) of that Act on a complaint by a person under whose supervision the child had been placed by an order under section 74(1)(c) of that Act).

4. An authorisation given by the Secretary of State under section 26(2) of the Children and Young Persons Act 1969 (except where the relevant order, within the meaning of that section, was made by virtue of the court which made it being satisfied that the child was guilty of an offence).

As amended by the Family Law Act 1986, ss67(1)–(5), 68(1), Schedule 1, paras 29, 30; Children Act 1989, s108(5), (7), Schedule 13, para 57(1)–(3), Schedule 15.

FAMILY LAW ACT 1986
(1986 c 55)

PART I

CHILD CUSTODY

CHAPTER I

PRELIMINARY

1   Orders to which Part I applies

(1) Subject to the following provisions of this section, in this Part
'Part I order' means –

> (a) a section 8 order made by a court in England and Wales under
> the Children Act 1989, other than an order varying or
> discharging such an order; ...

> (d) an order made by a court in England and Wales in the
> exercise of the inherent jurisdiction of the High Court with
> respect to children –

>> (i) so far as it gives care of a child to any person or provides
>> for contact with, or the education of, a child; but

>> (ii) excluding an order varying or revoking such an order. ...

(3) In this Part, 'Part I order' –

> (a) includes any order which would have been a custody order
> by virtue of this section in any form in which it was in force at
> any time before its amendment by the Children Act 1989 ...; and

> (b) (subject to section 32 and 40 of this Act) excludes any order
> which would have been excluded from being a custody order by
> virtue of this section in any such form. ...

CHAPTER II

JURISDICTION OF COURTS IN ENGLAND AND WALES

2   Jurisdiction: general

(1) A court in England and Wales shall not have jurisdiction to make a section 1(1)(a) order with respect to a child in or in connection with matrimonial proceedings in England and Wales unless the condition in section 2A of this Act is satisfied.

(2) A court in England and Wales shall not have jurisdiction to make a section 1(1)(a) order in a non-matrimonial case (that is to say, where the condition in section 2A of this Act is not satisfied) unless the condition in section 3 of this Act is satisfied.

(3) A court in England and Wales shall not have jurisdiction to make a section 1(1)(d) order unless –

(a) the condition in section 3 of this Act is satisfied, or

(b) the child concerned is present in England and Wales on the relevant date and the court considers that the immediate exercise of its powers is necessary for his protection.

2A   Jurisdiction in or in connection with matrimonial proceedings

(1) The condition referred to in section 2(1) of this Act is that the matrimonial proceedings are proceedings in respect of the marriage of the parents of the child concerned and –

(a) the proceedings –
(i) are proceedings for divorce or nullity of marriage, and
(ii) are continuing;
(b) the proceedings –
(i) are proceedings for judicial separation,
(ii) are continuing,

and the jurisdiction of the court is not excluded by subsection (2) below; or

(c) the proceedings have been dismissed after the beginning of the trial but –
(i) the section 1(1)(a) order is being made forthwith, or

(ii) the application for the order was made on or before the dismissal. ...

(4) Where a court –

(a) has jurisdiction to make a section 1(1)(a) order in or in connection with matrimonial proceedings, but

(b) considers that it would be more appropriate for Part I matters relating to the child to be determined outside England and Wales,

the court may by order direct that, while the order under this subsection is in force, no section 1(1)(a) order shall be made by any court in or in connection with those proceedings.

3   Habitual residence or presence of child

(1) The condition referred to in section 2(2) of this Act is that on the relevant date the child concerned –

(a) is habitually resident in England and Wales, or

(b) is present in England and Wales and is not habitually resident in any part of the United Kingdom or a specified dependent territory,

and, in either case, the jurisdiction of the court is not excluded by subsection (2) below.

(2) For the purposes of subsection (1) above, the jurisdiction of the court is excluded if, on the relevant date, matrimonial proceedings are continuing in a court in Scotland, Northern Ireland or a specified dependent territory in respect of the marriage of the parents of the child concerned. ...

5   Power of court to refuse application or stay proceedings

(1) A court in England and Wales which has jurisdiction to make a Part I order may refuse an application for the order in any case where the matter in question has already been determined in proceedings outside England and Wales.

(2) Where, at any stage of the proceedings on an application made to a court in England and Wales for a Part I order, or for the variation of a Part I order, it appears to the court –

(a) that proceedings with respect to the matters to which the application relates are continuing outside England and Wales, or

(b) that it would be more appropriate for those matters to be determined in proceedings to be taken outside England and Wales,

the court may stay the proceedings on the application.

(3) The court may remove a stay granted in accordance with subsection (2) above if it appears to the court that there has been unreasonable delay in the taking or prosecution of the other proceedings referred to in that subsection, or that those proceedings are stayed, sisted or concluded.

(4) Nothing in this section shall affect any power exercisable apart from this section to refuse an application or to grant or remove a stay.

6   Duration and variation of Part I orders

(1) If a Part I order made by a court in Scotland, Northern Ireland or a specified dependent territory (or a variation of such an order) comes into force with respect to a child at a time when a Part I order made by a court in England and Wales has effect with respect to him, the latter order shall cease to have effect so far as it makes provision for any matter for which the same or different provision is made by (or by the variation of) the order made by the court in Scotland, Northern Ireland or the territory.

(2) Where by virtue of subsection (1) above a Part I order has ceased to have effect so far as it makes provision for any matter, a court in England or Wales shall not have jurisdiction to vary that order so as to make provision for that matter.

(3) A court in England and Wales shall not have jurisdiction to vary a Part I order if, on the relevant date, matrimonial proceedings are continuing in Scotland, Northern Ireland or a specified dependent territory in respect of the marriage of the parents of the child concerned.

(3A) Subsection (3) above shall not apply if –

(a) the Part I order was made in or in connection with proceedings for divorce or nullity in England and Wales in respect of the marriage of the parents of the child concerned; and

(b) those proceedings are continuing.

(3B) Subsection (3) above shall not apply if –

(a) the Part I order was made in or in connection with proceedings for judicial separation in England and Wales;

(b) those proceedings are continuing; and

(c) the decree of judicial separation has not yet been granted. ...

(6) Subsection (7) below applies where a Part I order which is –

(a) a residence order (within the meaning of the Children Act 1989) in favour of a person with respect to a child,

(b) an order made in the exercise of the High Court's inherent jurisdiction with respect to children by virtue of which a person has care of a child, or

(c) an order –

(ii) under which a person is entitled to the actual possession of a child,

ceases to have effect in relation to that person by virtue of subsection (1) above.

(7) Where this subsection applies, any family assistance order made under section 16 of the Children Act 1989 with respect to the child shall also cease to have effect.

(8) For the purposes of subsection (7) above the reference to a family assistance order under section 16 of the Children Act 1989 shall be deemed to include a reference to an order for the supervision of a child made under –

(a) section 7(4) of the Family Law Reform Act 1969,

(b) section 44 of the Matrimonial Causes Act 1973,

(c) section 2(2)(a) of the Guardianship Act 1973,

(d) section 34(5) or 36(3)(b) of the Children Act 1975, or

(e) section 9 of the Domestic Proceedings and Magistrates' Courts Act 1978;

but this subsection shall cease to have effect once all such orders for the supervision of children have ceased to have effect in accordance with Schedule 14 to the Children Act 1989.

7   Interpretation of Chapter II

In this Chapter –

(a) 'child' means a person who has not attained the age of eighteen;

(b) 'matrimonial proceedings' means proceedings for divorce, nullity or marriage or judicial separation;

(c) 'the relevant date' means, in relation to the making or variation of an order –

(i) where an application is made for an order to be made or varied, the date of the application (or first application, if two or more are determined together), and

(ii) where no such application is made, the date on which the court is considering whether to make or, as the case may be, vary the order; and

(d) 'section 1(1)(a) order' and 'section 1(1)(d) order' means orders falling within section 1(1)(a) and (d) of this Act respectively.

CHAPTER V

RECOGNITION AND ENFORCEMENT

25 Recognition of Part I orders: general

(1) Where a Part I order made by a court in any part of the United Kingdom or in a specified dependent territory is in force with respect to a child who has not attained the age of sixteen, then, subject to subsection (2) below, the order shall be recognised in any other part or, in the case of a dependent territory order, any part of the United Kingdom as having the same effect in that part as if it had been made by the appropriate court in that part and as if that court had had jurisdiction to make it.

(2) Where a Part I order includes provision as to the means by which rights conferred by the order are to be enforced, subsection (1) above shall not apply to that provision.

(3) A court in a part of the United Kingdom in which a Part I order is recognised in accordance with subsection (1) above shall not enforce the order unless it has been registered in that part of the United Kingdom under section 27 of this Act and proceedings for enforcement are taken in accordance with section 29 of this Act.

27 Registration

(1) Any person on whom any rights are conferred by a Part I order

may apply to the court which made it for the order to be registered in another part of the United Kingdom under this section, or in a specified dependent territory under a corresponding provision.

(2) An application under this section shall be made in the prescribed manner and shall contain the prescribed information and be accompanied by such documents as may be prescribed.

(3) On receiving an application under this section the court which made the Part I order shall, unless it appears to the court that the order is no longer in force, cause the following documents to be sent to the appropriate court in the part of the United Kingdom or dependent territory specified in the application, namely –

(a) a certified copy of the order, and

(b) where the order has been varied, prescribed particulars of any variation which is in force, and

(c) a copy of the application and of any accompanying documents.

(4) Where the prescribed officer of the appropriate court in any part of the United Kingdom receives a certified copy of a Part I order under subsection (3) above or under a corresponding dependent territory provision, he shall forthwith cause the order, together with particulars of any variation, to be registered in that court in the prescribed manner.

(5) An order shall not be registered under this section in respect of a child who has attained the age of sixteen, and the registration of an order in respect of a child who has not attained the age of sixteen shall cease to have effect on the attainment by the child of that age.

28 Cancellation and variation of registration

(1) A court which revokes, recalls or varies an order registered under section 27 of this Act shall cause notice of the revocation, recall or variation to be given in the prescribed manner to the prescribed officer of the court in which it is registered and, on receiving the notice, the prescribed officer –

(a) in the case of the revocation or recall of the order, shall cancel the registration, and

(b) in the case of the variation of the order, shall cause particulars of the variation to be registered in the prescribed manner.

(2) Where –

(a) an order registered under section 27 of this Act ceases (in whole or in part) to have effect in the part of the United Kingdom or in a specified dependent territory in which it was made, otherwise than because of its revocation, recall or variation, or

(b) an order registered under section 27 of this Act in Scotland ceases (in whole or in part) to have effect there as a result of the making of an order in proceedings outside the United Kingdom and any specified dependent territory,

the court in which the order is registered may, of its own motion or on the application of any person who appears to the court to have an interest in the matter, cancel the registration (or, if the order has ceased to have effect in part, cancel the registration so far as it relates to the provisions which have ceased to have effect).

29   Enforcement

(1) Where a Part I order has been registered under section 27 of this Act, the court in which it is registered shall have the same powers for the purpose of enforcing the order as it would have if it had itself made the order and had jurisdiction to make it; and proceedings for or with respect to enforcement may be taken accordingly.

(2) Where an application has been made to any court for the enforcement of an order registered in that court under section 27 of this Act, the court may, at any time before the application is determined, give such interim directions as it thinks fit for the purpose of securing the welfare of the child concerned or of preventing changes in the circumstances relevant to the determination of the application.

(3) The references in subsection (1) above to a Part I order do not include references to any provision of the order as to the means by which rights conferred by the order are to be enforced.

30   Staying or sisting of enforcement proceedings

(1) Where in accordance with section 29 of this Act proceedings are taken in any court for the enforcement of an order registered in that court, any person who appears to the court to have an interest in the matter may apply for the proceedings to be stayed or sisted on the ground that he has taken or intends to take other proceedings (in the United Kingdom or elsewhere) as a result of which the order may

cease to have effect, or may have a different effect, in the part of the United Kingdom in which it is registered.

(2) If after considering an application under subsection (1) above the court considers that the proceedings for enforcement should be stayed or sisted in order that other proceedings may be taken or concluded, it shall stay or sist the proceedings for enforcement accordingly.

(3) The court may remove a stay or recall of sist granted in accordance with subsection (2) above if it appears to the court –

(a) that there has been unreasonable delay in the taking or prosecution of the other proceedings referred to in that subsection, or

(b) that those other proceedings are concluded and that the registered order, or a relevant part of it, is still in force.

(4) Nothing in this section shall affect any power exercisable apart from this section to grant, remove or recall a stay or sist.

31   Dismissal of enforcement proceedings

(1) Where in accordance with section 29 of this Act proceedings are taken in any court for the enforcement of an order registered in that court, any person who appears to the court to have an interest in the matter may apply for those proceedings to be dismissed on the ground that the order has (in whole or in part) ceased to have effect in the part of the United Kingdom or specified dependent territory in which it was made.

(2) Where in accordance with section 29 of this Act proceedings are taken in the Court of Session for the enforcement of an order registered in that court, any person who appears to the court to have an interest in the matter may apply for those proceedings to be dismissed on the ground that the order has (in whole or in part) ceased to have effect in Scotland as a result of the making of an order in proceedings outside the United Kingdom and any specified dependent territory.

(3) If, after considering an application under subsection (1) or (2) above, the court is satisfied that the registered order has ceased to have effect, it shall dismiss the proceedings for enforcement (or, if it is satisfied that the order has ceased to have effect in part, it shall dismiss the proceedings so far as they relate to the enforcement of provisions which have ceased to have effect).

32   Interpretation of Chapter V

(1) In this Chapter –

'the appropriate court', in relation to England and Wales or Northern Ireland, means the High Court and, in relation to Scotland, means the Court of Session and, in relation to a specified dependent territory, means the corresponding court in that territory;

'Part I order' includes (except where the context otherwise requires) any order within section 1(3) of this Act which, on the assumptions mentioned in subsection (3) below –

(a) could have been made notwithstanding the provisions of this Part or the corresponding dependent territory provisions;

(b) would have been a Part I order for the purposes of this Part; and

(c) would not have ceased to have effect by virtue of section 6, 15 or 23 of this Act.

(2) In the application of this Chapter to Scotland, 'Part I order' also includes (except where the context otherwise requires) any order within section 1(3) of this Act which, on the assumptions mentioned in subsection (3) below –

(a) would have been a Part I order for the purposes of this Part; and

(b) would not have ceased to have effect by virtue of section 6 or 23 of this Act,

and which, but for the provisions of this Part, would be recognised in Scotland under any rule of law.

(3) The said assumptions are –

(a) that this Part or the corresponding dependent territory provisions, as the case may be, had been in force at all material times; and

(b) that any reference in section 1 of this Act to any enactment included a reference to any corresponding enactment previously in force.

CHAPTER VI

MISCELLANEOUS AND SUPPLEMENTAL

33 Power to order disclosure of child's whereabouts

(1) Where in proceedings for or relating to a Part I order in respect of a child there is not available to the court adequate information as to where the child is, the court may order any person who it has reason to believe may have relevant information to disclose it to the court.

(2) A person shall not be excused from complying with an order under subsection (1) above by reason that to do so may incriminate him or his spouse of an offence; but a statement or admission made in compliance with such an order shall not be admissible in evidence against either of them in proceedings for any offence other than perjury.

(3) A court in Scotland before which proceedings are pending for the enforcement of an order for the custody of a child made outside the United Kingdom and any specified dependent territory which is recognised in Scotland shall have the same powers as it would have under subsection (1) above if the order were its own.

34 Power to order recovery of child

(1) Where –

(a) a person is required by a Part I order, or an order for the enforcement of a Part I order, to give up a child to another person ('the person concerned'), and

(b) the court which made the order imposing the requirement is satisfied that the child has not been given up in accordance with the order,

the court may make an order authorising an officer of the court or a constable to take charge of the child and deliver him to the person concerned.

(2) The authority conferred by subsection (1) above includes authority –

(a) to enter and search any premises where the person acting in pursuance of the order has reason to believe the child may be found, and

(b) to use such force as may be necessary to give effect to the purpose of the order.

(3) Where by virtue of –

(a) section 14 of the Children Act 1989, ...

a Part I order (or a provision of a Part I order) may be enforced as if it were an order requiring a person to give up a child to another person, subsection (1) above shall apply as if the Part I order had included such a requirement.

(4) This section is without prejudice to any power conferred on a court by or under any other enactment or rule of law.

36 Effect of orders restricting removal

(1) This section applies to any order made by a court in the United Kingdom or any specified dependent territory prohibiting the removal of a child from the United Kingdom or from any specified part of it or from any such territory.

(2) An order to which this section applies, made by a court in one part of the United Kingdom or in a specified dependent territory, shall have effect in each other part, or, in the case of an order made in a dependent territory, each part of the United Kingdom –

(a) as if it had been made by the appropriate court in that part, and

(b) in the case of an order which has the effect of prohibiting the child's removal to that part, as if it had included a prohibition on his further removal to any place except one to which he could be removed consistently with the order.

(3) The references in subsections (1) and (2) above to prohibitions on a child's removal include references to prohibitions subject to exceptions; and in a case where removal is prohibited except with the consent of the court, nothing in subsection (2) above shall be construed as affecting the identity of the court whose consent is required.

(4) In this section 'child' means a person who has not attained the age of sixteen; and this section shall cease to apply to an order relating to a child when he attains the age of sixteen.

37   Surrender of passports

(1) Where there is in force an order prohibiting or otherwise restricting the removal of a child from the United Kingdom or from any specified part of it or from a specified dependent territory, the court by which the order was in fact made, or by which it is treated under section 36 of this Act as having been made, may require any person to surrender any United Kingdom passport which has been issued to, or contains particulars of, the child.

(2) In this section 'United Kingdom passport' means a current passport issued by the Government of the United Kingdom.

38   Automatic restriction on removal of wards of court

(1) The rule of law which (without any order of the court) restricts the removal of a ward of court from the jurisdiction of the court shall, in a case to which this section applies, have effect subject to the modifications in subsection (3) below.

(2) This section applies in relation to a ward of court if –

(a) proceedings for divorce, nullity or judicial separation in respect of the marriage of his parents are continuing in a court in another part of the United Kingdom (that is to say, in a part of the United Kingdom) outside the jurisdiction of the court of which he is a ward), or in a specified dependent territory, or

(b) he is habitually resident in another part of the United Kingdom or in a specified dependent territory,

except where that other part is Scotland and he has attained the age of sixteen.

(3) Where this section applies, the rule referred to in subsection (1) above shall not prevent –

(a) the removal of the ward of court, without the consent of any court, to the other part of the United Kingdom or the specified dependent territory mentioned in subsection (2) above, or

(b) his removal to any other place with the consent of either the appropriate court in that other part of the United Kingdom or the specified dependent territory or the court mentioned in subsection (2)(a) above.

39 Duty to furnish particulars of other proceedings

Parties to proceedings for or relating to a Part I order shall, to such extent and in such manner as may be prescribed, give particulars of other proceedings known to them which relate to the child concerned (including proceedings instituted abroad and proceedings which are no longer continuing).

40 Interpretation of Chapter VI

(1) In this Chapter –

'the appropriate court' has the same meaning as in Chapter V;

'Part I order' includes (except where the context otherwise requires) any such order as is mentioned in section 32(1) of this Act. ...

41 Habitual residence after removal without consent, etc

(1) Where a child who –

    (a) has not attained the age of sixteen, and

    (b) is habitually resident in a part of the United Kingdom or in a specified dependent territory,

becomes habitually resident outside that part of the United Kingdom or that territory in consequence of circumstances of the kind specified in subsection (2) below, he shall be treated for the purposes of this Part as continuing to be habitually resident in that part of the United Kingdom or that territory for the period of one year beginning with the date on which those circumstances arise.

(2) The circumstances referred to in subsection (1) above exist where the child is removed from or retained outside, or himself leaves or remains outside, the part of the United Kingdom or the territory in which he was habitually resident before his change of residence –

    (a) without the agreement of the person or all the persons having, under the law of that part of the United Kingdom or that territory, the right to determine where he is to reside, or

    (b) in contravention of an order made by a court in any part of the United Kingdom or in a specified dependent territory.

(3) A child shall cease to be treated by virtue of subsection (1) above as habitually resident in a part of the United Kingdom or a specified dependent territory if, during the period there mentioned –

(a) he attains the age of sixteen, or

(b) he becomes habitually resident outside that part of the United Kingdom or that territory with the agreement of the person or persons mentioned in subsection (2)(a) above and not in contravention of an order made by a court in any part of the United Kingdom or in any specified dependent territory.

42 General interpretation of Part I

(1) In this Part –

'certified copy', in relation to an order of any court, means a copy certified by the prescribed officer of the court to be a true copy of the order or of the official record of the order;

'corresponding dependent territory order', 'corresponding dependent territory provision' and similar expressions, in relation to a specified dependent territory, shall be construed in accordance with Schedule 3 to the Family Law Act 1986 (Dependent Territories) Order 1991 as from time to time in force; 'dependent territory' has the meaning given by section 43(2) of this Act.

'part of the United Kingdom' means England and Wales, Scotland or Northern Ireland;

'prescribed' means prescribed by rules of court or act of sederunt;

'specified dependent territory' means a dependent territory for the time being specified in Schedule 1 to the said order of 1991.

(2) For the purposes of this Part proceedings in England and Wales, Northern Ireland or a specified dependent territory for divorce, nullity or judicial separation in respect of the marriage of the parents of a child shall, unless they have been dismissed, be treated as continuing until the child concerned attains the age of eighteen (whether or not a decree has been granted and whether or not, in the case of a decree of divorce or nullity of marriage, that decree has been made absolute).

(3) For the purposes of this Part, matrimonial proceedings in a court in Scotland which has jurisdiction in those proceedings to make a Part I order with respect to a child shall, unless they have been dismissed or decree of absolvitor has been granted therein, be treated as continuing until the child concerned attains the age of sixteen.

(4) Any reference in this Part to proceedings in respect of the marriage of the parents of a child shall, in relation to a child who, although not a child of both parties to the marriage, is a child of the family of those parties, be construed as a reference to proceedings in respect of that marriage; and for this purpose 'child of the family' –

(a) if the proceedings are in England and Wales, means any child who has been treated by both parties as a child of their family, except a child who is placed with those parties as foster parents by a local authority or a voluntary organisation; ...

(5) References in this Part to Part I orders include (except where the context otherwise requires) references to Part I orders as varied.

(6) For the purposes of this Part each of the following orders shall be treated as varying the Part I order to which it relates –

(a) an order which provides for a person to be allowed contact with or to be given access to a child who is the subject of a Part I order, or which makes provision for the education of such a child, ...

and for the purposes of chapter V of this Part and this Chapter, this subsection shall have effect as if any reference to any enactment included a reference to any corresponding enactment previously in force.

(7) In this Part –

(a) references to Part I proceedings in respect of a child are references to any proceedings for a Part I order or an order corresponding to a Part I order and include, in relation to proceedings outside the United Kingdom and any specified dependent territory, references to proceedings before a tribunal or other authority having power under the law having effect there to determine Part I matters; and

(b) references to Part I matters are references to matters that might be determined by a Part I order or an order corresponding to a Part I order.

PART II

RECOGNITION OF DIVORCES, ANNULMENTS AND LEGAL SEPARATIONS

44 Recognition in United Kingdom of divorces, annulments and judicial separations granted in the British Islands

(1) Subject to section 52(4) and (5)(a) of this Act, no divorce or annulment obtained in any part of the British Islands shall be regarded as effective in any part of the United Kingdom unless granted by a court of civil jurisdiction.

(2) Subject to section 51 of this Act, the validity of any divorce, annulment or judicial separation granted by a court of civil jurisdiction in any part of the British Islands shall be recognised throughout the United Kingdom.

45 Recognition in the United Kingdom of overseas divorces, annulments and legal separations

Subject to sections 51 and 52 of this Act, the validity of a divorce, annulment or legal separation obtained in a country outside the British Islands (in this Part referred to as an overseas divorce, annulment or legal separation) shall be recognised in the United Kingdom if, and only if, it is entitled to recognition –

(a) by virtue of sections 46 to 49 of this Act, or

(b) by virtue of any enactment other than this Part.

46 Grounds for recognition

(1) The validity of an overseas divorce, annulment or legal separation obtained by means of proceedings shall be recognised if –

(a) the divorce, annulment or legal separation is effective under the law of the country in which it was obtained; and

(b) at the relevant date either party to the marriage –

(i) was habitually resident in the country in which the divorce, annulment or legal separation was obtained; or

(ii) was domiciled in that country; or

(iii) was a national of that country.

(2) The validity of an overseas divorce, annulment or legal separation obtained otherwise than by means of proceedings shall be recognised if –

(a) the divorce, annulment or legal separation is effective under the law of the country in which it was obtained;

(b) at the relevant date –

(i) each party to the marriage was domiciled in that country; or

(ii) either party to the marriage was domiciled in that country and the other party was domiciled in a country under whose law the divorce, annulment or legal separation is recognised as valid; and

(c) neither party to the marriage was habitually resident in the United Kingdom throughout the period of one year immediately preceding that date.

(3) In this section 'the relevant date' means –

(a) in the case of an overseas divorce, annulment or legal separation obtained by means of proceedings, the date of the commencement of the proceedings;

(b) in the case of an overseas divorce, annulment or legal separation obtained otherwise than by means of proceedings, the date on which it was obtained.

(4) Where in the case of an overseas annulment, the relevant date fell after the death of either party to the marriage, any reference in subsection (1) or (2) above to that date shall be construed in relation to that party as a reference to the date of death.

(5) For the purpose of this section, a party to a marriage shall be treated as domiciled in a country if he was domiciled in that country either according to the law of that country in family matters or according to the law of the part of the United Kingdom in which the question of recognition arises.

47 Cross-proceedings and divorces following legal separations

(1) Where there have been cross-proceedings, the validity of an overseas divorce, annulment or legal separation obtained either in the original proceedings or in the cross-proceedings shall be recognised if –

(a) the requirements of section 46(1)(b)(i), (ii) or (iii) of this Act are satisfied in relation to the date of the commencement either of the original proceedings or of the cross-proceedings, and

(b) the validity of the divorce, annulment or legal separation is otherwise entitled to recognition by virtue of the provisions of this Part.

(2) Where a legal separation, the validity of which is entitled to recognition by virtue of the provisions of section 46 of this Act or of subsection (1) above, is converted, in the country in which it was obtained, into a divorce which is effective under the law of that country, the validity of the divorce shall be recognised whether or not it would itself be entitled to recognition by virtue of those provisions.

48   Proof of facts relevant to recognition

(1) For the purpose of deciding whether an overseas divorce, annulment or legal separation obtained by means of proceedings is entitled to recognition by virtue of section 46 and 47 of this court, any finding of fact made (whether expressly or by implication) in the proceedings and on the basis of which jurisdiction was assumed in the proceedings shall –

(a) if both parties to the marriage took part in the proceedings, be conclusive evidence of the fact found; and

(b) in any other case, be sufficient proof of that fact unless the contrary be shown.

(2) In this section 'finding of fact' includes a finding that either party to the marriage –

(a) was habitually resident in the country in which the divorce, annulment or legal separation was obtained; or

(b) was under the law of that country domiciled there; or

(c) was a national of that country.

(3) For the purposes of subsection (1)(a) above, a party to the marriage who has appeared in judicial proceedings shall be treated as having taken part in them.

49   Modifications of Part II in relation to countries comprising territories having different systems of law

(1) In relation to a country comprising territories in which different systems of law are in force in matters of divorce, annulment or legal

separation, the provisions of this Part mentioned in subsections (2) to (5) below shall have effect subject to the modifications there specified.

(2) In a case of a divorce, annulment or legal separation the recognition of the validity of which depends on whether the requirements of subsection (1)(b)(i) or (ii) of section 46 of this Act are satisfied, that section and, in the case of a legal separation, section 47(2) of this Act shall have effect as if each territory were a separate country.

(3) In the case of a divorce, annulment or legal separation the recognition of the validity of which depends on whether the requirements of subsection (1)(b)(iii) of section 46 of this Act are satisfied –

(a) that section shall have effect as if for paragraph (a) of subsection (1) there were substituted the following paragraph –

'(a) the divorce, annulment or legal separation is effective throughout the country in which it was obtained;'; and

(b) in the case of a legal separation, section 47(2) of this Act shall have effect as if for the words 'is effective under the law of that country' there were substituted the words 'is effective throughout that country'.

(4) In the case of a divorce, annulment or legal separation the recognition of the validity of which depends on whether the requirements of subsection (2)(b) of section 46 of this Act are satisfied, that section and section 52(3) and (4) of this Act and, in the case of a legal separation, section 47(2) of this Act shall have effect as if each territory were a separate country.

(5) Paragraphs (a) and (b) of section 48(2) of this Act shall each have effect as if each territory were a separate country.

50 Non-recognition of divorce or annulment in another jurisdiction no bar to remarriage

Where, in any part of the United Kingdom –

(a) a divorce or annulment has been granted by a court of civil jurisdiction, or

(b) the validity of a divorce or annulment is recognised by virtue of this Part,

the fact that the divorce or annulment would not be recognised elsewhere shall not preclude either party to the marriage from remarrying in that part of the United Kingdom or cause the remarriage of either party (wherever the remarriage takes place) to be treated as invalid in that part.

51   Refusal of recognition

(1) Subject to section 52 of this Act, recognition of the validity of –

(a) a divorce, annulment or judicial separation granted by a court of civil jurisdiction in any part of the British Islands, or

(b) an overseas divorce, annulment or legal separation,

may be refused in any part of the United Kingdom if the divorce, annulment or separation was granted or obtained at a time when it was irreconcilable with a decision determining the question of the subsistence or validity of the marriage of the parties previously given (whether before or after the commencement of this Part) by a court of civil jurisdiction in that part of the United Kingdom or by a court elsewhere and recognised or entitled to be recognised in that part of the United Kingdom.

(2) Subject to section 52 of this Act, recognition of the validity of –

(a) a divorce or judicial separation granted by a court of civil jurisdiction in any part of the British Islands, or

(b) an overseas divorce or legal separation,

may be refused in any part of the United Kingdom if the divorce or separation was granted or obtained at a time when, according to the law of that part of the United Kingdom (including its rules of private international law and the provisions of this Part), there was no subsisting marriage between the parties.

(3) Subject to section 52 of this Act, recognition by virtue of section 45 of this Act of the validity of the overseas divorce, annulment or legal separation may be refused if –

(a) in the case of a divorce, annulment or legal separation obtained by means of proceedings, it was obtained –

(i) without such steps having been taken for giving notice of the proceedings to a party to the marriage as, having regard to the nature of the proceedings and all the circumstances, should reasonably have been taken; or

(ii) without a party to the marriage having been given (for any reason other than lack of notice) such opportunity to take part in the proceedings as, having regard to those matters, he should reasonably have been given; or

(b) in the case of a divorce, annulment or legal separation obtained otherwise than by means of proceedings –

(i) there is no official document certifying that the divorce, annulment or legal separation is effective under the law of the country in which it was obtained; or

(ii) where either party to the marriage was domiciled in another country at the relevant date, there is no official document certifying that the divorce, annulment or legal separation is recognised as valid under the law of that other country; or

(c) in either case, recognition of the divorce, annulment or legal separation would be manifestly contrary to public policy.

(4) In this section –

'official', in relation to a document certifying that a divorce, annulment or legal separation is effective, or is recognised as valid, under the law of any country, means issued by a person or body appointed or recognised for the purpose under that law;

'the relevant date' has the same meaning as in section 46 of this Act;

and subsection (5) of that section shall apply for the purposes of this section as it applies for the purposes of that section.

(5) Nothing in this Part shall be construed as requiring the recognition of any finding of fault made in any proceedings for divorce, annulment or separation or of any maintenance, custody or other ancillary order made in any such proceedings.

52 Provisions as to divorces, annulments, etc obtained before commencement of Part II

(1) The provisions of this Part shall apply –

(a) to a divorce, annulment or judicial separation granted by a court of civil jurisdiction in the British Islands before the date of the commencement of this Part, and

(b) to an overseas divorce, annulment or legal separation obtained before that date,

as well as to one granted or obtained on or after that date.

(2) In the case of such a divorce, annulment or separation as is mentioned in subsection (1)(a) or (b) above, the provisions of this Part shall require or, as the case may be, preclude the recognition of its validity in relation to any time before that date as well as in relation to any subsequent time, but those provisions shall not –

(a) affect any property to which any person became entitled before that date, or

(b) affect the recognition of the validity of the divorce, annulment or separation if that matter has been decided by any competent court in the British Islands before that date.

(3) Subsections (1) and (2) above shall apply in relation to any divorce or judicial separation granted by a court of civil jurisdiction in the British Islands before the date of the commencement of this Part whether granted before or after the commencement of section 1 of the Recognition of Divorces and Legal Separations Act 1971.

(4) The validity of any divorce, annulment or legal separation mentioned in subsection (5) below shall be recognised in the United Kingdom whether or not it is entitled to recognition by virtue of any of the foregoing provisions of this Part.

(5) The divorces, annulments and legal separations referred to in subsection (4) above are –

(a) a divorce which was obtained in the British Islands before 1 January 1974 and was recognised as valid under rules of law applicable before that date;

(b) an overseas divorce which was recognised as valid under the Recognition of Divorces and Legal Separations Act 1971 and was not affected by section 16(2) of the Domicile and Matrimonial Proceedings Act 1973 (proceedings otherwise than in a court of law where both parties resident in the United Kingdom);

(c) a divorce of which the decree was registered under section 1 of the Indian and Colonial Divorce Jurisdiction Act 1926;

(d) a divorce or annulment which was recognised as valid under section 4 of the Matrimonial Causes (War Marriages) Act 1944; and

(e) an overseas legal separation which was recognised as valid under the Recognition of Divorces and Legal Separations Act 1971.

PART III

DECLARATIONS OF STATUS

55 Declarations as to marital status

(1) Subject to the following provisions of this section, any person may apply to the court for one or more of the following declarations in relation to a marriage specified in the application, that is to say –

(a) a declaration that the marriage was at its inception a valid marriage;

(b) a declaration that the marriage subsisted on a date specified in the application;

(c) a declaration that the marriage did not subsist on a date so specified;

(d) a declaration that the validity of a divorce, annulment or legal separation obtained in any country outside England and Wales in respect of the marriage is entitled to recognition in England and Wales;

(e) a declaration that the validity of a divorce, annulment or legal separation so obtained in respect of the marriage is not entitled to recognition in England and Wales.

(2) A court shall have jurisdiction to entertain an application under subsection (1) above if, and only if, either of the parties to the marriage to which the application relates –

(a) is domiciled in England and Wales on the date of the application, or

(b) has been habitually resident in England and Wales throughout the period of one year ending with that date, or

(c) died before that date and either –

(i) was at death domiciled in England and Wales, or

(ii) had been habitually resident in England and Wales throughout the period of one year ending with the date of death.

(3) Where an application under section (1) above is made by any person other than a party to the marriage to which the application relates, the court shall refuse to hear the application if it considers that the applicant does not have a sufficient interest in the determination of that application.

56 Declarations of parentage, legitimacy or legitimation

(1) Any person may apply to the court for a declaration –

(a) that a person named in the application is or was his parent; or

(b) that he is the legitimate child of his parents.

(2) Any person may apply to the court for one (or for one or, in the alternative, the other) of the following declarations, that is to say –

(a) a declaration that he has become a legitimated person;

(b) a declaration that he has not become a legitimated person.

(3) A court shall have jurisdiction to entertain an application under this section if, and only if, the applicant –

(a) is domiciled in England and Wales on the date of the application, or

(b) has been habitually resident in England and Wales throughout the period of one year ending with that date.

(4) Where a declaration is made on an application under subsection (1) above, the prescribed officer of the court shall notify the Registrar General, in such a manner and within such period as may be prescribed, of the making of that declaration.

(5) In this section 'legitimated person' means a person legitimated or recognised as legitimated –

(a) under section 2 or 3 of the Legitimacy Act 1976;

(b) under section 1 or 8 of the Legitimacy Act 1926; or

(c) by a legitimation (whether or not by virtue of the subsequent marriage of his parents) recognised by the law of England and Wales and effected under the law of another country.

57 Declarations as to adoptions effected overseas

(1) Any person whose status as an adopted child of any person depends on whether he has been adopted by that person by either –

(a) an overseas adoption as defined by section 72(2) of the Adoption Act 1976, or

(b) an adoption recognised by the law of England and Wales and effected under the law of any country outside the British Islands, may apply to the court for one (or for one or, in the alternative, the other) of the declarations mentioned in subsection (2) below.

(2) The said declarations are –

(a) a declaration that the applicant is for the purposes of section 39 of the Adoption Act 1976 the adopted child of that person;

(b) a declaration that the applicant is not for the purposes of that section the adopted child of that person.

(3) A court shall have jurisdiction to entertain an application under subsection (1) above if, and only if, the applicant –

(a) is domiciled in England and Wales on the date of the application, or

(b) has been habitually resident in England and Wales throughout the period of one year ending with that date.

58 General provisions as to the making and effect of declarations

(1) Where on an application for a declaration under this Part the truth of the proposition to be declared is proved to the satisfaction of the court, the court shall make that declaration unless to do so would manifestly be contrary to public policy.

(2) Any declaration made under this Part shall be binding on Her Majesty and all other persons.

(3) The court, on the dismissal of an application for a declaration under this Part, shall not have power to make any declaration for which an application has not been made.

(4) No declaration which may be applied for under this Part may be made otherwise than under this Part by any court.

(5) No declaration may be made by any court, whether under this Part or otherwise –

(a) that a marriage was at its inception void;

(b) that any person is or was illegitimate.

(6) Nothing in this section shall affect the powers of any court to grant a decree of nullity of marriage.

59   Provisions relating to the Attorney-General

(1) On an application for a declaration under this Part the court may at any stage of the proceedings, of its own motion or on the application of any party to the proceedings, direct that all necessary papers in the matter be sent to the Attorney-General.

(2) The Attorney-General, whether or not he is sent papers in relation to an application for a declaration under this Part, may –

(a) intervene in the proceedings on that application in such manner as he thinks necessary or expedient, and

(b) argue before the court any question in relation to the application which the court considers it necessary to have fully argued.

(3) Where any costs are incurred by the Attorney-General in connection with any application for a declaration under this Part, the court may make such order as it considers just as to the payment of those costs by parties to the proceedings.

60   Supplementary provisions as to declarations

(1) Any declaration made under this Part, and any application for such a declaration, shall be in the form prescribed by rules of court.

(2) Rules of court may make provision –

(a) as to the information required to be given by any applicant for a declaration under this Part;

(b) as to the persons who are to be parties to proceedings on an application under this Part;

(c) requiring notice of an application under this Part to be served on the Attorney-General and on persons who may be affected by any declaration applied for.

(3) No proceedings under this Part shall affect any final judgment or decree already pronounced or made by any court of competent jurisdiction.

(4) The court hearing an application under this Part may direct that the whole or any part of the proceedings shall be heard in camera, and an application for a direction under this subsection shall be heard in camera unless the court otherwise directs.

As amended by the Family Law Reform Act 1987, ss22, 33(1), Schedule 2, para 96; Children Act 1989, s108(5), (7), Schedule 13, paras 62(1), (2)(a), (b), (3), 63, 64, 65, 66(1), (2), (3), 70, 71, Schedule 15; Age of Legal Capacity (Scotland) Act 1991, s10(1), Schedule 10, para 47; Family Law Act 1986 (Dependent Territories) Order 1991.

RECOGNITION OF TRUSTS ACT 1987
(1987 c 14)

1   Applicable law and recognition of trusts

(1) The provisions of the Convention set out in the Schedule to this Act shall have the force of law in the United Kingdom.

(2) Those provisions shall, so far as applicable, have effect not only in relation to the trusts described in Articles 2 and 3 of the Convention but also in relation to any other trusts of property arising under the law of any part of the United Kingdom or by virtue of a judicial decision whether in the United Kingdom or elsewhere.

(3) In accordance with Articles 15 and 16 such provisions of the law as are there mentioned shall, to the extent there specified, apply to the exclusion of the other provisions of the Convention.

(4) In Article 17 the reference to a State includes a reference to any country or territory (whether or not a party to the Convention and whether or not forming part of the United Kingdom) which has its own system of law.

(5) Article 22 shall not be construed as affecting the law to be applied in relation to anything done or omitted before the coming into force of this Act.

SCHEDULE

CONVENTION ON THE LAW APPLICABLE TO TRUSTS AND ON THEIR RECOGNITION

CHAPTER 1 – SCOPE

ARTICLE 1

This Convention specifies the law applicable to trusts and governs their recognition.

ARTICLE 2

For the purposes of this Convention, the term 'trust' refers to the legal relationship created – inter vivos or on death – by a person, the settlor, when assets have been placed under the control of a trustee for the benefit of a beneficiary or for a specified purpose.

A trust has the following characteristics –

(a) the assets constitute a separate fund and are not a part of the trustee's own estate;

(b) title to the trust assets stands in the name of the trustee or in the name of another person on behalf of the trustee;

(c) the trustee has the power and the duty, in respect of which he is accountable, to manage, employ or dispose of the assets in accordance with the terms of the trust and the special duties imposed upon him by law.

The reservation by the settlor of certain rights and powers, and the fact that the trustee may himself have rights as a beneficiary, are not necessarily inconsistent with the existence of a trust.

ARTICLE 3

The Convention applies only to trusts created voluntarily and evidenced in writing.

ARTICLE 4

The Convention does not apply to preliminary issues relating to the validity of wills or of other acts by virtue of which assets are transferred to the trustee.

ARTICLE 5

The Convention does not apply to the extent that the law specified by Chapter II does not provide for trusts or the category of trusts involved.

CHAPTER II – APPLICABLE LAW

ARTICLE 6

A trust shall be governed by the law chosen by the settlor. The choice must be express or be implied in the terms of the instrument creating or the writing evidencing the trust, interpreted, if necessary, in the light of the circumstances of the case.

Where the law chosen under the previous paragraph does not provide for trusts or the category of trusts involved, the choice shall not be effective and the law specified in Article 7 shall apply.

ARTICLE 7

Where no applicable law has been chosen, a trust shall be governed by the law with which it is most closely connected.

In ascertaining the law with which a trust is most closely connected reference shall be made in particular to –

(a) the place of administration of the trust designated by the settlor;

(b) the situs of the assets of the trust;

(c) the place of residence or business of the trustee;

(d) the objects of the trust and the places where they are to be fulfilled.

ARTICLE 8

The law specified by Article 6 or 7 shall govern the validity of the trust, its construction, its effects and the administration of the trust.

In particular that law shall govern –

(a) the appointment, resignation and removal of trustees, the capacity to act as a trustee, and the devolution of the office of trustee;

(b) the rights and duties of trustees among themselves;

(c) the right of trustees to delegate in whole or in part the discharge of their duties or the exercise of their powers;

(d) the power of trustees to administer or to dispose of trust assets, to create security interests in the trust assets, or to acquire new assets;

(e) the powers of investment of trustees;

(f) restrictions upon the duration of the trust, and upon the power to accumulate the income of the trust;

(g) the relationships between the trustees and the beneficiaries including the personal liability of the trustees to the beneficiaries;

(h) the variation of termination of the trust;

(i) the distribution of the trust assets;

(j) the duty of trustees to account for their administration.

ARTICLE 9

In applying this chapter a severable aspect of the trust, particularly matters of administration, may be governed by a different law.

ARTICLE 10

The law applicable to the validity of the trust shall determine whether that law or the law governing a severable aspect of the trust may be replaced by another law.

CHAPTER III – RECOGNITION

ARTICLE 11

A trust created in accordance with the law specified by the preceding chapter shall be recognised as a trust.

Such recognition shall imply, as a minimum, that the trust property constitutes a separate fund, that the trustee may sue and be sued in his capacity as trustee, and that he may appear or act in this capacity before a notary or any person acting in an official capacity.

In so far as the law applicable to the trust requires or provides, such recognition shall imply in particular –

(a) that personal creditors of the trustee shall have no recourse against the trust assets;

(b) that the trust assets shall not form part of the trustee's estate upon his insolvency or bankruptcy;

(c) that the trust assets shall not form part of the m﹡trimonial property of the trustee or his spouse nor part of the trustee's estate upon his death;

(d) that the trust assets may be recovered when the trustee, in breach of trust, has mingled trust assets with his own property or has alienated trust assets. However, the rights and obligations of any third party holder of the assets shall remain subject to the law determined by the choice of law rules of the forum.

ARTICLE 12

Where the trustee desires to register assets, movable or immovable, or documents of title to them, he shall be entitled, in so far as this is not prohibited by or inconsistent with the law of the State where registration is sought, to do so in his capacity as trustee or in such other way that the existence of the trust is disclosed.

ARTICLE 14

The Convention shall not prevent the application of rules of law more favourable to the recognition of trusts.

CHAPTER IV – GENERAL CLAUSES

ARTICLE 15

The Convention does not prevent the application of provisions of the law designated by the conflicts rules of the forum, in so far as those provisions cannot be derogated from by voluntary act, relating in particular to the following matters –

(a) the protection of minors and incapable parties;

(b) the personal and proprietary effects of marriage;

(c) succession rights, testate and intestate, especially the indefeasible shares of spouses and relatives;

(d) the transfer of title to property and security interests in property;

(e) the protection of creditors in matters of insolvency;

(f) the protection, in other respects, of third parties acting in good faith.

If recognition of a trust is prevented by application of the preceding paragraph, the court shall try to give effect to the objects of the trust by other means.

ARTICLE 16

The Convention does not prevent the application of those provisions of the law of the forum which must be applied even to international situations, irrespective of rules of conflict of laws.

ARTICLE 17

In the Convention the word 'law' means the rules of law in force in a State other than its rules of conflict of laws.

ARTICLE 18

The provisions of the Convention may be disregarded when their application would be manifestly incompatible with public policy.

ARTICLE 22

The Convention applies to trusts regardless of the date on which they were created.

DIPLOMATIC AND CONSULAR PREMISES ACT 1987

(1987 c 46)

PART I

DIPLOMATIC AND CONSULAR PREMISES

1 Acquisition and loss by land of diplomatic or consular status

(1) Subject to subsection (2) below, where a State desires that land shall be diplomatic or consular premises, it shall apply to the Secretary of State for his consent to the land being such premises.

(2) A State need not make such an application in relation to land if the Secretary of State accepted it as diplomatic or consular premises immediately before the coming into force of this section.

(3) In no case is land to be regarded as a State's diplomatic or consular premises for the purposes of any enactment or rule of law unless it has been so accepted or the Secretary of State has given that State consent under this section in relation to it; and if –

(a) a State ceases to use land for the purposes of its mission or exclusively for the purposes of a consular post; or

(b) the Secretary of State withdraws his acceptance or consent in relation to land,

it thereupon ceases to be diplomatic or consular premises for the purposes of all enactments and rules of law.

(4) The Secretary of State shall only give or withdraw consent or withdraw acceptance if he is satisfied that to do so is permissible under international law.

(5) In determining whether to do so he shall have regard to all

material considerations, and in particular, but without prejudice to the generality of this subsection –

(a) to the safety of the public;

(b) to national security; and

(c) to town and country planning.

(6) If a State intends to cease using land as premises of its mission or as consular premises, it shall give the Secretary of State notice of that intention, specifying the date on which it intends to cease so using them.

(7) In any proceedings a certificate issued by or under the authority of the Secretary of State stating any fact relevant to the question whether or not land was at any time diplomatic or consular premises shall be conclusive of that fact.

2 Vesting of former diplomatic or consular premises

(1) Where –

(a) the Secretary of State formerly accepted land as diplomatic or consular premises but did not accept it as such premises immediately before the coming into force of this section; or

(b) land has ceased to be diplomatic or consular premises after the coming into force of this section but not less than 12 months before the exercise of the power conferred on the Secretary of State by this subsection,

the Secretary of State may by order provide that this section shall apply to that land.

(2) The Secretary of State shall only exercise the power conferred by subsection (1) above if he is satisfied that to do so is permissible under international law.

(3) In determining whether to exercise it he shall have regard to all material considerations, and in particular, but without prejudice to the generality of its subsection, to any of the considerations mentioned in section 1(5) above that appears to him to be relevant.

(4) An order under subsection (1) above shall be made by statutory instrument, and a statutory instrument containing any such order shall be subject to annulment in pursuance of a resolution of either House of Parliament.

(5) The Secretary of State may by deed poll vest in himself such estate or interest in land to which this section applies as appears to him to be appropriate.

(6) A deed poll under this section may also comprise any portion of a building in which the former diplomatic or consular premises are situated.

(7) In relation to land in Scotland this section shall have effect with the substitution of references to an order for references to a deed poll, and such an order shall take effect immediately it is made.

(8) Subject to subsection (9) below, in a case falling within paragraph (a) of subsection (1) above the Secretary of State may only exercise the power conferred by that subsection before the end of the period of two months beginning with the date on which this section comes into force.

(9) In such a case the power continues to be exercisable after the end of that period if the Secretary of State within that period –

(a) certifies that he reserves the right to exercise it; and

(b) unless he considers it inappropriate or impracticable to do so, serves a copy of the certificate on the owner of any estate or interest in the land.

(10) Where –

(a) circumstances have arisen in consequence of which the power conferred by subsection (1) above is exercisable; but

(b) the Secretary of State serves on the owner of the land in relation to which it has become exercisable notice that he does not intend to exercise the power in relation to that land,

it shall cease to be exercisable in relation to it in consequence of those circumstances.

(11) If –

(a) the Secretary of State has exercised the power conferred by subsection (1) above in relation to land; but

(b) serves on the owner notice that he does not intend to execute a deed poll under this section, or if the land is in Scotland to make an order under it, relating to the land,

the power to vest conferred by this section shall cease to be exercisable.

3   Duty of sale

(1) Where an estate or interest in land has vested in the Secretary of State under section 2 above, it shall be his duty to sell it as soon as it is reasonably practicable to do so, taking all reasonable steps to ensure that the price is the best that can reasonably be obtained.

(2) The Secretary of State shall apply the purchase money –

(a) firstly in payment of expenses properly incurred by him as incidental to the sale or any attempted sale;

(b) secondly in discharge of prior incumbrances to which the sale is not made subject or in the making of any payments to mortgagees required by Schedule 1 to this Act;

(c) thirdly in payment of expenses relating to the land reasonably incurred by him on repairs or security;

(d) fourthly in discharge of such liabilities to pay rates or sums in lieu of rates on the land or on any other land as the Secretary of State thinks fit;

(e) fifthly in discharge of such judgment debts arising out of matters relating to the land or to any other land as he thinks fit,

and, subject to subsection (3) below, shall pay any residue to the person divested of the estate or interest.

(3) Where a State was divested but there is no person with whom Her Majesty's Government of the United Kingdom has dealings as the Government of that State, the Secretary of State shall hold the residue until there is such a person and then pay it.

(4) A sum held by the Secretary of State under subsection (3) above shall be placed in a bank account bearing interest at such rate as the Treasury may approve.

5   Interpretation of Part I

In this Part of this Act –

'consular post' and 'consular premises' have the meanings given by the definitions in paragraph 1(a) and (j) of Article 1 of the 1963 Convention as that Article has effect in the United Kingdom by virtue of section 1 of and Schedule 1 to the Consular Relations Act 1968;

'diplomatic premises' means premises of the mission of a State;

'mortgage' includes a charge of lien for securing money or money's worth, and references to mortgagees shall be construed accordingly;

'premises of the mission' has the meaning given by the definition in Article 1(i) of the 1961 Convention as that Article has effect in the United Kingdom by virtue of section 2 of and Schedule 1 to the Diplomatic Privileges Act 1964;

'the 1961 Convention' means the Vienna Convention on Diplomatic Relations signed in 1961; and

'the 1963 Convention' means the Vienna Convention on Consular Relations signed in 1963.

FAMILY LAW REFORM ACT 1987
(1987 c 42)

1   General principle

(1) In this Act and enactments passed and instruments made after the coming into force of this section, references (however expressed) to any relationship between two persons shall, unless the contrary intention appears, be construed without regard to whether or not the father and mother of either of them, or the father and mother of any person through whom the relationship is deduced, have or had been married to each other at any time.

(2) In this Act and enactments passed after the coming into force of this section, unless the contrary intention appears –

(a) references to a person whose father and mother were married to each other at the time of his birth include; and

(b) references to a person whose father and mother were not married to each other at the time of his birth do not include,

references to any person to whom subsection (3) below applies, and cognate references shall be construed accordingly.

(3) This subsection applies to any person who –

(a) is treated as legitimate by virtue of section 1 of the Legitimacy Act 1976;

(b) is a legitimated person within the meaning of section 10 of that Act;

(c) is an adopted child within the meaning of Part IV of the Adoption Act 1976; or

(d) is otherwise treated in law as legitimate.

(4) For the purpose of construing references falling within subsection (2) above, the time of a person's birth shall be taken to include any time during the period beginning with –

(a) the insemination resulting in his birth; or

(b) where there was no such insemination, his conception,

and (in either case) ending with his birth.

18 Succession on intestacy

(1) In Part IV of the Administration of Estates Act 1925 (which deals with the distribution of the estate of an intestate), references (however expressed) to any relationship between two persons shall be construed in accordance with section 1 above.

(2) For the purposes of subsectiopn (1) above and that Part of that Act, a person whose father and mother were not married to each other at the time of his birth shall be presumed not to have been survived by his father, or by any person related to him only through his father, unless the contrary is shown. ...

(4) This section does not affect any rights under the intestacy of a person dying before the coming into force of this section.

19 Dispositions of property

(1) In the following dispositions, namely –

(a) dispositions inter vivos made on or after the date on which this section comes into force; and

(b) dispositions by will or codicil where the will or codicil is made on or after that date,

references (whether expressed or implied) to any relationship between two persons shall be construed in accordance with section 1 above. ...

(5) This section is without prejudice to section 42 of the Adoption Act 1976 (construction of dispositions in cases of adoption).

(6) In this section 'disposition' means a disposition, including an oral disposition, of real or personal property whether inter vivos or by will or codicil.

(7) Notwithstanding any rule of law, a disposition made by will or codicil executed before the date on which this section comes into force shall not be treated for the purposes of this section as made on or after that date by reason only that the will or codicil is confirmed by a codicil executed on or after that date.

27   Artificial insemination

(1) Where after the coming into force of this section a child is born in England and Wales as the result of the artificial insemination of a woman who –

(a) was at the time of the insemination a party to a marriage (being a marriage which had not at that time been dissolved or annulled); and

(b) was artificially inseminated with the semen of some person other than the other party to that marriage,

then, unless it is proved to the satisfaction of any court by which the matter has to be determined that the other party to that marriage did not consent to the insemination, the child shall be treated in law as the child of the parties to that marriage and shall not be treated as the child of any person other than the parties to that marriage.

(2) Any reference in this section to a marriage includes a reference to a void marriage if at the time of the insemination resulting in the birth of the child both or either of the parties reasonably believed that the marriage was valid; and for the purposes of this section it shall be presumed, unless the contrary is shown, that one of the parties so believed at that time that the marriage was valid.

(3) Nothing in this section shall affect the succession to any dignity or title of honour or render any person capable of succeeding to or transmitting a right to succeed to any such dignity or title.

CHILDREN ACT 1989

(1989 c 41)

PART I

INTRODUCTORY

1 Welfare of the child

(1) When a court determines any question with respect to –

(a) the upbringing of a child; or

(b) the administration of a child's property or the application of any income arising from it,

the child's welfare shall be the court's paramount consideration.

(2) In any proceedings in which any question with respect to the upbringing of a child arises, the court shall have regard to the general principle that any delay in determining the question is likely to prejudice the welfare of the child.

(3) In the circumstances mentioned in subsection (4), a court shall have regard in particular to –

(a) the ascertainable wishes and feelings of the child concerned (considered in the light of his age and understanding);

(b) his physical, emotional and educational needs;

(c) the likely effect on him of any change in his circumstances;

(d) his age, sex, background and any characteristics of his which the court considers relevant;

(e) any harm which he has suffered or is at risk of suffering;

(f) how capable each of his parents, and any other person in relation to whom the court considers the question to be relevant, is of meeting his needs;

(g) the range of powers available to the court under this Act in the proceedings in question.

(4) The circumstances are that –

(a) the court is considering whether to make, vary or discharge a section 8 order, and the making, variation or discharge of the order is opposed by any party to the proceedings; or

(b) the court is considering whether to make, vary or discharge an order under Part IV.

(5) Where a court is considering whether or not to make one or more orders under this Act with respect to a child, it shall not make the order or any of the orders unless it considers that doing so would be better for the child than making no order at all.

2 Parental responsibility for children

(1) Where a child's father and mother were married to each other at the time of his birth, they shall each have parental responsibility for the child.

(2) Where a child's father and mother were not married to each other at the time of his birth –

(a) the mother shall have parental responsibility for the child;

(b) the father shall not have parental responsibility for the child, unless he acquires it in accordance with the provisions of this Act.

(3) References in this Act to a child whose father and mother were, or (as the case may be) were not, married to each other at the time of his birth must be read with section 1 of the Family Law Reform Act 1987 (which extends their meaning). ...

3 Meaning of 'parental responsibility'

(1) In this Act 'parental responsibility' means all the rights, duties, powers, responsibilities and authority which by law a parent of a child has in relation to the child and his property.

(2) It also includes the rights, powers and duties which a guardian of the child's estate (appointed, before the commencement of section 5, to act generally) would have had in relation to the child and his property.

(3) The rights referred to in subsection (2) include, in particular, the right of the guardian to receive or recover in his own name, for

the benefit of the child, property of whatever description and wherever situated which the child is entitled to receive or recover.

(4) The fact that a person has, or does not have, parental responsibility for a child shall not affect –

(a) any obligation which he may have in relation to the child (such as a statutory duty to maintain the child); or

(b) any rights which, in the event of the child's death, he (or any other person) may have in relation to the child's property.

(5) A person who –

(a) does not have parental responsibility for a particular child; but

(b) has care of the child,

may (subject to the provisions of this Act) do what is reasonable in all the circumstances of the case for the purpose of safeguarding or promoting the child's welfare.

4   Acquisition of parental responsibility by father

(1) Where a child's father and mother were not married to each other at the time of his birth –

(a) the court may, on the application of the father, order that he shall have parental responsibility for the child; or

(b) the father and mother may by agreement ('a parental responsibility agreement') provide for the father to have parental responsibility for the child.

(2) No parental responsibility agreement shall have effect for the purposes of this Act unless –

(a) it is made in the form prescribed by regulations made by the Lord Chancellor; and

(b) where regulations are made by the Lord Chancellor prescribing the manner in which such agreements must be recorded, it is recorded in the prescribed manner.

(3) Subject to section 12(4), an order under subsection (1)(a), or a parental responsibility agreement, may only be brought to an end by an order of the court made on the application –

(a) of any person who has parental responsibility for the child; or

(b) with leave of the court, of the child himself.

(4) The court may only grant leave under subsection (3)(b) if it is satisfied that the child has sufficient understanding to make the proposed application.

PART II

ORDERS WITH RESPECT TO CHILDREN IN FAMILY PROCEEDINGS

8 Residence, contact and other orders with respect to children

(1) In this Act –

'a contact order' means an order requiring the person with whom a child lives, or is to live, to allow the child to visit or stay with the person named in the order, or for that person and the child otherwise to have contact with each other;

'a prohibited steps order' means an order that no step which could be taken by a parent in meeting his parental responsibility for a child, and which is of a kind specified in the order, shall be taken by any person without the consent of the court;

'a residence order' means an order settling the arrangements to be made as to the person with whom a child is to live; and

'a specific issue order' means an order giving directions for the purpose of determining a specific question which has arisen, or which may arise, in connection with any aspect of parental responsibility for a child.

(2) In this Act 'a section 8 order' means any of the orders mentioned in subsection (1) and any order varying or discharging such an order. ...

9 Restrictions on making s8 orders

(1) No court shall make any section 8 order, other than a residence order, with respect to a child who is in the care of a local authority.

(2) No application may be made by a local authority for a residence order or contact order and no court shall make such an order in favour of a local authority.

(3) A person who is, or was at any time within the last six months, a local authority foster parent of a child may not apply for leave to apply for a section 8 order with respect to the child unless –

(a) he had the consent of the authority;

(b) he is a relative of the child; or

(c) the child has lived with him for at least three years preceding the application.

(4) The period of three years mentioned in subsection (3)(c) need not be continuous but must have begun not more than five years before the making of the application.

(5) No court shall exercise its powers to make a specific issue order or prohibited steps order –

(a) with a view to achieving a result which could be achieved by making a residence or contact order; or

(b) in any way which is denied to the High Court (by section 100(2)) in the exercise of its inherent jurisdiction with respect to children.

(6) No court shall make any section 8 order which is to have effect for a period which will end after the child has reached the age of sixteen unless it is satisfied that the circumstances of the case are exceptional.

(7) No court shall make any section 8 order, other than one varying or discharging such an order, with respect to a child who has reached the age of sixteen unless it is satisfied that the circumstances of the case are exceptional.

10   Power of court to make s8 orders

(1) In any family proceedings in which a question arises with respect to the welfare of any child, the court may make a section 8 order with respect to the child if –

(a) an application for the order has been made by a person who –

(i) is entitled to apply for a section 8 order with respect to the child; or

(ii) has obtained the leave of the court to make the application; or

(b) the court considers that the order should be made even though no such application has been made.

(2) The court may also make a section 8 order with respect to any child on the application of a person who –

(a) is entitled to apply for a section 8 order with respect to the child; or

(b) has obtained the leave of the court to make the application.

(3) This section is subject to the restrictions imposed by section 9.

(4) The following persons are entitled to apply to the court for any section 8 order with respect to a child –

(a) any parent or guardian of the child;

(b) any person in whose favour a residence order is in force with respect to the child.

(5) The following persons are entitled to apply for a residence or contact order with respect to a child –

(a) any party to a marriage (whether or not subsisting) in relation to whom the child is a child of the family;

(b) any person with whom the child has lived for a period of at least three years;

(c) any person who –

(i) in any case where a residence order is in force with respect to the child, has the consent of each of the persons in whose favour the order was made;

(ii) in any case where the child is in the care of a local authority, has the consent of that authority; or

(iii) in any other case, has the consent of each of those (if any) who have parental responsibility for the child.

(6) A person who would not otherwise be entitled (under the previous provisions of this section) to apply for the variation or discharge of a section 8 order shall be entitled to do so if –

(a) the order was made on his application; or

(b) in the case of a contact order, he is named in the order.

(7) Any person who falls within a category of person prescribed by

rules of court is entitled to apply for any such section 8 order as may be prescribed in relation to that category of person.

(8) Where the person applying for leave to make an application for a section 8 order is the child concerned, the court may only grant leave if it is satisfied that he has sufficient understanding to make the proposed application for the section 8 order.

(9) Where the person applying for leave to make an application for a section 8 order is not the child concerned, the court shall, in deciding whether or not to grant leave, have particular regard to –

(a) the nature of the proposed application for the section 8 order;

(b) the applicant's connection with the child;

(c) any risk there might be of that proposed application disrupting the child's life to such an extent that he would be harmed by it; and

(d) where the child is being looked after by a local authority –

(i) the authority's plans for the child's future; and

(ii) the wishes and feelings of the child's parents.

(10) The period of three years mentioned in subsection (5)(b) need not be continuous but must not have begun more than five years before, or ended more than three months before, the making of the application.

CONTRACTS (APPLICABLE LAW) ACT 1990
(1990 c 36)

1 Meaning of 'the Conventions'

In this Act –

(a) 'the Rome Convention' means the Convention on the law applicable to contractual obligations opened for signature in Rome on 19 June 1980 and signed by the United Kingdom on 7 December 1981;

(b) 'the Luxembourg Convention' means the Convention on the accession of the Hellenic Republic to the Rome Convention signed by the United Kingdom in Luxembourg on 10 April 1984; and

(c) 'the Brussels Protocol' means the first Protocol on the interpretation of the Rome Convention by the European Court signed by the United Kingdom in Brussels on 19 December 1988;

(d) 'the Funchal Convention' means the Convention on the accession of the Kingdom of Spain and the Portuguese Republic to the Rome Convention and the Brussels Protocol, with adjustments made to the Rome Convention by the Luxembourg Convention, signed by the United Kingdom in Funchal on 18 May 1992;

and these Conventions and this Protocol are together referred to as 'the Conventions'.

2 Conventions to have force of law

(1) Subject to sub-sections (2) and (3) below, the Conventions shall have the force of law in the United Kingdom.

(1A) The internal law for the purposes of Article 1(3) of the Rome Convention is whichever of the following are applicable, namely –

(a) the provisions of Schedule 3A to the Insurance Companies Act 1982 (law applicable to certain contracts of insurance with insurance companies), and

(b) the provisions of Schedule 20 to the Friendly Societies Act 1992 as applied by sub-sections (1)(a) and (2)(a) of section 101 of that Act (law applicable to certain contracts of insurance with friendly societies).

(2) Articles 7(1) and 10(1)(e) of the Rome Convention shall not have the force of law in the United Kingdom.

(3) Notwithstanding Article 19(2) of the Rome Convention, the Conventions shall apply in the case of conflicts between the laws of different parts of the United Kingdom.

(4) For ease of reference there are set out in Schedules 1, 2 3 and 3A to this Act respectively the English texts of –

(a) the Rome Convention;

(b) the Luxembourg Convention;

(c) the Brussels Protocol; and

(d) the Funchal Convention.

3   Interpretation of Conventions

(1) Any question as to the meaning or effect of any provision of the Conventions shall, if not referred to the European Court in accordance with the Brussels Protocol, be determined in accordance with the principles laid down by, and any relevant decision of, the European Court.

(2) Judicial notice shall be taken of any decision of, or expression of opinion by, the European Court on any such question.

(3) Without prejudice to any practice of the courts as to the matters which may be considered apart from this subsection –

(a) the report on the Rome Convention by Professor Mario Giuliano and Professor Paul Lagarde which is reproduced in the Official Journal of the Communities of 31 October 1980 may be considered in ascertaining the meaning or effect of any provision of that Convention; and

(b) any report on the Brussels Protocol which is reproduced in the Official Journal of the Communities may be considered in ascertaining the meaning or effect of any provision of that Protocol.

SCHEDULE 1

THE ROME CONVENTION ...

TITLE 1

SCOPE OF THE CONVENTION

ARTICLE 1

1. The rules of this Convention shall apply to contractual obligations in any situation involving a choice between the laws of different countries.

2. They shall not apply to:

(a) questions involving the status or legal capacity of natural persons, without prejudice to Article 11;

(b) contractual obligations relating to:

– wills and succession,

– rights in property arising out of a matrimonial relationship,

– rights and duties arising out of a family relationship, parentage, marriage or affinity, including maintenance obligations in respect of children who are not legitimate;

(c) obligations arising under bills of exchange, cheques and promissory notes and other negotiable instruments to the extent that the obligations under such other negotiable instruments arise out of their negotiable character;

(d) arbitration agreements and agreements on the choice of court;

(e) questions governed by the law of companies and other bodies corporate or unincorporate such as the creation, by registration or otherwise, legal capacity, internal organisation or winding up of companies and other bodies corporate or unincorporate and the personal liability of officers and members as such for the obligations of the company or body;

(f) the question whether an agent is able to bind a principal, or an organ to bind a company or body corporate or unincorporate, to a third party;

(g) the constitution of trusts and the relationship between settlors, trustees and beneficiaries;

(h) evidence and procedure, without prejudice to Article 14.

3. The rules of this Convention do not apply to contracts of insurance which cover risks situated in the territories of the Member States of the European Economic Community. In order to determine whether a risk is situated in these territories the court shall apply its internal law.

4. The preceding paragraph does not apply to contracts of re-insurance.

ARTICLE 2

Any law specified by this Convention shall be applied whether or not it is the law of a Contracting State.

TITLE II

UNIFORM RULES

ARTICLE 3

1. A contract shall be governed by the law chosen by the parties. The choice must be express or demonstrated with reasonable certainty by the terms of the contract or the circumstances of the case. By their choice the parties can select the law applicable to the whole or a part only of the contract.

2. The parties may at any time agree to subject the contract to a law other than that which previously governed it, whether as a result of an earlier choice under this Article or of other provisions of this Convention. Any variation by the parties of the law to be applied made after the conclusion of the contract shall not prejudice its formal validity under Article 9 or adversely affect the rights of third parties.

3. The fact that the parties have chosen a foreign law, whether or not accompanied by the choice of a foreign tribunal, shall not, where all the other elements relevant to the situation at the time of the choice are connected with one country only, prejudice the application of rules of the law of that country which cannot be derogated from by contract, hereinafter called 'mandatory rules'.

4. The existence and validity of the consent of the parties as to the choice of the applicable law shall be determined in accordance with the provisions of Articles 8, 9 and 11.

ARTICLE 4

1. To the extent that the law applicable to the contract has not been chosen in accordance with Article 3, the contract shall be governed by the law of the country with which it is most closely connected. Nevertheless, a severable part of the contract which has a closer connection with another country may by way of exception be governed by the law of that other country.

2. Subject to the provisions of paragraph 5 of this Article, it shall be presumed that the contract is most closely connected with the country where the party who is to effect the performance which is characteristic of the contract has, at the time of conclusion of the contract, his habitual residence, or, in the case of a body corporate or unincorporate, its central administration. However, if the contract is entered into in the course of that party's trade or profession, that country shall be the country in which the principal place of business is situated or, where under the terms of the contract the performance is to be effected through a place of business other than the principal place of business, the country in which that other place of business is situated.

3. Notwithstanding the provisions of paragraph 2 of this Article, to the extent that the subject matter of the contract is a right in immovable property or a right to use immovable property it shall be presumed that the contract is most closely connected with the country where the immovable property is situated.

4. A contract for the carriage of goods shall not be subject to the presumption in paragraph 2. In such a contract if the country in which, at the time the contract is concluded, the carrier has his principal place of business is also the country in which the place of loading or the place of discharge or the principal place of business of the consignor is situated, it shall be presumed that the contract is most closely connected with that country. In applying this paragraph single voyage charter-parties and other contracts the main purpose of which is the carriage of goods shall be treated as contracts for the carriage of goods.

5. Paragraph 2 shall not apply if the characteristic performance cannot be determined, and the presumptions in paragraphs 2, 3 and 4 shall be disregarded if it appears from the circumstances as a whole that the contract is more closely connected with another country.

ARTICLE 5

1. This Article applies to a contract the object of which is the supply of goods or services to a person ('the consumer') for a purpose which can be regarded as being outside his trade or profession, or a contract for the provision of credit for that object.

2. Notwithstanding the provisions of Article 3, a choice of law made by the parties shall have the result of depriving the consumer of the protection afforded to him by the mandatory rules of the law of the country in which he has habitual residence:

   – if in that country the conclusion of the contract was preceded by a specific invitation addressed to him or by advertising, and he had taken in that country all the steps necessary on his part for the conclusion of the contract, or

   – if the other party or his agent received the consumer's order in that country, or

   – if the contract is for the sale of goods and the consumer travelled from that country to another country and there gave his order, provided that the consumer's journey was arranged by the seller for the purpose of inducing the consumer to buy.

3. Notwithstanding the provisions of Article 4, a contract to which this Article applies shall, in absence of choice in accordance with Article 3, be governed by the law of the country in which the consumer has his habital residence if it is entered into in the circumstances described in paragraph 2 of this Article.

4. This Article shall not apply to:

   (a) a contract of carriage;

   (b) a contract for the supply of services where the services are to be supplied to the consumer exclusively in a country other than that in which he has his habital residence.

5. Notwithstanding the provisions of paragraph 4, this Article shall apply to a contract which, for an inclusive price, provides for a combination of travel and accommodation.

ARTICLE 6

1. Notwithstanding the provisions of Article 3, in a contract of employment a choice of law made by the parties shall not have the result of depriving the employee of the protection afforded to him

by the mandatory rules of the law which would be applicable under paragraph 2 in the absence of choice.

2. Notwithstanding the provisions of Article 4, a contract of employment shall, in the absence of choice in accordance with Articel 3, be governed:

(a) by the law of the country in which the employee habitually carries out his work in performance of the contract, even if he is temporarily employed in another country; or

(b) if the employee does not habitually carry out his work in any one country, by the law of the country in which the place of business through which he was engaged is situated;

unless it appears from the circumstances as a whole that the contract is more closely connected with another country, in which case the contract shall be governed by the law of that country.

ARTICLE 7

1. When applying under this Convention the law of a country, effect may be given to the mandatory rules of the law of another country with which the situation has a close connection, if and in so far as, under the law of the latter country, those rules must be applied whatever the law applicable to the contract. In considering whether to give effect to these mandatory rules, regard shall be had to their nature and purpose and to the consequences of their application or non-application.

2. Nothing in this Convention shall restrict the application of the rules of the law of the forum in a situation where they are mandatory irrespective of the law otherwise applicable to the contract.

ARTICLE 8

1. The existence and validity of a contract, or of any term of a contract, shall be determined by the law which would govern it under this Convention if the contract or term were valid.

2. Nevertheless a party may rely upon the law of the country in which he has his habitual residence to establish that he did not consent if it appears from the circumstances that it would not be reasonable to determine the effect of his conduct in accordance with the law specified in the preceding paragraph.

ARTICLE 9

1. A contract concluded between persons who are in the same country is formally valid if it satisfies the formal requirements of the law which governs it under this Convention or of the law of the country where it is concluded.

2. A contract concluded between persons who are in different countries is formally valid if it satisfies the formal requirements of the law which governs it under this Convention or of the law of one of those countries.

3. Where a contract is concluded by an agent, the country in which the agent acts is the relevant country for the purposes of paragraphs 1 and 2.

4. An act intended to have legal effect relating to an existing or contemplated contract is formally valid if it satisfies the formal requirements of the law which under this Convention governs or would govern the contract or of the law of the country where the act was done.

5. The provisions of the preceding paragraphs shall not apply to a contract to which Article 5 applies, concluded in the circumstances described in paragraph 2 of Article 5. The formal validity of such a contract is governed by the law of the country in which the consumer has his habital residence.

6. Notwithstanding paragraphs 1 to 4 of this Article, a contract the subject matter of which is a right in immovable property or a right to use immovable property shall be subject to the mandatory requirements of form of the law of the country where the property is situated if by that law those requirements are imposed irrespective of the country where the contract is concluded and irrespective of the law governing the contract.

ARTICLE 10

1. The law applicable to a contract by virtue of Articles 3 to 6 and 12 of this Convention shall govern in particular:

   (a) interpretation;

   (b) performance;

   (c) within the limits of the powers conferred on the court by its procedural law, the consequences of breach, including the assessment of damages in so far as it is governed by rules of law;

(d) the various ways of extinguishing obligations and prescription and limitation of actions;

(e) the consequences of nullity of the contract.

2. In relation to the manner of performance and the steps to be taken in the event of defective performance regard shall be had to the law of the country in which performance takes place.

ARTICLE 11

In a contract concluded between persons who are in the same country, a natural person who would have capacity under the law of that country may invoke his incapacity resulting from another law only if the other party to the contract was aware of this incapacity at the time of the conclusion of the contract or was not aware thereof as a result of negligence.

ARTICLE 12

1. The mutal obligations of assignor and assignee under a voluntary assignment of a right against another person ('the debtor') shall be governed by the law which under this Convention applies to the contract between the assignor and assignee.

2. The law governing the right to which the assignment relates shall determine its assignability, the relationship between the assignee and the debtor, the conditions under which the assignment can be invoked against the debtor and any question whether the debtor's obligations have been discharged.

ARTICLE 13

1. Where a person ('the creditor') has a contractual claim upon another ('the debtor'), and a third person has a duty to satisfy the creditor, or has in fact satisfied the creditor in discharge of that duty, the law which governs the third person's duty to satisfy the creditor shall determine whether the third person is entitled to exercise against the debtor the rights which the creditor had against the debtor under the law governing their relationship and, if so, whether he may do so in full or only to a limited extent.

2. The same rule applies where several persons are subject to the same contractual claim and one of them has satisfied the creditor.

ARTICLE 14

1. The law governing the contract under this Convention applies to the extent that it contains, in the law of contract, rules which raise presumptions of law or determine the burden of proof.

2. A contract or an act intended to have legal effect may be proved by any mode of proof recognised by the law of the forum or by any of the laws referred to in Article 9 under which that contract or act is formally valid, provided that such mode of proof can be administered by the forum.

ARTICLE 15

The application of the law of any country specified by this Convention means the application of the rules of law in force in that country other than its rules of private international law.

ARTICLE 16

The application of a rule of the law of any country specified by this Convention may be refused only if such application is manifestly incompatible with the public policy ('ordre public') of the forum.

ARTICLE 17

This Convention shall apply in a Contracting State to contracts made after the date on which this Convention has entered into force with respect to that State.

ARTICLE 18

In the interpretation and application of the preceding uniform rules, regard shall be had to their international character and to the desirability of achieving uniformity in their interpretation and application.

ARTICLE 19

1. Where a State comprises several territorial units each of which has its own rules of law in respect of contractual obligations, each

territorial unit shall be considered as a country for the purposes of identifying the law applicable under this Convention.

2. A State within which different territorial units have their own rules of law in respect of contractual obligations shall not be bound to apply this Convention to conflicts solely between the laws of such units.

ARTICLE 20

This Convention shall not affect the application of provisions which, in relation to particular matters, lay down choice of law rules relating to contractual obligations and which are or will be contained in acts of the institutions of the European Communities or in national laws harmonised in implementation of such acts.

ARTICLE 21

This Convention shall not prejudice the application of international conventions to which a Contracting State is, or becomes, a party.

ARTICLE 22

1. Any Contracting State may, at the time of signature, ratification, acceptance or approval, reserve the right not to apply:

(a) the provisions of Article 7(1);
(b) the provisions of Article 10(1)(e).

3. Any Contracting State may at any time withdraw a reservation which it has made; the reservation shall cease to have effect on the first day of the third calendar month after notification of the withdrawal.

TITLE III

FINAL PROVISIONS

ARTICLE 23

1. If, after the date on which this Convention has entered into force for a Contracting State, that State wishes to adopt any new choice of

law rule in regard to any particular category of contract within the scope of this Convention, it shall communicate its intention to the other signatory States through the Secretary-General of the Council of the European Communities.

2. Any signatory State may, within six months from the date of the communication made to the Secretary-General, request him to arrange consultations between signatory States in order to reach agreement.

3. If no signatory State has requested consultations within this period or if within two years following the communication made to the Secretary-General no agreement is reached in the course of consultations, the Contracting State concerned may amend its law in the manner indicated. The measures taken by that State shall be brought to the knowledge of the other signatory States through the Secretary-General of the Council of the European Communities. ...

SCHEDULE 3

THE BRUSSELS PROTOCOL ...

ARTICLE 1

The Court of Justice of the European Communities shall have jurisdiction to give rulings on the interpretation of –

(a) the Convention on the law applicable to contractual obligations, opened for signature in Rome on 19 June 1980, hereinafter referred to as 'the Rome Convention';

(b) the Convention on accession to the Rome Convention by the States which have become Members of the European Communities since the date on which it was opened for signature;

(c) this Protocol.

ARTICLE 2

Any of the courts referred to below may request the Court of Justice to give a preliminary ruling on a question raised in a case pending before it and concerning interpretation of the provisions contained in the instruments referred to in Article 1 if that court considers that a decision on the question is necessary to enable it to give judgment:

(a) ... in the United Kingdom:

the House of Lords and other courts from which no further appeal is possible;

(b) the courts of the Contracting States when acting as appeal courts. ...

As amended by the Friendly Societies (Amendment) Regulations 1993, reg 6(5); Contracts (Applicable Law) Act 1990 (Amendment) Order 1994, arts 3–7.

FOREIGN CORPORATIONS ACT 1991
(1991 c 44)

1 Recognition of corporate status of certain foreign corporations

(1) If at any time –

(a) any question arises whether a body which purports to have or, as the case may be, which appears to have lost corporate status under the laws of a territory which is not at that time a recognised State should or should not be regarded as having legal personality as a body corporate under the law of any part of the United Kingdom, and

(b) it appears that the laws of that territory are at that time applied by a settled court system in that territory,

that question and any other material question relating to the body shall be determined (and account shall be taken of those laws) as if that territory were a recognised State.

(2) For the purposes of subsection (1) above –

(a) 'a recognised State' is a territory which is recognised by Her Majesty's Government in the United Kingdom as a State;

(b) the laws of a territory which is so recognised shall be taken to include the laws of any part of the territory which are acknowledged by the federal or other central government of the territory as a whole; and

(c) a material question is a question (whether as to capacity, constitution or otherwise) which, in the case of a body corporate, falls to be determined by reference to the laws of the territory under which the body is incorporated.

(3) Any registration or other thing done at a time before the coming into force of this section shall be regarded as valid if it would have been valid at that time, had subsections (1) and (2) above then been in force.

SOCIAL SECURITY CONTRIBUTIONS AND BENEFITS ACT 1992
(1992 c 4)

121 Treatment of certain marriages

(1) Regulations may provide –

(a) for a voidable marriage which has been annulled, whether before or after the date when the regulations come into force, to be treated for the purposes of the provisions to which this subsection applies as if it had been a valid marriage which was terminated by divorce at the date of annulment;

(b) as to the circumstances in which, for the purposes of the enactments to which this section applies, a marriage during the subsistence of which a party to it is at any time married to more than one person is to be treated as having, or as not having, the same consequences as any other marriage.

(2) Subsection (1) above applies –

(a) to any enactment contained in Parts I to V or this Part of this Act; and

(b) to regulations under any such enactment.

147 Interpretation of Part IX and supplementary provisions
...

(5) Regulations may make provisions as to the circumstances in which a marriage during the subsistence of which a party to it is at any time married to more than one person is to be treated for the purposes of this Part of this Act as having, or not having, the same consequences as any other marriage.

As amended by the Private International Law (Miscellaneous Provisions) Act 1995, s8(2), Schedule, para 4.

MAINTENANCE ORDERS
(RECIPROCAL ENFORCEMENT)
ACT 1992
(1992 c 56)

1 Amendment of the 1920 and 1972 Acts

(1) The Maintenance Orders (Facilities for Enforcement) Act 1920 shall have effect (until its repeal by the Maintenance Orders (Reciprocal Enforcement) Act 1972 comes into force) with the amendments set out in Part I of Schedule 1 to this Act.

(2) The Maintenance Orders (Reciprocal Enforcement) Act 1992 shall have effect with the amendments set out in Part II of Schedule 1 to this Act.

NB These amendments have been included in the texts of the 1920 and 1972 Acts, as appropriate.

EUROPEAN COMMUNITIES (AMENDMENT) ACT 1993
(1993 c 32)

1   Treaty on European Union

(2) For the purposes of section 6 of the European Parliamentary Elections Act 1978 (approval of treaties increasing the Parliament's powers) the Treaty on European Union signed at Maastricht on 7 February 1992 is approved.

2   Economic and monetary union

No notification shall be given to the Council of the European Communities that the United Kingdom intends to move to the third stage of economic and monetary union (in accordance with the Protocol on certain provisions relating to the United Kingdom adopted at Maastricht on 7 February 1992) unless a draft of the notification has first been approved by Act of Parliament and unless Her Majesty's Government has reported to Parliament on its proposals for the coordination of economic policies, its role in the European Council of Finance Ministers (ECOFIN) in pursuit of the objectives of Article 2 of the Treaty establishing the European Community as provided for in Articles 103 and 102a, and the work of the European Monetary Institute in preparation for economic and monetary union.

3   Annual report by Bank of England

In implementing Article 108 of the Treaty establishing the European Community, and ensuring compatibility of the statutes of the national central bank, Her Majesty's Government shall, by order, make provision for the Governor of the Bank of England to make an annual report to Parliament, which shall be subject to approval by a Resolution of each House of Parliament.

4 Information for Commission

In implementing the provisions of Article 103(3) of the Treaty establishing the European Community, information shall be submitted to the Commission from the United Kingdom indicating performance on economic growth, industrial investment, employment and balance of trade, together with comparisons with those items of performance from other member States.

5 Convergence criteria: assessment of deficits

Before submitting the information required in implementing Article 103(3) of the Treaty establishing the European Community, Her Majesty's Government shall report to Parliament for its approval an assessment of the medium term economic and budgetary position in relation to public investment expenditure and to the social, economic and environmental goals set out in Article 2, which report shall form the basis of any submission to the Council and Commission in pursuit of their responsibilities under Articles 103 and 104c.

6 Committee of the Regions

A person may be proposed as a member or alternative member for the United Kingdom of the Committee of the Regions constituted under Article 198a of the Treaty establishing the European Community only if, at the time of the proposal, he is an elected member of a local authority.

7 Commencement (Protocol on Social Policy)

This Act shall come into force only when each House of Parliament has come to Resolution on a motion tabled by a Minister of the Crown considering the question of adopting the Protocol on Social Policy.

PRIVATE INTERNATIONAL LAW (MISCELLANEOUS PROVISIONS) ACT 1995

(1995 c 42)

PART I

INTEREST ON JUDGMENT DEBTS AND ARBITRAL AWARDS

1   Interest on judgment debts generally

[Inserts s44A of the Administration of Justice Act 1970]

2   Interest on county court judgment debts

[Inserts s74(5) of the County Courts Act 1984]

3   Interest on arbitral awards

[Substitutes s20 of the Arbitration Act 1950]

PART II

VALIDITY OF MARRIAGES UNDER A LAW WHICH PERMITS POLYGAMY

5   Validity in English law of potentially polygamous marriages

(1) A marriage entered into outside England and Wales between parties neither of whom is already married is not void under the law of England and Wales on the ground that it is entered into under a law which permits polygamy and that either party is domiciled in England and Wales.

(2) This section does not affect the determination of the validity of a marriage by reference to the law of another country to the extent that it falls to be so determined in accordance with the rules of private international law.

6 Application of s5 to prior marriages

(1) Section 5 above shall be deemed to apply, and always to have applied, to any marriage entered into before commencement which is not excluded by subsection (2) or (3) below.

(2) That section does not apply to a marriage a party to which has (before commencement) entered into a later marriage which either –

(a) is valid apart from this section but would be void if section 5 above applied to the earlier marriage; or

(b) is valid by virtue of this section.

(3) That section does not apply to a marriage which has been annulled before commencement, whether by a decree granted in England and Wales or by an annulment obtained elsewhere and recognised in England and Wales at commencement.

(4) An annulment of a marriage resulting from legal proceedings begun before commencement shall be treated for the purposes of subsection (3) above as having taken effect before that time.

(5) For the purposes of subsections (3) and (4) above a marriage which has been declared to be invalid by a court of competent jurisdiction in any proceedings concerning either the validity of the marriage or any right dependent on its validity shall be treated as having been annulled.

(6) Nothing in section 5 above, in its application to marriages entered into before commencement –

(a) gives or affects any entitlement to an interest –

(i) under the will or codicil of, or on the intestacy of, a person who died before commencement; or

(ii) under a settlement or other disposition of property made before that time (otherwise than by will or codicil);

(b) gives or affects any entitlement to a benefit, allowance, pension or other payment –

(i) payable before, or in respect of a period before, commencement; or

(ii) payable in respect of the death of a person before that time;

(c) affects tax in respect of a period or event before commencement; or

(d) affects the succession to any dignity or title of honour.

(7) In this section 'commencement' means the commencement of this Part.

8   Part II: supplemental

(1) Nothing in this Part affects any law or custom relating to the marriage of members of the Royal Family. ...

PART III

CHOICE OF LAW IN TORT AND DELICT

9   Purpose of Part III

(1) The rules in this Part apply for choosing the law (in this Part referred to as 'the applicable law') to be used for determining issues relating to tort or (for the purposes of the law of Scotland) delict.

(2) The characterisation for the purposes of private international law of issues arising in a claim as issues relating to tort or delict is a matter for the courts of the forum.

(3) The rules in this Part do not apply in relation to issues arising in any claim excluded from the operation of this Part by section 13 below.

(4) The applicable law shall be used for determining the issues arising in a claim, including in particular the question whether an actionable tort or delict has occurred.

(5) The applicable law to be used for determining the issues arising in a claim shall exclude any choice of law rules forming part of the law of the country or countries concerned.

(6) For the avoidance of doubt (and without prejudice to the operation of section 14 below) this Part applies in relation to events occurring in the forum as it applies in relation to events occurring in any other country.

(7) In this Part as it extends to any country within the United

Kingdom, 'the forum' means England and Wales, Scotland or Northern Ireland, as the case may be. ...

10 Abolition of certain common law rules

The rules of the common law, in so far as they –

(a) require actionability under both the law of the forum and the law of another country for the purpose of determining whether a tort or delict is actionable; or

(b) allow (as an exception from the rules falling within paragraph (a) above) for the law of a single country to be applied for the purpose of determining the issues, or any of the issues, arising in the case in question,

are hereby abolished so far as they apply to any claim in tort or delict which is not excluded from the operation of this Part by section 13 below.

11 Choice of applicable law: the general rule

(1) The general rule is that the applicable law is the law of the country in which the events constituting the tort or delict in question occur.

(2) Where elements of those events occur in different countries, the applicable law under the general rule is to be taken as being –

(a) for a cause of action in respect of personal injury caused to an individual or death resulting from personal injury, the law of the country where the individual was when he sustained the injury;

(b) for a cause of action in respect of damage to property, the law of the country where the property was when it was damaged; and

(c) in any other case, the law of the country in which the most significant element or elements of those events occurred.

(3) In this section 'personal injury' includes disease or any impairment of physical or mental condition.

12 Choice of applicable law: displacement of general rule

(1) If it appears, in all the circumstances, from a comparison of –

(a) the significance of the factors which connect a tort or delict with the country whose law would be the applicable law under the general rule; and

(b) the significance of any factors connecting the tort or delict with another country,

that it is substantially more appropriate for the applicable law for determining the issues arising in the case, or any of those issues, to be the law of the other country, the general rule is displaced and the applicable law for determining those issues or that issue (as the case may be) is the law of that other country.

(2) The factors that may be taken into account as connecting a tort or delict with a country for the purposes of this section include, in particular, factors relating to the parties, to any of the events which constitute the tort or delict in question or to any of the circumstances or consequences of those events.

13 Exclusion of defamation claims from Part III

(1) Nothing in this Part applies to affect the determination of issues arising in any defamation claim.

(2) For the purposes of this section 'defamation claim' means –

(a) any claim under the law of any part of the United Kingdom for libel or slander or for slander of title, slander of goods or other malicious falsehood and any claim under the law of Scotland for verbal injury; and

(b) any claim under the law of any other country corresponding to or otherwise in the nature of a claim mentioned in paragraph (a) above.

14 Transitional provision and savings

(1) Nothing in this Part applies to acts or omissions giving rise to a claim which occur before the commencement of this Part.

(2) Nothing in this Part affects any rules of law (including rules of private international law) except those abolished by section 10 above.

(3) Without prejudice to the generality of subsection (2) above, nothing in this Part –

(a) authorises the application of the law of a country outside the forum as the applicable law for determining issues arising in any claim in so far as to do so –

(i) would conflict with principles of public policy; or

(ii) would give effect to such a penal, revenue or other public law as would not otherwise be enforceable under the law of the forum; or

(b) affects any rules of evidence, pleading or practice or authorises questions of procedure in any proceedings to be determined otherwise than in accordance with the law of the forum.

(4) This Part has effect without prejudice to the operation of any rule of law which either has effect notwithstanding the rules of private international law applicable in the particular circumstances or modifies the rules of private international law that would otherwise be so applicable.

15 Crown application

(1) This Part applies in relation to claims by or against the Crown as it applies in relation to claims to which the Crown is not a party.

(2) In subsection (1) above a reference to the Crown does not include a reference to Her Majesty in Her private capacity or to Her Majesty in right of Her Duchy of Lancaster or to the Duke of Cornwall.

(3) Without prejudice to the generality of section 14(2) above, nothing in this section affects any rule of law as to whether proceedings of any description may be brought against the Crown.

PART IV

SUPPLEMENTAL

16 Commencement

(1) Part I shall come into force on such day as the Lord Chancellor may by order made by statutory instrument appoint; and different days may be appointed for different provisions.

(2) Part II shall come into force at the end of the period of two months beginning with the day on which this Act is passed.

(3) Part III shall come into force on such day as the Lord Chancellor and the Lord Advocate may by order made by statutory instrument

appoint; and different days may be appointed for the commencement of Part III as it extends to England and Wales, Scotland or Northern Ireland.

RULES OF THE SUPREME COURT 1965

ORDER 11
(as amended)

1 Principal cases in which service of writ out of jurisdiction is permissible

(1) Provided that the writ does not contain any claim mentioned in Order 75, r.2(1) and is not a writ to which paragraph (2) of this rule applies, service of a writ out of the jurisdiction is permissible with the leave of the Court if in the action begun by the writ –

(a) relief is sought against a person domiciled within the jurisdiction;

(b) an injunction is sought ordering the defendant to do or refrain from doing anything within the jurisdiction (whether or not damages are also claimed in respect of a failure to do or the doing of that thing);

(c) the claim is brought against a person duly served within or out of the jurisdiction and a person out of the jurisdiction is a necessary or proper party thereto;

(d) the claim is brought to enforce, rescind, dissolve, annul or otherwise affect a contract, or to recover damages or obtain other relief in respect of the breach of a contract, being (in either case) a contract which –

(i) was made within the jurisdiction, or

(ii) was made by or through an agent trading or residing within the jurisdiction on behalf of a principal trading or residing out of the jurisdiction, or

(iii) is by its terms, or by implication, governed by English law, or

(iv) contains a term to the effect that the High Court shall have jurisdiction to hear and determine any action in respect of the contract;

(e) the claim is brought in respect of a breach committed within the jurisdiction of a contract made within or out of the jurisdiction, and irrespective of the fact, if such be the case, that the breach was preceded or accompanied by a breach committed out of the jurisdiction that rendered impossible the performance of so much of the contract as ought to have been performed within the jurisdiction;

(f) the claim is founded on a tort and the damage was sustained, or resulted from an act committed, within the jurisdiction;

(g) the whole subject-matter of the action is land situate within the jurisdiction (with or without rents of profits) or the perpetuation of testimony relating to land so situate;

(h) the claim is brought to construe, rectify, set aside or enforce an act, deed, will, contract, obligation or liability affecting land situate within the jurisdiction;

(i) the claim is made for a debt secured on immovable property or is made to assert, declare or determine proprietary or possessory rights, or rights of security, in or over movable property, or to obtain authority to dispose of movable property, situate within the jurisdiction;

(j) the claim is brought to execute the trusts of a written instrument being trusts that ought to be executed according to English law and of which the person to be served with the writ is a trustee, or for any relief or remedy which might be obtained in any such action;

(k) the claim is made for the administration of the estate of a person who died domiciled within the jurisdiction or for any relief or remedy which might be obtained in any such action;

(l) the claim is brought in a probate action within the meaning of Order 76;

(m) the claim is brought to enforce any judgment or arbitral award;

(n) the claim is brought against a defendant not domiciled in Scotland or Northern Ireland in respect of a claim by the Commissioners of Inland Revenue for or in relation to any of the duties or taxes which have been, or are for the time being, placed under their care and management;

(o) the claim is brought under the Nuclear Installations Act 1965 or in respect of contributions under the Social Security Act 1975;

(p) the claim is made for a sum to which the Directive of the Council of the European Communities dated 15th March 1976 No.76/308/EEC applies, and service is to be effected in a country which is a member State of the European Economic Community.

(q) the claim is made under the Drug Trafficking Offences Act 1986;

(r) the claim is made under the Financial Services Act 1986 or the Banking Act 1987;

(s) the claim is made under Part VI of the Criminal Justice Act 1988;

(t) the claim is brought for money had and received or for an account or other relief against the defendant as constructive trustee, and the defendant's alleged liability arises out of acts committed, whether by him or otherwise, within the jurisdiction.

(u) the claim is made under the Immigration (Carriers' Liability) Act 1987.

(2) Service of a writ out of the jurisdiction is permissible without the leave of the Court provided that each claim made by the writ is either:–

(a) a claim which by virtue of the Civil Jurisdiction and Judgments Act 1982 the Court has power to hear and determine, made in proceedings to which the following conditions apply –

(i) no proceedings between the parties concerning the same cause of action are pending in the courts of any other part of the United Kingdom or of any other Convention territory, and

(ii) either –

the defendant is domiciled in any part of the United Kingdom or in any other Convention territory, or

the proceedings begun by the writ are proceedings to which Article 16 of Schedule 1, 3C or 4 refers, or the defendant is a party to an agreement conferring jurisdiction to which Article 17 of Schedule 1, 3C or 4 to the Act applies,

or

(b) a claim which by virtue of any other enactment the High Court has power to hear and determine notwithstanding that the person against whom the claim is made is not within the jurisdiction of the Court or that the wrongful act, neglect or default giving rise to the claim did not take place within its jurisdiction.

(3) Where a writ is to be served out of the jurisdiction under paragraph (2), the time to be inserted in the writ within which the defendant served therewith must acknowledge service shall be –

(a) 21 days where the writ is to be served out of the jurisdiction under paragraph (2)(a) in Scotland, Northern Ireland or in the European territory of another Contracting State, or

(b) 31 days where the writ is to be served under paragraph (2)(a) in any other territory of a Contracting State, or

(c) limited in accordance with the practice adopted under r.4(4) where the writ is to be served under paragraph (2)(a) in a country not referred to in sub-paragraphs (a) or (b) or under paragraph (2)(b).

(4) For the purposes of this rules, and of r.9 of this Order, domicile is to be determined in accordance with the provisions of sections 41 to 46 of the Civil Jurisdictions and Judgments Act 1982 and 'Convention territory' means the territory or territories of any Contracting State, as defined by s1(3) of that Act, to which, as defined in s1(1) of that Act, the Brussels or the Lugano Convention apply.

4 Application for, and grant of, leave to serve writ out of jurisdiction

(1) An application for the grant of leave under rule 1(1) must be supported by an affidavit stating –

(a) the grounds on which the application is made,

(b) that in the deponent's belief the plaintiff has a good cause of action,

(c) in what place or country the defendant is, or probably may be found, and

(d) where the application is made under rule 1(1)(c), the grounds for the deponent's belief that there is between the plaintiff and the person on whom a writ has been served a real issue which the plaintiff may reasonably ask the Court to try.

(2) No such leave shall be granted unless it shall be made sufficiently to appear to the Court that the case is a proper one for service out of the jurisdiction under this Order.

(3) Where the application is for the grant of leave under rule 1 to serve a writ in Scotland or Northern Ireland, if it appears to the Court that there may be a concurrent remedy there, the Court, in deciding whether to grant leave shall have regard to the comparative cost and convenience of proceeding there or in England, and (where that is relevant) to the powers and jurisdiction of the

sheriff court in Scotland or the county courts or courts of summary jurisdiction in Northern Ireland.

(4) An order granting under rule 1 leave to serve a writ, out of the jurisdiction must limit a time within which the defendant to be served must acknowledge service.

5   Service of writ abroad: general

(1) Subject to the following provisions of this rule, Order 10, rule 1(1), (4), (5) and (6) and Order 65, rule 4, shall apply in relation to the service of a writ, notwithstanding that the writ is to be served out of the jurisdiction, save that the accompanying form of acknowledgement of service shall be modified in such a manner as may be appropriate.

(2) Nothing in this rule or in any order or direction of the Court made by virtue of it shall authorise or require the doing of anything in a country in which service is to be effected which is contrary to the law of that country.

(3) A writ which is to be served out of the jurisdiction –

(a) need not be served personally on the person required to be served so long as it is served on him in accordance with the law of the country in which service is effected; and

(b) need not be served by the plaintiff or his agent if it is served by a method provided for by rule 6 or rule 7.

(5) An official certificate stating that a writ as regards which rule 6 has been complied with has been served on a person personally, or in accordance with the law of the country in which service was effected, on a specified date, being a certificate –

(a) by a British consular authority in that country, or

(b) by the government or judicial authorities of that country, or

(c) by any other authority designated in respect of that country under the Hague Convention,

shall be evidence of the facts so stated.

(6) An official certificate by the Secretary of State stating that a writ has been duly served on a specified date in accordance with a request made under rule 7 shall be evidence of that fact.

(7) A document purporting to be such a certificate as is mentioned in paragraph (5) or (6) shall, until the contrary is proved, be deemed to be such a certificate.

(8) In this rule and rule 6 'the Hague Convention' means the Convention on the service abroad of judicial and extra-judicial documents in civil or commercial matters signed at the Hague on November 15, 1965.

6   Service of writ abroad through foreign governments, judicial authorities and British consuls

(1) Save where a writ is to be served pursuant to paragraph (2A) this rule does not apply to service in –

(a) Scotland, Northern Ireland, the Isle of Man or the Channel Islands;

(b) any independent Commonwealth country;

(c) any associated state;

(d) any colony;

(e) the Republic of Ireland.

(2) Where in accordance with these rules a writ is to be served on a defendant in any country with respect to which there subsists a Civil Procedure Convention (other than the Hague Convention) providing for service in that country of process of the High Court, the writ may be served –

(a) through the judicial authorities of that country; or

(b) through a British consular authority in that country (subject to any provision of the convention as to the nationality of persons who may be so served).

(2A) Where in accordance with these rules, a writ is to be served on a defendant in any country which is a party to the Hague Convention, the writ may be served –

(a) through the authority designated under the Convention in respect of that country; or

(b) if the law of that country permits –

(i) through the judicial authorities of that country, or

(ii) through a British consular authority in that country.

(3) Where in accordance with these rules a writ is to be served on a

defendant in any country with respect to which there does not subsist a Civil Procedure Convention providing for service in that country of process of the High Court, the writ may be served –

(a) through the government of that country, where that government is willing to effect service; or

(b) through a British consular authority in that country, except where service through such an authority is contrary to the law of that country.

(4) A person who wishes to serve a writ by a method specified in paragraph (2), (2A) or (3) must lodge in the Central Office a request for service of the writ by that method, together with a copy of the writ and an additional copy thereof for each person to be served.

(5) Every copy of a writ lodged under paragraph (4) must be accompanied by a translation of the writ in the official language of the country in which service is to be effected or, if there is more than one official language of that country, in any one of those languages which is appropriate to the place in that country where service is to be effected: Provided that this paragraph shall not apply in relation to a copy of a writ which is to be served in a country the official language of which is, or the official languages of which include, English, or is to be served in any country by a British consular authority on a British subject, unless the service is to be effected under paragraph (2) and the Civil Procedure Convention with respect to that country expressly requires the copy to be accompanied by a translation.

(6) Every translation lodged under paragraph (5) must be certified by the person making it to be a correct translation; and the certificate must contain a statement of that person's full name, of his address and of his qualifications for making the translation.

(7) Documents duly lodged under paragraph (4) shall be sent by the Senior Master to the Parliamentary Under-Secretary of State to the Foreign Office with a request that he arrange the writ to be served by the method indicated in the request lodged under paragraph (4) or, where alternative methods are so indicated, by such one of those methods as is most convenient.

7 Service of writ in certain actions under certain Acts

(1) Subject to paragraph (4) where a person to whom leave has been granted under rule 1 to serve a writ on a State, as defined in section

14 of the State Immunity Act 1978, wishes to have the writ served on that State, he must lodge in the Central Office –

(a) a request for service to be arranged by the Secretary of State; and

(b) a copy of the writ; and

(c) except where the official language of the State is, or the official languages of the State include, English, a translation of the writ in the official language or one of the official languages of that State.

(2) Rule 6(6) shall apply in relation to a translation lodged under paragraph (1) of this rule as it applies in relation to a translation lodged under paragraph (5) of that rule.

(3) Documents duly lodged under this Rule shall be sent by the Senior Master to the Secretary of State with a request that the Secretary of State arrange for the writ to be served.

(4) Where section 12(6) of the State Immunity Act 1978 applies and the State has agreed to a method of service other than that provided by the preceding paragraphs, the writ may be served either by the method agreed or in accordance with the preceding paragraphs of this rule. ...

INDEX